ROBERT LOWELL

ROBERT LOWELL

Interviews and Memoirs

Edited by
JEFFREY MEYERS

Ann Arbor   *The University of Michigan Press*

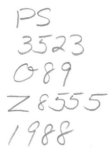

6/1988
antil

Library of Congress Cataloging-in-Publication Data

Robert Lowell, interviews and memoirs.

  Bibliography: p.
  1. Lowell, Robert, 1917–1977. 2. Lowell, Robert,
1917–1977—Interviews. 3. Poets, American—20th century—
Biography. I. Lowell, Robert 1917–1977. II. Meyers,
Jeffrey.
PS3523.089Z8555   1988   811'.52 [B]   87-19172
ISBN 0-472-10089-0 (alk. paper)

*I am grateful to the University of Colorado Committee on
University Scholarly Publications, which awarded a grant for
permission fees.*

To Denis Donoghue

Contents

Works by Robert Lowell

Land of Unlikeness (1944)
Lord Weary's Castle (1946)
The Mills of the Kavanaughs (1951)
Life Studies (1959)
Imitations (1961)
Phaedra (1961)
For the Union Dead (1964)
The Old Glory (1965)
Near the Ocean (1967)
The Voyage and Other Versions of Poems by Baudelaire (1968)
Prometheus Bound (1969)
Notebook 1967–68 (1969)
Notebook (1970)
The Dolphin (1973)
For Lizzie and Harriet (1973)
History (1973)
Day by Day (1977)
The Oresteia of Aeschylus (1979)

Introduction

Jeffrey Meyers

Robert Lowell (1917–77) is the most important American poet since World War Two. The wide range of essays in *Robert Lowell: Interviews and Memoirs*—written between 1953 and 1985 by distinguished poets, novelists and critics, including John Crowe Ransom and Seamus Heaney, Norman Mailer and V. S. Naipaul, Alfred Kazin and Helen Vendler—is an essential source for the study of Lowell's life and work. They illuminate the meaning of his poetry, suggest the development of his reputation and provide a vivid complement to his biography.[1]

Lowell's reputation developed in four stages. He established his fame as a poet by winning the Pulitzer Prize for *Lord Weary's Castle* in 1947. *Life Studies,* a major breakthrough that influenced two generations of confessional poets, confirmed his stature and won the National Book Award in 1960. Lowell's commitment to political protest against the Vietnam war in the mid-1960s—his campaigning with Senator Eugene McCarthy, his March on the Pentagon with Norman Mailer and his refusal to attend the White House Arts Festival—brought him to the attention of a mass audience. During the 1970s, when his work was more prolific but less impressive than *For the Union Dead* (1964), he became a celebrity and was recognized as the greatest poet of his time.

Lowell's witty anecdotes, vivid character sketches of teachers and friends, incisive comments on poets and their poems, and idealistic political beliefs reveal a sophisticated, urbane, learned and allusive mind. Though the interviewers focus on his work and do not ask personal questions, Lowell freely refers to his personal life in order to explain the development of his poetry and his ideas. He discusses his family background, early life, education at Harvard and Kenyon, conversion to Catholicism, jail term as a conscientious objector during the Second World War, work habits, teaching experience at Boston University and Harvard, expatriate years in Europe and England as well as his three turbulent marriages and his mental illness.

A few of the twenty interviews (about half of this book) were inspired by particular occasions: Lowell teaching at Salzburg or winning the National Book Award, publishing a major work or staging a play in New York or London. Some of the interviews take the form of formal questions and answers, others are narratives that describe his appearance and character, and incorporate his conversation. Some of the interviews (on metrics and translation) are specialized; others consider numerous topics. Though there is a significant difference between his substantial discussions with Frederick Seidel, Stanley Kunitz and Ian Hamilton, and the brief statements included in stories that appeared in *Newsweek, Life* and *Time,* in each interview Lowell, instead of repeating the same prepared statements, welcomes the opportunity to express his ideas and answer his critics, and responds sincerely and seriously to the individual questions. Lowell had a fine ability to manipulate the media and used the interviews to project himself as an authoritative public figure.

I. Interviews

Lowell taught at the American-organized Salzburg Seminars in July and August 1952. John McCormick's leisurely account (1953) of a day with Lowell describes his physical appearance, education, conviction as a conscientious objector during the War, knowledge of languages and work habits. It also considers the style and content of Lowell's lecture on Hart Crane, his discussion of Emerson and Melville, his affection for the dramatic monologue, and the influence of historians and of expatriate life on his poetry. McCormick notes that "like many poets, [Lowell] does not read his own verse well; his voice is rather high and lacks range, but his feeling and inflection add a depth which a better but less sensitive voice would often miss." McCormick also perceives that "the violence, the sense that in the case of each poet [Hart Crane and Lowell] you must say, here is a man who devours himself, was inescapable" (No. 1).

John Fuller's brief interview (1960) in his "Trade Winds" column appeared just after Lowell had won the National Book Award for *Life Studies.* His poems were cited for their "fierce and immediate compassion . . . which strike through the private dimension to document the pressures of an age." Lowell sees *Life Studies* as a turning point in his career but does not know whether it is a "life line or a death rope." He discusses the technique in his current book, which he calls *Imitations* because "they're not completely accurate translations, but rather poetic interpretations of them" (No. 2).

Lowell, whose savage side was reflected in his nickname Cal (short for Caligula and Caliban), had studied with Cleanth Brooks and Robert Penn Warren at Louisiana State University during 1940–41. Their formal interview (1961) emphasized technique: the meter, rhythm and rhyme of Lowell's poems. Lowell begins by analyzing the opening lines of Milton's "Lycidas" and Donne's "If Poysonous Mineralls," and recounts Frost's valuable advice about poetic compression during their first meeting in 1936. Lowell acknowledges the influence of Milton, Melville and Allen Tate on his major poem, "The Quaker Graveyard in Nantucket." He then turns to the technique of *Life Studies:* the visual quality of the line lengths, the fact that his poem to Delmore Schwartz was "written in perfectly regular meter and then taken out of that and irregularized," and that "My Last Afternoon with Uncle Devereux Winslow" was originally "four or five prose pages that [he] rewrote into lines" (No. 3).

The *Paris Review* interview (1961) with Frederick Seidel, Lowell's most substantial and significant statement, covers a great range of topics and has been quarried and quoted by numerous scholars. Lowell discusses the influence of his poetic ancestors, his study with Richard Eberhart at St. Mark's School, his rejection by the staff of the *Harvard Advocate,* his reasons for transferring from Harvard to Kenyon, his training in Classics, the difficulty of publishing his early poetry, the Catholic element in his work ("I was much more interested in being a Catholic than in being a writer"), the change in style from the "twisting and disgust" of *Land of Unlikeness* to the breaking of forms in *Life Studies,* his friendship with Ford Madox Ford and Allen Tate, the controversy surrounding the award of the 1948 Bollingen Prize to Ezra Pound, his teaching at Boston University, his literary criticism and translations: "both a continuation of my own bias and a release from myself." He praises the poetry of Frost, Pound, Eliot, Crane, Roethke, Bishop, Jarrell, Schwartz and Snodgrass; and observes that "almost the whole problem of writing poetry is to bring it back to what you really feel" (No. 4).

In Lowell's first English interview (1963), which appeared in a leading Sunday newspaper and was written by his greatest admirer in England, A. Alvarez, he discusses the limitations of confessional poetry ("often you have nothing to confess that makes a poem") as well as the unpleasant truths about himself that may strike the fire of inspiration. Lowell compares his poems to action painting; praises the work of Philip Larkin and the "thunderbolt" animal poems of Ted Hughes; and comments on the politics of the Thirties, the Second World War and the Atomic Age. He also voices a characteristically witty epigram: "I thought that civilisation was going to break down, and instead *I* did" (No. 5). In the second interview with Alvarez (1963), a continuation of the previous one, Lowell describes the composition of *Life Studies* and reveals that "Skunk Hour," which was influenced by Elizabeth Bishop's "The Armadillo," was written before the other poems in the book and "written backwards, more or less, and I added the first four stanzas after I'd finished it" (No. 6).

At the time of his five-hour interview (1964) with Stanley Kunitz (whose poetry he had praised in the *Paris Review* piece), Lowell was "without doubt the most celebrated poet in English of his generation." Kunitz, who notes Lowell's "air of affectionate dependency" with his friends, begins with a description of Lowell's voice and of his apartment in New York. Lowell contrasts literary life in New York and Boston, and states that from the beginning of his career he "was preoccupied with technique, fascinated by the past, and tempted by other languages." He mentions the conflict between the conservative and liberal aspects of his character; and makes the astonishing claim that "what saved [Pound] as a poet was his bad politics, which got him involved in the contemporary world." Lowell speaks of his work habits and of his independent income (unusual for a poet) which made it unnecessary for him to work for a living. He comments on his sources of inspiration and how he decides when a poem is finished. "We are more conscious of our wounds than the poets before us," he shrewdly remarks, "but we are not necessarily more wounded" (No. 7).

Lowell's anonymous interview (1964) with the staff writers of *Newsweek,* a few days after his talk with Kunitz appeared in the *New York Times Book Review,* celebrated the publication of *For the Union Dead* and first brought him to the attention of a mass audience. It was ironic that Lowell, at the peak of his reputation, claimed "the small audience is a blessing" for a poet. During the time of student riots and protests against the war in Vietnam, Lowell became a famous public figure and felt called upon to utter vatic pronouncements: "We're decaying. . . . The old morality doesn't hold. . . . Genocide has stunned us; we have a curious dread it will be repeated" (No. 8). Lowell's aphoristic views about words and the world were extracted from his *Life* magazine interview (1965) with Jane Howard and from his published statements, and printed separately. He spoke of his nickname, the autobiographical basis of his poetry, the advantage of myopia, our few cultured presidents, his Jewish ancestors and the Jewish contribution to the arts, his favorite poets and painters, the particular quality of alcoholic poetry, his teaching at Harvard, his relations with his daughter and his opposition to nuclear war: "I believe we should rather die than drop our own bombs" (No. 9).[2]

Time's cover story on Lowell (1967), even more extensive than the *Newsweek* article of 1964, was the first to mention his recurrent mental illness. The six quotations by Lowell (extracted here from the *Time* story) concern the place of poetry in society, a comparison of poetry and the novel, his method of composing poems, his criticism of Lyndon Johnson's policy on Vietnam, the future of American poetry and the aphorism (a reversal of Lytton Strachey's ironic remark, "It is perhaps as difficult to write a good life as to live one"), "It is harder to be a good man than a good poet" (No. 10).

In his third interview (1965) with Lowell, which was political rather than literary and took place shortly after the assassination of President Kennedy, Alvarez again claims that Lowell's manner is "almost saintly." Lowell comments on the cultural significance of Kennedy, and the difference between the artist's and the politician's view of the world. He compares Freud's case histories to Russian novels, notes the connection between poetry and power, and is somewhat sceptical about Norman Mailer's ambitious attempts to create the great American novel. Lowell perceives that America "always had the ideal of 'saving the world.' And that comes close to perhaps destroying the world" (No. 11).

Goddard Lieberson's interview (1965) appeared as liner notes to the recording of Lowell's dramatic adaptation of Melville's *Benito Cereno,* the story of the suppression of a slave revolt aboard ship. Lowell relates how he decided to write a play rather than an opera based on the novella, and quotes his letter to the *Village Voice*—in response to criticism that he was anti-Negro—about the meaning of the play: "The terrible injustice, in the past and in the present, of the American treatment of the Negro is of the greatest urgency to me as a man and as a writer" (No. 12). Michael Billington's interview (1967) also concerns Lowell's *Benito Cereno* and notes that his "work for the theatre has consisted entirely of adaptations and translations." Lowell acknowledges that he put a great deal of himself into the central character and that the Civil Rights movement dominated his mind when he wrote the play (No. 13). John Gale's interview (1967) appeared in London three days after Billington's. Lowell admits the reviews of the play were poor, but thinks the critics may have missed its subtlety. He mentions the difficulties of writing plays about contemporary figures like Leon Trotsky and Malcolm X. He fears a Third World War and the recurrent threat of Fascism, and believes Robert Kennedy might possibly get America out of the Vietnam War: "Our whole life is torn by it" (No. 14).

The interview (1968) with Richard Gilman concentrates on the theater: the unity of the three plays in *The Old Glory* trilogy, the definition of the dramatic, the role of language and the current interest in the stage. Lowell indicates a technical weakness in his loosely structured plays by admitting: "Plots are boring anyway. We all hate the sort of play where one thing leads to another and everything is drawn tight." He also mentions campaigning with Senator Eugene McCarthy (Lowell's close friendship with McCarthy distracted the senator from serious political responsibilities during his presidential campaign) and the role of the writer in politics: "When your private experience converges on the nation's experience, you feel you have to do something. Writers have to act publicly sometimes from private experience" (No. 15).

Lowell's fourth interview (1976) with Alvarez was prompted by the revival of *The Old Glory* in New York. Lowell explains what inspired him to write for the theater and how far the author can control his work when writing poems and plays. He acknowledges that he uses the theater to express his political views: "I think that what I have written is almost tame compared to what has happened. . . . We've just had one of the most disastrous wars we have ever fought, in Vietnam, and one of the most disastrous Presidents who has ever served, Nixon" (No. 16).

The interview (1968) with D. S. Carne-Ross was devoted to Lowell's translations and imitations of plays and poems. Lowell explains why his *Prometheus Bound* was written in prose rather than verse, how a translator can approximate different languages and how he translates from languages he does not know. He comments on the merits of Greek and Italian translations by Richmond Lattimore and Laurence Binyon, and on the metrical distinction of Auden's verse. He believes the contemporary interest in translation is inspired by the "discovery of what we lack" and by the excitement of bringing "into English something that didn't exist in English before." Lowell tries "to give an accurate, eloquent photograph of the original" and is fascinated by "this sort of mosaic-work, transferring pebble by pebble into meter" (No. 17).

When asked by V. S. Naipaul (1969) about his distinguished lineage, Lowell refers to his uneasy "relations with my parents" (whom he lacerates in his poetry) and admits: "I felt I was born in a kind of illiterate culture, a kind of decadence." While speaking of intellectual life in New York, he says: "Most of my friends are Jewish, and the people I've learned most from and that I like best . . . are Jewish." He speaks of the need for political engagement; notes the conservatism of the greatest modern satirists: Wyndham Lewis, Waugh, Lardner and Genet; and he discusses egoism (including his own) in contemporary literature (No. 18).

Lowell seemed to be in a rather difficult and defensive mood during his talk with Dudley Young (1971). He says his audience lives in "an alien age for poetry," notes that even Shakespeare was not very popular in his own time and comments on Yeats' role as an Irish poet. He responds to the negative criticism of *Notebook* and compares it to his previous work: "the spine of the book is my own life, more or less like an early book of mine, *Life Studies*. It's about as personal as that and I wanted to make it more difficult and complicated" (No. 19).

The second interview (1972) in the *Review,* one of the best and most aphoristic, was conducted by his future biographer, Ian Hamilton. Lowell ranges from his reasons for living in England to the publicity provoked by his refusal to attend the White House Festival of the Arts in June 1965, from competition in American literary life to the advantages of the fourteen-line unrhymed sonnet in *Notebook:* "[It] allowed me rhetoric, formal construction, and quick breaks. . . . Words came rapidly, almost four hundred sonnets in four years." He is witty about his ancestors: James Russell Lowell was "a poet pedestalled for oblivion," his relation to Amy Lowell was like having Mae West for a cousin. He explains the influence of Catholicism, and of Ransom and Tate on his poetry; and describes himself as an "idealist felon." He admits that poetry readings exhaust him; praises Pound ("more heart than any poet since Hardy") and his sometime student, Sylvia Plath: "I glory in her. . . . In an extreme Life-and-Death style, she is as good as Sir Walter Raleigh." He finds it "disgusting when professors look to the young for vision"; calls Eugene McCarthy "a lost cause man"; says theater is "a trapped and thwarted art"; and characterizes *For the Union Dead* as "lemony, soured and dry, the drouth I had touched with my own hands." Lowell also allows a dark glimpse into his mental illness: "I have been through mania and depression. . . . Mania is extremity for one's friends, depression for one's self. Both are chemical. In depression, one wakes, is happy for about two minutes, probably less, and then fades into the dread of the day" (No. 20).

II. Memoirs

Lowell was big, strong, ruggedly handsome and aristocratic. He had tremendous personal authority, was preeminent in his circle and dominated the literary arena. He had a distinguished background, studied with influential teachers, was exceptionally talented, earned many awards and prizes, had a powerful personality, attracted devoted friends, married brilliant wives, was engaged in political events, established an impressive public image, and survived to bury and elegize all his poetic competitors.

The twenty-seven memoirs of Lowell reprinted here fall into four general categories. Four memoirs were published in his lifetime, nine obituary notices appeared shortly after his death in September 1977, ten essays were published in the memorial issue of the *Harvard Advocate* (November 1979) and in *Robert Lowell: A Tribute* (Pisa, 1979), and four retrospective memoirs appeared between 1982 and 1985. The memoirs were written by old friends who had known Lowell for a long time, by former students who later became his disciples, by younger intimates and by acquaintances who knew him only slightly. The most penetrating and honest memoirs are by his literary and intellectual equals—Norman Mailer and Seamus Heaney—as well as by Stanley Kunitz, Blair Clark, Esther Brooks and Helen Vendler.

Mary Jane Baker, Lowell's freshman student at the University of Iowa in 1953, offers a gushing view of her teacher (1954).[3] She found him shy and mumbling when she bravely signed up for his advanced course in the spring term. On the first day of class he said they would attempt to read the poets in the original languages—which the students did not know. He read French poems with an atrocious accent in order to show the class "how they sounded." He was a learned and exciting, but disorganized and confusing, teacher. He never mastered the names of the thirty students and was not interested in their comprehension or opinions. Their final paper could either criticize or translate the poems. In the fall term Lowell, with a Classics professor, taught a Greek poetry workshop on Homer and Pindar, and his wife, Elizabeth Hardwick, was among the pupils. Baker seems more awed by Lowell the famous poet than by his actual performance in class.

In a brief paternal essay (1961), John Crowe Ransom recalls that Lowell—and Randall Jarrell—actually lived in his house during their first year at Kenyon: that "Lowell's animal spirits were high, his personality was spontaneous, so that he was a little bit overpowering. . . . His way of reading literature was to devour it, to get it quickly into his blood stream." Ransom particularly praises the weight of Classical learning in Lowell's "Falling Asleep over the Aeneid" (No. 21).

Anne Sexton's short, informal essay on Lowell's pedagogy (1961) also expresses awe of her teacher but is more sophisticated than Mary Jane Baker's piece. Sexton found Lowell "formal in a rather awkward New England sense. His voice was soft and slow." His "method of teaching is intuitive and open," but he can be harsh and "works with a cold chisel with no more mercy than a dentist." She summarizes his influence on her work by stating: "he helped me to distrust the easy musical phrase and to look for the frankness of ordinary speech. If you have enough natural energy he can show you how to chain it in" (No. 22).

During the interview with V. S. Naipaul (No. 18), Lowell had praised Norman Mailer: "His description of me is one of the best things ever written about me, and most generous—what my poetry is like and that sort of thing. He records a little speech I made about draft-dodgers and I felt he was very good on that. . . . Of my contemporaries in poetry or prose Mailer is the most talented." Mailer begins the portrait of Lowell in *Armies of the Night* (1968), one of his finest books, by mentioning their initial bond: "their secret detestation of liberal academic parties to accompany worthy causes." At the party, they engaged in deep conversation to avoid the crashing bores. Mailer found his coeval immensely attractive: "his features were at once virile and patrician and his characteristic manner turned up facets of the grim, the gallant, the tender and the solicitous as if he were the nicest Boston banker one had ever hoped to meet." Yet "the hollows in his cheeks gave a hint of the hanging judge," and Lowell had irritated the prickly and competitive novelist by engaging in literary logrolling and sending postcards of insincere praise. "Obviously spoiled by everyone for years," Mailer notes, "he seemed nonetheless to need the spoiling."

Mailer introduces Lowell's speech by reminding the audience that the poet's refusal to attend the White House Festival of the Arts "was one of the first dramatic acts of protest against the war in Vietnam." As Lowell slouches to the podium to read his poems in a weak, indifferent voice, Mailer is astonished and annoyed that the people adored him. He seemed to have effortlessly stolen the affection that Mailer would have to work hard to earn. In his second speech, Lowell pledged to support the young men who had burned their draft cards. "It was said softly,"

Mailer reports, "on a current of intense indignation and Lowell had never looked more dignified nor more admirable." It seemed as if Lowell were "repaying the moral debts of ten generations of ancestors." At the end of the Pentagon March, Mailer was arrested for trying to cross the police lines while Lowell was turned back and then ignored by the police as he joined a sit-down demonstration outside the Pentagon.

Writing in a highly-charged style, and with gentle irony about both Lowell and himself, Mailer's antagonistic and affectionate portrait brilliantly captures the conflict in Lowell between action and reflection. Both were Harvard men (Mailer is witty about how they came from opposite ends of the social scale), both were the acknowledged leaders in their literary territory, and both competed for public attention and personal glory (No. 23).

Donald Newlove's satiric essay (1969) is a peculiar mixture of fact and fantasy, which he calls "fantijournalism."[4] He apparently went to dinner at the Lowells' New York apartment in the winter of 1968, but deliberately exaggerates what actually happened. He admits that he scarcely knew Lowell and was invited by chance to interpret for a visiting Chilean, who was supposed to be writing a book on contemporary American poets but was deeply confused about Lowell's work. When Newlove arrives at the door, Lowell tells him that he was *not* expected for dinner, but he crashes the party anyway. Newlove, in the first negative memoir about Lowell, expresses his animosity toward the "greying, bespectacled, skulking" poet. They discuss the dubious value of poetry workshops; the difference between writing poetry and prose, between British and American poets, between German and Anglo-Saxon. They consider the reputations of contemporary writers, the merits of Randall Jarrell, Shakespeare's late plays and Ben Jonson's *The Alchemist,* King James's *Daemonologie,* the Southern Fugitive poets, Mozart and Freemasonry, the work of Dylan Thomas and Pablo Neruda, and South American politics. Writing with license to catch the bizarre tone of the evening, Newlove savages the other (invited) guests and maliciously portrays Lowell as rude, arrogant, egoistic, overbearing and gauche.

The last memoir (1977) to be published during Lowell's lifetime provides reverential, chummy, fussily-detailed and mock-modest snapshots of the Maine village where he spent eleven summers. Philip Booth portrays Lowell holding up traffic while absorbed in his own poetry, burning the baby's food, sailing and playing tennis ineptly. He advises his younger colleague to read "Empson for intellect, Marianne

Moore for observation, Frost for how a poem gets organized." Booth mentions that the tone of "Skunk Hour" has offended the local inhabitants; and discusses the stylistic change in Lowell's later poetry, his generous party for Theodore Roethke and his daily work schedule: "Breakfast, postoffice, Barn; work and lunch there until it is time for tennis and people again." The essay ends with the sudden landfall of Ted Kennedy and his friends, and a lively discussion about Vietnam. Booth's piece is flawed by his awkward, adolescent viewpoint. When he receives instruction from the "master teacher," he feels "like a new boy taken out behind the gym by a Sixth Former, being told quietly that one isn't living up to the school's best traditions" (No. 24).

The literary world was shocked by Lowell's sudden death from a heart attack, in a taxi traveling from Kennedy airport to his Manhattan flat, on 12 September 1977. Alvarez was first off the mark with an obituary that appeared six days later in the London *Observer*. Alvarez places Lowell in the modern tradition, links him to the manic American poets of his generation (Roethke, Berryman, Jarrell and Schwartz) and describes him as "a tall, stooping man with a benign, vaguely puzzled air but shrewd eyes which missed nothing." He calls *Life Studies* as revolutionary and influential as *The Waste Land* and says you looked through these poems "to see the man as he was, troubled, witty, vulnerable, balancing precariously between tenderness and violence." Alvarez's crisp account of Lowell's career convincingly concludes that he was "the finest poet of his greatly gifted generation" (No. 25).

The composite obituary in the *Listener* (22 September) includes tributes from poets, professors and critics—Seamus Heaney (who had seen Lowell a week before his death), Peter Levi, Richard Ellmann, M. L. Rosenthal and Alvarez—that had been broadcast on BBC Radio 3 the previous week. All agreed about Lowell's poetic stature. Levi reflected that "he was a very loving man but that also was affected by the madness, so that although he could give such happiness to other people, there was also pain, and he knew a lot about that" (No. 26).

Patrick Cosgrave recalls (24 September) Lowell inviting him to lunch shortly after the publication of his rather critical book about the poet. He stresses Lowell's hypersensitivity, for it seemed that "writing, even feeling, caused in [Lowell] an agony that . . . could be assuaged only by drink or mania." He also records Lowell's profound conviction that "poetry was a necessary public activity, an essential method of judging the affairs of men and of state" (No. 27).

Robert Fitzgerald's rather disappointing obituary (1 October)[5] praises Lowell's neglected criticism as well as his "scope and grasp and largeness of mind." Fitzgerald reports that Lowell exclaimed (with considerable exaggeration) that he could no longer be a Catholic because "it set him on fire," that he "had to govern his greatness with his illness in mind." Fitzgerald's second memoir (May 1978) was originally read at a Harvard memorial service on 2 March 1978. He briefly comments on Lowell's ancestry and education; the course of his career; his friendships with Jarrell, Berryman and George Santayana; his marriages, teaching and translations; his recent illness and the impact of his work. He found Lowell "myopic, hulking, diffident, formidable, wry, companionable, sombre"; and categorized Lowell, in the extremities of his Baroque poetry, as "working with intensities close to madness" (No. 28).

Stanley Kunitz, who knew Lowell best of all the writers, was more personal and critical in his obituary (16 October). He speaks of Lowell's competition with other poets. "His concentration on the literary land-scape was unremitting" and he loved to rate his contemporaries at par-ties, "especially when inferiors were present, with high-keyed zest and malice." He considers Lowell's friendships, revisions, reaction to crit-icism; his use of Elizabeth Hardwick's letters in *The Dolphin,* his mega-lomania and his manic attacks: "He makes us excruciatingly aware of the thrashing of the self behind the lines, of the intense fragility of the psyche trying to get a foothold in an 'air of lost connections'" (No. 29).

John Thompson's incisively etched portrait (24 October) begins with a description of Lowell's learned awkwardness at Kenyon and with his dreadful parents: "Charlotte was a Snow Queen who flirted coldly and shamelessly with her son. His father once ordered a half-bottle of wine for five at dinner." He depicts Lowell's marriages, breakdown, poetic style, personal appearance, character, habits and tastes: "Fame, titles, great names attracted him as they do all those who know their souls belong on the upper slopes. . . . He was also dangerous, as men in his dimensions can be" (No. 30).

The memoir of Helen Ransom Forman (November 1977), a teen-ager when Lowell lived in her father's house at Kenyon, recalls his messy room, his zealous snow-shoveling, games with the family and ingenious charades. The accompanying excerpt from Peter Taylor's "1939," a slightly fictionalized account of life with Lowell at the sleepy Ohio col-lege, describes Lowell's slovenly habits and their passionate determina-tion to become writers.[6]

Vereen Bell (January 1978) met Lowell only twice: when he read his poems—in a "halting, disorganized, and diffident" fashion—at a scholarly conference and at Vanderbilt University. Bell mentions Lowell's "strangely neurasthenic and animated conversation," his poetic celebration of the psychopathology of everyday life; and states that Lowell, like Roethke, "was intoxicated by the knowledge of his own mortality" (No. 31).

The moving memorial address of Seamus Heaney was read at St. Luke's Church in London on 5 October 1977. With an oratorical grandeur worthy of his subject, Heaney places Lowell in the modern poetic tradition. He speaks of Lowell's lineal descent from Frost, Pound, Eliot, Ransom and Tate; of the "nimbus of authority that ringed his writings and his actions"; and of his oracular and penitential voice whose purpose was redemptive. He weaves personal memories with poetic praise, describes their recent meeting and his response to Lowell's death, and ruminates on the themes of memory, history, love and renewal in Lowell's work (No. 32).

Alfred Kazin's brief notes in his autobiography (1978) depict Lowell's friendship with Jarrell and Hannah Arendt, Kazin's meeting with Lowell at Yaddo in 1949 and Lowell's manic belief that the director of the artists' colony was a Soviet agent. Kazin portrays Lowell as "handsome, magnetic, rich, wild with excitement about his powers, wild over the many tributes to him from Pound [and] Santayana." He calls the "straightforward 'confessional' mode [of his poetry] perfect for his literary instinct and troubled life in an age merciless with guilt" (No. 33).

Peter Taylor's rather rambling snippets of conversations, anecdotes, remarks and letters (1979)[7] describe Lowell in church and in Kenyon College, as a would-be writer and a Catholic convert, as a political protester and a campaigner: "He wanted to participate in every intellectual activity that it was conceivable he might. Moreover, he wanted to *possess* the experience. And once he had participated in something, he was never willing to give up his part in it—not even old opinions that no longer suited him. In a sense, he was a Roman Catholic till the end, and would say so, though he would also almost simultaneously declare that he was in no sense a believer. He would boast at times that he had never lost a friend. He never even wanted to give up a marriage entirely. He wanted his wife and children around him in an old fashioned household, and yet he wanted to be free and on the town. . . . One could not help feeling that he had had everything, even the kind of death he had always said he wanted." The best part of Taylor's piece is the extract from Lowell's letters. In November 1955, shortly after his return to live in Boston, Lowell wrote in high spirits: "We're having a good fall, and feel very lordly and pretentious in our new Boston house. It's just exactly a block from the one I grew up in. It's not really little, and not at all unpretentious, and we despise everyone whose nerve for cities has failed, all country people, all suburbanites, and all people who live in apartments."

The nine memoirs in the special Lowell issue of the *Harvard Advocate* (November 1979) were written by two boyhood friends, two publishers, a former pupil, and four poets and critics who had studied with Lowell and become his disciples. Francis Parker recalls Lowell's interest in art at St. Mark's School; and explains that the experiences of the moody, solitary, antisocial and unnaturally fervid Lowell, who had worked at a summer camp for under-privileged boys, taught the poet the gratification of satisfied willpower, which he later harnessed to the chariot of literary fame (No. 34). Blair Clark's memoir is frank and incisive. He reports (like John Thompson) that "Charlotte Lowell's white gloves sheathed steely hands determined to wrest victory from her strange, rebellious only child." Clark lacked the confidence to challenge the boyhood bullying of Lowell, the undisputed leader of the Parker-Clark gang; and reports that Lowell was considered odd, not crazy, by his classmates. He points out that Lowell systematically apprenticed himself to older writers so "he could learn from them not just the craft of poetry but [also] something about how to think and live as a poet." He frequently rescued Lowell during bouts of mania; and concludes that there were "two dynamos within him, spinning in opposite directions and tearing him apart, and that these forces would kill him at last" (No. 35).

Robert Giroux's remarks (like Fitzgerald's and Heaney's) were spoken at a memorial service for Lowell—in New York on 25 September 1977. After mentioning his first meeting with Lowell in 1940 and their visit to Pound in St. Elizabeth's in 1948, he quotes Lowell's letters about the death of Eliot in 1965 and his plans for future work: "I must say that there was no one who spoke with such authority as Tom, and so little played the role of the great man." After the publication of *History* in 1973, Lowell intended to translate ten or twelve cantos of Dante and to continue his "prose reminiscences, more or less like what I've done, if I can find a new form that will let me write at greater length" (No. 36). Charles Monteith's slight piece recalls meeting Lowell at Harvard, seeing

him in Boston, attending the opera with him in New York, visiting him
at his country house in Kent and calling on him at a nursing home in
Hampstead.[8]

Richard Tillinghast sees Lowell as a profoundly divided person, in
whom "radicalism was balanced by a rock-ribbed, atavistic sense of
tradition." Lowell both rejected and embodied his guilt-ridden New
England heritage, and was "trapped by fate in a tragically flawed person-
ality." He describes a lively meeting between Lowell and James Dickey,
and affords a rare glimpse into Lowell's extraordinary letters. When he
urged the poet to accept an invitation to teach at Berkeley during the
revolutionary sixties, Lowell replied with a witty analogy: "Your saying
that I 'should be in on it' is as tho I were to offer you Castine by saying
'we seem likely to have a tidal wave and you should see the morale of a
village in danger'" (No. 37).

Alan Williamson focuses on Lowell's friendships, his effectiveness in
political protest and the influence of madness on his character. Lowell's
own "hypersensitivity mixed badly with the hypersensitivity and self-
consciousness his fame evoked in most people who met him." His rela-
tion to others "was at once dominating and expansive and curiously,
even poignantly, dependent." Lowell inspired the radical movement by
"his refusal to fall for easy hopes or to relinquish any imaginatively
valuable point of view." His mere presence "seemed to prove that the
best . . . of traditional culture was on the dissenting side." Lowell
seemed heroic to many people, for "living in the imminence of an inter-
nal chaos that would have wrecked many lives, he so often seemed
stronger and not weaker than the normal person"—in work, in physical
courage, in capacity for friendship and "in his ability to synthesize harsh
truths with deeply felt values" (No. 38). Frank Bidart, thinking particu-
larly of *The Dolphin,* emphasizes (like Stanley Kunitz) the human cost of
Lowell's poems. He writes of Lowell's strange impact on his friends, of
"the inextricable mixture of love, expectation, frustration, *rancor* Lowell
aroused in many," and concludes: "In a central way, Robert Lowell was
not quite civilized" (No. 39).

Judith Baumel recalls that all the student writers at Harvard wanted
to take Lowell's poetry workshop and that he selected his pupils quixot-
ically. He was "a great teacher of literature and an awful workshop
teacher. . . . Lowell had very little help to offer in the form of direct,
constructive criticism of line, structure, intent, execution of student
drafts." In his judgment of pupils, as of fellow poets, he "could be

arbitrary, petty and even cruel." But he was excellent at synthesizing a poet's work in an epigrammatic and often self-reflective sentence. Browning "invented the mystery novel in verse [*The Ring and the Book*] and wrote more good lines than any nineteenth-century poet." Tennyson (who seems like Lowell) was "an intense, moody, clumsy young man with an enormous metrical skill" (No. 40).

In 1979 Rolando Anzilotti—professor at Pisa, mayor of a small Tuscan town and Italian translator of Lowell—edited a bilingual volume of tributes that were offered at a literary conference in May 1978. There were five memoirs among the critical essays—three by Italian poets, two by Lowell's friends. None of the poets knew him well, and all write in a florid and sentimental Latin style. Giorgio Caproni reverently recounts his only meeting with Lowell during a poetry reading in Pisa in May 1973. He praises Lowell's insight, says that he looks like "a sympathetic tapeworm" and notes that "he speaks very softly, but with an almost Japanese smile, gently ironic."[9] Carlo Betocchi contrasts his own humble origins to Lowell's aristocratic wealth and compares their rebellion against the torments of the Catholic Church. He praises the depth of Lowell's culture, recalls a dinner party and poetry reading in the hills of Tuscany, and exclaims that Lowell's books "have moved me and have had the function of liberating my spirit."[10] Francesco Tentori considers the importance of Lowell's work, which "was distinguished, like that of Eliot, by an allegorical and moral dimension . . . tradition and renewal, dramatic intensity, visionary fantasy and irony seem deeply fused." To Tentori, Lowell "seemed to have a solid structure . . . but lightened by the spirit . . . a presence attentive and at the same time abstracted."[11]

Esther Brooks begins her lively memoir with an account of Lowell's appearance, conversation and air of abstraction, and then comments on his interest in painting. She says that when he was well he was enormous fun to be with and had one of the most knowledgeable minds she had ever encountered: "he was riveting, fascinating, funny, odd, and completely, interestingly original and serious." His anguish about Vietnam was extreme, but he "managed to remain lucid, independent, and courageously non-violent. . . . [He had] an almost infallible instinct for making the right [political] gesture at the right time." Brooks perceives that in Lowell "the well person and the unwell person seemed to rub together in a strange kind of muted euphoria." When he recovered from his mental breakdowns, he could remember all he had said and done when he was ill: "Yes, everything. And that is the worst part of it."

Brooks is also strikingly frank about what she considers his disastrous third marriage, to Caroline Blackwood, and states that he was returning to Elizabeth Hardwick when he died of a heart attack (No. 41).

Helen Vendler's essay, based on her classroom notes, is the most intelligent and substantial description of Lowell as a teacher. Citing his extensive discussion of Matthew Arnold (as well as of Clare, Coleridge, Hopkins and Whitman), Vendler explains that his murmured monologues were "a form of teaching that had nothing to do with the imposition of a body of knowledge, but rather aimed at the example of a mind in action." He gave his students a sense of how poems are created, "of a life, a spirit, a mind, and a set of occasions from which writing issues. . . . Lowell's sense of the poem as event, together with his equal sense of the living voice speaking the lines out of some occasion, made the poems instantly available as experience," though he tended to "rearrange poetic features till they resembled his own." In his response to poetry, "familiarity and reverence went hand in hand . . . technique and vision were indissoluble." Lowell's mode of perception is synthesized in his aphoristic praise of Frost, who possessed "faith incorrupt from subversion, subversion unillumined by faith" (No. 42). Vendler's second memoir of Lowell (also 1979), weaves personal memories into her reading—and her defense—of his last book, *Day by Day*. She finds it a stern and touching volume; and commends its techniques and themes: "The poems drift from one focus to another; they avoid the histrionic; they sigh more often than they expostulate. They acknowledge exhaustion; they expect death." Lowell appears in the memoir—teaching, responding to criticism, wanting to be "heartbreaking" in his work—as modest, thoughtful, dedicated to his craft and to his calling (No. 43).

Dudley Young (1982)—Lowell's sometime colleague, housemate and manservant at Essex University during 1970–71—records their long conversations about Lowell's current style of poetry and stresses the manic side of his personality: "that voluminous brain, the relentless talk, the charm, the wit, the malice: all driven by a deceptively powerful body burning manic energy and whisky at about twice the rate" of people half his age (No. 44).

James Atlas' digressive, denigrating piece (1982)—as much, unfortunately, about Atlas as about Lowell—resembles those by Donald Newlove and Dudley Young: "Lowell would shuffle into the crowded room looking hung over and pale, his forehead damp, a watery remoteness in his eyes." Atlas describes the difficulty of getting into

Lowell's class at Harvard, his secret office hours, his chaotic mode of teaching, his gossip about English poets, his indiscriminate curiosity about his students' work, his delight in "ranking poets, assigning them their place on the ladder—beneath him, it was understood" (No. 45).

Anthony Hecht brings memories of Lowell into his review-essay (1983) of Ian Hamilton's biography. Hecht discusses the influence of "Lycidas" on "The Quaker Graveyard in Nantucket," the sources (Holbein's portrait and Roper's life) of his sonnet on Sir Thomas More ("terrifying in its awareness of the hideous cost of greatness"), his tendency to reverse his meaning in revisions and to convert great foreign poetry into "Lo-Cal." He considers Lowell's use of Hardwick's letters in *The Dolphin* and Auden's dislike of that volume. In the comparison of Lowell and Byron, which gives the essay its title, Hecht writes: "Both poets were public figures and involved in the political events of their time; both were capable of devastating expressions of scorn for their opponents; both were powerful and handsome men; both were crippled, each in his own way; both were astonishingly attractive to women; both were aristocrats by inheritance (somewhat shabby aristocrats) and democrats by generous instinct; both were the subject of scandalous gossip during and after their lifetime; and both were poets of acknowledged international stature, who *found themselves famous* quite early in life. It may be added that both were bedeviled by a strict and relentlessly Puritan conscience, and Calvinistic anguish" (No. 46).

Kathleen Spivack's first memoir (1985)—which has the same pedagogical emphasis as Tillinghast, Baumel and Vendler—concentrates on Lowell's greatness as poet and teacher, the reverence and timidity of the students in his classes, his belief that poetry was the central thing in life, and his relations with women poets: Anne Sexton, Adrienne Rich, Denise Levertov and Elizabeth Bishop. To Spivack, who did not know Lowell well and was puzzled by his bizarre mania, "the whole series of swings in Lowell's moods seemed very mysterious, and what later struck others as 'signs' seemed, in fact, to be normal Lowell behavior. I was never able to shake a slight fear of his unpredictability, the flashes of cruelty that could and did emerge" (No. 47). Spivack's second memoir (also 1985)[12] tends to avoid a direct discussion of Lowell. She begins with an account of her unapproachable fellow-pupil, Sylvia Plath—who made even Lowell feel ill at ease in her presence, and of Anne Sexton—whom Lowell admired and treated as an equal. Like Anne Sexton, Spivack is honest about the dark side of Lowell's character, especially as he moved closer to a breakdown: "Lowell had the capacity for extreme cruelty where the living . . . were concerned. He liked to pit student against student, friend against friend, hopefully, to draw the listener into the role of conspirator against the other, less fortunate contenders for his favor. . . . Cal, although pretending to be half-mad, knew exactly what he was doing."

Lowell's letter to his wife Caroline, written in February 1977, captures his indomitable irony and stoic resignation, and expresses the essence of the gifted and tormented man portrayed in the memoirs: "The hospital business, despite the rough useless and dramatic ambulance at McLean's, was painless eventless; perhaps what death might be at best. A feeling that one was doomed like Ivan Illich, but without suffering. There seemed to be no danger at all, except that there still may be—but all so quiet it hardly seemed to matter. . . . If that's all life is, it's a coldly smiling anti-climax. Gone the great apocalypse of departure" (No. 32).[13]

1. The memoirs also complement the imaginative portraits of Lowell's powerful personality in poems, plays, stories and novels. See I. A. Richards, "For a Miniature of Robert Lowell," *Harvard Advocate* 145 (November 1961): 4; and "For the 50th Birthday of Robert Lowell," *Internal Colloquies* (New York, 1971), p. 55.

Joseph Brodsky, "Elegy: For Robert Lowell" (1977), *A Part of Speech* (New York, 1980), pp. 135–137.

Seamus Heaney, *Robert Lowell: A Memorial Address and Elegy* (London, 1978).

Elizabeth Bishop, "North Haven," *Harvard Advocate* 113 (November 1979): 25.

Andrei Voznesensky, "Family Graveyard" and "Lines to Robert Lowell," *Nostalgia for the Present* (Garden City, N.Y., 1978), pp. 7, 109–115.

Richard Eberhart, "The Mad Musician," *Collected Verse Plays of Richard Eberhart* (Chapel Hill, N.C., 1962), pp. 131–166.

Jean Stafford, "A Country Love Story," "The Home Front" and "The Interior Castle," *Children Are Bored on Sunday* (New York, 1953), pp. 41–60, 105–142, 195–217; and "An Influx of Poets," *New Yorker* 54 (6 November 1978): 43–60.

Peter Taylor, "1939," *The Collected Stories* (New York, 1969), pp. 336–359.

Paul Theroux, "The Exile," *The London Embassy* (Boston, 1983), pp. 82–100.

Vladimir Nabokov, *Ada* (New York, 1969)—in which Lowell appears as Lowden.

Caroline Blackwood, *The Step-Daughter* (London, 1976).

Elizabeth Hardwick, *Sleepless Nights* (New York, 1979).

2. Lowell first said this in "The Cold War and the West," *Partisan Review* 29 (Winter 1962): 47.

3. Mary Jane Baker, "Classes with a Poet," *Mademoiselle* 40 (November 1954): 106, 137, 139–141.

4. Donald Newlove, "Dinner at the Lowells'," *Esquire* 72 (September 1969): 128–129, 168, 170, 176–178, 180, 184.

5. Robert Fitzgerald, "Robert Lowell, 1917–1977," *New Republic* 177 (1 October 1977): 10–12.

6. Helen Ransom Forman and Peter Taylor, "Robert Lowell: The Years at Kenyon, A Remembrance," *Kenyon College Alumni Bulletin* 1 (November 1977): 22–24.

7. Peter Taylor, "Robert Traill Spence Lowell, 1917–1977," *Ploughshares* 5 (1979): 74–81.

8. Charles Monteith, "From Faber and Faber," *Harvard Advocate* 113 (November 1979): 29.

9. Giorgio Caproni, "Leaves From My Diary: May 1973," *Robert Lowell: A Tribute,* edited by Rolando Anzilotti (Pisa, 1979), pp. 47–49.

10. Carlo Betocchi, "My Friend Lowell," *Robert Lowell: A Tribute,* edited by Rolando Anzilotti (Pisa, 1979), pp. 28–32.

11. Francesco Tentori, "Memories of Lowell," *Robert Lowell: A Tribute,* edited by Rolando Anzilotti (Pisa, 1979), pp. 55–56.

12. Kathleen Spivack, "Lear in Boston: Robert Lowell as Teacher and Friend," *Ironwood* 13 (Spring 1985): 76–92.

13. For other aspects of Lowell's life and work, see Jeffrey Meyers, *Manic Power: Robert Lowell and His Circle* (London: Macmillan; New York: Arbor House, 1987).

"Review-essay of Ian Hamilton's *Robert Lowell,*" *Virginia Quarterly Review* 59 (Summer 1983): 516–522.

"Lowell as Critic," *Journal of Modern Literature* (1987).

"Robert Lowell: The Paintings in the Poems," *Papers on Language and Literature* 23 (Spring 1987): 218–239.

Note on the text: The interviews and memoirs printed in this volume follow the original texts and appear in roughly chronological order. Typographical errors have been corrected, exact repetitions have been deleted and quotations from Lowell's works have been retained—and identified. Memoirs described in the Introduction but not reprinted in this collection are identified in notes 3 through 12.

I. Interviews

1 • Falling Asleep over Grillparzer: An Interview with Robert Lowell

John McCormick

After swimming, we lolled on the grass of the terrace before the Schloss[1] in the full morning sun; it was a day without haze and in the near distance, across from Leopoldskron-Teich, we could see the Untersberg, where, according to local legend and some written history, Charlemagne lies buried. To the left, deceptively close, Hohensalzburg and the lower ridge of Hitler's Berchtesgaden (pronounced Birchesgarden by the local American troops) dominated the horizon. Lowell and I talked about Germany and Austria. During the winter in Amsterdam he had gone through most of the Nürnberg Trial Reports.

Obviously from his conversation and his verse Lowell had read a good deal of history. Had he seen a recent article by an American poet who said that "The subject farthest from the poet's interests and sympathy will probably be history"? No, he had not read it, and he could not agree. He had spent the winter with Lord Macaulay as well as with the Nürnberg Trials. How inexhaustibly mature were Macaulay, Burke, and Halifax[2] on the balances and complexities of parliamentary government. North's Plutarch was a great favorite of his along with Thucydides, Tacitus, Clarendon,[3] and Toynbee. The greatest historians were those who re-created people, not simply those who gave an accurate or even an interesting account of events. Then possibly he would agree with a further remark in the same article I had mentioned, which said in effect "The positivism of modern historians is almost the perfect foil for the poet." Certainly; history is an art, not a science. A historian must be at least as intelligent as his subjects.

Before coming to the Salzburg Seminar, where Lowell was lecturing on American poetry, he had spent three weeks in Vienna. The opera was the big thing there; he had attended almost every night. We talked

Poetry 81 (January 1953): 269–279. Reprinted by permission of John McCormick.

about the tombs of the Hapsburgs and the fact that the Hapsburg entrails were distributed all over the churches and monuments of Vienna in jars and urns and pots.

Later in the evening we had hoped to listen to the final nominations from the Democratic Convention, until we remembered that a poetry reading had been arranged which would conflict with the broadcast. It was, unfortunately, to be a busy day: a lecture on Hart Crane immediately after lunch, a seminar at five, then the reading in the evening.

I gathered myself together, book, a pen, sun glasses, while Lowell strode off to make some last-minute preparation for his lecture. "Strode" is not the verb. He walks on tip-toe, rather on the balls of his feet, clumsily, not from lack of bodily grace but because he is near-sighted. Like a small child who distrusts his sense of equilibrium, he has trouble turning corners. In his swimming trunks he looked like an athlete slightly out of shape; broad shoulders and an oarsman's wrists and forearms, but the thin and unathletic legs of a nervous and possibly sedentary man. It was easy to see why, on the first day of the seminar, one of the Germans who had not yet been introduced to him had referred to him as "ein grosse, schwarze Mann."[4] (This was the same person who later in the day had asked Mrs. Lowell if it were true that Randall Jarrell was a negro. Lowell, standing near, had replied that if Jarrell *were* a negro, he was the finest negro poet of all time.) In spite of Lowell's dark hair sprinkled with grey, he did not look thirty-five. After a week's association, I had come to realize that he is fundamentally a serious man who has achieved the confidence that permits and indeed encourages the frivolous. I was never to think of him without using one of his own terms about Pound's *Cantos*—hilarity.

During luncheon in the pink Baroque dining hall I asked Lowell about his background and education. After an undistinguished career at St. Mark's, he made a conventional, brief, and doomed assault upon Harvard. There he wrote a long heroic poem, garbled from Michaud's[5] (illustrations by Doré)[6] *History of the Crusades* and met Robert Frost, who turned him obliquely and gently to other and more rewarding models. Merrill Moore[7] was partially responsible for his transfer to Kenyon, where he arrived at the age of nineteen in a filthy white suit, carrying a suitcase full of stinking laundry and drafts of verses, to live first in John Crowe Ransom's house and later in a detached dormitory where Randall Jarrell, a year older, was Proctor and Peter Taylor and Robie Macauley[8] were also residents. Under Ransom's protection, and in a sense, patronage, he specialized in Classics (thus fulfilling Pound's dictum about the ideal training for poets), studied French and philosophy, talked much, wrote more, and completed an apprenticeship. Lowell's living in the South and with Southern poets has influenced his speech, which is soft and given to Southern inflections. He emphasizes auxiliaries and adverbs, and plays down nouns and verbs. It is a gentle speech in which New England hardnesses only occasionally intrude.

The war loomed large. At the beginning, Lowell volunteered for the Navy (his father had been a Naval officer: one remembers *The Mills of the Kavanaughs*), but he was rejected for near-sightedness. By 1943 his constitutional docility had become a militant pacifism of an unorthodox nature; he was tried in New York City in 1943 and offered in defense not religious convictions or standard pacifistic volutions but arguments against the Allied, and specifically American, demand for unconditional surrender, and against saturation bombing. His sentence was a year and a day (making it a felony, he points out) in the penitentiary at Danbury, Connecticut. Lowell remarked at this point that the Judge was not too hard on him, since the standard sentence was three years; he rather enjoyed his companions at Danbury, mostly well-heeled gentlemen from the New York black markets, fallen, momentarily, from grace. His poem "The Exile's Return," as I read it, was worth the felony: *Voi ch'entrate,*[9] *and your life is in your hands.*

After lunch we sat on at the table, smoking and talking. Lowell is a man who smokes a great deal but rarely has either cigarettes or matches on his person. A Milanese poet asked Lowell about New England and the South. Lowell replied by talking with deceptive irrelevance about the wonderful age of both New England and the mid-Southern landscape, the landscape of Vermont, of rural Massachusetts, of Tennessee and Kentucky. "Its ancientness makes you feel the vulgar modernity of Europe," he said ironically. In the same fashion he talked about Ransom's "Conrad,"[10] describing the rheumatic Conrad sitting in his doorway perversely inducing more rheumatism: "You see, Conrad's a Platonist." The Milanese, unlike most literate Italians, had read Ransom thoroughly, and Lowell went on with reminiscences of Ransom, of his gentle and civilized reception of Dylan Thomas when Thomas reached Kenyon on one of his shattering lecture tours, of Ransom on Aristotle. "It was wonderful to see Ransom playing with Aristotle. Like a cat toying with an enormous tortoise—each keeping its dignity."

Suddenly we realized it was almost time for Lowell's lecture. His chair screeched on the marble floor as he struggled away from the table, putting my cigarettes in his pocket and saying, "Here I've been talking about Mr. Ransom when I should have been thinking about Hart Crane."

As always, the lecture on Hart Crane was seemingly off the cuff but actually a complete and nice piece of organization; thoughtful and original and wilful and entirely successful with its audience of poets and writers and literary students from a dozen-odd countries. Lowell's method—he is a first-rate teacher who enjoys teaching—is to circle in upon his man like a dog upon a bird; he came to Crane by way of Tate, Emerson, Dante, and Vergil. All were relevant, sometimes surprising, and always enlightening. The method is personal, it brooks no questioning or resistance, and it is highly effective, even though, in the diction of the social-relations people, on the authoritarian side. You accepted, even when you silently questioned, for the man had clearly sweated through to his position. Lowell described his own view of Crane by saying that "Allen Tate always speaks of Crane with awe and vexation." Lowell's own awe is for the intensity and mastery, and his vexation, of a very mild variety, for the "gaiety and innocence that prevent Crane from being one of the greatest poets."

As anyone must who talks publicly in Europe of Crane, Lowell discussed Crane's fondness for sailors, drink, and violence not in fashionable terms borrowed from psychiatry, but by saying that we must go to Dante for a parallel in treatment. We must put Crane with the homosexual Arnaut Daniel[11] (*il miglior fabbro*) in the *Purgatorio,* not with Brunetto Latini in the *Inferno.*[12] How better say it? He went on to the obvious layers of Whitman in such places as the invocation to the *Bridge,* and to the not so obvious kinship between Crane and Emerson. Listening to the lecture and checking off the poems of Crane which Lowell selected to read, I thought again, as I had when I first read *Lord Weary's Castle,* that Lowell, while he does not borrow from Crane, owes much to him; the authority of precedent, perhaps. He read "Black Tambourine," the invocation to *The Bridge,* the extraordinary Pocahontas poem, "The Dance," from *The Bridge,* and finally "National Winter Garden" and "Voyages II." This forty-minute anthology was a masterpiece of selection and understanding, and in the tenderness and carnality of the Pocahontas poem, the rhetoric of the invocation, the mysticism (Lowell's word) of the burlesque-show "National Winter Garden" (about which he added that Crane was "one of the few American poets we can call religious"),

the Classical aura, the "Vergilian freshness" of "Voyages," you per-
ceived the qualities Lowell seeks and frequently achieves in his own
poetry. Even the prosody, the classicism, the suggestion of monologue
in Crane which Lowell makes specific and dramatic; the violence, the
sense that in the case of each poet you must say, here is a man who
devours himself, was inescapable. Only a relationship which is not that
of teacher to student, not imitation, not mere influence, but rather identi-
fication, could lead Lowell to the suggestion with which he ended his
lecture: that when Crane leapt off the fantail of the ship into the Mexican
Gulf he did not wish to commit suicide, but rather that he had only an
intense desire to cool and wet his exhausted body.

Later in the day I asked Lowell about the possible "influence" of
Crane in his work, for I was anxious to check my conviction. He was
embarrassed at the directness of my question, and noncommittal.
Couldn't I be more specific? Well, then, how did he come to his affection
for the dramatic monologue? Through Pound? Chaucer? Crane?
Browning?

"I'm not evading," he said, "but once Delmore Schwartz said to me
that if you had people in a poem, the right people, you can say anything.
Of course, I had already begun with dramatic monologues—"Mr. Ed-
wards and the Spider" and the one "To Peter Taylor" were the first. But
Schwartz had thought through the possibilities much more profoundly
than I had."

What about habits of work? People always wanted to know these
things. How much revision did he make? Did he work by day or at
night?

"The best thing about writing verse is that you can work lying
down. I like a small room, to myself, that I can stack as high as I want
with books and papers, with a cot where I can write on my back, take
naps, wake up and go back to the painful, necessary, and fascinating
business of changing around the words and the lines. Sometimes there
are as many as thirty versions of one poem, and I usually make more
changes between magazine publication and book publication. And even
when it's in a book, I want to change it again." Lowell described how he
might work on five or six poems at a time, when he was going well; that
he might begin a poem in the Fall and not "finish" it until the next
Spring.

Late in the afternoon we all trailed half-way around the lake to a
Bierstube[13] where Lowell once or twice held his seminar; no one could

endure Max Reinhardt's[14] Baroque-Rococo taste in Schloss Leopolds-kron twenty-four hours a day, and particularly not as a back-drop for Poe, Emerson, and Melville, whose poems were the subject of the day's meeting. The fine weather of the morning still held, although it was chilly in the shade of the chestnuts at the Biergarten, and occasionally our voices would be lost in the nerve-shattering splutter of the single-cylinder Austrian motorcycles on the nearby road.

Lowell was clearly tired; his lecture had taken a good deal of energy. His weariness emphasized his intolerance of dissenting, and, sometimes, idiotic opinions. Again the poems he had selected for discussion were favorites: "To Helen," "The Concord Hymn," and Melville's fine "March into Virginia" and "The Maldive Shark." Lowell asserted, in contradiction to an American student, that "To Helen" was not metronomic, and when someone said that the images in the "Concord Hymn" came from a library, Lowell asked "What library?" An Italian said of the "Hymn," "I feel Horace here," and Lowell answered, "I do too." "It's patriotic," an Irish poet said, "and you can't write patriotic verse anymore." Lowell answered, "You never could—not even in Emerson's time. Read again about the river *which seaward creeps*. A fine line." The Irishman was nettled, and Lowell was aware of it. He made amends, in his fashion. "When I interrupt people I'm not trying to be arrogant." There was ground to cover, was the implication, and certain things had to be said, put aright. "And what about *the shot heard round the world?* Another fine line—conscious, urbane exaggeration. Emerson always maintains an ironic and urbane distance from the Concord farmers who themselves simply thought they were out-shooting the English tax collectors. In this poem you've got freshness, gentleness, calmness. And the most exciting work is in the last stanza. The poem becomes more internal as it goes on, and you find Emerson's old themes—time, world, spirit—flashing in one historic moment."

Did Lowell consider Emerson a finished craftsman? someone asked. "Certainly not. He only hit it in some poems, like this one, but then he was superior to Poe. People underrate him. A good poem always seems fresh, and Emerson's poetry is so often fresh and alive." The Irishman still was not satisfied, but we went on to Melville. Lowell read "The March into Virginia" and said it gave you the feeling of daguerreotypes of the American Civil War combined with Wilfred Owen. "The Maldive Shark" was one of those poems which renews itself continually; what more terrifying symbol of the intelligence that served Hitler like pilot fish. At this point we were aware of the hovering bar-keep, himself a corpulent maldive shark in a dirty denim apron and a cigarette behind his ear; we realized it was time to pay up and return to dinner. Lowell asked in his bad German whether they sold de-nicotinized cigarettes in Austria. The shark answered in worse English that he had not understood Herr-Professor, but that his daughter spoke fine English; we endured the *Bezahlen*[15]-litany and straggled back to the Schloss. On the way, Lowell explained to a Finn how Robert Herrick would have ended "The Humble-Bee" at the conclusion of the second stanza.

At dinner an Austrian radio script-writer talked about Grillparzer's *Sappho*,[16] and Lowell remarked that Grillparzer sounded like the name of an unsuccessful Hapsburg general, one of those you saw brooding on horseback in magnificent etchings in the Albertina.[17]

Nine poets from nine different countries participated in the poetry reading. With gentle justice Lowell introduced each one, and read in his alphabetical turn two of his own poems, "The Exile's Return" and "Mother Marie Thérèse." Like many poets, he does not read his own verse well; his voice is rather high and lacks range, but his feeling and inflection add a depth which a better but less sensitive voice would often miss. At ten o'clock Mrs. Lowell appeared to announce triumphantly that Stevenson[18] had been nominated. The Europeans were puzzled by the American reaction to the news; the reading broke up, and in spite of a wearying day, a slight case of sunburn, and the fact that we had all talked too much and were exhausted, we agreed that Stevenson deserved a celebration. We would walk to town and drink a bottle of Gumpoldskirchner.

Anna, my Dachshund, rated an evening promenade, so she came along. The Weinstube near the Dom[19] for once was not crowded; the wall facing us was a perpendicular boneyard devoted to the skulls and antlers of various mountain goats and deer, surmounted by a painted wooden Crucifixion. Anna ranged the floor scrounging bits of food, while the Lowells, an Englishman, the Irishman, two Italians, and I talked about Europe, Stevenson's prospects, history, and architecture. "It's good to be away from home for a bit," Lowell said, "to have a let-up from the unavoidable idea, a Promethean illusion perhaps, that the future of the world depends upon what your country does every day." I was pleased by this turn in the conversation; I knew the Lowells had been abroad a long time. After a winter in Florence, a long trip to the Near East, and a winter in Amsterdam, next winter, probably, they would take a flat in Rome. I wanted to know how Lowell felt about his European experience, about the classic difficulty which an American who writes must always feel in the course of a long residence abroad; his vision of his own country changes, his view of himself is fortified or destroyed by the impact of the alien, no matter how agreeable, culture.

"Before I came abroad," Lowell said, "I had always wanted to live in Europe for perhaps a year, or two years. Now I'm beginning my third. I'm always very conscious of being an American, in Europe, far more so than at home, but that's as it should be. I haven't got the real expatriate temperament, as I see all the time; only England, in my view, is possible for an American forever—look at Eliot . . . . You see the risk and reward wonderfully in Pound. He didn't think of himself as an Italian, but as a sort of Idaho, patrician exile, a Landor . . . . With that conception and being, at the same time, intense about the present, he naturally suffered long, barren periods. Still when Pound was a bookless prisoner of the American Army, his twenty seemingly wasted years at Rapallo suddenly flowered in those magnificent reveries of recollection in the *Pisan Cantos*."

We discussed the importance to a poet of familiarity with many languages and literatures. Lowell himself is a good passive linguist, and a bad but brave active one. Each morning we were reading *Faust* with a tutor for an hour after breakfast; in Holland he had struggled with Dutch poetry, and his Italian was improving. I mentioned the frequency with which he makes a poem "after" a foreign writer, and he said, "Every writer has to be a thief. He has to be *childishly* ambitious and even say to himself, like Racine, what would Sophocles think of this?"

What about American poets? I asked. With the exception of Elizabeth Bishop and Randall Jarrell, he confined his remarks carefully to the older poets. Frost and Eliot seemed the greatest; certainly no one had written religious verse like the *Quartets*. Williams, Ransom, Tate, Pound, Crane, Marianne Moore, and Stevens—these will be read as long as Catullus and Tibullus. And what of prose in the United States? the Englishman asked. Lowell said he had just read a wonderful essay by Eleanor Clark[20] on the Roman poet, Belli.[21] Lowell and the Englishman argued about the stature of Fitzgerald; Lowell thought him, with Hemingway and Faulkner, among our best. But Faulkner towered. Katherine Anne Porter stood out in her perfection; he didn't care for Dos Passos or know much about him. At the moment he was reading Lord Acton[22] and Goethe—he could never be a professional novel-reader.

As we talked, a twenty-piece band dressed in the red and green of the Tyrol crowded into the Stube; they were fairly well tanked, and at least ten of them were tooting different songs all at once on brass instruments, while the others shouted dull jokes in their heavy, xenophobic dialect. Anna was frightened, and we could not hear one another. We decided that in justice to Stevenson, to say nothing of Sparkman[23] and Anna, we would have to finish the evening with coffee and a final Weinbrand in the third-class restaurant at the Bahnhof.[24] The Bahnhof was always dependable, for it was large as a barn, at once pleasantly anonymous and cosmopolitan, and it never closed. It was raining outside, but one of the Swedes who had joined us was celebrating his winning of a literary prize and offered to finance a taxi.

I asked Lowell about his plans for the winter. Maybe he'd visit me in Berlin? He wanted to come to Berlin very much; he had heard the RIAS[25] Symphony do an all-Bartok concert in Paris in May, and he'd heard a lot about the Berlin opera companies, East Zone and West. But most of all he wanted to settle for the winter in Rome and get to work.

Late in the evening we made off again. Lowell, unconscious of the rain, was discussing with a student—the mayor of a small Tuscan city— the grotesque possibility of selling his poem "Falling Asleep over the Aeneid" to Hollywood. "How would you translate that title into Italian? Can't you see it now in neon lights at Mantua?"

John McCormick (b. 1918), Professor of Comparative Literature at Rutgers University, is the author of *Catastrophe and Imagination* (1957), *The Middle Distance* (1971) and *Fiction as Knowledge* (1975). McCormick taught at the Salzburg Seminars with Lowell in the summer of 1952. His title alludes to Lowell's poem, "Falling Asleep over the Aeneid."

1. Schloss Leopoldskron was the castle where the Salzburg Seminars were held.

2. George Savile, Marquess of Halifax (1633–95), political pamphleteer, author of *Character of a Trimmer* (1688).

3. Edward Hyde, First Earl of Clarendon (1609–74), British statesman and historian, author of *The True Historical Narrative of the Rebellion and Civil Wars in England* (1704–07).

4. German: a big, dark man.

5. Joseph Michaud (1767–1839), French historian, author of *The History of the Crusades* (1812–22).

6. Gustave Doré (1832–83), French painter and illustrator.

7. Merrill Moore (1903–57), psychiatrist and sonneteer who treated Lowell and was probably the lover of Lowell's mother.

8. Robie Macauley (b. 1919), American novelist, author of *The Disguises of Love* (1951) and editor at Houghton Mifflin.

9. Part of Dante's phrase about Hell: "abandon hope all ye who enter here."

10. See Ransom's poem "Conrad in Twilight" (1922).

11. Arnaut Daniel (fl. 1180–1200), celebrated Provencal poet and troubadour.

12. Brunetto Latini (ca. 1220–94), Florentine scholar and leading member of the Guelph party. In *Inferno* XV he is condemned for sodomy, but addressed with great respect by Dante.

13. German: beer cellar.

14. Max Reinhardt (1873–1943), Austrian theatrical director, producer and actor.

15. German: paying the bill.

16. Franz Grillparzer (1791–1872), Austrian poet and dramatist, author of *Sappho* (1818).

17. The great art museum in Vienna.

18. Adlai Stevenson (1900–65), Democratic candidate for president in 1952.

19. German: cathedral.

20. Eleanor Clark (b. 1913), American writer and wife of Robert Penn Warren, author of *Rome and a Villa* (1952) and *The Oysters of Locmariaquer* (1964).

21. Giuseppe Belli (1791–1863), Roman satirical sonneteer.

22. John Dahlberg-Acton, First Baron (1834–1902), British historian and moralist, author of essays on the history of freedom and on the study of history.

23. John Sparkman (1899–1985), senator from Alabama, ran for vice-president with Adlai Stevenson.

24. German: railway station.

25. RIAS: Rundfunk im Amerikanischen Sektor Berlins (Radio in the American Sector, West Berlin).

2 • From "Trade Winds"

John Fuller

Cited for poems ". . . of fierce and immediate compassion . . . which strike through the private dimension to document the pressures of an age," Mr. Lowell went on in his acceptance speech [of the National Book Award] to describe a recent phone call to his publisher.

A reluctant secretary asked: "*What* Mr. Lowell? What firm do you belong to?"

After telling of this rebuff, he went on to conclude that when he had finished *Life Studies,* his career was left hanging on a question mark—and he doesn't yet know whether it is a "life line or a death rope."

Revealing his characteristic New England thrift, Lowell said that he was planning to lay aside his $1,000 in prize money while he continued teaching at Boston University and working on translations into English of several foreign poets, including Pasternak.

"I'm calling the collection *Imitations,* because they're not completely accurate translations, but rather poetic interpretations of them. For instance, I'm working from a literal English translation as far as Pasternak is concerned, and the final result will be a poem combining both our poetic efforts."

Mr. Lowell writes slowly, with gruelling discipline, and does not believe that the Beat school of rapid-fire writing has yet produced a genuine master.

"The Beat movement has a great many things to recommend it," he told us. "But it seems to be in suspense right now, and tough, hard discipline is still lacking."

His favorite poets at the moment are Williams, Tate, Frost, and a few others—and of course the classics of the past.

"They can never be ignored in poetry," he said.

John G. Fuller was a staff writer for the *Saturday Review.*

Saturday Review 43 (9 April 1960): 12, 16. Reprinted by permission of *Saturday Review.*

3 • Robert Lowell

Cleanth Brooks and Robert Penn Warren

B: *Well, Cal—because I'm not going to call you Robert; after this many years, all your friends are bound to call you Cal—let me begin by asking, what is meter to you?*

L: Well, meter is the rules you go by, the measured definite thing in a poem, and I think of rhythm as the beat that's unmeasured.

W: *May I break in, Cal, for a moment? Let me make a statement and see how you respond to it. Meter is, as you have said, a measure, is a count. The rhythm is what you experience; you never experience the meter; the rhythm is what you get, what you experience in the verse line. But, now what would make that difference? Between the meter and the rhythm?*

L: I think of a figure of speech, that the meter is like the bone structure of the body, and God knows what the rhythm would be; it's not just the flesh and blood, it's the whole character, the whole flux of things that aren't visible at all, that are going in there. And, I'm sure the rhythm is the person himself.

B: *Would you be willing to go this far, that the meter strictly considered is always an abstraction; the rhythm is a concrete thing, that's the thing itself. . . .*

L: Yes, I think meter is as abstract as geometry, say. Yet its . . . when they come together, somehow, the meter becomes alive and it changes the rhythm a great deal, eventually it no longer exists as an abstraction.

It's a mystery I can't solve that at least nine-tenths of the great poetry of the world is in meter, that's something that can be measured. Then there's a large body of free verse, and then there's prose, which isn't radically different from poetry, I think. And it's impossible to say that Milton is better than Melville because he wrote *Paradise Lost* in meter and *Moby Dick* is in rhythm, in paragraphs and rhythm. That's myste-

Conversations on the Craft of Poetry, edited by Cleanth Brooks and Robert Penn Warren (New York: Holt, Rinehart and Winston, 1961), pp. 33–47. Reprinted by permission of Cleanth Brooks and Robert Penn Warren.

34

rious to me! I mean, for a writer, it's, meter's, very useful for revision, and you can tinker with your blank verse-line or your rhymed line in a way you can't quite if you're free. I don't think you can imagine quite rewriting the end of *Moby Dick* the way perhaps Milton rewrote the beginning of *Paradise Lost*. Equally inspired passages, but I can't see one superior and I can't really . . . I don't know what Milton does that Melville doesn't—I don't know that he does anything—but I know the form is utterly different and the rules are . . . .

B: *I wonder, Cal, whether you would like to make a few concrete illustrations oh, from let's say a traditional poet like, say, Donne or Milton, of this special character that metered rhythm gives to poetry.*

L: Well, take the opening stanza of "Lycidas," and it's quite mysterious why that's very great poetry. It's a very conventional subject, and the expression is conventional, but the ear is what's magical. I think particularly the first line, which has very little remarkable content yet is a tremendous thing rhythmically. "Yet once more, O ye Laurels, and once more."

> Yet once more, O ye Laurels, and once more
> Ye Myrtles brown, with Ivy never sere,
> I come to pluck your Berries harsh and crude,
> And with forc'd fingers rude,
> Shatter your leaves before the mellowing year.

What's so striking about this is that it's extremely formal, extremely conventional, yet when he does these unusual things that you'd never find in Spenser, like "Shatter your leaves" or "Berries harsh and crude," they seem shatteringly original in this very tight form.

W: *Just saying those lines is a pleasure, even if you aren't thinking about their content.*

L: Yes.

W: *And one thing is a pleasure, just the way the muscles get into play. In your whole vocal apparatus, even if you're reading them to yourself and not articulating them. It's just a wonderful workout, a sense of kinetic involvement in the lines. This release, this muscular play, which that kind of simple, unlabelled vitalness evoked over and against this elaboration of form and the elaboration of idea, whatever it is in any given poem. But just the physical pleasure in a well-turned line is something. To me it is.*

L: I think particularly I like "I come to pluck your Berries harsh and crude." That's a very great line in its context, and it's largely through sound. And I'd say this: That someone who was sensitive to poetry but didn't read English very well but knew French poetry would say this is a great poet. But if he knew no English and just heard them read aloud, he wouldn't know, you couldn't tell.

W: *It has to be tied to something.*

L: Yes, he has to have a feeling what it's about. But it's quite mysterious. I mean we can't go into the infinite amount of what "Lycidas" is about; it's a very personal poem in a queer way, but it . . . this armor of convention is incredible. So that whole sections won't seem original at all except verbally.

W: *Well, what you have said about the armor of convention is part of the great excitement of the poem, the sense of the breaking through of the personal elements in the poem, through this armor of convention.*

L: It's fascinating that the man who is probably one of the two or three most personal poets in English, Milton, should have come in this Goliath's armor of brazen metric, and felt that was necessary. Well, that's heroic.

B: *Would you say a word or two, Cal, maybe illustrating from a line or two of Donne, whom we think also of as a great personal, immediate poet and yet so very, very different from Milton in his handling of conventions.*

W: *And meter.*

L: I'm trying to think of a passage. I've always had a feeling that Donne is much less personal, curiously enough, than Milton, though the opposite would seem to be true.

W: *Would you care, Cal, to glance at that Donne poem?*

B: *Would you give us the title?*

L: It's "Poysonous Mineralls." Let me read the beginning:

> If poysonous mineralls, and if that tree,
> Whose fruit threw death on else immortall us,
> If lecherous goats, if serpents envious
> Cannot be damn'd; Alas; why should I bee?

You feel the rhythm of this couldn't be written by anybody but Donne, or some imitator.

W: *Some gifted imitator . . .*

L: Very gifted imitator. And it didn't exist in English, even in drama until this was done. Unlike the "Lycidas," which is just Spenser a thousand times better. But the two things that interest me are, one, that this has a kind of agonized, wonderful directness, like Baudelaire, that is quite unlike Milton or unlike almost anybody of Donne's period; and the other is that in a way, it's a much more old-fashioned poem than, not "Lycidas," but say, one of Milton's sonnets—the one on his blindness, which is also a religious poem, but it's much more abstract and theological and I think Milton would disdain to put in the tree; he'd say that was too symbolic. I'm thinking of the most famous of the blindness sonnets. That would never use this kind of symbol. Baudelaire would, more than Milton and less than Donne. Fascinating is "Whose fruit threw death on else immortall us," which sounds like Milton but isn't. It's more dramatic than Milton would do it.

W: *You almost have two kinds of poetry here, without choosing between them. They're both of enormous power, but they're somehow different dimensions of poetry.*

L: I take it Donne never would allow a line like "Ye Myrtles brown, with Ivy never sere"; and he never could have had an effect like "Shatter your leaves before the mellowing year."

W: *No.*

L: Do you feel "I come to pluck your Berries harsh and crude," which in its harshness sounds a little like a Donne line, yet it couldn't be Donne; it's another kind of, much more measured harshness.

B: *Yes, definitely.*

L: I'm sure it's trying to do something entirely different from "Whose fruit threw death on else immortall us."

W: *Milton would never have written that line.*

L: No, he couldn't have.

W: *It's not just the massing of accents there, it's the sudden sort of strange twisting of and unresolvement of those accents. Milton would have found a way to absorb them, I believe.*

L: Yes. It's funny—the line is perfectly regular except for the pauses and "a" sounds—"Cannot be damn'd; Alas; why should I bee?" There is a great . . . "I" struggles for the accent.

W: *That's a great stroke, isn't it?*

L: Terrific, yes. But it's a line Baudelaire would have been proud of, and would have had that kind of sound effect. Hèlas—it's almost a French word.

W: *I remember now our talk with Frost some time back. He said: "What*

makes a line stick in your head?" That's the whole question. Like a burr that
catches on your clothes when you pass. He said, "A good line's got to be catchy.
A good poem's got to be catchy." Now you want to say "catchy" is based on a
dramatic element in the poem.

L: I remember Frost was the first poet I ever met who told me about
this. But I went to him in Cambridge when I was a freshman at Harvard
and I had a huge blank verse epic on the First Crusade and took it to him
all in my uncipherable pencil-writing, and he read a little of it, and said,
"It goes on rather a bit, doesn't it?" And then he read me the opening of
Keats's "Hyperion," the first version, and I thought all of that was
sublime. It's Miltonic verse and every line was equally good and terrific
and unapproachable. And Frost just passed through the opening and then
came to that line about the naiad, "No stir of air was there." He said,
"There it comes alive." Now that's not superficially a dramatic line, and
he didn't mean the other lines were poor, but he meant that it was
building up for that, and the voice tone is something I think he's just
extraordinarily sensitive to.

W: *That's what we ultimately mean by "dramatic" in poetry, isn't it? At*
least in lyric poetry.

L: Yes. And I'd say "Yet once more, O ye Laurels, and once more"
is dramatic in that sense.

B: *In this sense, yes. Yes.*

W: *Cal, we'd certainly like for you to read some of your own poems; I'll*
nominate some of the Warren Winslow elegy.

L: Well, I'll read Section Two, which is an eighteen-line rhymed
section.

B: *This is "The Quaker Graveyard at Nantucket" isn't it?*

L: Yes.

> Whenever winds are moving and their breath
> Heaves at the roped-in bulwarks of this pier,
> The terns and sea-gulls tremble at your death
> In these home waters. Sailor, can you hear
> The Pequod's sea wings, beating landward, fall
> Headlong and break on our Atlantic wall
> Off 'Sconset, where the yawing S-boats splash
> The bellbuoy, with ballooning spinnakers,
> As the entangled, screeching mainsheet clears
> The blocks: off Madaket, where lubbers lash
> The heavy surf and throw their long lead squids
> For blue-fish? Sea-gulls blink their heavy lids

Seaward. The winds' wings beat upon the stones,
Cousin, and scream for you and the claws rush
At the sea's throat and wring it in the slush
Of this old Quaker graveyard where the bones
Cry out in the long night for the hurt beast
Bobbing by Ahab's whaleboats in the East.

Well, it's all very regular meter, which doesn't tell too much, does
it?

W: *It's regular with an enormous amount of variation absorbed in terms of
accent and . . .*

L: I'd say, I mean for influences which go into the whole rhythm of
it, that this is a poem by someone who's read Milton very carefully, and
yet it's not very Miltonic and some sort of current of Donne-like rough-
ness in it, to get the most distinguished ancestors to this, and certainly
Melville comes into it in some way. . . . Personally, Allen Tate was the
poet who was closest to me and I feel it's like his poetry and yet unlike it,
and I've never quite known how. He never would have written this.

B: *It is very much like it and yet quite unlike it.*

L: I never could have written one of his, any of his, typical passages.
And they're somehow different from this entirely. Yet he was the closest
direct influence.

W: *Yet your rhythm is entirely different from his.*

L: I think it's more regular or something.

W: *It's just different. It has a different feel to it. It'd be very hard to prove it
by a graph but no one could miss that difference.*

L: I wanted to write the way [Tate wrote] the opening of "Aeneas at
Washington" in parts of "The Graveyard," but I never could and I did
something else. And I don't . . . no one has ever compared us in any
detail. I always wondered how we resemble each other . . .

W: *You mind reading the third section too? It's one of the best, I think.*

All you recovered from Poseidon died
With you, my cousin, and the harrowed brine
Is fruitless on the blue beard of the god,
Stretching beyond us to the castles in Spain,
Nantucket's westward haven. To Cape Cod
Guns, cradled on the tide,
Blast the eelgrass about a waterclock
Of bilge and backwash, roil the salt and sand
Lashing earth's scaffold, rock

> Our warships in the hand
> Of the great God, where time's contrition blues
> Whatever it was these Quaker sailors lost
> In the mad scramble of their lives. They died
> When time was open-eyed,
> Wooden and childish; only bones abide
> There, in the nowhere, where their boats were tossed
> Sky-high, where mariners had fabled news
> Of IS, the whited monster. What it cost
> Them is their secret. In the sperm-whale's slick
> I see the Quakers drown and hear their cry:
> "If God himself had not been on our side,
> If God himself had not been on our side,
> When the Atlantic rose against us, why
> Then it had swallowed us up quick."

W: *Two wonderful effects in there: the line "mad scramble for their lives" and then the last line has sudden shifts of rhythm and general feeling in that poem. Great strokes, there, I think.*

L: They were hard ones to get in writing it.

W: *I'll bet.*

L: They're both slightly prosy and harsh.

W: *Prosy and harsh, yet they come with a great shiver, both of them.*

L: And idiom comes in, "mad scramble" is very dramatic and "quick" with its pun on quickly and alive. That does something to the rhythm, doesn't it?

B: *I would like to ask another kind of question, shifting a little from meter to rhyme. I think one of the most interesting things about this poem and many of your other poems is the way in which you use rhyme. In this case it's almost as if the rhyme were being—were being constantly overwhelmed.*

L: Yes.

B: *So that we find it just coming through. What's your conscious feeling about that, were you playing down the rhyme rather than playing it up, or what were you using it for?*

L: I've been told I did something original in running on lines; I felt the line gave the impression that the rhyme word was there because it was a rhyme word and so that perhaps to ease that effect that I'd run the line on. Yet the rhymes are supposed to scream out and sound important in the sound effect, and the two sections I read, the first has a regular rhyme scheme. I've forgotten what it is but there are eighteen lines and there are three groups of six lines that are exactly alike, while the second one, every line rhymes but there's no pattern, there's no rule. What difference that makes in the final effect I don't . . . I'm not sure, but the second one can range about more, and somehow counterpoints the first.

B: *Well, certainly one's impression of this fine point is made—is colored to a great extent by what is happening to the rhyme, the way in which the rhymes ride up through the surf of the words, as it were, so that you just get glimpses and flickers of them. It's an entirely different effect, let's say, from the rhyming as used in most traditional poetry. Very different.*

L: [agrees] I think we're doing something that Milton did with blank verse, of running on the line, only doing that with rhyme. I noticed something I hadn't noticed before, that Spain doesn't rhyme, yet it sounds like "brine" but I don't know, it wasn't meant to be an off-rhyme, it was just in there.

B: *I noticed too, Cal, that in some of your later poems—your poems from your most recent volume—the rhyming is used very, very interestingly. It will come out in very pronounced form and then the rhyme will subside completely. I'm thinking of poems like the "Sailing Home from Rapallo" or the poem, "To Delmore Schwartz," for example, which begins with a very firm couplet.*

W: *Why don't we read those poems?*

L: Could I talk a little first, on the general metrics of the book. . . .

W: *By "the book" now you mean your current book, your most recent book,* Life Studies.

W: *Yes. That's fine.*

L: Most of it is free verse. But then that has to be specified. That there are four or five different ways I started a poem, roughly; that some, such as the "Delmore Schwartz," were written in perfectly regular meter and then taken out of that and irregularized and it once had two regular stanzas which disappeared. Bits of them remain in the poem and that was one extreme, and in fact, that even was quite a finished poem in regular meter which somehow never came off and I dug out of old manuscript. Then there are others where I wrote specifically at the time in regular meter and just felt they didn't work at all and ripped them up, like the Commander Lowell one. It was once a couplet poem and like "Marble Faun" it was perfectly regular. I just knocked it out but a lot of the couplets remain as rhymes. Then there were poems that were written in prose first and then were rewritten as poems. The "Uncle Devereux," the first poem of the *Life Studies* series, was four or five prose pages that I rewrote into lines. And a poem like "Homecoming" was written after I'd written a great deal in this meter where I'm deliberately—its first version was something like the final one, though much revised, but metrically the same—where I was trying to be lyrical and make the rhyme stand out and it was supposed to end a section and sound like a lyrical poem and it certainly shifts into iambic pattern which is the meter I'm most familiar with, yet it didn't—I didn't write it scanning. I was much more conscious of a metrical poem in the background. And then "Skunk Hour," the last poem of the sequence was written in six-line stanzas where every line rhymes, though they're odd, off-rhymes, some of them. And then there's no meter within the line; they could be any length. And then there's even a poem like "Man" and "The Woe That Is in Marriage" and most of "Man and Wife" which are perfectly regular metrical poems somehow meant to contrast with other poems. The free-verse poems—I think that the whole trick is that you've got to say to yourself, this isn't going to be scanned while you write it, that you're not given any rules. Then you may toss in little rhymes, or toss in lines where the beat is quite marked and an iambic line comes through. And if the iambic thing is too regular, you lose most of the advantages of free verse. That it ought to have rhythms that are not meant to be any way a wrenched, Donne-like iambic pentameter line. It just doesn't have any rules; it has that freedom.

W: *Cal, may I ask if you have any principle about your line lengths. Do you hear your line . . . and God tells you? Is that it?*

L: I think it's partly visual, sometimes I like to see a poem go down the page in short lines, and when there's a long, looping line, I'm very conscious of that and I couldn't say why it's good, or if it's good, I mean, but part of it's visual and you wonder in a free-verse poem, if you read it aloud to someone, if that person could ever—copying down every word—could ever get your line pattern. And a very funny thing happened. I wrote out a Williams poem about parking lots and it read like a very clouded, rhetorical Faulkner paragraph. But when you read it in quatrains of lines all equal length in Williams, it looked very light and springy. I don't know. It doesn't disturb me that someone couldn't get your line scheme from just knowing the words.

B: *Well, Cal, I noticed this in looking over these last poems; as we all know in poetry which is frequently very much wrenched, the norm will be asserted in an early line, or more frequently reasserted for the ear to pick up or the eye to pick up, later on. I noticed, for example, that some of your free verse poems, as you've already suggested, will begin in a quiet scannable iambic pentameter and then depart from it, but then will return. It doesn't matter I suppose in one sense whether that is consciously thought out, as you work or do the poem, or not, but would you agree that probably that's a help to the reader, as he reads the poem, to have these little landing stages, these little places to which he returns to some kind of normal pattern.*

L: I think I understand, Cleanth, and I both agree and disagree that I've written so much meter that when I write free verse, it is bound to run through it. And some of the poems are meant to be rather regular, or regular with irregularities standing out; but others are not meant to have any norm, and the whole point is that you're not meant to say, here's an anapaestic line or iambic pentameter line, just to get free of that, utterly.

B: *Free of it utterly in the sense that nobody's bothering now with scanning—still, there is a sense in which the rhythms don't seem just random, at least in the total context of the poems they seem right. This line ought to be this shape.*

L: Yes.

B: *This line ought to be this length and not another length. I'm trying to account for that.*

L: I don't. . . . I mean I've never thought it out but it seems to me poetry differs from prose, if you want a sort of definition, that it's written in lines not paragraphs. Which tells you nothing about the content. And if you write free verse, you're very conscious of some line unit; you feel that rhythm and in a sense the rhythm stops and you have another line, something you don't feel in prose. It would be terribly stupid and confusing to write the freest poetry without this line feeling. And then the rightness may be just removing any resemblance to blank verse line.

B: *I wonder if you mind reading one of these freer poems in whole or part to give us a notion of what kind of length you give to these lines that are so irregular.*

L: I'll just read the first section of "The Terminal Days at Beverly Farms":

> At Beverly Farms, a portly, uncomfortable boulder
> bulked in the garden's center—
> an irregular Japanese touch.
> After his Bourbon "old fashioned," Father,
> bronzed, breezy, a shade too ruddy,
> swayed as if on deck-duty
> under his six pointed star-lantern—
> last July's birthday present.
> He smiled his oval Lowell smile,
> he wore his cream gabardine dinner-jacket,

and indigo cummerbund.
His head was efficient and hairless,
his newly dieted figure was vitally trim.

Now, I never—when I read this or when I wrote it—had any idea of
meter, but I did do certain things, like "boulder" and "center," and
"father" where there are sort of rhymes, not too strong, "ruddy" and
"duty." And then there was a certain feeling of release with "lantern,"
"present." From there on the stanza drops these rhymes.

B: *Yes.*

L: I was aware of it; now why they seemed right in the beginning
and seemed pleasant to get away from later on I'm not sure.

B: *Surely part of the story is that a writer who has a great deal of this in his
experience and in his bones can work out a free verse which sounds right and
inevitable whereas a great deal of free verse sounds entirely too free in the sense
it's merely random and therefore meaningless.*

L: I never dared write it until I was almost forty. If it doesn't work,
if the rhythm isn't right and the experience isn't right, you have nothing,
I think. You do have a little to fall back on in meter. Not too much, but a
little. One of the pleasures in doing these poems was that reading them
aloud to friends, who, such as my wife, who are good prose readers but
know nothing about meter, that if they objected to something, you
could make any change you pleased and though there's still rhythm and
that was very important, yet innumerable line lengths could be sub-
stituted for each other and you could make amazing changes in meter and
rhythm that you couldn't in regular verse and still have the . . .

W: *I find this remark interesting, Cal, in the light of a remark you made in
a letter to me earlier this year. You said how much more difficult it was to file a
line of free verse than one of metrical verse, to quote you.*

L: Well, I'm very clumsy, and it really is very hard for me to write a
sonnet and not have padding and clumsiness in it.

W: *Well, you've covered your tracks pretty well.*

L: But it killed me to do it and that's part of the joy of meter. Well,
you don't have that problem in free verse—you have something else but
it's a different agony and a different joy. But I feel, again going back to
Tate, that he's unusually clumsy and obscure often in his verse and not in
his prose, and I like his verse in the end, better than the prose. The
quatrain that looks easy for the superficial poet is hard for him. It hasn't
anything to do with greatness; very good poets are very slick and at ease

often or they can be very awkward. But me, I've always been very awkward and it's been very hard to do and taken endless revision to write decent meter. I've always wanted to write a northern Civil War poem. And finally at forty-three I did and it's about Colonel Shaw who commanded the first Negro regiment from Boston.

W: *He was killed at Fort Wagner, wasn't he?*

L: Fort Wagner, yes. Technically it's an interesting problem. It's written in quatrains that have no meter and it's quite long—I mean it's a page and a half—it's quite a formal problem and I'd stopped writing a poem as impersonal as that. It's sort of a return to the earlier poems, yet the meter's like the late ones. It's called "To the Union Dead" or "Colonel Shaw and the Massachusetts 54th."

> The old South Boston Aquarium stands
> in a Sahara of snow now. Its broken windows are boarded.
> The bronze weathervane cod has lost half its scales.
> The airy tanks are dry.
>
> Once my nose crawled like a snail on the glass;
> my hand tingled
> to burst the bubbles
> drifting from the noses of the cowed, compliant fish.
>
> My hand draws back. I often sigh still
> for the dark downward and vegetating kingdom
> of the fish and reptile. One morning last March,
> I pressed against the new barbed and galvanized
>
> fence on the Boston Common. Behind their cage,
> yellow dinosaur steamshovels were grunting
> as they cropped up tons of mush and grass
> to gouge their underworld garage.
>
> Parking-spaces luxuriate like civic
> sandpiles in the heart of Boston.
> A girdle of orange, Puritan-pumpkin colored girders
> braces the tingling Statehouse,
>
> shaking over the excavations, as it faces Colonel Shaw
> and his bell-cheeked Negro infantry
> on St. Gaudens' shaking Civil War relief,
> propped by a plank splint against the garage's earthquake.
>
> Two months after marching through Boston,
> half the regiment was dead;
> at the dedication,
> William James could almost hear the bronze Negroes breathe.

Their monument sticks like a fishbone
in the city's throat.
Its Colonel is as lean
as a compass-needle.

He has an angry wrenlike vigilance,
a greyhound's gentle tautness;
he seems to wince at pleasure,
and suffocate for privacy.

He is out of bounds now. He rejoices in man's lovely,
peculiar power to choose life and die—
when he leads his black soldiers to death,
he cannot bend his back.

On a thousand small town New England greens,
the old white churches hold their air
of sparse, sincere rebellion; frayed flags
quilt the graveyards of the Grand Army of the Republic.

The stone statues of the abstract Union Soldier
grow slimmer and younger each year—
wasp-waisted, they doze over muskets
and muse through their sideburns . . .

Shaw's father wanted no monument
except the ditch,
where his son's body was thrown
and lost with his "niggers."

The ditch is nearer.
There are no statues for the last war here;
on Boylston Street, a commercial photograph
shows Hiroshima boiling

over a Mosler Safe, the "Rock of Ages"
that survived the blast. Space is nearer.
When I crouch to my television set,
the drained faces of Negro school-children rise like balloons.

Colonel Shaw
is riding on his bubble,
he waits
for the blessèd break.

The Aquarium is gone. Everywhere,
giant finned cars nose forward like fish;
a savage servility
slides by on grease.

W: *Very fine. That's one of your best, I expect. One of your very best.*

L: It's an interesting thing, though; the technical problem isn't so important, but it is important too. This must be a formal poem. The parts hold together yet there's no meter. And the quatrain is, in a certain sense, an artificial one. It's sometimes kept and sometimes run on and the lines vary greatly in length; they may be three or four syllables for fifteen, yet I feel the quatrain is important. . . .

W: *As a minimal thing, anyway, I suppose it's something for the poet to hang on to in the process, to . . .*

L: Yes. You know, just as I do, that sometimes you want something to hold on to, sometimes you want much less.

Cleanth Brooks (b. 1906), influential New Critic and Emeritus Professor of English at Yale University, is the author of *Modern Poetry and the Tradition* (1939), *The Well-Wrought Urn* (1947) and *William Faulkner: The Yoknapatawpha Country* (1963). Robert Penn Warren (b. 1905), American novelist and poet, and Emeritus Professor of English at Yale University, is the author of *All the King's Men* (1946), *Band of Angels* (1955), *Flood* (1964); *Brother to Dragons* (1953) and *Promises* (1957). Lowell studied with Brooks and Warren at Louisiana State University during 1940–41.

4 • The Art of Poetry: Robert Lowell

Frederick Seidel

On one wall of Mr. Lowell's study was a large portrait of Ezra Pound, the tired, haughty outlines of the face concentrated as in the raised outlines of a ring seal in an enlargement. Also bearded, but on another wall, over the desk, James Russell Lowell looked down from the gray old-fashioned photograph on the apex of the triangle thus formed, where his great-grand-nephew sat and answered questions.

Mr. Lowell had been talking about the classes he teaches at Boston University.

Four floors below the study window, cars whined through the early spring rain on Marlborough Street toward the Boston Public Garden.

Seidel: *What are you teaching now?*

Lowell: I'm teaching one of these poetry-writing classes and a course in the novel. The course in the novel is called Practical Criticism. It's a course I teach every year, but the material changes. It could be anything from Russian short stories to Baudelaire, a study of the New Critics, or just fiction. I do whatever I happen to be working on myself.

Seidel: *Has your teaching over the last few years meant anything to you as a writer?*

Lowell: It's meant a lot to me as a human being, I think. But my teaching is part time and has neither the merits nor the burdens of real teaching. Teaching is entirely different from writing. You're always up to it, or more or less up to it; there's no question of it's clogging, of it's not coming. It's much less subjective, and it's a very pleasant pursuit in itself. In the kind of teaching I do, conversational classes, seminars, if the students are good, which they've been most of the time, it's extremely entertaining. Now, I don't know what it has to do with writing. You

Paris Review 7 (Winter–Spring 1961): 56–95. Reprinted in *Writers at Work: The "Paris Review" Interviews, Second Series,* edited by George Plimpton (New York: Viking, 1963), pp. 336–368. Copyright © 1963 by The Paris Review, Inc. Reprinted by permission of Viking Penguin, Inc.

review a lot of things that you like, and you read things that you haven't read or haven't read closely, and read them aloud, go into them much more carefully than you would otherwise; and that must teach you a good deal. But there's such a jump from teaching to writing.

Seidel: *Well, do you think the academic life is liable to block up the writer-professor's sensitivity to his own intuitions?*

Lowell: I think it's possible to give a general answer. Almost all the poets of my generation, all the best ones, teach. I only know one, Elizabeth Bishop, who doesn't. They do it for a livelihood, but they also do it because you can't write poetry all the time. They do it to extend themselves, and I think it's undoubtedly been a gain to them. Now the question is whether something else might be more of a gain. Certainly the danger of teaching is that it's much too close to what you're doing— close and not close. You can get expert at teaching and be crude in practice. The revision, the consciousness that tinkers with the poem— that has something to do with teaching and criticism. But the impulse that starts a poem and makes it of any importance is distinct from teaching.

Seidel: *And protected, you think, from whatever you bring to bear in the scrutiny of parts of poems and aspects of novels, etc.?*

Lowell: I think you have to tear it apart from that. Teaching may make the poetry even more different, less academic than it would be otherwise. I'm sure that writing isn't a craft, that is, something for which you learn the skills and go on turning out. It must come from some deep impulse, deep inspiration. That can't be taught, it can't be what you use in teaching. And you may go further afield looking for that than you would if you didn't teach. I don't know, really; the teaching probably makes you more cautious, more self-conscious, makes you write less. It may make you bolder when you do write.

Seidel: *You think the last may be so?*

Lowell: The boldness is ambiguous. It's not only teaching, it's growing up in this age of criticism which we're all so conscious of, whether we like it or don't like it, or practice it or don't practice it. You think three times before you put a word down, and ten times about taking it out. And that's related to boldness; if you put words down they must do something, you're not going to put clichés. But then it's related to caution; you write much less.

Seidel: *You yourself have written very little criticism, haven't you? You did once contribute to a study of Hopkins.*

Lowell: Yes, and I've done a few omnibus reviews. I do a review or two a year.

Seidel: *You did a wonderful one of Richards' poems.*

Lowell: I felt there was an occasion for that, and I had something to say about it. Sometimes I wish I did more, but I'm very anxious in criticism not to do the standard analytical essay. I'd like my essay to be much sloppier and more intuitive. But my friends are critics, and most of them poet-critics. When I was twenty and learning to write, Allen Tate, Eliot, Blackmur, and Winters, and all those people were very much news. You waited for their essays, and when a good critical essay came out it had the excitement of a new imaginative work.

Seidel: *Which is really not the case with any of the critics writing today, do you think?*

Lowell: The good critics are almost all the old ones. The most brilliant critic of my generation, I think, was Jarrell, and he in a way connects with that older generation. But he's writing less criticism now than he used to.

Seidel: *In your schooling at St. Mark's and Harvard—we can talk about Kenyon in a minute—were there teachers or friends who had an influence on your writing, not so much by the example of their own writing as by personal supervision or direction—by suggesting certain reading, for instance?*

Lowell: Well, my school had been given a Carnegie set of art books, and I had a friend, Frank Parker, who had great talent as a painter but who'd never done it systematically. We began reading the books and histories of art, looking at reproductions, tracing the Last Supper on tracing paper, studying dynamic symmetry, learning about Cézanne, and so on. I had no practical interest in painting, but that study seemed rather close to poetry. And from there I began. I think I read Elizabeth Drew[1] or some such book on modern poetry. It had free verse in it, and that seemed very simple to do.

Seidel: *What class were you in then?*

Lowell: It was my last year. I'd wanted to be a football player very much, and got my letter but didn't make the team. Well, that was satisfying but crushing too. I read a good deal, but had never written. So this was a recoil from that. Then I had some luck in that Richard Eberhart was teaching there.

Seidel: *I'd thought he'd been a student there with you.*

Lowell: No, he was a young man about thirty. I never had him in class, but I used to go to him. He'd read aloud and we'd talk, he was very pleasant that way. He'd smoke honey-scented tobacco, and read Baudelaire and Shakespeare and Hopkins—it made the thing living—and he'd read his own poems. I wrote very badly at first, but he was encouraging and enthusiastic. That probably was decisive, that there was someone there whom I admired who was engaged in writing poetry.

Seidel: *I heard that a very early draft of "The Drunken Fisherman" appeared in the St. Mark's magazine.*

Lowell: No, it was the Kenyon college magazine that published it. The poem was very different then. I'd been reading Winters, whose model was Robert Bridges, and what I wanted was a rather distant, quiet, classical poem without any symbolism. It was in four-foot couplets as smooth as I could write them. The *Kenyon Review* had published a poem of mine and then they'd stopped. This was the one time they said, if you'd submitted this we'd have taken it.

Seidel: *Then you were submitting other poems to the* Review?

Lowell: Yes, and that poem was rather different from anything else I did. I was also reading Hart Crane and Thomas and Tate and Empson's *Seven Types of Ambiguity;* and each poem was more difficult than the one before, and had more ambiguities. Ransom, editing the *Kenyon Review,* was impressed, but didn't want to publish them. He felt they were forbidding and clotted.

Seidel: *But finally he did come through.*

Lowell: Well, after I'd graduated. I published when I was a junior, then for about three years no magazine would take anything I did. I'd get sort of pleasant letters—"One poem in this group interests us, if you can get seven more." At that time it took me about a year to do two or three poems. Gradually I just stopped, and really sort of gave it up. I seemed to have reached a great impasse. The kind of poem I thought was interesting and would work on became so cluttered and overdone that it wasn't really poetry.

Seidel: *I was struck on reading* Land of Unlikeness *by the difference between the poems you rejected for* Lord Weary's Castle *and the few poems and passages that you took over into the new book.*

Lowell: I think I took almost a third, but almost all of what I took was rewritten. But I wonder what struck you?

Seidel: *One thing was that almost all the rejected poems seemed to me to be those that Tate, who in his introduction spoke about two kinds of poetry in the book, said were the more strictly religious and strictly symbolic poems, as against the poems he said were perhaps more powerful because more experienced or relying more on your sense of history. What you took seemed really superior to what you left behind.*

Lowell: Yes, I took out several that were paraphrases of early Christian poems, and I rejected one rather dry abstraction, then whatever seemed to me to have a messy violence. All the poems have religious imagery, I think, but the ones I took were more concrete. That's what the book was moving toward: less symbolic imagery. And as I say, I tried to take some of the less fierce poems. There seemed to be too much twisting and disgust in the first book.

Seidel: *I wondered how wide your reading had been at the time. I wondered, when I read in Tate's introduction that the stanza in one of your poems was based on the stanza in "The Virginian Voyage," whether someone had pointed out Drayton's poem to you.*

Lowell: Tate and I started to make an anthology together. It was a very interesting year I spent with Tate and his wife. He's a poet who writes in spurts, and he had about a third of a book. I was going to do a biography of Jonathan Edwards and he was going to write a novel, and our wives were going to write novels. Well, the wives just went humming away. "I've just finished three pages," they'd say at the end of the day; and their books mounted up. But ours never did, though one morning Allen wrote four pages to his novel, very brilliant. We were in a little study together separated by a screen. I was heaping up books on Jonathan Edwards and taking notes, and getting more and more numb on the subject, looking at old leather-bound volumes on freedom of the will and so on, and feeling less and less a calling. And there we stuck. And then we decided to make an anthology together. We both liked rather formal, difficult poems, and we were reading particularly the sixteenth and seventeenth centuries. In the evening we'd read aloud, and we started a card catalogue of what we'd make for the anthology. And then we started writing. It seems to me we took old models like Drayton's Ode—Tate wrote a poem called "The Young Proconsuls of the Air" in that stanza. I think there's a trick to formal poetry. Most poetry is very formal, but when a modern poet is formal he gets more attention for it than old poets did. Somehow we've tried to make it look difficult. For example, Shelley can just rattle off terza rima by the page, and it's very smooth, doesn't seem an obstruction to him—you sometimes wish it were more difficult. Well, someone does that today and in modern style it looks as though he's wrestling with every line and may be pushed into confusion, as though he's having a real struggle with form and content. Marks of that are in the finished poem. And I think both Tate and I felt that we wanted our formal patterns to seem a hardship and something that we couldn't rattle off easily.

Seidel: *But in* Lord Weary's Castle *there were poems moving toward a sort of narrative calm, almost a prose calm— "Katherine's Dream," for example, or the two poems on texts by Edwards, or "The Ghost"—and then, on the other hand, poems in which the form was insisted upon and maybe shown off, and where the things that were characteristic of your poetry at that time—the kind of enjambments, the rhyming, the meters, of course—seem willed and forced, so that you have a terrific log jam of stresses, meanings, strains.*

Lowell: I know one contrast I've felt, and it takes different forms at different times. The ideal modern form seems to be the novel and certain short stories. Maybe Tolstoy would be the perfect example—his work is imagistic, it deals with all experience, and there seems to be no conflict of the form and content. So one thing is to get into poetry that kind of human richness in rather simple descriptive language. Then there's another side of poetry: compression, something highly rhythmical and perhaps wrenched into a small space. I've always been fascinated by both these things. But getting it all on one page in a few stanzas, getting it all done in as little space as possible, revising and revising so that each word and rhythm though not perfect is pondered and wrestled with—you can't do that in prose very well, you'd never get your book written. "Katherine's Dream" was a real dream. I found that I shaped it a bit, and cut it, and allegorized it, but still it was a dream someone had had. It was material that ordinarily, I think, would go into prose, yet it would have had to be much longer or part of something much longer.

Seidel: *I think you can either look for forms, you can do specific reading for them, or the forms can be demanded by what you want to say. And when the material in poetry seems under almost unbearable pressure you wonder whether the form hasn't cookie-cut what the poet wanted to say. But you chose the couplet, didn't you, and some of your freest passages are in couplets.*

Lowell: The couplet I've used is very much like the couplet Browning uses in "My Last Duchess," in *Sordello*, run-on with its rhymes buried. I've always, when I've used it, tried to give the impression that I had as much freedom in choosing the rhyme word as I had in any of the other words. Yet they were almost all true rhymes, and maybe half the time there'd be a pause after the rhyme. I wanted something as fluid as prose; you wouldn't notice the form, yet looking back you'd find that great obstacles had been climbed. And the couplet is pleasant in this way—once you've got your two lines to rhyme, then that's done and you can go on to the next. You're not stuck with the whole stanza to round out and build to a climax. A couplet can be a couplet or can be split and left as one line, or it can go on for a hundred lines; any sort of compression or expansion is possible. And that's not so in a stanza. I think a couplet's much less lyrical than a stanza, closer to prose. Yet it's an honest form, its difficulties are in the open. It really is pretty hard to rhyme each line with the one that follows it.

Seidel: *Did the change of style in* Life Studies *have something to do with working away from that compression and pressure by way of, say, the kind of prose clarity of "Katherine's Dream"?*

Lowell: Yes. By the time I came to *Life Studies* I'd been writing my autobiography and also writing poems that broke meter. I'd been doing a lot of reading aloud. I went on a trip to the West Coast and read at least once a day and sometimes twice for fourteen days, and more and more I found that I was simplifying my poems. If I had a Latin quotation I'd translate it into English. If adding a couple of syllables in a line made it clearer I'd add them, and I'd make little changes just impromptu as I read. That seemed to improve the reading.

Seidel: *Can you think of a place where you added a syllable or two to an otherwise regular line?*

Lowell: It was usually articles and prepositions that I added, very slight little changes, and I didn't change the printed text. It was just done for the moment.

Seidel: *Why did you do this? Just because you thought the most important thing was to get the poem over?*

Lowell: To get it over, yes. And I began to have a certain disrespect for the tight forms. If you could make it easier by adding syllables, why not? And then when I was writing *Life Studies,* a good number of the poems were started in very strict meter, and I found that, more than the rhymes, the regular beat was what I didn't want. I have a long poem in there about my father, called "Commander Lowell," which actually is largely in couplets, but I originally wrote perfectly strict four-foot couplets. Well, with that form it's hard not to have echoes of Marvell. That regularity just seemed to ruin the honesty of sentiment, and became rhetorical; it said, "I'm a poem"—though it was a great help when I was revising having this original skeleton. I could keep the couplets where I wanted them and drop them where I didn't; there'd be a form to come back to.

Seidel: *Had you originally intended to handle all that material in prose?*

Lowell: Yes. I found it got awfully tedious working out transitions and putting in things that didn't seem very important but were necessary to the prose continuity. Also, I found it hard to revise. Cutting it down into small bits, I could work on it much more carefully and make fast transitions. But there's another point about this mysterious business of prose and poetry, form and content, and the reasons for breaking forms. I don't think there's any very satisfactory answer. I seesaw back and forth between something highly metrical and something highly free; there isn't any one way to write. But it seems to me we've gotten into a sort of Alexandrian[2] age. Poets of my generation and particularly younger ones have gotten terribly proficient at these forms. They write a very musical, difficult poem with tremendous skill, perhaps there's never been such skill. Yet the writing seems divorced from culture somehow. It's become too much something specialized that can't handle much experience. It's become a craft, purely a craft, and there must be some breakthrough back into life. Prose is in many ways better off than poetry. It's quite hard to think of a young poet who has the vitality, say, of Salinger or Saul Bellow. Yet prose tends to be very diffuse. The novel is really a much more difficult form than it seems; few people have the wind to write anything that long. Even a short story demands almost poetic perfection. Yet on the whole prose is less cut off from life than poetry is. Now, some of this Alexandrian poetry is very brilliant, you would not have it changed at all. But I thought it was getting increasingly stifling. I couldn't get my experience into tight metrical forms.

Seidel: *So you felt this about your own poetry, your own technique, not just about the general condition of poetry?*

Lowell: Yes, I felt that the meter plastered difficulties and mannerisms on what I was trying to say to such an extent that it terribly hampered me.

Seidel: *This then explains, in part anyway, your admiration for Elizabeth Bishop's poetry. I know that you've said the qualities and the abundance of its descriptive language reminded you of the Russian novel more than anything else.*

Lowell: Any number of people are guilty of writing a complicated poem that has a certain amount of symbolism in it and really difficult meaning, a wonderful poem to teach. Then you unwind it and you feel that the intelligence, the experience, whatever goes into it, is skin-deep. In Elizabeth Bishop's "Man-Moth" a whole new world is gotten out and you don't know what will come after any one line. It's exploring. And it's as original as Kafka. She's gotten a world, not just a way of writing. She seldom writes a poem that doesn't have that exploratory quality; yet it's very firm, it's not like beat poetry, it's all controlled.

Seidel: *What about Snodgrass?*[3] *What you were trying to do in* Life Studies *must have something to do with your admiration for his work.*

Lowell: He did these things before I did, though he's younger than I am and had been my student. He may have influenced me, though people have suggested the opposite. He spent ten years at the University of Iowa, going to writing classes, being an instructor; rather unworldly, making little money, and specializing in talking to other people writing poetry, obsessed you might say with minute technical problems and rather provincial experience—and then he wrote about just that. I mean, the poems are about his child, his divorce, and Iowa City, and his child is a Dr. Spock child—all handled in expert little stanzas. I believe that's a new kind of poetry. Other poems that are direct that way are slack and have no vibrance. His experience wouldn't be so interesting and valid if it weren't for the whimsy, the music, the balance, everything revised and placed and pondered. All that gives light to those poems on agonizing subjects comes from the craft.

Seidel: *And yet his best poems are all on the verge of being slight and even sentimental.*

Lowell: I think a lot of the best poetry is. Laforgue—it's hard to think of a more delightful poet, and his prose is wonderful too. Well, it's on the verge of being sentimental, and if he hadn't dared to be sentimental he wouldn't have been a poet. I mean, his inspiration was that. There's some way of distinguishing between false sentimentality, which is blowing up a subject and giving emotions that you don't feel, and using whimsical, minute, tender, small emotions that most people don't feel but which Laforgue and Snodgrass do. So that I'd say he had pathos and fragility—but then that's a large subject too. He has fragility along the edges and a main artery of power going through the center.

Seidel: *Some people were disappointed with* Life Studies *just because earlier you had written a kind of heroic poetry, an American version of heroic poetry, of which there had been none recently except your own. Is there any chance that you will go back to that?*

Lowell: I don't think that a personal history can go on forever, unless you're Walt Whitman and have a way with you. I feel I've done enough personal poetry. That doesn't mean I won't do more of it, but I don't want to do more now. I feel I haven't gotten down all my experience, or perhaps even the most important part, but I've said all I really have much inspiration to say, and more would just dilute. So that you need something more impersonal, and other things being equal it's better to get your emotions out in a Macbeth than in a confession. Macbeth must have tons of Shakespeare in him. We don't know where, nothing in Shakespeare's life was remotely like Macbeth, yet he somehow gives the feeling of going to the core of Shakespeare. You have much more freedom that way than you do when you write an autobiographical poem.

Seidel: *These poems, I gather from what you said earlier, did take as much working over as the earlier ones.*

Lowell: They were just as hard to write. They're not always factually true. There's a good deal of tinkering with fact. You leave out a lot, and emphasize this and not that. Your actual experience is a complete flux. I've invented facts and changed things, and the whole balance of the poem was something invented. So there's a lot of artistry, I hope, in the poems. Yet there's this thing: if a poem is autobiographical—and this is true of any kind of autobiographical writing and of historical writing— you want the reader to say, this is true. In something like Macaulay's *History of England* you think you're really getting William III.[4] That's as good as a good plot in a novel. And so there was always that standard of truth which you wouldn't ordinarily have in poetry—the reader was to believe he was getting the *real* Robert Lowell.

Seidel: *I wanted to ask you about this business of taking over passages from earlier poems and rewriting them and putting them in new contexts. I'm thinking of the passage at the end of the "Cistercians in Germany," in* Land of Unlikeness, *which you rewrote into those wonderful lines that end "At the Indian Killer's Grave." I know that Hart Crane rewrote early scraps a great deal and used most of the rewrites. But doesn't doing this imply a theory of poetry that would talk much more about craft than about experience?*

Lowell: I don't know, it's such a miracle if you get lines that are halfway right; it's not just a technical problem. The lines must mean a good deal to you. All your poems are in a sense one poem, and there's always the struggle of getting something that balances and comes out right, in which all parts are good, and that has experience that you value. And so if you have a few lines that shine in a poem or are beginning to shine, and they fail and get covered over and drowned, maybe their real form is in another poem. Maybe you've mistaken the real inspiration in the original poem and they belong in something else entirely. I don't think that violates experience. The "Cistercians" wasn't very close to me, but the last lines seemed felt; I dropped the Cistercians and put a Boston graveyard in.

Seidel: *But in Crane's "Ode to an Urn," a poem about a personal friend, there are lines which originally applied to something very different, and therefore, in one version or the other, at least can't be called personal.*

Lowell: I think we always bring over some unexplained obscurities by shifting lines. Something that was clear in the original just seems odd and unexplained in the final poem. That can be quite bad, of course; but you always want—and I think Chekhov talks about this—the detail that you can't explain. It's just there. It seems right to you, but you don't have to have it; you could have something else entirely. Now if everything's like that you'd just have chaos, but a few unexplained difficult things—they seem to be the life-blood of variety—they may work. What may have seemed a little odd, a little difficult in the original poem, gets a little more difficult in a new way in the new poem. And that's purely accidental, yet you may gain more than you lose—a new suggestiveness and magic.

Seidel: *Do you revise a very great deal?*

Lowell: Endlessly.

Seidel: *You often use an idiom or a very common phrase either for the sake of irony or to bear more meaning than it's customarily asked to bear—do these come late in the game, do you have to look around for them?*

Lowell: They come later because they don't prove much in themselves, and they often replace something that's much more formal and worked-up. Some of my later poetry does have this quality that the earlier doesn't: several lines can be almost what you'd say in conversation. And maybe talking with a friend or with my wife I'd say, "This doesn't sound quite right," and sort of reach in the air as I talked and change a few words. In that way the new style is easier to write; I sometimes fumble out a natural sequence of lines that will work. But a whole poem won't come that way; my seemingly relaxed poems are just about as hard as the very worked-up ones.

Seidel: *That rightness and familiarity, though, is in "Between the Porch and the Altar" in several passages which are in couplets.*

Lowell: When I am writing in meter I find the simple lines never come right away. Nothing does. I don't believe I've ever written a poem in meter where I've kept a single one of the original lines. Usually when I was writing my old poems I'd write them out in blank verse and then put in the rhymes. And of course I'd change the rhymes a lot. The most I could hope for at first was that the rhymed version wouldn't be much inferior to the blank verse. Then the real work would begin, to make it something much better than the original out of the difficulties of the meter.

Seidel: *Have you ever gone as far as Yeats and written out a prose argument and then set down the rhymes?*

Lowell: With some of the later poems I've written out prose versions, then cut the prose down and abbreviated it. A rapidly written prose draft of the poem doesn't seem to do much good, too little pain has gone into it; but one really worked on is bound to have phrases that are invaluable. And it's a nice technical problem: how can you keep phrases and get them into meter?

Seidel: *Do you usually send off your work to friends before publishing it?*

Lowell: I do it less now. I always used to do it, to Jarrell and one or two other people. Last year I did a lot of reading with Stanley Kunitz.

Seidel: *At the time you were writing the poems for* Lord Weary's Castle, *did it make a difference to you whether the poet to whom you were sending your work was Catholic?*

Lowell: I don't think I ever sent any poems to a Catholic. The person I was closest to then was Allen Tate, who wasn't a Catholic at the time; and then later it became Jarrell, who wasn't at all Catholic. My two close Catholic writer friends are prose writers, J. F. Powers and Flannery O'Connor, and they weren't interested in the technical problems of poems.

Seidel: *So you feel that the religion is the business of the poem that it's in and not at all the business of the Church or the religious person.*

Lowell: It shouldn't be. I mean, a religion ought to have objective validity. But by the time it gets into a poem it's so mixed up with technical and imaginative problems that the theologian, the priest, the serious religious person isn't of too much use. The poem is too strange for him to feel at home and make any suggestions.

Seidel: *What does this make of the religious poem as a religious exercise?*

Lowell: Well, it at least makes this: that the poem tries to be a poem and not a piece of artless religious testimony. There is a drawback. It seems to me that with any poem, but maybe particularly a religious one where there are common interests, the opinion of intelligent people who are not poets ought to be useful. There's an independence to this not getting advice from religious people and outsiders, but also there's a narrowness. Then there is a question whether my poems are religious, or whether they just use religious imagery. I haven't really any idea. My last poems don't use religious imagery, they don't use symbolism. In many ways they seem to me more religious than the early ones, which are full of symbols and references to Christ and God. I'm sure the symbols and the Catholic framework didn't make the poems religious experiences. Yet I don't feel my experience changed very much. It seems to me it's clearer to me now than it was then, but it's very much the same sort of thing that went into the religious poems—the same sort of struggle, light and darkness, the flux of experience. The morality seems much the same. But the symbolism is gone; you couldn't possibly say what creed I believed in. I've wondered myself often. Yet what made the earlier poems valuable seems to be some recording of experience, and that seems to be what makes the later ones.

Seidel: *So you end up saying that the poem does have some integrity and can have some beauty apart from the beliefs expressed in the poem.*

Lowell: I think it can only have integrity apart from the beliefs; that no political position, religious position, position of generosity, or what have you, can make a poem good. It's all to the good if a poem *can* use politics, or theology, or gardening, or anything that has its own validity aside from poetry. But these things will never *per se* make a poem.

Seidel: *The difficult question is whether when the beliefs expressed in a poem are obnoxious the poem as a whole can be considered to be beautiful—the problem of the* Pisan Cantos.

Lowell: The *Pisan Cantos* are very uneven, aren't they? If you took what most people would agree are maybe the best hundred passages, would the beliefs in those passages be obnoxious? I think you'd get a very mixed answer. You could make quite a good case for Pound's good humor about his imprisonment, his absence of self-pity, his observant eye, his memories of literary friends, for all kinds of generous qualities and open qualities and lyrical qualities that anyone would think were good. And even when he does something like the death of Mussolini, in the passage that opens the *Pisan Cantos,* people debate about it. I've talked to Italians who were partisans, and who said that this is the only poem on Mussolini that's any good. Pound's quite wily often: Mussolini hung up like an ox—his brutal appearance. I don't know whether you could say the beliefs there are wrong or not. And there are other poems that come to mind: in Eliot, the Jew spelled with a small j in "Gerontion," is that anti-Semitism or not? Eliot's not anti-Semitic in any sense, but there's certainly a dislike of Jews in those early poems. Does he gain in the fierceness of writing his Jew with a small *j*? He says you write what you have to write and in criticism you can say what you think you should believe in. Very ugly emotions perhaps make a poem.

Seidel: *You were on the Bollingen Committee at the time the award was made to Pound. What did you think of the great ruckus?*

Lowell: I thought it was a very simple problem of voting for the best book of the year; and it seemed to me Pound's was. I thought the *Pisan Cantos* was the best writing Pound had ever done, though it included some of his worst. It is a very mixed book: that was the question. But the consequences of not giving the best book of the year a prize for extraneous reasons, even terrible ones in a sense—I think that's the death of art. Then you have Pasternak suppressed and everything becomes stifling. Particularly in a strong country like ours you've got to award things objectively and not let the beliefs you'd like a man to have govern your choice. It was very close after the war, and anyone must feel that the poetry award was a trifling thing compared with the concentration camps. I actually think they were very distant from Pound. He had no political effect whatsoever and was quite eccentric and impractical. Pound's social credit, his Fascism, all these various things, were a tremendous gain to him; he'd be a very Parnassian[5] poet without them. Even if they're bad beliefs—and some were bad, some weren't, and some were just terrible, of course—they made him more human and more to do with life, more to do with the times. They served him. Taking what interested him in these things gave a kind of realism and life to his poetry that it wouldn't have had otherwise.

Seidel: *Did you become a translator to suit your own needs or because you wanted to get certain poems, most of them not before translated, into English? Or was it a matter of both, as I suppose it usually is, and as it was for Pound?*

Lowell: I think both. It always seemed to me that nothing very close to the poems I've translated existed in English; and on the other hand, there was some kind of closeness, I felt a kinship. I felt some sort of closeness to the Rilke and Rimbaud poems I've translated, yet they were doing things I couldn't do. They were both a continuation of my own bias and a release from myself.

Seidel: *How did you come to translate Propertius—in fact, how did you come to have such a great interest in Roman history and Latin literature?*

Lowell: At Harvard my second year I took almost entirely English courses—the easiest sort of path. I think that would have been a disaster. But before going to Kenyon I talked to Ford Madox Ford and Ransom, and Ransom said you've just got to take philosophy and logic, which I did. The other thing he suggested was classics. Ford was rather flippant about it, said of course you've got to learn classics, you'll just cut yourself off from humanity if you don't. I think it's always given me some sort of yardstick for English. And then the literature was amazing, particularly the Greek; there's nothing like Greek in English at all. Our plays aren't formally at all like Aeschylus and Sophocles. Their whole inspiration was unbelievably different, and so different that you could hardly think of even the attempt to imitate them, great as their prestige was. That something like *Antigone* or *Oedipus* or the great Achilles moments in the Iliad would be at the core of a literature is incredible for anyone brought up in an English culture—Greek wildness and sophistication all different, the women different, everything. Latin's of course much closer. English is a half-Latin language, and we've done our best to absorb the Latin literature. But a Roman poet is much less intellectual than the Englishman, much less abstract. He's nearer nature somehow— somewhat what we feel about a Frenchman but more so still. And yet he's very sophisticated. He has his way of doing things, though the number of forms he explored is quite limited. The amount he could take from the Greeks and yet change is an extraordinary piece of firm discipline. Also, you take almost any really good Roman poet—Juvenal, or Vergil, or Propertius, Catullus—he's much more raw and direct than anything in English, and yet he has this blocklike formality. The Roman frankness interests me. Until recently our literature hasn't been as raw as the Roman, translations had to have stars. And their history has a terrible human frankness that isn't customary with us—corrosive attacks on the establishment, comments on politics and the decay of morals, all felt terribly strongly, by poets as well as historians. The English writer who reads the classics is working at one thing, and his eye is on something else that can't be done. We will always have the Latin and Greek classics, and they'll never be absorbed. There's something very restful about that.

Seidel: *But, more specifically, how did Latin poetry—your study of it, your translations—affect your measure of English poetry?*

Lowell: My favorite English poetry was the difficult Elizabethan plays and the Metaphysicals, then the nineteenth century, which I was aquiver about and disliked but which was closer to my writing than anything else. The Latin seemed very different from either of these. I immediately saw how Shelley wasn't like Horace and Vergil or Aeschylus—and the Latin was a mature poetry, a realistic poetry, which didn't have the contortions of the Metaphysicals. What a frail, bony, electric person Marvell is compared with Horace!

Seidel: *What about your adaptation of Propertius?*

Lowell: I got him through Pound. When I read him in Latin I found a kind of Propertius you don't get in Pound at all. Pound's Propertius is a rather Ovidian figure with a great deal of Pound's fluency and humor and irony. The actual Propertius is a very excited, tense poet, rather desperate; his line is much more like parts of Marlowe's *Faustus*. And he's of all the Roman poets the most like a desperate Christian. His experiences, his love affair with Cynthia, are absolutely rending, destroying. He's like a fallen Christian.

Seidel: *Have you done any other translations of Latin poems?*

Lowell: I did a monologue that started as a translation of Vergil and then was completely rewritten, and there are buried translations in several other poems. There's a poem called "To Speak of Woe That Is in Marriage" in my last book that started as a translation of Catullus. I don't know what traces are left, but it couldn't have been written without the Catullus.

Seidel: *You've translated Pasternak. Do you know Russian?*

Lowell: No, I have rewritten other English translations, and seldom even checked with Russian experts. I want to get a book of translations together. I read in the originals, except for Russian, but I have felt quite free to alter things, and I don't know that Pasternak would look less close than the Italian, which I have studied closely. Before I publish, I want to check with a Russian expert.

Seidel: *Can I get you back to Harvard for a minute? Is it true you tried out for the Harvard* Advocate, *did all the dirty work for your candidacy, and then were turned down?*

Lowell: I nailed a carpet down. I forget who the editor was then, but he was a man who wrote on Frost. At that time people who wrote on Frost were quite different from the ones who write on him now; they tended to be conservative, out of touch. I wasn't a very good writer then, perhaps I should have been turned down. I was trying to write like William Carlos Williams, very simple, free verse, imagistic poems. I had a little group I was very proud of which was set up in galleys; when I left Harvard it was turned down.

Seidel: *Did you know any poets at the time?*

Lowell: I had a friend, Harry Brown, who writes dialogue for movies and has been in Hollywood for years. He was a terribly promising poet. He came to Harvard with a long correspondence with Harriet Monroe[6] and was much more advanced than anyone else. He could write in the style of Auden or Webster or Eliot or Crane. He'd never graduated from high school, and wasn't a student, but he was the person I felt closest to. My other friends weren't writers.

Seidel: *Had you met any older poets—Frost, for instance, who must have been around?*

Lowell: I'd gone to call on Frost with a huge epic on the First Crusade, all written out in clumsy longhand on lined paper. He read a page of that and said, "You have no compression." Then he read me a very short poem of Collins, "How Sleep the Brave," and said, "That's not a great poem, but it's not too long." He was very kindly about it. You know his point about the voice coming into poetry: he took a very unusual example of that, the opening of *Hyperion;* the line about the Naiad, something about her pressing a cold finger to her cold lips, which wouldn't seem like a voice passage at all. And he said, "Now Keats comes alive here." That was a revelation to me; what had impressed me was the big Miltonic imitation in *Hyperion*. I don't know what I did with that, but I recoiled and realized that I was diffuse and monotonous.

Seidel: *What decided you to leave Harvard and go to Kenyon?*

Lowell: I'd made the acquaintance of Merrill Moore, who'd been at Vanderbilt and a Fugitive. He said that I ought to study with a man who was a poet. He was very close to Ransom, and the plan was that I'd go to Vanderbilt; and I would have, but Ransom changed to Kenyon.

Seidel: *I understand you left much against the wishes of your family.*

Lowell: Well, I was getting quite morose and solitary, and they sort of settled for this move. They'd rather have had me a genial social Harvard student, but at least I'd be working hard this way. It seemed to them a queer but orderly step.

Seidel: *Did it help you that you had had intellectual and literary figures in your family?*

Lowell: I really didn't know I'd had them till I went to the South. To my family, James Russell Lowell was the ambassador to England, not a writer. Amy seemed a bit peculiar to them. When I began writing I think it would have been unimaginable to take either Amy or James Russell Lowell as models.

Seidel: *Was it through Ransom that you met Tate?*

Lowell: I met them at more or less the same time, but actually stayed with Tate before I knew Ransom very well.

Seidel: *And Ford Madox Ford was there at some time, wasn't he?*

Lowell: I met Ford at a cocktail party in Boston and went to dinner with him at the Athens Olympia. He was going to visit the Tates, and said, "Come and see me down there, we're all going to Tennessee." So I drove down. He hadn't arrived, so I got to know the Tates quite well before his appearance.

Seidel: *Staying in a pup-tent.*

Lowell: It's a terrible piece of youthful callousness. They had one Negro woman who came in and helped, but Mrs. Tate was doing all the housekeeping. She had three guests and her own family, and was doing cooking and writing a novel. And this young man arrived, quite ardent and eccentric. I think I suggested that maybe I'd stay with them. And they said, "We really haven't any room, you'd have to pitch a tent on the lawn." So I went to Sears, Roebuck and got a tent and rigged it on their lawn. The Tates were too polite to tell me that what they'd said had been just a figure of speech. I stayed two months in my tent and ate with the Tates.

Seidel: *And you were showing him your work all the while.*

Lowell: Oh, I became converted to formalism and changed my style from brilliant free verse, all in two months. And everything was in rhyme, and it still wasn't any good. But that was a great incentive. I poured out poems and went to writers' conferences.

Seidel: *What about Ford?*

Lowell: I saw him out there and took dictation from him for a while. That was hell, because I didn't know how to type. I'd take the dictation down in longhand, and he rather mumbled. I'd ask him what he'd said, and he'd say, "Oh, you have no sense of prose rhythm," and mumble some more. I'd get most of his words, then I'd have to improvise on the typewriter.

Seidel: *So for part of Ford's opus we're indebted to you.*

Lowell: A handful of phrases in *The March of Literature*, on the Provençal poets.

Seidel: *That was the summer before you entered Kenyon; but most of the poems in* Land of Unlikeness *were written after you'd graduated, weren't they?*

Lowell: Yes, they were almost all written in a year I spent with the Tates, though some of them were earlier poems rewritten. I think becoming a Catholic convert had a good deal to do with writing again. I was much more interested in being a Catholic than in being a writer. I read Catholic writers but had no intention of writing myself. But somehow, when I started again, I won't say the Catholicism gave me subject matter, but it gave me some kind of form, and I could begin a poem and build it to a climax. It was quite different from what I'd been doing earlier.

Seidel: *Why, then, did you choose to print your work in the small liberal magazines whose religious and political positions were very different from yours? Have you ever submitted to the* New Yorker *or the* Atlantic Monthly?

Lowell: I think I may have given something to the *Atlantic* on Santayana; the *New Yorker* I haven't given anything. I think the *New Yorker* does some of the best prose in the country, in many ways much more interesting than the quarterlies and little magazines. But poems are lost in it; there's no table of contents, and some of their poetry is light verse. There's no particular continuity of excellence. There just seems no point in printing there. For a while the little magazines, whose religious-political positions *were* very different from mine, were the only magazines that would publish me, and I feel like staying with them. I like magazines like the *New Statesman*, the *Nation*, the *New Republic*—something a little bit off the track.

Seidel: *Just because they are off the track?*

Lowell: I think so. A political position I don't necessarily agree with which is a little bit adverse seems to me just more attractive than a time-serving, conventional position. And they tend to have good reviews, those magazines. I think you write for a small audience, an ardent critical audience. And you know Graves says that poets ought to take in each other's washing because they're the only responsible audience. There's a danger to that—you get too specialized—but I pretty much agree that's the audience you do write for. If it gets further, that's all fine.

Seidel: *There is, though, a certain inbred, in-group anemia to those magazines, at least to the literary quarterlies. For instance, it would have been almost inconceivable for* Partisan Review, *which is the best of them, I think, to give your last book a bad review or even a sharp review.*

Lowell: I think no magazine likes to slam one of its old contributors. *Partisan* has sometimes just not reviewed a book by someone they liked very much and their reviewer didn't. I know [Karl] Shapiro has been attacked in *Partisan* and then published there, and other people have been unfavorably reviewed and made rather a point of sending them something afterwards. You want to feel there's a certain degree of poorer writing that wouldn't get published in the magazine your work appears in. The good small magazine may publish a lot of rather dry stuff, but at least it's serious, and if it's bad it's not bad by trying to be popular and put something over on the public. It's a wrenched personal ineptitude that will get published rather than a public slickness. I think that has something to do with good reviews coming out in the magazine. We were talking about *Partisan's* not slamming one of its contributors, but *Partisan* has a pretty harsh, hard standard of reviewing, and they certainly wouldn't praise one of their contributors who'd gone to pot.

Seidel: *What poets among your contemporaries do you most admire?*

Lowell: The two I've been closest to are Elizabeth Bishop—I spoke about her earlier—and Jarrell, and they're different. Jarrell's a great man of letters, a very informed man, and the best critic of my generation, the best professional poet. He's written the best war poems, and those poems are a tremendous product of our culture, I feel. Elizabeth Bishop's poems, as I said, are more personal, more something she did herself, and she's not a critic but has her own tastes, which may be very idiosyncratic. I enjoy her poems more than anybody else's. I like some of Shapiro very much, some of Roethke and Stanley Kunitz.

Seidel: *What about Roethke, who tries to do just about everything you don't try to do?*

Lowell: We've read to each other and argued, and may be rather alike in temperament actually, but he wants a very musical poem and always would quarrel with my ear as I'd quarrel with his eye. He has love poems and childhood poems and startling surrealistic poems, rather simple experience done with a blaze of power. He rejoices in the rhetoric and the metrics, but there's something very disorderly working there. Sometimes it will smash a poem and sometimes it will make it. The things he knows about I feel I know nothing about, flowers and so on. What we share, I think, is the exultant moment, the blazing out. Whenever I've tried to do anything like his poems, I've felt helpless and realized his mastery.

Seidel: *You were apparently a very close friend of Delmore Schwartz's.*

Lowell: Yes, and I think that I've never met anyone who has somehow as much seeped into me. It's a complicated personal thing to talk about. His reading was very varied, Marx and Freud and Russell, very catholic and not from a conservative position at all. He sort of grew up knowing those things and has a wonderful penetrating humorous way of talking about them. If he met T. S. Eliot his impressions of Eliot would be mixed up with his impressions of Freud and what he'd read about Eliot; all these things flowed back and forth in him. Most of my writer friends were more specialized and limited than Schwartz, most of them took against-the-grain positions which were also narrow. Schwartz was a revelation. He felt the poet who had experience was very much better than the poet with polish. Wordsworth would interest him much more than Keats—he wanted openness to direct experience. He said that if you got people talking in a poem you could do anything. And his own writing, *Coriolanus* and *Shenandoah,* is interesting for that.

Seidel: *Isn't this much what you were saying about your own hopes for* Life Studies?

Lowell: Yes, but technically I think that Delmore and I are quite different. There have been very few poets I've been able to get very much from technically. Tate has been one of the closest to me. My early poems I think grew out of my admiration for his poems.

Seidel: *What about poets in the past?*

Lowell: It's hard for me to imitate someone; I'm very self-conscious about it. That's an advantage perhaps—you don't become too imitative—but it's also a limitation. I tremble when I feel I'm being like someone else. If it's Rilke or Rimbaud or Propertius, you know the language is a big bar and that if you imitate you're doing something else. I've felt greater freedom that way. I think I've tried to write like some of the Elizabethans.

Seidel: *And Crane? You said you had read a good deal of Crane.*

Lowell: Yes, but his difficult style is one I've never been able to do much with. He can be very obscure and yet write a much more inspired poem than I could by being obscure. There's a relationship between Crane and Tate, and for some reason Tate was much easier for me. I could see how Tate was done, though Tate has a rhythm that I've never been able to imitate. He's much more irregular than I am, and I don't know where the rhythm comes from, but I admire it very much. Crane said somewhere that he could write five or six good lines but Tate could write twelve that would hang together, and you'd see how the twelve were built. Tate was somehow more of a model: he had a lot of wildness and he had a lot of construction. And of course I knew him and never knew Crane. I think Crane is the great poet of that generation. He got out more than anybody else. Not only is it the tremendous power there, but he somehow got New York City; he was at the center of things in the way that no other poet was. All the chaos of his life missed getting sidetracked the way other poets' did, and he was less limited than any other poet of his generation. There was a fullness of experience; and without that, if you just had his mannerisms, and not his rather simple writing—which if done badly would be sentimental merely—or just his obscure writing, the whole thing would be merely verbal. It isn't with Crane. The push of the whole man is there. But his style never worked for me.

Seidel: *But something of Crane does seem to have gotten into your work—or maybe it's just that sense of power thrashing about. I thought it had come from a close admiring reading of Crane.*

Lowell: Yes, some kind of wildness and power that appeals to me, I guess. But when I wrote difficult poems they weren't meant to be difficult, though I don't know that Crane meant his to be. I wanted to be loaded and rich, but I thought the poems were all perfectly logical. You can have a wonderful time explaining a great poem like "Voyages II," and it all can be explained, but in the end it's just a love poem with a great confusion of images that are emotionally clear; a prose paraphrase wouldn't give you any impression whatever of the poem. I couldn't do that kind of poem, I don't think; at least I've never been able to.

Seidel: *You said that most of the writers you've known have been against the grain. What did you mean?*

Lowell: When I began writing most of the great writers were quite unpopular. They hadn't reached the universities yet, and their circulation was small. Even Eliot wasn't very popular then. But life seemed to be there. It seemed to be one of those periods when the lid was still being blown. The great period of blowing the lid was the time of Schönberg and Picasso and Joyce and the early Eliot, where a power came into the arts which we perhaps haven't had since. These people were all rather traditional, yet they were stifled by what was being done, and they almost wrecked things to do their great works—even rather minor but very good writers such as Williams or Marianne Moore. Their kind of protest and queerness has hardly been repeated. They're wonderful writers. You wouldn't see anyone as strange as Marianne Moore again, not for a long while. Conservative and Jamesian as she is, it was a terrible, private, and strange revolutionary poetry. There isn't the motive to do that now. Yet those were the classics, and it seems to me they were all against the grain, Marianne Moore as much as Crane. That's where life was for the small audience. It would be a tremendous subject to say whether the feelings were against the grain too, and whether they were purifying, nihilistic, or both.

Seidel: *Have you had much contact with Eliot?*

Lowell: I may have seen him a score of times in my life, and he's always been very kind. Long before he published me he had some of my poems in his files. There's some kind of New England connection.

Seidel: *Has he helpfully criticized your work?*

Lowell: Just very general criticism. With the first book of mine Faber did he had a lot of little questions about punctuation, but he never said he liked this or disliked that. Then he said something about the last book—"These are first-rate, I mean it"—something like that that was very understated and gratifying. I feel Eliot's less tied to form than a lot of people he's influenced, and there's a freedom of the twenties in his work that I find very sympathetic. Certainly he and Frost are the great New England poets. You hardly think of Stevens as New England, but you have to think of Eliot and Frost as deeply New England and puritanical. They're a continuation and a criticism of the tradition, and they're probably equally great poets. Frost somehow put life into a dead tradition. His kind of poetry must have seemed almost unpublishable, it was so strange and fresh when it was first written. But still it was old-fashioned poetry and really had nothing to do with modern writing—except that he is one of the greatest modern writers. Eliot was violently modern and unacceptable to the traditionalist. Now he's spoken of as a literary dictator,[7] but he's handled his position with wonderful sharpness and grace, it seems to me. It's a narrow position and it's not one I hold particularly, but I think it's been held with extraordinary honesty and finish and development. Eliot has done what he said Shakespeare had done: all his poems are one poem, a form of continuity that has grown and snowballed.

Seidel: *I remember Jarrell in reviewing* Mills of the Kavanaughs[8] *said that Frost had been doing narrative poems with ease for years, and that nobody else had been able to catch up.*

Lowell: And what Jarrell said is true: nobody except Frost can do a sort of Chaucerian narrative poem that's organized and clear. Well, a lot of people do them, but the texture of their verse is so limp and uninspired. Frost does them with great power. Most of them were done early, in that *North of Boston* period. That was a miracle, because except for Robinson—and I think Frost is a very much greater poet than Robinson—no one was doing that in England or America.

Seidel: *But you hadn't simply wanted to tell a story in* Mills of the Kavanaughs.

Lowell: No, I was writing an obscure, rather Elizabethan, dramatic

and melodramatic poem. I don't know quite how to describe this busi-
ness of direct experience. With Browning, for instance, for all his gifts—
and there is almost nothing Browning couldn't use—you feel there's a
glaze between what he writes and what really happened, you feel the
people are made up. In Frost you feel that's just what the farmers and so
on were like. It has the virtue of a photograph but all the finish of art.
That's an extraordinary thing; almost no other poet can do that now.

Seidel: *What do you suppose are the qualities that go into that ability?*

Lowell: I don't know. Prose writers have it much more, and quite a
few prose writers have it. It's some kind of sympathy and observation of
people. It's the deep, rather tragic poems that I value most. Perhaps it's
been overdone with Frost, but there's an abundance and geniality about
those poems that isn't tragic. With this sense of rhythm and words and
composition, and getting into his lines language that is very much like
the language he speaks—which is also a work of art, much better than
other people's ordinary speech and yet natural to him; he has that con-
tinuity with his ordinary self and his poetic self—he's made what with
anyone else would be just flat. A very good prose writer can do this and
make something of it. You get it quite often in Faulkner. Though he's an
Elizabethan sort of character, rather unlike Frost, he can get this amazing
immediacy and simplicity. When it comes to verse the form is so hard
that all of that gets drained out. In a very conventional old-fashioned
writer, or someone who's trying to be realistic but also dramatic and
inspired, though he may remain a good poet, most of that directness and
realism goes. It's hard for Eliot to be direct that way, though you get it in
bits of *The Waste Land,* that marvelous Cockney section. And he can be
himself; I feel Eliot's real all through the *Quartets.* He can be very intel-
ligent or very simple there, and *he's* there, but there are no other people
in the *Quartets.*

Seidel: *Have many of your poems been taken from real people and real
events?*

Lowell: I think, except when I've used myself or occasionally named
actual people in poems, the characters are purely imaginary. I've tried to
buttress them by putting images I've actually seen and in indirect ways
getting things I've actually experienced into the poem. If I'm writing
about a Canadian nun the poem may have a hundred little bits of things
I've looked at, but she's not remotely anyone I've ever known. And I
don't believe anybody would think my nun was quite a real person. She
has a heart and she's alive, I hope, and she has a lot of color to her and

drama, and has some things that Frost's characters don't, but she doesn't have their wonderful quality of life. His Witch of Coös is absolutely there. I've gathered from talking to him that most of the *North of Boston* poems came from actual people he knew shuffled and put together. But then it's all-important that Frost's plots are so extraordinary, so carefully worked out though it almost seems that they're not there. Like some things in Chekhov, the art is very well hidden.

Seidel: *Don't you think a large part of it is getting the right details, symbolic or not, around which to wind the poem tight and tighter?*

Lowell: Some bit of scenery or something you've felt. Almost the whole problem of writing poetry is to bring it back to what you really feel, and that takes an awful lot of maneuvering. You may feel the doorknob more strongly than some big personal event, and the doorknob will open into something that you can use as your own. A lot of poetry seems to me very good in the tradition but just doesn't move me very much because it doesn't have personal vibrance to it. I probably exaggerate the value of it, but it's precious to me. Some little image, some detail you've noticed—you're writing about a little country shop, just describing it, and your poem ends up with an existentialist account of your experience. But it's the shop that started it off. You didn't know why it meant a lot to you. Often images and often the sense of the beginning and end of a poem are all you have—some journey to be gone through between those things; you know that, but you don't know the details. And that's marvelous; then you feel the poem will come out. It's a terrible struggle, because what you really feel hasn't got the form, it's not what you can put down in a poem. And the poem you're equipped to write concerns nothing that you care very much about or have much to say on. Then the great moment comes when there's enough resolution of your technical equipment, your way of constructing things, and what you can make a poem out of, to hit something you really want to say. You may not know you have it to say.

Frederick Seidel (b. 1936), American poet and editor, is the author of *Final Solutions* (1963) and *Sunrise* (1979).

1. See Elizabeth Drew, *Discovering Poetry* (1933) and *Directions in Modern Poetry* (1940).

2. Elaborate and complex, from the pagan school of literature that flourished when the Greeks ruled Alexandria, in Egypt, from 325 B.C. to the beginning of the Christian era.

3. W. D. Snodgrass (b. 1926), won the Pulitzer Prize for *Heart's Needle* in 1959.

4. William III (1650–1702), King of England, 1689–1702.

5. A group of nineteenth-century French poets who stressed restraint, objectivity and technical perfection in reaction against the emotionalism of the Romantics.

6. Harriet Monroe (1860–1936), founder and editor of *Poetry* in Chicago.

7. See Delmore Schwartz, "The Literary Dictatorship of T. S. Eliot," *Partisan Review* 16 (February 1949): 119–137.

8. Randall Jarrell, "Poetry in War and Peace," *Partisan Review* 12 (Winter 1945): 120–126.

5 • Robert Lowell in Conversation

A. Alvarez

Robert Lowell, who was in London briefly for last week's Poetry Festival, is a tall, stooping man of great sensitivity, tact and an almost saint-like gentleness; he is also the foremost poet to emerge from America since the days of Eliot, Pound and Stevens. He is one of the Boston Lowells—who "talk to the Cabots"[1]—and like Eliot he is a Harvard man, though he didn't stick it out, finishing at Kenyon College under the poet John Crowe Ransom.

He published his first two books, *Land of Unlikeness* and *Lord Weary's Castle,* in 1944 and 1946, when he himself was in his middle twenties. They caused an explosion in the literary world. Not only did they earn him all the usual prizes—and some unusual ones, including a Pulitzer—but they also clearly signalled the arrival of a totally new and independent talent, who had learned and assimilated the lessons of the great moderns, and applied them in ways wholly his own.

Thirteen years later, in 1959, came *Life Studies,* a complete and unexpected change in direction. In it he turned away from the more formal subjects and methods, and from the Catholic symbolism of his earlier work, and wrote rather loose, highly varied poems of an intimately autobiographical kind. It was another breakthrough in verse and has been much imitated.

Last year his volume of very free translations, *Imitations,* showed his style changing yet again. The poems since then have left *Life Studies* a long way behind. Now, at forty-six, he is at the height of his powers, the mature master of his own poetic world and style.

Alvarez: *People are continually claiming to find new directions in poetry—in your own included. How do you feel about it?*

Lowell: Literary life is just one little wave after another: there was

Observer, 21 July 1963, p. 19. Reprinted by permission of Aitken & Stone, Ltd.

the Auden wave and the Dylan Thomas and the anti-Dylan Thomas, and we've had similar things in America. Most of the good poetry does seem to come out of these waves, though you occasionally get solitary figures who have nothing to do with them. The waves usually recede. There are few survivors: most people are left stranded on the beach.

One manner seems as bad or as good as another; it freshens the atmosphere for a moment and then seems to have faults as disastrous as the ones they were fighting against. Every so often something enormous opens, such as French symbolism, which will go on for fifty or sixty years with enormous talents one after another taking it up and changing it.

Alvarez: *Yet you yourself have certainly added something quite new to modern poetry. As I read it, it's a matter of coping with material which has not really been coped with before—taboo material, about a nervous breakdown and so on. There had been poems about these things before, but they were all in regular metre. What you've done is to let the metrical form shape itself out of the feelings.*

Lowell: Well, I remember I started one of these poems in Marvell's four-foot couplet and showed it to my wife. And she said "Why not say what really happened?" (It wasn't the one about her.) The metre just seemed to prevent any honesty on the subject, it got into the cadence of the four-foot couplet. The style came out of a whole lot of things, and I don't know myself what was the dominating influence.

In the beginning you got people who said this was prose and so forth and didn't want to see the skill, I think. Now you're beginning to get a time when there's too much of this confessional verse—in my own country it's one of the trends—and you feel that a lot of the poems don't have enough lyrical concentration.

I think a confessional poem is a possibility but you shouldn't over-work it. Often you have nothing to confess that makes a poem. The problem is to use a little of all that and be inventive. I think of several possibilities, of strings one might be able to pull: one is the confession given rather directly with hidden artifice; the other is a more rhetorical poem that doesn't use natural language at all; and then there are ways of distorting the experience, bringing in invention.

Alvarez: *The inspiration of this has nothing to do with "True Confes-sions." It's in recognizing what makes you tick, isn't it?*

Lowell: Well, the needle that prods into what really happened may be the same needle that writes a good line, I think. There's some sort of technical connection; there must be at best. Inspiration's such a tricky word, but we all know poetry isn't a craft that you can just turn on and off. It has to strike fire somewhere, and truth, maybe unpleasant truth about yourself, may be the thing that does that.

It's puzzling. You may be in a very sunny mood and the poem that comes out is not at all sunny; and to a certain extent vice versa. You can say that what comes out is your real self in some queer way, but it may be one that you're not particularly aware of at the time. Certainly, you can't trust your feelings and put them down and say "That's the truth." You find that often you're working with something that isn't your immediate feeling at all. I think it must be worked up.

When I was writing my book I had a lot of argument with action painters. I wanted to return to a sort of Tolstoyan fullness of representation, and their technical freedom came from doing the opposite. Yet I suppose there's some connection. Something pushed the two of us at the same time, it seems to me: action painting and my kind of writing. Mine seemed to bring in more and more human experience. Theirs left it out entirely. I feel it's a narrow kind of painting and that it reaches a limit, whereas the kind of thing I do, if someone of greater power did it, is limitless, it seems to me.

Alvarez: *Obviously, this kind of writing involves a great deal of strain. Was it to alleviate that that you turned to plays?*

Lowell: Yes, and on a small scale—I mean, I don't know too much about writing plays. I found it a great relief to have a plot and people who weren't me at all. I could say things that were personal that I couldn't say in a confessional poem. I don't mean that I know how to write a play as well as a poem, but the medium gave a certain freedom.

Alvarez: *Is this why you do translations as well?*

Lowell: I think so. The centre's provided, the plot of the poem, even the tone, and then you're free to let yourself go at that point. When I was doing Villon and Rimbaud and Baudelaire I tried to live through the plots of their poems. It was as if I'd been given Villon's costume for a little while. It's a great soothing.

Alvarez: *Do you think that the seriousness of your verse—your willingness and ability to tackle difficult new subjects—is linked with the professionalism of American literary life? We, by contrast, seem so debilitatingly amateur.*

Lowell: I think it's the sort of "all-outness" which the Americans perhaps have that's a virtue. But the trouble with our professionalism is that it becomes a little bit too much an abstract technique which really, I think, isn't technique in some sense. There's too much concentration on how a poem's made. And actually someone who seems rather imperfect such as Wordsworth, who can write bad lines and good lines, is a master technician in the kind of resources he can use and put into poetry.

From my point of view Philip Larkin is the English poet I follow most carefully. He seems utterly professional and a technician in a way almost no American is. As for Ted Hughes, I find him just a sort of thunderbolt. His animal poems are some of the best poems in English. I wouldn't know whether he could influence anybody; whether he's typical of any country.

Alvarez: *What about Auden and Dylan Thomas? Do you feel any links with them?*

Lowell: Well, when I first read Thomas in the Faber book about 1935 he appealed to me very much in that he was metrical and splendid and non-political in any direct sense. But I think it's a poetry that's limited. He's certainly a great poet in about ten poems, the sheer energy of it. But I find him less interesting than Auden. Auden has made that period immortal, that period of waiting for the war.

My first book was written *during* the war, which was a very different time from the Thirties. Then violence, heroism, things like that, seemed much more natural to life. They seemed everyday matters and that governed my style. Things seemed desperate. Even though our cities weren't bombed you felt they might be, and we were destroying thousands of people. The world seemed apocalyptic at that time, and heroically so. I thought that civilisation was going to break down, and instead *I* did.

Alvarez: *What connection do you think there is between your present verse and your political situation—or your country's?*

Lowell: I'm very conscious of belonging to the country I do, which is a very powerful country and, if I have an image of it, it would be one taken from Melville's *Moby Dick:* the fanatical idealist who brings the world down in ruins through some sort of simplicity of mind. I believe that's in our character and in my own personal character; I reflect that it's a danger for us. It's not all on the negative side, but there's power there and energy and freshness and the possibility of ruin. I'm very aware of that.

I lost sleep about the atom bomb, of course. I don't think this is a period of parties and politics, the way the Thirties were. Here and in America that all seems to have calmed down to something we imagine is more the way life ordinarily is. While in the Thirties everybody was taking sides on something, usually very violently. The whole thing was almost like snakes twisting and hissing at each other. Things couldn't be more different now, in fact people are rather nostalgic for it.

Alvarez: *Well, how do you see the situation now?*

Lowell: I think the thing Pasternak expressed is universal . . . and it's certainly very strong in my country: that is, the danger of the great impersonal bureaucratic machine rolling over everything and flattening out humanity; the danger of luxury and organisation and all this slick stuff, this vulgarity and so forth. That's the terrible danger.

Alfred Alvarez (b. 1929), English critic and editor, is the author of *The Shaping Spirit* (1958), *The School of Donne* (1961), *The Savage God* (1971) and *Life After Marriage* (1982).

1. See John Collins Brossidy, "Toast, Holy Cross Alumni Dinner" (1910):

> And this is good old Boston,
> The home of the bean and the cod,
> Where the Lowells talk to the Cabots
> And the Cabots talk only to God.

6 • Robert Lowell in Conversation

A. Alvarez

Alvarez: *Your verse has changed a great deal, hasn't it? Most of the mannerisms of rhythm and imagery that you used in your early poems have disappeared, and yet you now have something much more personal. Is this how you see your own work?*

Lowell: When my second book came out the most interesting review of it was by Randall Jarrell. Though he liked the book, he made the point that I was doing things I could do best quite often, and I think he quoted Kipling—when you learn how to do something, don't do it again.[1] I think you should always do something a little longer than you should, go on until it gives out. There was a long pause between the second and the third. I didn't want to go on just cranking the same machine.

Alvarez: *When your first poems came out you were a Catholic, weren't you? You've ceased to be one since. Has the change in style anything to do with this change in allegiance?*

Lowell: It may have. In the second book I wasn't a Catholic but I was using Catholic material from a non–Catholic point of view, a neutral one. In *Life Studies* I was very anxious to get a tone that sounded a little like conversation.

Alvarez: *I felt that in* Life Studies *you were setting your personal house in order, you were dealing with the very personal material almost as you would in psychoanalysis. It seemed that, having left behind the dogmatic Catholic base and the dogmatic rhythms and symbols that went with it, you were trying to build a new base from which you could work.*

Lowell: I had in the back of my mind something like the prose of a Chekhov short story. The poems came in two spurts. The first was more intense when two-thirds of the autobiographical poems were written.

The Review 8 (August 1963): 36–40. Reprinted in *The Modern Poet,* edited by Ian Hamilton (New York: Horizon, 1969), pp. 188–193. Reprinted by permission of Aitken & Stone, Ltd.

This was a period of, at most, three months. Then there was a second period which finished that group and filled in blank spaces.

Alvarez: *I remember someone in* The Review *saying that the prose section in your book—which unfortunately wasn't published in the English version—was often more concentrated than one or two of the poems about your relatives. Do you think that's a fair comment?*

Lowell: There's a long first section in *Life Studies* called "Last Afternoon with Uncle Devereux Winslow" which was originally written in prose. I put it aside and I later cut things out and re-arranged it and made different transitions and put it into verse, so there is that connection and perhaps the style comes out of writing prose. But I'd say that the prose was an awful job to do. It took a long time and I think it could be less concentrated with more sting or something like that.

Alvarez: *You don't find prose comes naturally?*

Lowell: I find it very hard. I like to revise and when you have something of thirty or forty pages written as carefully as a poem—and it was written that carefully—it's very hard.

Alvarez: *Do you revise your poems much?*

Lowell: Usually. I think my record is a poem that was finished in one day. Usually it's a long time. I would have said that writing free verse you're more likely to get a few lines that are right in the beginning than you are in metre.

Alvarez: *My own interpretation of* Life Studies *is that the family poems cleared the ground and that, with the now very famous poems like "Man and Wife," "Home After Three Months Away," and "Waking in the Blue," your own choice came up absolutely clear—they have this unmistakable Lowell rhythm.*

Lowell: They are not written chronologically. Actually the first poem finished was "Skunk Hour" and I think the second was "Man and Wife," though they were all going on at the same time. But the first nut to crack really was "Skunk Hour"—that was the hardest. I cast about . . . it was written backwards, more or less, and I added the first four stanzas after I'd finished it.

Alvarez: *It came before these family poems?*

Lowell: Yes, actually it was the first, although the others were sort of started. I guess the first thing I had was a very imperfect version of "Man and Wife," which I dropped, and then I wrote "Skunk Hour." "Skunk Hour" was the first one completed. I was reading Elizabeth

Bishop's poems very carefully at the time and imitating the loose formality of her style.

Alvarez: *It seems to me that that poem is less successful in its opening lines. It suddenly gets down to what you're really talking about in the last part.*

Lowell: The opening's sort of cotton-nosed, it's supposed to let you sink into the poem and then it tenses up. I don't know whether it works or not. You dawdle in the first part and suddenly get caught in the poem.

Alvarez: *Confessional verse as you write it isn't simply an outpouring, is it? It's very strict, although the rules are hard to find.*

Lowell: You're asking how a confessional poem that's a work of art differs from someone's outpourings, sensational confessions for the newspapers or confessions to one's analyst. It seems to me there is some connection. When I was doing what might be called confessional poems there was a big chunk of something to be gotten out, but a great deal of it was very tame; the whole thing wasn't any very great story, but still there were things I wanted to say. Then the thing was the joy of composition, to get some music and imagination and form into it and to know just when to stop and what sort of language to put it in—it was pure joy writing it and I think it was pure technical joy, and poems are dull if you don't have that.

Alvarez: *What about the technique? You were saying that you have a great love for William Carlos Williams, who I would say seems to be the antithetical poet to you. Has he had any effect?*

Lowell: I always liked Williams, since I was a young man. But I don't think I've ever written anything that's very much like him. He really is utterly carried away into the object, it intoxicated him in describing it, and his way of composition's so different from mine. He was an active doctor and he wrote in snatches; he developed a way of writing in which he could get things out very quickly. I find him a very artful poet, but his art was largely cutting what he poured out. My things are much more formal, much more connected with older English poetry; there's a sort of formal personality in myself. I think anyone could tell that my free verse was written by someone who'd done a lot of formal verse. I began writing in the thirties and the current I fell into was the southern group of poets—John Crowe Ransom and Allen Tate—and that was partly a continuation of Pound and Eliot and partly an attempt to make poetry much more formal than Eliot and Pound did: to write in metres but to make the metres look hard and make them hard to write. It was the period of the famous book *Understanding Poetry,*[2] of analysing poems to see how they're put together; there was a great emphasis on craftsmanship. Out of that, though it came later, were poetry workshops and all that sort of thing. Well, that's in my blood very much, and about 1950 it was prevailing everywhere in America. There were poets trained that way, writing in the style, writing rather complicated, difficult, laboured poems, and it was getting very dry. You felt you had to get away from that at all costs. Yet still it's in one's blood. We're trained that way and I admire Tate and Ransom as much as ever. But in England that was the period of Auden and poetry was trying to express the times, politics, psychology, economics, the war and everything that somehow wasn't very strong with us. We had such poets and we had a lot of Auden imitators, but the strongest feeling seemed to be to get away from that and just write a poem. We talked a lot about form, craft, tragic experience and things like that.

Alvarez: *On this question of Auden, you seem to feel apparently quite strongly about not being political.*

Lowell: Well, yes, and that's quite misleading because it now seems to me that Auden's glory is that he caught all those things with much greater power than any of the people of his group. He's made the period immortal, of waiting for the war. At that time it seemed so stifled in controversy that it wasn't possible for us. People tried it in our country.

Alvarez: *What he got really was not the politics but the neurotic tension.*

Lowell: That's a better description. He caught the air and it was air in which events were hovering over your shoulder at every point, the second war was boiling into existence. Freud and Marx and a host of thinkers who were the most alive at that time—and still are in many ways—all do get into his poetry, and the idiom of those people waiting! I find that marvellous. I don't think this is a period of parties and politics the way the Thirties were. Here and in America that all seems to have calmed down to something we imagine is more the way life ordinarily is. I don't meet people who are violently anti-Russian very often. That doesn't seem to be [in] the air.

Alvarez: *They still exist though.*

Lowell: They exist, but they don't exist very much in the intellectual world. While in the Thirties everybody was taking sides on something, usually very violently—violent conversions, violent Marxist positions, violent new deal, violent anti-new deal—things couldn't be more different now. The terrible danger now is of the great impersonal bureaucratic machinery rolling over everything and flattening out humanity.

Alvarez: *The poets over here, and I would say in the States too, with the Beats, are rather cashing in on this.*

Lowell: Well, some of the Beats are quite good, but no mass movement like that can be of much artistic importance. It was a way for people to get away from the complexities of life. You've got to remain complicatedly civilised and organised to keep your humanity under the pressures of our various governments, not go into a bohemian wildness. Quite a few people are genuinely bohemian; the real bohemia is something tremendous, of course. I think someone really good, some Hart Crane, might swoop down on all this material and take it up and make art out of it. It's useful in a way that a certain amount of ice has been broken.

The Review was an English magazine of poetry and criticism, edited by Ian Hamilton.

1. Randall Jarrell, "From the Kingdom of Necessity," *Nation* 164 (18 January 1947): 74, 76. Jarrell actually wrote: "[Jean] Cocteau said to poets: *Learn what you can do and then don't do it.*"

2. An influential poetry textbook by Cleanth Brooks and Robert Penn Warren, first published in 1938, 4th edition 1975.

7 • Talk with Robert Lowell

Stanley Kunitz

Robert Lowell speaks with an air of gentle authority. Surprisingly, for a New Englander, his voice has a soft Southern tincture, which may be traced back to his formative years when he modeled himself on the Southerners Allen Tate and John Crowe Ransom. His wife, who supplies another auditory influence, is the Kentucky-born novelist and critic Elizabeth Hardwick, one of the founding editors of the *New York Review of Books*. Since 1960, when the Lowells braved the shock of transplanting themselves from Boston, they have figured prominently in the literary and intellectual life of New York. With their daughter Harriet, an ebullient seven-year-old, from whose flights of fancy and rhetoric her father has been known to borrow, they occupy a cooperative duplex apartment in mid-Manhattan, off Central Park.[1] The Victorian décor, dominated by "an unauthenticated Burne-Jones" hanging above the fireplace, and the majestic proportions of the book-lined living room, with its twenty-foot ceiling, recall the turn of the century, when the building was designed as a luxurious nest of studio apartments for non-struggling artists.

"Our move from Boston to New York gave me a tremendous push," says Lowell. "Boston is all history and recollection; New York is ahead of one. Sympathetic spirits are a rarity elsewhere. Here there is a whole community of the arts, an endlessly stimulating fellowship . . . at times too stimulating. No one is too great for New York, and yet I grant there is something frightening about it."

He is asked to comment on a passage from his remarks at the Boston Arts Festival in 1960, when he was the honored poet: "Writing is neither transport nor a technique. My own owes everything to a few of our poets who have tried to write directly about what mattered to them, and

New York Times Book Review, 4 October 1964, pp. 34–38. Reprinted in Stanley Kunitz, *A Kind of Order, a Kind of Folly* (Boston: Atlantic–Little Brown, 1975), pp. 153–160. Reprinted here by permission of Stanley Kunitz.

yet to keep faith with their calling's tricky, specialized, unpopular possibilities for good workmanship. . . .

"Thankfully," he responds with the hint of a smile, "the lifeline seems to me both longer and stronger than I thought at that time."

He notes that he is feeling unusually fit, as his bronzed look confirms, after a summer in Castine, Maine, where the Lowells have an old Colonial house on the Common, a gift from his cousin Harriet Winslow. His weight—he has a tendency to gain—is down to 170 pounds, ideal for his six-foot frame.

"In *Life Studies,*" he continues, "I wanted to see how much of my personal story and memories I could get into poetry. To a large extent, it was a technical problem, as most problems in poetry are. But it was also something of a cause: to extend the poem to include, without compromise, what I felt and knew. Afterwards, having done it, I did not have the same necessity. My new book, *For the Union Dead,* is more mixed, and the poems in it are separate entities. I'm after invention rather than memory, and I'd like to achieve some music and elegance and splendor, but not in any programmatic sense. Some of the poems may be close to symbolism. After all, it's a bore to keep putting down just the things you know."

As Lowell talks, slumped in his chair until he is practically sitting on his spine, he knits his brow in the effort to concentrate and stirs an invisible broth with his right index finger. The troubled blue eyes, intense and roving behind the thick glasses, rarely come to rest.

"The kind of poet I am was largely determined by the fact that I grew up in the heyday of the New Criticism, with Eliot's magical scrutiny of the text as a critical example. From the beginning I was preoccupied with technique, fascinated by the past, and tempted by other languages. It is hard for me to imagine a poet not interested in the classics. The task is to get something new into old forms, even at the risk of breaking them.

"So much of the effort of the poem is to arrive at something essentially human, to find the right voice for what we have to say. In life we speak with many false voices; occasionally, if we are lucky, we find a true one in our poems. A poem needs to include a man's contradictions. One side of me, for example, is a conventional liberal, concerned with causes, agitated about peace and justice and equality, as so many people are. My other side is deeply conservative, wanting to get at the roots of things, wanting to slow down the whole modern process of mechanization and dehumanization, knowing that liberalism can be a form of death too. In the writing of a poem all our compulsions and biases should get in, so that finally we don't know what we mean."

The contradictions of which Lowell speaks are present in his face and manner. The sensitive curved mouth contrasts with the jutting, fleshy chin; the nose is small, with wide circular nostrils; he is articulate, informed, and positive, but his gestures are vague and rather endearingly awkward. With his friends he has an air of affectionate dependency, which makes him seem perpetually boyish, despite the forty-seven years, the grizzled hair, the deep parentheses etched at the corners of his mouth. He is knowing about fame and power, but no less knowing about his weaknesses. His ambition and pride are real, but so is his modesty. It would be hard to imagine another poet of comparable stature saying to his interviewer and meaning it, "I should be interviewing you," or prefacing a book of his poems with such a disarmingly candid note as the one that introduces *For the Union Dead:*

> I want to make a few admissions and disclosures. My poems on Hawthorne and Edwards draw heavily on prose sentences by their subjects. "The Scream" owes everything to Elizabeth Bishop's beautiful, calm story, *In the Village.* "The Lesson" picks up a phrase or two from Rafael Alberti.[2] "Returning" was suggested by Giuseppe Ungaretti's[3] "Canzone." "The Public Garden" is a recasting and clarification of an old confusing poem of mine called "David and Bathsheba in the Public Garden." "Beyond the Alps" is the poem I published in *Life Studies,* but with a stanza restored at the suggestion of John Berryman. . . .

He has a great gift for friendship. No one is more generous than Robert Lowell in acknowledging his indebtedness to anybody who has ever helped him with a problem or with a poem.

"The poets who most directly influenced me," he says, "were Allen Tate, Elizabeth Bishop, and William Carlos Williams. An unlikely combination! . . . but you can see that Bishop is a sort of bridge between Tate's formalism and Williams's informal art. For sheer language, Williams beats anybody. And who compares with him for aliveness and keenness of observation? I admire Pound but find it impossible to imitate him. Nor do I know how to use Eliot or Auden—their voice is so personal. Williams can be used, partly because he is somewhat anonymous.

His poems are as perfect as anybody's, but they lead one to think of the possibility of writing them in different ways—for example, putting them into rhyme."

Lowell has no secondary skills or hobbies to distract him from his absorption in literature. At 9:30 every morning, when he is in the city, he retires to his separate and private apartment on an upper floor of the building in which he lives. There he spends at least five or six hours reading and writing. He reads only three or four novels a year now, but is quite omnivorous in his capacity for literary periodicals and for books of poetry, criticism, and history. He makes a point of returning regularly to the classics "with the aid of some sort of trot." Recently he has been reading Juvenal and Dante. Some of his scholarship is specifically designed to prepare him for his courses at Harvard, where he teaches two days a week. "I have had the advantage," he reflects, "of an independent income, which made it unnecessary for me to work for a living. I came to teaching voluntarily and quite late, having been unfit for it in my youth."

Lowell occupies himself tirelessly with literary evaluations, comparisons, and ratings. "The modern poem of length that interests me most," he remarks sweepingly, "is Pound's *Cantos,* the only long poem of the century that really comes off, even with all its flaws. One reason for my sustained interest in it is that it continues to puzzle me. In so many respects Pound remains a pre-Raphaelite figure, filled with nostalgia for the pure song of the troubadours and a lost pre-Renaissance innocence. What saved him as a poet was his bad politics, which got him involved in the contemporary world. The *Cantos* are not so good as Faulkner, but they are better than Hemingway and better than the work of any other novelist we've had since James. Dreiser's *American Tragedy,* which is comparable in scale, is humanly superior to the *Cantos,* but technically and stylistically inferior."

His taste for fine prose is as keen as his taste for verse. "As Pound said, poetry ought to be at least as well-written as prose. Furthermore, if you have sufficient control of the measure, you ought to be able to say anything in poetry that you can say in prose. The main difference between prose and poetry is a matter of technique: prose is written in paragraphs, poetry in lines. I am fascinated by the prose grip on things that somehow lets the music in and invites the noble splendor of a formal art. Swinburne's voice is dead because it's all music and no experience. Hardy owed a great deal to Swinburne, as we know from his elegy, but

his grasp on reality put him out of Swinburne's class. Both Hardy and
John Clare[4] were clumsy but honest craftsmen who sometimes wrote
remarkably well. Some of the intricate musical stanzas in Hardy have the
solidity of a stone-mason's job. In an anthology that I was reading the
other day I came across "The Frigate Pelican" of Marianne Moore's with
a sense of relief and liberation, not because it wasn't well-made but
because it was made differently, outside the groove of conventional poet-
ics. It caused the other poems to wither. I am still tempted by metrical
forms and continue to write them on occasion, but I am aware that meter
can develop into a kind of paralysis. Sometimes I start regular and end
irregular; sometimes the other way around."

With an accelerated stir of his finger, Lowell tries to sum up his
argument on the relationship between prose and poetry. "In general, the
poets of the last generation have lasted much better than the novelists. By
way of illustration, contrast Williams with Thomas Wolfe. Yet the poets
need the prose-writers and have a lot to learn from them. The style of a
Flaubert or of a Faulkner affects the tradition of poetry as much as it af-
fects the tradition of fiction. An ideal poetic language is more likely to re-
semble the art of Chekhov than that of Dylan Thomas. Maybe Thomas's
language is too sonorous to be at the center of poetry. The best poets have
an enormous respect for prose. After all, the great novelists of the nine-
teenth century make *Idylls of the King* seem frivolous. The supreme epic of
the last 150 years is *War and Peace;* of the last 50 years, *Ulysses.*"

The conversation veers to the subject of poetic reputation. Lowell is
without doubt the most celebrated poet in English of his generation.
Almost from the beginning it seemed that he could do no wrong. Why?
After several false starts and a deepening of the furrows in his brow,
Lowell proposes a tentative reply:

"I can't really explain why that much attention has been paid to me.
Looking back at *Lord Weary's Castle,* for example, my first full-length
collection, I see it as out of the mainstream, a rather repellent, odd,
symbolic Catholic piece of work. It may be that some people have turned
to my poems because of the very things that are wrong with me. I mean
the difficulty I have with ordinary living, the impracticability, the myo-
pia. Seeing less than others can be a great strain. One has to learn how to
live with one's limitations. I don't like to admit that my gift is for short
pieces, but I'm better off knowing it."

The British critic A. Alvarez has paired Lowell with John Berryman
as writers of "poetry of immense skill and intelligence which coped

openly with the quick of their experience, experience sometimes on the edge of disintegration and breakdown. . . . Where once Lowell tried to externalize his disturbances theologically in Catholicism and rhetorically in certain mannerisms of language and rhythm, he is now . . . trying to cope with them nakedly, and without evasion."5

Lowell does not try to skirt the issue, though it is difficult for him to discuss. "We are more conscious of our wounds," he ruminates, "than the poets before us, but we are not necessarily more wounded. Is Stevens or Eliot or Pound really any sadder at the heart or more vulnerable than Keats or Coleridge? The difference may be that modern art tries more deliberately to save the unsavable by giving it form. I am inclined to argue that it is better to be happy and kind than to be a poet. The truth is that no sort of life seems to preclude poetry. Poetry can come out of utterly miserable or disorderly lives, as in the case of a Rimbaud or a Hart Crane. But to make the poems possible a huge amount of health has to go into the misery."

Lowell finds the sources of his poems, variously, in a theme, an image, a musical phrase, sometimes in a prose passage or in another poem, preferably in a foreign language. The first draft is only a beginning. Only once did he ever complete a poem in a day. That was "The Tenth Muse," a poem about sloth! He makes a practice of showing his original draft to his poet friends, whose criticisms and suggestions he dutifully studies. A poem for him does not, as for Yeats, close shut with a click like a box. It only becomes less blurred. He does not believe in perfectibility. "In a way a poem is never finished. It simply reaches a point where it isn't worth any more alteration, where any further tampering is liable to do more harm than good. There are passages in all my books that make me wince, but I can't do anything with them. The worst grievance is the limitation inherent in any poet's character—the fact that Wordsworth, for example, can't be turned into Falstaff. That central limitation is far more serious than a few bad lines."

At the door, where he offers a warm valedictory hand, Lowell stands for a moment surveying the pantheon of his friends and heroes whose photographs adorn the staircase wall. These cherished countenances, who are very much a part of the Lowell life and household, include—in so far as one remembers—T. S. Eliot, Ezra Pound, William Carlos Williams, Robert Frost, Boris Pasternak, John Crowe Ransom, Edmund Wilson, the Allen Tates, I. A. Richards, William Empson, Randall Jarrell, Flannery O'Connor, and Elizabeth Bishop.

Exhausted as he is, at two in the morning, after more than five vehement hours of conversation, he is loath to let you go until the final resolving word has been spoken.

"You wouldn't write poetry unless you felt it had some chance of lasting. But if you get too concerned about posterity, you're in danger of becoming pompous and fraudulent. The poet needs to keep turning to something immediate and alive . . . something impertinent, engaging, un-Olympian. It's a waste of time to dream about immortality, but it's important to try for a poem that continues to be good, even though you realize that it's somehow a mockery for a poem to last longer than you do.

"You write poetry without hoping to attract too much attention, and it would be foolish to aim for a great audience that doesn't exist. Most people have a contempt for poetry—it's so ineffectual—but there may be some envy mixed up in that reaction. Today 'poet' is a slightly laughable and glamorous word."

Stanley Kunitz (b. 1905), American poet and author of *Intellectual Things* (1930), *The Testing Tree* (1971) and *Poems, 1928–1978* (1979), was Lowell's friend.

1. The Dakota, at 15 West Sixty-seventh Street.

2. Rafael Alberti (b. 1902), Spanish poet and playwright, author of an autobiography, *The Lost Grove* (1942).

3. Giuseppe Ungaretti (1888–1970), Italian poet, founder of the Hermetic movement.

4. John Clare (1793–1864), author of *Poems Descriptive of Rural Life* (1820) and *The Shepherd's Calendar* (1827), spent the last twenty years of his life in an insane asylum.

5. A. Alvarez, "Beyond the Gentility Principle" (1962), *Beyond All This Fiddle* (London, 1968), p. 41.

8 • In Bounds

Robert Lowell is one of the best, one of the most important American writers. He has won a Pulitzer Prize and a National Book Award, and many academic honors. He is a poet, and all his readers together could be put comfortably in one large lecture hall. But his new book, *For the Union Dead,* is an important literary event, and his publishers are understandably "astonished" by an advance sale of 1,500 copies in just two days.

"In a way," Lowell told *Newsweek* last week, "the small audience is a blessing. Too much success can be fatal to a poet—Byron, for example, had much too much for his own good." Most poets today live by teaching, and Lowell remembered Randall Jarrell's line—"God who took away the poet's audience gave him students instead." But the cadre of students who read poetry is largely a craft-oriented audience, and Lowell has said that poetry is becoming "purely a craft, and there must be some breakthrough back into life."

Lowell's poetry itself has become perhaps the sharpest and heaviest wedge in that breakthrough. His work is a precise and powerful example of what modern poetry does that no other mode of expression can do. If the avalanche of "ologies" has chipped and shattered the poet's role all the way down, Lowell's work shows how paradoxically important and powerful that role has become.

The role, quite simply, is to express what it feels like to be a living creature in the universe. The modern lyric poem is a small but explosive unit of expression which no novel, no play, no film can replace. The lives of most people are not epics, nor dramas—in many cases they are hardly narratives. But all are *lives*—this is the irreducible human state that the lyric poem addresses itself to.

In Robert Lowell's family there is an old bookplate motto: "I prefer to bend than to break." The poet comes as close as he can to the human

Newsweek 64 (12 October 1964): 120, 122. Copyright © 1964 by *Newsweek,* Inc. All rights reserved. Reprinted by permission.

breaking point. In these new poems Lowell is closer to that point than he has ever been, and the poems have therefore a new isometric tension and latent fatality.

The tense grating sound of the breaking point has never been absent from Lowell's poetry. For a while a Catholic, he was a conscientious objector in World War II. The poems in *Lord Weary's Castle* (which won the Pulitzer in 1947) are clenched, jammed—eloquent stammerings like pneumatic drills of language. These were a young man's poems—expressions of a powerful ego seeking exaltation, and knowing where to look for it—in the rainbow of God's will.

But as one grows older, the certainty and the possibility of exaltation diminish. The sense of life itself—growth eventuating in decay—takes over. Glory becomes retrospective rather than prospective; the future is simply the snapped tension of the present moment. This is the feeling in Lowell's new book. Middle age which in Dante produced the moment of his most supernal vision, produces in the modern poet a moment just as clear, but more earth-bound, more touching for us.

"The midwinter grind" has come, "the weary hours" that pile up to replace "the hour of credulity / and young summer." Lowell's words about a picture of Hawthorne are true for himself:

> . . . His hard
> survivor's smile is touched with fire . . .
>
> eyes fixed on some chip . . .
> the commonest thing,
> as if it were the clue.[1]

These poems search for clues to life's "rot and renewal," and find them. Mostly the finding occurs in the dark hours, with "Night Sweat" and "Myopia" and all the infirmities of the flesh crowding the soul to the breaking point.

The poems bend—but the poet doesn't break. Sometimes he reaches outside himself for leverage. Here he watches, and identifies with, some dying turtles:

> . . . I rub my skull,
> that turtle shell,
> and breathe their dying smell,
> still watch their crippled last survivors pass,
> and hobble humpbacked through the grizzled grass.[2]

The sense of survival is strong in this book, and that sense is in harmony with ripeness. Modern science treats man as a problem-solving animal, but poets like Lowell treat man as a mistake-making animal, and this is what makes these poems seem so much a part of the reader's own life, the reader's potential, the reader's felt humanity.

In this service Lowell brings magnificent resources of language. His descriptions ignite into images that sear and cauterize: ". . . and yet I saw the bouillon of his eye / was the same color as his frayed mustache . . ." "On a thousand small town New England greens, / the old white churches hold their air / of sparse, sincere rebellion . . ." And this about a drinker: "His despair has the galvanized color / of the mop and water in the galvanized bucket."

Last week in his New York apartment, Robert Lowell talked in his slow, careful, half-Boston, half-Carolina accent about despair: "We're turning, we're decaying, we're in mid-century. We feel the death of some tropical warmth. Mechanical time is replacing organic time. We're in some great midstream of morality; the old morality doesn't hold, no new one has been born. Genocide has stunned us; we have a curious dread it will be repeated."[3] Against this glacial drift of our age the poet's weapon—language—is small but supreme. Poetry is language conscious of its history, and making of that consciousness a moral responsibility. This is the supreme existential therapy we call art. In his title poem, "For the Union Dead," Lowell says of the Union general:

> He is out of bounds now. He rejoices in man's lovely,
> peculiar power to choose life and die—

While he is in bounds, every human being must wonder: what is the glory in being mortal? This is the answer, as only a great poet can give it.

1. Lowell, "Hawthorne."
2. Lowell, "The Neo-Classical Urn."
3. See W. B. Yeats, "The Second Coming" (1920):

> Things fall apart; the centre cannot hold;
> Mere anarchy is loosed upon the world.

9 • From "Applause for a Prize Poet"

Jane Howard

These opinions of Robert Lowell came from his interviews with Jane Howard of
Life *and from his published statements.*

My "autobiographical" poems are not always factually true. I've tin-
kered a lot with fact. You leave out a lot, and emphasize this and not
that. Your actual experience is a complete flux. I've invented facts and
changed things, and the whole balance of the poem was something
invented.

Not since Lincoln—a great prose writer and artist as well as statesman—
have we had a really cultured President. Theodore Roosevelt came clos-
est, but he was quite a drop. Kennedy? He was a step in the right
direction. Both he and his brother Bobby really have appeared to care
about history.

Jewishness, and not just of the New York variety, is the theme of today's
literature as the Middle West was the theme of Veblen's time and the
South in the Thirties. These regions have burnt out, and now we're
lucky to have the Jewish influence. It's what keeps New York alive; not
only writers and painters but also the good bourgeois who support the
arts. Consider the list of patrons and benefactors of any cultural
enterprise.

Do I feel left out in a Jewish age? Not at all. Fortunately, I'm one-eighth
Jewish myself, which I do feel is a saving grace. It's not a lot of Jewish
blood, but I think it would have been enough to come under the Nurem-
berg laws. My Jewish ancestors, oddly enough, were named Moses
Mordecai and Mordecai Moses.

From *Life* 58 (19 February 1965): 55–56, 58. Reprinted by permission of Jane Howard.

I suppose Rilke and Hardy are the best poets of this century, in any language. Of poets alive now my favorites are Elizabeth Bishop and Randall Jarrell. Eliot made an achievement unparalleled in our time: his work all hangs together and his greatest poems are long ones. Not since Pope, perhaps, has anyone written so well at such consistent length.

This has been an age of barbarous manslaughter. . . . We face the precariousness of keeping alert, of staying alive in the triple conflict between madness, death and life. We must bend, not break.

I believe we should rather die than drop our own bombs. Every man belongs to his own nation and to the world. He can only, as things are, belong to the world by belonging to his own nation. Yet the sovereign nations, despite their feverish last-minute existence, are really obsolete. They imperil the lives they were created to protect.

My kind of teaching—two seminars in one semester at Harvard—doesn't intrude on my writing. It doesn't do me any particular *good* but that isn't the point. You shouldn't think of writing while you teach; you should think of English and American classics, which is what I do.

The poetry of alcoholic men can be discerned from that of others: it has a kind of sleepwalking, musical quality to it.

In preparatory school, before I got to Harvard and eventually to Kenyon College, I was for some reason nicknamed "Caligula." That was shortened to "Cal," which is what I'm still called.

Advising, as Sartre has, that fathers and their own children can't get on together is utter rot. To say that's a reason not to have children is to say, "Don't go out for a walk, because if you do your feet might get hurt." I am quite optimistic about getting along with my daughter.

Being myopic has its advantages. It's like having two different visions, the world you see through glasses and the one you see without them—a blurred, romantic and much more mysterious, provocative one.

Our great museum in this country is the National Gallery in Washington, but of course the Metropolitan Museum's Rembrandt Room is one of the supreme things in any museum. Rembrandt is incomparably greater than any painter of this century, just as Shakespeare is a much greater poet.

My renowned forebears weren't a direct literary influence on me at all, highly though I regard my great-granduncle James Russell Lowell. . . . My distant cousin Amy, some of whose poetry really is rather good, struck her brothers Percival and Lawrence as being a bit odd. They wished her well, but didn't quite understand what she was about. The one I'd most like to have known myself is my military cousin, Charles Russell Lowell.

Jane Howard (b. 1935), editor at *Life* magazine, is the author of *Please Touch* (1970), *A Different Woman* (1973) and *Margaret Mead: A Life* (1984).

10 • From "The Second Chance"

"There's poetry all over the place," says Robert Lowell. "The world is swimming with it. I think more people write it and there are more ways to write it. It's almost pointless—there's no money in it—but a lot of them become teachers, and a lot of them write quite good poems and read to a lot of people. Poets are a more accepted part of society, and I don't know if it's bad for us or not, but it's pleasanter. I don't suppose even now parents are very glad when their children become poets, but it's not such a desperate undertaking. Still, being good isn't any easier."

. . . Says Lowell: "The strength of the novel is that it tells a story and has real people. But so many novels have been written that when you pick one up you feel you've read it before. The problem with poetry is that it doesn't necessarily have the connection with life and can be rather obscure. But poetry has the wonderful short thrust. By the time you get to the end of a poem, there's a whole interpretation of life in seventy lines or less. It's hard to get that in a novel, hard to get the heightening, hard to leave things out. And amid the complex, dull horrors of the 1960s, poetry is a loophole. It's a second chance of some sort: things that the age turns thumbs down on you can get out in poetry."

. . . When he has finished his rough draft, he begins fashioning rhymes. Later comes the "real work," which is "to make it something much better than the original out of the difficulties of the meter." He adds: "If you don't know a good deal about what you're saying, you're an idiot. But if you know too well what you're doing, you are a pedant."

. . . At Manhattan's Town Hall recently, he introduced Soviet poet Andrei Voznesensky to the audience and let loose with a curious political remark—his first such public utterance since his telegram to L.B.J. "This is indiscreet," he said, "but both our countries, I think, have really terrible governments. But we do the best we can with them, and they

Time 89 (2 June 1967): 67, 73–74. Copyright 1967 Time Inc. All rights reserved. Reprinted by permission from *Time*.

better do the best they can with each other or the world will cease to be here." Some people in the hall applauded; others gasped. Voznesensky, asked later for comment, merely turned away without a word.

. . . "It's a very dark crystal," he says. "I don't know what poetry needs now. Something's happening now, but it's hard to tell what it is. Half of it is very difficult, and half of it is very quiet." He guesses that perhaps "there has been too much confessional poetry."

. . . "It is harder to be a good man than a good poet."

11 • A Talk with Robert Lowell

A. Alvarez

This conversation took place in the studio where Robert Lowell works, a couple of floors above his family apartment. It's a high, very private room in a pleasantly old-fashioned block just off Central Park West. The view is undramatic yet specifically New York: the oddly shapeless backs of big buildings, water-towers, airshafts, and those deep narrow wells called "backyards." Unlike most New York flats, this one is peculiarly silent. The perpetual honking of car horns never penetrates this far back. Only occasionally the central heating creaks and bangs mildly. Otherwise there is nothing to distract you.

Lowell himself, now in his middle forties, is a big man, yet rather frail. His manner is gentle, almost saintly, although he can, when appropriate, be tart enough in his comments, a mixture of shyness and stringency, relaxed yet with a great deal in reserve. He is now at the height of his creative powers as a poet. He began his career as something of a prodigy, with two brilliant and influential books published in his middle twenties: *Land of Unlikeness* and *Lord Weary's Castle*. Like Dylan Thomas, he seemed to have given a new edge to poetic language, post-Eliot, symbolic, Catholic, and with powerfully original rhythms. Then there was a long pause, until thirteen years later he produced *Life Studies*— totally new, moving in a totally different direction, and even more influential. The Catholicism and symbolism had gone; the texture was simpler and the effort was to deal with his experience as nakedly as possible, letting the flow of feeling regulate the rhythmical pattern, which remained as insistently individual as ever. That was in 1959. In 1962 he published an extraordinary book of free translations called *Imitations,* really original variations by Lowell on themes from other poets. He has also translated Racine's *Phèdre* and recently completed a play of his own,

Encounter 24 (February 1965): 39–43. Reprinted in A. Alvarez, *Under Pressure* (London: Pelican, 1965), pp. 101, 108, 130–132, 163–164, 168, 173. Reprinted here by permission of Aitken & Stone, Ltd.

The Old Glory, based on short stories by Nathaniel Hawthorne and Herman Melville, which Jonathan Miller has just directed in New York with success. In *Imitations* and in the collection of new poems which he has made since then and which has just been published in the States, Lowell seems to have reached a new stage of technical and emotional fluency. In his early poems the power was sometimes short-circuited by mannerisms: the language could be too clotted, the rhythms almost predictably idiosyncratic. In *Life Studies* these mannerisms were reversed: some of the weaker poems were so loose, almost prattling, that the poetic urgency seemed to drain away in personal reminiscence. (I had better admit that this is critical hindsight. Each book of Lowell's seems, to an extraordinary degree, complete and resolved in itself. Then the next one appears and goes so unexpectedly far beyond the last that you have to revise your demands. He has, in short, a genius for constantly setting and then raising the standards by which his own work is to be judged.) But since *Imitations* the barriers have been down between his technique and his emotional resources, his imaginative power effortlessly matching the depth and scope and continual richness of his responses. His work now has that rare aliveness and vibration that comes only in the maturity of a major artist.

When we talked he had recently been ill and his reactions had the slightly tentative directness and openness, that curiously new-born quality, which goes with convalescence. And this tone seemed to match very precisely the raw, nervous atmosphere of New York in the period following President Kennedy's assassination, with its odd feeling of general psychic shock and displacement.

I began by asking him why the American artists, who are usually not in the least concerned with politicians, seemed to identify so closely with the dead President.

Lowell: Well, Kennedy represents a side of America that is appealing to the artist in retrospect, a certain heroism. You feel in certain terms he really was a martyr in his death; that he was reckless, went further than the office called for, and perhaps that he was fated to be killed. That's an image one could treasure, and it stirs one.

Alvarez: *But it's not just an image that concerns you. Don't you identify more with Kennedy than with other Presidents, because he somehow changed the position of the artist in American society, raised his status, and made him more acceptable by his obvious and publicly manifested interest in the cultural life of the country? I mean he invited artists and intellectuals to the Inauguration and to those White House dinner parties, he gave them medals and awards, he brought August Heckscher to the White House as his Special Consultant on the Arts, and so on.*

Lowell: I think you can take two more or less opposed lines on Kennedy: that the arts were in some way getting, though they haven't become more popular, more and more prestige, so that finally (as Hannah Arendt[1] says) it wasn't so much that Kennedy wanted to do anything for the arts but just his own personal ambition wanted to include the arts, and have the artists come to the White House. . . . But it was part of his ambition to tap this latent prestige of the arts. Well, the other line is that he was really a very exceptional President who broke the ice and put the artists sort of in the front window for a moment.

Alvarez: Yet those dinner parties of Kennedy's did have some curious side-effects, didn't they? Weren't they, if nothing else, a sign of change? I mean when Eisenhower was President you felt that the country was being run exclusively by the Pentagon and those awful golfing big-business cronies of his. With Kennedy there did seem some vague, fragile possibility of some kind of connection, even mutual interchange, between the representatives of the cultural life of the country and those of the world of power.

Lowell: I think of Edmund Wilson's comment. Arthur Schlesinger asked him how he felt about being invited to the White House to dinner and Wilson said "Oh, it was bigger than other dinners! . . ." I was invited to the White House for Malraux's dinner there. Kennedy made a rather graceful joke that "the White House was becoming almost a café for intellectuals. . . ." Then we all drank a great deal at the White House, and had to sort of be told not to take our champagne into the concert, and to put our cigarettes out like children—though nicely, it wasn't peremptory. Then the next morning you read that the Seventh Fleet had been sent somewhere in Asia and you had a funny feeling of how unimportant the artist really was: that this was sort of window dressing and that the real government was somewhere else, and that something much closer to the Pentagon was really ruling the country. And maybe this is how it must be.

You see, I have a feeling that the arts are in a very funny position now—that we are free to say what we want to, and somehow what we want to say is the confusion and sadness and incoherence of the human condition. Anyone running a government must say the opposite of that: that it can be solved. He must take an optimistic stance. I don't know why the arts say this so strongly. It may be a more miserable time, more than others, with the world liable to blow up. We're in some transition domestically; I mean in one's family life and everything else. There are new moral possibilities, new moral incoherence. It's a very confused moment. And for some reason it's almost a dogma with us: we'll show that confusion.

Alvarez: *The confusion has been staring right at you since the events in Dallas, hasn't it? But I wonder if the pervasiveness and inescapability of it all isn't emphasized by the American preoccupation with psycho-analysis. Every-body is in analysis. It's the dominant mode for the American interpretation of reality. And whatever you think about it, it does at least force one to recognise the answering confusion in oneself. Analysis has made it very difficult to live purely rationally and on the surface, at least with any conviction.*

Lowell: Well, I get a funny thing from psycho-analysis. I mean Freud is the man who moves me most: and his case histories, and the book on dreams, read almost like a late Russian novel to me—with a scientific rather than a novelist's mind. They have a sort of marvellous old-order quality to them, though he is the father of the new order, almost the opposite of what psycho-analysis has been since. All that human sort of colour and sadness, that long German-Austrian and Jew-ish culture that Freud had, seems something in the past; but it was still real to him. There is something rather beautiful and sad and intricate about Freud that seems to have gone out of psycho-analysis; it's become a way of looking at things.

Alvarez: *What I suppose you're getting at is a certain moral rooted quality in Freud—a sense of continuing cultural tradition which you don't get in the orthodox Freudians.*

Lowell: I was brought up as an Episcopalian Protestant, with a good deal of Bible reading at school. We had a rather sceptical attitude, but we were rather saturated (even in this late day) with it. And it strikes me this may be just true of my own peculiar history: brought up as a Protestant, then a Catholic convert. When that goes and we look at it another way, Freud seems the only religious teacher. I have by no means a technical understanding of Freud, but he's very much part of my life. He seems unique among the non-fictional teachers of the century. He's a prophet. I think somehow he continues both the Jewish and Christian tradition, and puts it maybe in a much more rational position. I find nothing bores me more than someone who has all the orthodox sort of Freudian answers like the Catechism, but what I find about Freud is that he provides the conditions that one must think in. I'm thinking of my own case: I'm one-eighth Jewish and seven-eighths non-Jewish and our culture seems sort of that way. We never supplied what the Jewish tradition did—our culture never supplied the equivalent of that. And now to-day, we can't. The two thinkers, non-fictional thinkers, who influence and are never out of one's mind are Marx and Freud.

Alvarez: *Now this, of course, is particularly so in New York, which is enormously Jewish in its whole atmosphere, isn't it? The intellectual life is almost entirely Jewish, most of the entertaining is Jewish, the ways of eating are Jewish, and so on.*

Lowell: Yes, and I think there wouldn't be any active American culture now without the Jewish element. They are small in numbers, but they're a leaven that changes the whole intellectual, cultural world of America. And it's a painful reality, I think, that a minority should have such liveliness and vigour that you're at a loss why the rest of the country doesn't equal that.

Alvarez: *There is every reason why the Jews should feel at home in the States. I mean American democracy was based, theoretically, on certain abstract principles which were lacking in Europe. So the Jews, as more or less permanent outsiders in Europe, would have responded to America very strongly.*

Lowell: I think of Jefferson and the whole idealism—there are very few countries founded on a declaration the way ours was. There's something biblical and Jewish about that—Messianic. It is both what is unreal about America and what's noble about America. Violence and idealism have some occult connection. I remember reading Henry Adams' *History of Jefferson and Madison*—it's rather sceptical history, far from idealising America (though it's different from Adams' later position). I noticed the strange pride that Adams takes in American gunnery—it's almost wild-Western: that the American ships shot better than the English ships and that Andrew Jackson's artillery shot better than the British artillery. All that had some great symbolic significance to him. We seem to be a very sheer country: I mean power is something everyone must have, because the country's powerful. The ideal isn't real unless it's somehow backed by power. Robert Frost was very much criticised for his remark about poetry and power: "We must have more of both." Well, he seemed to rejoice in that. But in a way I feel it is our curse that we can't disentangle those two things.

Alvarez: *Well, power and violence—above all, violence—are things you simply can't get away from in the States: they seem to come in at you from every direction.*

Lowell: I don't know where it comes from—whether it's the American genius, or just the chaos of our schools and that young people are badly brought up—but I think it has something to do with both the idealism and the power of the country. Other things are boring for these young people, and violence isn't boring. We have a thing for the Western movie: some sort of faith that the man who can draw most quickly is the real hero. He's proved himself. Yet that is a terribly artificial standard; the real hero might be someone who'd never get his pistol out of the holster, stumbling about, near-sighted. We don't want to admit that. It's deep in us that the man who draws first somehow has proved himself.

Alvarez: *But this violence and heroism is in key with the tone of the country: with the speed, the rawness, the vast size, the emptiness and the aggression of the cities.*

Lowell: I feel that it's a very naked country; the sort of flesh that goes on the skeleton and the nervous system that works is very meagre. And we come to Norman Mailer—he has this peculiar thing, he's cursed with it. The country works so well; it's powerful; therefore the writers should be on an enormous scale. And why can't we produce an enormous novel, the way the Russians did in the nineteenth century? It's quite beyond our powers, apparently, though maybe some American will appear who'll disprove that. But there's a burden on Mailer to make that attempt, and we're cursed with the ambitious big novel. Yet it's not entirely a curse and Mailer is genuinely a hero and every so often he really does have the flesh so that he's at least the greatest of our journalists, I think; suddenly all those enormous ambitions get clothed for a moment.

Alvarez: *So you think that this ambition and power—the kind of thing you get in Mailer—is specifically an American characteristic?*

Lowell: We have some impatience with prosaic, everyday things of life—I think those hurt us. That sort of whimsical patience that other countries may have—that's really painful to endure: to be minor. We leap for the sublime. You might almost say American literature and culture begins with *Paradise Lost*. I always think there are two great symbolic figures that stand behind American ambition and culture. One is Milton's Lucifer and the other is Captain Ahab: these two sublime ambitions that are doomed and ready, for their idealism, to face any amount of violence.

Alvarez: *Does this literary, spiritual quality also affect America's political behaviour?*

Lowell: Our world position is a curious sort of fulfilment of a national characteristic: that we're a country founded on a constitution. That makes us rather different from the usual country founded on a history and a culture. We were founded on a Declaration, on the Constitution, on Principles, and we've always had the ideal of "saving the world." And that comes close to perhaps destroying the world. Suddenly it is as though this really terrible nightmare has come true, that we are suddenly in a position where we might destroy the world, and that is very closely allied to saving it. We might blow up Cuba to save ourselves and then the whole world would blow up. Yet it would come in the guise of an idealistic stroke.

Alvarez: *But the trouble with this idealism is that it seems so unqualified at times: I mean the anti-Communism, you know. The anti-totalitarianism is so overwhelming that it becomes at times something very like another form of totalitarianism, certainly, a kind of total stupidity.*

Lowell: Yes, I suppose this is too apocalyptic to put it this way, but it is the Ahab story of having to murder evil: and you may murder all the good with it if it gets desperate enough to struggle. Russia is in somewhat the same position, of course. It is a world situation now. But it hits our genius in a very strange way, and what's best in our country in a way is united with this, and what's worst and most dangerous and naked and inhuman about us gets swept up into this ideal. And also this thing that we won't let go, a kind of energy and power of imagination, of throwing yourself all out into something.

Alvarez: *And does this affect the arts—the idea of never having minor art, the one thing no one can bear to be is minor?*

Lowell: Yes. It's often said that we have no minor poets in America, though of course we do; but that seems an oddly ignoble ambition. Even the minor poet reaches for the sublime.

Alvarez: *What about the theory that sociology is taking over the arts? Isn't there a perfectly good case to be made for the first great American novel being not* Moby Dick *or* The Scarlet Letter *but de Tocqueville's* Democracy in America?

Lowell: But would you call de Tocqueville a sociologist? His book still seems the best book on America, and it's an oddly unique book. He somehow lived it, yet it's a rather abstract book. Still, it's a book he couldn't have written without having visited America and lived through it; that's always there.

Alvarez: *But this abstractness is somehow typical: for example, the big political issues which are plaguing you now—"Civil rights" and "poverty"— are essentially moral, slightly abstract issues, not party issues. I mean that, except for the extremists on the right, both parties agree that these are national sicknesses that must be cured. They merely disagree about the kind and the quantity of medicine needed.*

Lowell: This may not answer what you're after at all. The biggest issue in the country now is civil rights. We're bound to act morally on this and, of course, there's the danger that the morals may cut people's legs off; they may be simplified. The only opposition to civil rights is an inarticulate immoral position that has a certain human appeal, I think— the Southern. But it's morally indefensible. This seems to come down all the way from the Civil War, that the Southerner's morally inarticulate. One felt this more strongly in the Thirties when there was a "Southern Renaissance" in culture. It was, perhaps, the strongest single element in American culture: this Southern position which somehow was quite human and observant (in some ways typically American, but in others not), and it was a sort of position with its moral head cut off. Somehow this whole Southern view didn't make sense morally; but it was observant of life and talked a great deal about the "tragedy of life." The Southerners no longer seem to have that strength. When you have a rather disagreeable reactionary Southerner talking, it is terrible that he doesn't make more sense, moral sense.

Alvarez: *Does this lack of "moral sense" have something to do with the general rootlessness and mobility of American life? It is something that strikes the visitor very hard: nothing seems to last, neither objects, nor relationships, nor even the landscape. And people are always drifting restlessly from one city to another, eternally migrating.*

Lowell: The mobility I know most about in America is New York City. And this is such a cliché I blush to utter it. But you go from New York to London—and they're two cities in many ways much alike, maybe essentially alike—but the superficial difference hits you terribly hard. You can't touch a stone in London that doesn't point backwards into history; while even for an American city, New York seems to have no past. And yet it's the only city that sort of provides an intellectual, human continuum to live in. Of course you don't have to live in New York. Many people loathe living in it. But still, if you removed it, you'd be cutting out the heart of American culture. Yet it is a heart with no past. The New York of fifty years ago is utterly gone and there are no landmarks; the record of the city doesn't point back into the past. It has that sheer presence which, I think, is not the image of mobility you talk about.

Alvarez: *This kind of driving force, moving into the future all the time, without a past at all, as though the wake were closing up behind it. . . .*

Lowell: And it has a great sheer feeling of utter freedom. And then when one thinks back a little bit, it seems all confused and naked.

Alvarez: *Do you think this freedom is behind the cult of experimentalism of America in the arts, the demand that no two poets, no two major poets in America ever write the same?*

Lowell: Well, certainly they are not burdened down with this sort of baggage of life the English poet carries. I mean what everyone finds wrong with American culture is the monotony of the sublime. I've never lived anywhere else, but I feel it is extreme (and perhaps unique, even) about America, that the artist's existence becomes his art. He is re-born in it, and he hardly exists without it. There's that feeling, perhaps.

Alvarez: *That he himself is as mobile as the society, he has no roots in the family, no real social niche, no sense of permanence?*

Lowell: A friend of mine went to London this summer. He was utterly delighted with it and said, "It's so human" (he comes from the South). "And its people were so polite, and it just seemed unimaginably gentle and wonderful in a way an American city isn't." But he avoided meeting any English literary people; he felt that England was a disaster for the literary man, that he was hampered at every step with "cautions and nots and things." That shows the American temperament, the impatience.

Alvarez: *Well, the major part of these "cautions and nots and things" is the compulsory Cult of the Amateur in England—which you certainly don't suffer from in the States.*

Lowell: We are talking about the arts being, perhaps, more a profession in the States. I don't know enough about Englishmen or any other country to make a comparison. But I feel this in meeting people, that we have a feeling the arts should be "all out"—you're in it, you're all out in it, and you're not ashamed to talk about it endlessly, sheerly. That would seem embarrassing to an Englishman, and inhuman, probably, to be that "all out" about it. I guess the American finds something a little unin-vigorating about the Englishman that he doesn't do that.

Alvarez: *There is this terrible feeling in England that excellence is some-thing that, in a sense, one ought to feel apologetic about.*

Lowell: Done with your left hand, and it's always done with both your hands in America. We were talking about it earlier: the artist finds new life in his art and almost sheds his other life.

1. Hannah Arendt (1906–75), German-born political scientist and philoso-pher, author of *Origins of Totalitarianism* (1951) and *Eichmann in Jerusalem* (1963).

12 • An Interview with the Author

Goddard Lieberson

Goddard Lieberson: *When you were writing* Benito Cereno, *were you writing it with the conscious thought that the lines would be spoken? Did you hear them?*

Robert Lowell: Oh yes. But let me say first of all, I think your record is the finest performance the play has ever had. I can't read the plays as well as first-rate actors. In writing *The Old Glory* I found that wherever I tried to write fine poetry, I had to junk it. You have to leave something for the actors to add. That explains why I can read my poems far better than any actor can, but not the plays. I can get certain rhythmical things that no actor gets in the plays, but that's secondary to the projection of the figure.

Goddard Lieberson: *Whether you were consciously writing poetry or not, in* Benito, *or* The Old Glory *if you like, what we hear is so much more poetry than anything that usually goes on in the theater today. On the other hand, I can't conceive of some poets as playwrights.*

Robert Lowell: Most poets.

Goddard Lieberson: *Exactly. Dramaturgical talent is something quite separate from being a poet.*

Robert Lowell: Only about ten first-rate poets have written plays, isn't that true? I never counted—but Milton, Ben Jonson, Shakespeare. . . .

Goddard Lieberson: *As to Shakespeare, I find your play owes less to Melville than Shakespeare owed to Plautus or Plutarch, or any of the works he used as a basis for his plays. I've been reading the Melville novella, as somebody called it—I can't believe that's the right description of it—*

Robert Lowell: I like your objection: "short novel" would be a better description.

Liner notes for *Benito Cereno by Robert Lowell* (New York: Columbia Records, 1965). Reprinted by permission of Brigitta Lieberson.

Goddard Lieberson: *—but tell me, how did you decide to write* Benito Cereno *as a play?*

Robert Lowell: I'll tell you literally.

Goddard Lieberson: *Yes, I want to know.*

Robert Lowell: I was given a Ford grant to go either to plays or opera, and I chose opera. I spent three weeks or a month going to the City Center, and then five months going to Met rehearsals. A friend of mine, Bill Meredith,[1] had the same fellowship, and he went to the Met, too. He had the idea of writing an opera on *Benito Cereno.* We decided we'd collaborate. But, instead, I immediately discovered I didn't want to do a libretto of *Benito* but an acting play, because in a libretto the plot is all-important, not the language, while what I was interested in was the plot plus language. So I went ahead on my own.

Goddard Lieberson: *In rereading the Melville, I could find only the barest kind of jumping-off places for you.*

Robert Lowell: It doesn't concern me how much is Melville and how much is Lowell. I first read *Benito Cereno* in college, some twenty-five years ago. There's a masterpiece of an essay on it by Yvor Winters.[2] He places it next to *Moby Dick,* among Melville's works, and I agree. I've read it a number of times since: it's been in my blood and haunted me. In some ways it's a more human novel than *Moby Dick.* But I'll tell you how I went about turning *Benito* into a play.

I'd already translated Racine's *Phèdre.* There, I got the trick of the confidant, a character in whom the hero confides. Perkins is my invention—that's pure Racine—French classical tragedy, not Melville.

Goddard Lieberson: *Putting Perkins in makes a play of it. Do you think that Perkins is a part of Delano?—that the two of them together are America, in a way, at the same time?*

Robert Lowell: But they're different, they're distinct people. Perkins starts as a confidant and ends up superior to Delano.

Goddard Lieberson: *Where does the superiority first show, do you think?—where Perkins says, "I only have one life"?*

Robert Lowell: "I only have one life, *Sir.*" The "*Sir*" is very important; it puts Delano in his place. That, and also then at the end, when Perkins says, "We have to save someone. . . ." There he proves himself superior to Delano.

Goddard Lieberson: *That's right. I read* Benito Cereno *years and years ago, and I'd forgotten the device of the diary and the official documents in the Melville story.*

Robert Lowell: Those are real. Melville didn't make them up, they're official documents.

Goddard Lieberson: *Suddenly, when Melville brings them in at the end, I feel they're not digested—it's like seeing a play and then suddenly having part of a newsreel brought in.*

Robert Lowell: Undigested, yes.

Goddard Lieberson: *One more question: some people seem to be unsure just what you meant by ending* Benito Cereno *as you did. Do you care to comment?*

Robert Lowell: I wrote a letter to the *Village Voice* about that. Someone accused me of wishing to put down the present Negro revolt by guns. They had me confused with Captain Delano. I'd like to quote from my letter: "The play is set about 1803, in Jefferson's time, and the remarks so outrageously attributed to my own feelings are meant to show the ambivalence toward salvery, even in the mind of a Northerner like Captain Delano. He literally cannot see what is before his eyes because he thinks of the Negroes only as servants and primitives. . . . The terrible injustice, in the past and in the present, of the American treatment of the Negro is of the greatest urgency to me as a man and as a writer."[3]

Goddard Lieberson (1911–77), American composer and president of Columbia Records, was the editor of *John Fitzgerald Kennedy* (1965) and *The Irish Rising, 1916–1922* (1966).

1. William Meredith (b. 1919), American poet and Professor of English at Connecticut College, is the author of *The Open Sea* (1958) and *The Cheer* (1980).

2. See Ivor Winters, "Herman Melville and the Problems of Moral Navigation," *Maule's Curse* (1938).

3. Robert Lowell, "Mr. Lowell Rebuts," *Village Voice,* 19 November 1964, p. 4.

13 • Mr. Robert Lowell on T. S. Eliot and the Theatre

Michael Billington

"Beautifully civil" was how someone described Robert Lowell's translation of *Phèdre*. The same words might be applied to the American poet himself. His manner is gracious and friendly, his appearance slightly suggestive of a don engrossed with problems of scholarship. But just as Lowell's poetry seems to have enormous reserves of strength under its usually calm surface, so the man himself can be unyielding on matters of principle, as his public actions have proved.

He is in London for the opening of his play, *Benito Cereno,* at the Mermaid tonight; and in the theatre foyer one morning this week, surrounded by a small band of cleaners with mops and pails, he talked concisely and openly about his work. The Herman Melville short story from which he has adapted this particular play has always been one of his favourite books: he first read it as a student thirty years ago and he ranks it second only to *Moby Dick* in the Melville canon. In translating it to the stage, he has tried to keep faith with the original while adding a number of details: "An Argentinian writer, Borges, once said that you could tell the Koran was genuine because it didn't mention camels, whereas if you were translating it you would put the camels in. This happens with a dramatization. For instance, here, I've included a lot about the French Revolution not in the original. I've also put a lot of myself into the central character and I've disregarded exact historical chronology. If anyone wanted to check the text, he would probably find a network of tiny errors."

Between Melville and Lowell himself, however, one senses unusual affinities. Like the author of *Moby Dick,* Lowell seems to have the sea in his blood. "I grew up every summer by the sea and as a boy I often went sailing. I've never sailed in a whaling boat, of course, but I wouldn't ever

---

The Times (London), 8 March 1967, p. 10. Reprinted by permission of Michael Billington.

want to live far away from the sea." Issues that unconsciously stirred Melville are consciously present in his adapter: "Melville wrote his story on the eve of the Civil War and it came into his work in an intuitive, clairvoyant way. All kinds of things were in my mind when I wrote the play—the Civil Rights issue most of all." Finally, Melville had what Lowell calls "a feeling for operatic melodrama": and before sitting down to write his play, Lowell had been studying exactly that subject and attending hundreds of opera rehearsals.

To date, Lowell's work for the theatre has consisted entirely of adaptations and translations, but these obviously carry his own distinctive imprint. His next work, a new version of Aeschylus's *Prometheus,* will be twice as long as the original and applicable to our own age. "The story is of a guy chained to a rock, but it's what goes through his mind that's important. I didn't have to put in cigarette lighters or motor cycles to make it up to date. His thoughts all come out of our world." But Lowell would also like to write plays about twentieth-century figures, and he mentions Trotsky and Malcolm X as examples. The difficulty, he feels, would be partly one of idiom and partly the weight of documentary evidence: as he says, Shakespeare had only Holinshed[1] and Plutarch to work from when writing his histories.

Although *Benito Cereno* has an undeniably poetic feel to it, Lowell seems a little wary of the term "poetic drama." "For me, poetic drama means anything non-naturalistic or heightened. The sort of thing that Christopher Fry[2] does I'm not interested in. I find it better to write in paragraphs than lines because one can sustain an idea that way." Eliot's suggestion that there are certain states of being that can achieve theatrical expression only in verse does not strike a chord with him. "I knew Eliot well. His essays on Elizabethan dramatists were almost my introduction to drama. But I wish that he himself had tried to use a more gaudy style, something more like the Elizabethans themselves. In trying to throw out the purple passages, he sometimes threw out the poetry as well."

When the question of modern American poetry is raised, Lowell finds little to cheer. "I see oceans of competence in every kind of style. There have never been so many competent people writing poetry. But there needs to be more personality—not just technique or the imitation of something better. Most of the poets I admire at the moment are women—Sylvia Plath, for instance." Lowell himself combines writing poetry with three months' academic work every year. "My old friend, Randall Jarrell, once said that he liked teaching so much that, if he were rich enough, he'd pay to be a teacher. I don't go so far as that but I do like it. Besides a poet can get awfully full of himself if he works alone."

No one could accuse Robert Lowell of being full of himself: there is about him a hint of that "triumphant diffidence" he once praised in a friend. At the same time, he has not been afraid to stand publicly by his principles: he was gaoled in wartime as a conscientious objector and he refused an invitation to the White House because of his feelings about Vietnam.[3] About this, he says reasonably: "It's all to the good if a gesture of protest can be symbolic—it helps if it's more than verbal, anyway. But there's no reason why a poet shouldn't simply write poetry like Herrick or de la Mare if he wants to." In its combination of tolerance with strong personal convictions this says a lot about the spirit of Robert Lowell.

Michael Billington (b. 1939), drama critic of the London *Guardian,* is the author of *The Modern Actor* (1974), *How Tickled I Am* (1977) and *Alan Ayckbourn* (1983).

1. Raphael Holinshed (d. ?1580), English chronicler, author of *Chronicles of Englande, Scotlande and Irelande* (1577), a major source for Shakespeare's history plays.

2. Christopher Fry (b. 1907), English playwright, author of *A Phoenix Too Frequent* (1946), *The Lady's Not For Burning* (1949) and *The Dark is Light Enough* (1954).

3. See Robert Lowell, "Letter to Lyndon Johnson," *New York Times,* 3 June 1965, p. 1.

14 • Keeping the Lid on the World

John Gale

Mr. Lowell came into the room quickly, stooping a little to one side. He had a rather sad smile, yet the blue eyes behind the glasses seemed amused. He tended to look down when he talked.

He had spoken somewhere of the danger of the great impersonal bureaucratic machine flattening out humanity. Would he elaborate?

"Once you get that enormous Government machine connected with power and world ambition it's terrifying. And there are a lot of other machines in the world besides America's: Russia is another. I'm haunted by the First World War, when these huge countries, despite inertia—or through inertia—went to war. Nobody could stop it; not even the people running the Governments. We've seen this twice in one century, and it's impossible to see that very much has been done to prevent a third.

The Kaiser was an unattractive character, but not a villain; most of the heads of State were the same. Even the Kaiser, when he got cold feet, couldn't stop the train schedules when the German trains were going to the frontier. I'm sure you've been in something where the thing's been set up and something goes wrong with the schedule and it's too expensive to change it. In television, say. Think of a nation in that state.

Another frightening thing in our country is that if we begin to lose in the world-juggling, the country could go fascist. Again, it's not us alone: I think Europe's fairly dangerous; and Russia's certainly dangerous; and China, if she had any power.

There there's another thing. Isaiah Berlin[1] and I were talking about war, and he said there's one thing worse than war: massacre. I feel very gloomy about the future: the Indonesian massacre and the Hindu-Muslim thing. That seems bound to happen in South Africa and elsewhere.

Observer, 12 March 1967, p. 11. Reprinted by permission of the *Observer*.

I think the best thing—it's a little chilly to me—would be a sort of pax America-Russiana: just coming to terms by trying to keep the lid on the world; and Europe might be in this. I think that's a strong possibility. It will be very much 'Two Cheers For Democracy';[2] *faute de mieux* kind of thing: an attempt at peace and just-under-peace."

Was it true that he often wrote a very gloomy poem when in a very happy mood?

"I write rather slowly, and a lot boils up and changes in the course of a poem. In a poem you don't try to give the reader distress and disorder: you want to give him something well made and organized, with loveliness to it: and that's exhilarating even with subjects that are apocalyptic. You don't want to be mannered about these things, or else people think they've heard you before you begin speaking.

I think it should be very hard to say whether life is joyful or tragic: it's all that. Henry Adams's brother, Charles Francis Adams, wrote about the eighteenth-century Frenchman who said he'd had fourteen happy hours in his life. Charles Francis Adams didn't know whether he'd had that many, but he was certain that he'd had more than all his family put together."

It was the morning after the first night of his play.

"The reviews are rather lousy. That's the kind they had in New York. I thought the company did a beautiful job last night: I was very pleased with the performance. It's rather a delicate play: a lot of nuances. Maybe they [the critics] don't get that. There were a lot of complaints about its being too short. It was one of three plays.[3]

The first begins with seventeenth-century New England, Puritan and anti-Puritan. Cromwell's Civil War is already brewing. The play's built around an incident when the English flag is cut down by the Puritan Governor. The second is the American Revolution. [*The third,* Benito Cereno, *is based on a slave-trading incident.*]

He discussed plans for future writing. Was it true that he might write plays on Trotsky and Malcolm X?

"I just can't find any language. With Trotsky I was going to do just his exile, beginning in Turkey and ending with his murder in Mexico. It's very difficult to get anyone to speak. Trotsky's almost too much to handle: it's very hard to get that sort of person talking at all. But it's a terrific thing: all his entourage, the daughter that went insane. You immediately think Dostoevsky could have handled the Trotsky story, but it probably wouldn't have been Trotsky any more: he'd have been a rather minor figure. I'd have made Trotsky a hero and sympathetic; but he's very mixed: there's a great deal that's terrifying about him.

With Malcolm X there are even greater difficulties. I could probably get him talking. But all the Negroes round him—I don't know how they'd talk. And there's the problem of Negroes murdered by Negroes. What sort of public would follow that? He wrote a fascinating auto-biography. He's the most fascinating of the Negro leaders.

And of course he can say all these things about Negroes that no white person dare say. And yet he's a Negro hero. Dramatically you feel that neither he nor Trotsky could have escaped being murdered. They weren't bent on being murdered: they were bent on succeeding as politicians. Then they suddenly found themselves doomed."

Perhaps he would rather not say any more about Vietnam?

"It's peculiarly hideous and useless right now. We were just talking at breakfast of the chances of Bobby Kennedy running against Johnson next year and ending the war. But the odds are against that. It would have taken a million years for North Vietnam to have done as much harm to us as we've done to ourselves. Our whole life is torn by it. And our students are about to be drafted. It absorbs conversation and the cost and brutality are appalling.

I suppose it's a small minority in America that's disgusted with the war. But it's almost universal with intellectuals. Kennedy has changed and grown, I think. You're not sure of any person in power. He could take a very bad turn. He's about the best we could hope for, I think: he's about as open morally as a politician could be. I don't mean that if he was elected we wouldn't object to a great deal he did. But it would be an enormous relief. Of course he has odds against him. But it does look more likely; and I think the country as a whole is sicker of the war than they know: the ugliness and unsuccess."

A last question. He had once spoken of the "sheerness" of America. Could he say any more?

"I've got a phrase out of that interview I used later in a poem: the 'monotonous sublime.' It can get too sheer in that way. It has something to do with our character. It's probably harder in America to be a first-class minor poet. Most people are ruined. They feel immoral not doing what the national genius expects. They've got to do something on a big scale."

1. Sir Isaiah Berlin (b. 1909), British philosopher and intellectual historian, author of *Karl Marx* (1939) and *The Hedgehog and the Fox* (1951).

2. The title of E. M. Forster's essay of 1938.

3. The other two plays in *The Old Glory* trilogy are *Endecott and the Red Cross* and *My Kinsman, Major Molineux*.

15 • "Life Offers No Neat Conclusions"

Richard Gilman

I talked to Robert Lowell on Easter Sunday. Half a block away from the large, beautifully unmodern apartment in the West Sixties where he lives with his wife Elizabeth Hardwick and their eleven-year-old daughter Harriet, Central Park was jumping with hippies, yippies and others of the disaffected and affected, gathered for an impromptu spring be-in. A few blocks south, the Coliseum was holding the first International Motorcycle show, and Columbus Circle was ringed with shining cycles whose leather-clad owners were being amiably stared at by Indian-clad hippies.

Lowell, who is fifty-one, and I talked at first about early America, the period from the origins to the early nineteenth century, the span in which his trilogy, *The Old Glory,* is set. *Endecott and the Red Cross,* the first play in the sequence but the last to be staged, takes place in a colonial settlement in Massachusetts in the 1630s. It has been playing at the American Place Theater since April 18 although, in keeping with its usual practice, the church-theater has asked critics to hold off their reviews until this Tuesday.

The three plays, which obviously can be staged separately, do, however, have a unity, which Lowell regards as roughly having to do with certain basic American experiences, more particularly New England experiences, whose effects and implications run through all our history. When I mentioned the flag as a unifying symbol, he said that he didn't think too much should be made of that, since it was there largely for "harmonic repetition." I then remarked that it seemed to me that what really binds the three plays together is their dealing with certain generally ignored tensions in American experience, specifically the tensions and

New York Times, 5 May 1968, sec. 2, pp. 1, 5. Reprinted by permission of Richard Gilman.

antinomies rising from the hidden painfulness of our origins, the contradictions of our freedom and self-definition, the losses that all aggressive gains entail. He nodded in agreement, his long, rather quizzical, grayhaired, civilized head bobbing slowly up and down.

Endecott has been considerably revised from the version I'd read and also seen in a staged reading several years ago. "I've shortened [lengthened?] it, for one thing," Lowell said, "and I think it's more actable now." This led us to a wide-ranging discussion of the present-day theater, of what constitutes the dramatic, the role of language, the question of whether the stage is as boring today as many people say: the sort of conversation, in short, it would be difficult to imagine having with an "established," institutionalized playwright.

Lowell said: "I know much less about plays than you do. I don't go to the theater very much . . . and I mostly like old plays. The great moments I remember are a Chekhov powerfully done, or an Ibsen . . . something like that. The rest is reading plays. You know, I find fragments more interesting usually than whole plays. Plots are boring anyway. We all hate the sort of play where one thing leads to another and everything is drawn tight."

I said that most good playwrights didn't care very much about plots, and that in fact he had taken his from Hawthorne and Melville. "Yes, using Hawthorne and Melville spared me a lot of work and gave me confidence that something was there. Of course, Shakespeare is the great example of borrowing plots. You know, recently I read *Macbeth,* skipping all the places where he or his wife don't speak. What I found was that it would have made a great poem, one of the greatest, with all those plot elements removed. But at the same time I think that to write a 'poetic' play now is death—all that emotion *pumped* into the theater."

I mentioned Cocteau's distinction between poetry *of* the theater and in it, and he nodded once again in agreement that the theater had its own poetry which certainly wasn't a matter of formal verse. "That's when you get Christopher Fry," he said, to which I added, "or Maxwell Anderson."

We talked then about the "new" theater, Off Off Broadway and its environs, happenings, mixed-media events and so on. "I'm not very much in touch with the new theater," Lowell said, "although I can't stand naturalistic theater, the usual thing, either. I think the new movements are perfectly legitimate, but as a word-man I can't be interested in anything that wants to do without language or restrict it so heavily. To me words are all-important, and you're giving up a lot, I think, when you give up words or give up using them well."

We agreed that the impulse against texts, against the sovereignty of language on the stage, was part of larger cultural and esthetic change, something about which Marshall McLuhan has, it seemed to me, said useful if also muddying things. Lowell spoke of having met McLuhan and liked him, and when I remarked that many writers I knew, or whose comments on McLuhan I'd read, regarded him with something close to fury or dread, he replied, "Oh, no, I find his ideas rather dull, not a menace. I remember thinking of him as a huge machine that could turn anything into anything else without regard to quality."

As to the position of language in drama, where it still mostly held its own, we agreed that, like poetry, drama has its own nonverbal element, a reality *beneath* the words. In a piece like *Marat/Sade*[1] the words have very little importance, he said, but the dramatic occasion works. His own plays are written "carefully but plainly" and he knows that "a really good production would be better than any reading." But though they're essentially verbal, he would want them to be seen for the "nonverbal element in them."

I told him I thought his own plays were closer, for all their seeming traditionalism, to the works of certain experimental playwrights than they were, say to Arthur Miller's. "Yes," he replied, after meditating for a few moments (conversations with Lowell always contain these silences, good opportunities for the other party, if he wants them, to find out what he himself thinks), "this business of naturalistic plays: life doesn't offer such neat conclusions."

From here we went off into politics, which doesn't offer neat conclusions either. Lowell had recently returned from Wisconsin, where he had accompanied Senator Eugene McCarthy on the latter's campaigning. I asked him when and how he had met McCarthy. "I do most things accidentally,"he said, "although the accidents are in character. A couple of years ago my wife was preparing a piece on senators for the *New York Review*. McCarthy was one of the few we were able to meet. I liked him from the start. It turned out he knew friends of mine from Minnesota—J. F. Powers[2] and other writers—but more important, I felt a temperamental affinity between us. Oh, I don't mean we're alike—there are lots of differences—but we share certain attitudes and values.

"I like his humor. It mostly has to do with political jokes, but they're honest jokes, and they're connected with a deeper vein of seriousness."

I asked him to give me an example and he told me about a quip McCarthy had made at a luncheon at Harvard two years ago. The lunch was an informal occasion in which students could meet public men, and Lowell, who was teaching a seminar there, dropped in. Someone asked McCarthy what he thought of George Romney and Charles Percy as Presidential possibilities, to which he replied, "You know, America has given two original religions to the world. The Mormons believe what isn't true, and the Christian Scientists don't believe what is true."

(I refrained from telling Lowell of my strong feeling of having heard this before, mostly because I liked the fact that McCarthy had used the joke, so that its possible lack of originality didn't trouble me.)

His own role in the McCarthy campaign, Lowell went on to say, had nothing directly political about it. When I said that it seemed to me that he was there simply as human contact, to give McCarthy that kind of support, he agreed, adding that the men whom McCarthy, like any political person, was surrounded by were rather narrow and lacking in wit and humor.

He is probably going to accompany McCarthy during the California campaign, he said. When I asked him about Bobby Kennedy, he said that Kennedy would be his choice if McCarthy didn't make it. "I know him fairly well, and he's a lot better than he seems to a lot of people."

We talked then about the role of the writer in politics. "This whole peace business," Lowell said. "When your private experience converges on the nation's experience, you feel you have to do something. Writers have to act publicly sometimes from private experience. . . . You know, when you have relations, as a writer, with public men, there has to be equality. I went to John Kennedy's inauguration, but before going I sent him a copy of one of my books of poetry. When I was introduced to him he gave me the kind of compliment that indicated he'd really read the book, so I said to him, 'You're the first President who's treated your peers as equals.'

"This kind of equality—it's an ideal to be aspired to by both writers and public persons."

The afternoon was dying. We talked then about his writing again, about the mysteries of decision and procedure in the making of poems and plays. I mentioned Hebbel's[3] rather wonderful statement that the secret of dramatic art lay in presenting the necessary in the form of the accidental. Lowell nodded vigorously. "That's it," he said. "You're free to pick up anything and put it in, and if it's right it points through to some deep meaning. I'm always happy when I toss something in and it works."

Outside, as evening came on, the hippies and yippies were still trying to toss something in, but despite all my sympathy I didn't think it seemed to be working.

Richard Gilman (b. 1925), theater critic and Professor of Drama at Yale University, is the author of *The Confusion of Realms* (1969), *The Making of Modern Drama* (1974) and *Decadence* (1979).

1. Peter Weiss' play of 1964.

2. J. F. Powers (b. 1917), superb American story writer and novelist, author of *Prince of Darkness* (1947), *Presence of Grace* (1956) and *Morte D'Urban* (1962), which won the National Book Award.

3. Christian Hebbel (1813–63), German lyric poet and playwright.

16 • A Poet Talks About Making History into Theater

A. Alvarez

The American poet Robert Lowell has been living in England for the last few years, and that chastening experience seems, understandably, to have turned his floating hair white. Otherwise, he seems not much changed by the years or the place: a tall, stooping figure in a brilliant tweed coat, his expression is benign, almost puzzled, though his eyes are shrewd and miss nothing.

We met recently to talk about *The Old Glory,* Lowell's dramatic trilogy on themes from American history, based on two stories by Nathaniel Hawthorne and one by Herman Melville, which will be revived in New York later this week. The Hawthorne stories are "Endecott and the Red Cross," about the Puritan governor of a colonial settlement in seventeenth-century Massachusetts, and "My Kinsman, Major Molineux," set in Boston on the eve of the American Revolution. The Melville, entitled "Benito Cereno," concerns a rebellion aboard a slave ship in the year 1800. "My Kinsman" and "Benito" were the inaugural productions of the American Place Theater in New York in 1964. "Endecott" was not presented there until 1968. Now, as a Bicentennial contribution, the American Place is staging the trilogy in its entirety. Performances begin this Friday and the plays will be done in a variety of combinations during the six-week run.

I began by asking Lowell what had originally given him the idea of writing for the theater.

Lowell: Two things, both accidents. I was asked by Eric Bentley[1] to translate Racine's *Phèdre* for a classic theater anthology he was editing,

---

New York Times, 4 April 1976, sec. 2, pp. 1, 5. Reprinted by permission of Aitken & Stone, Ltd.

and I spent a summer doing that. It was something I had always wanted to do and the experience stuck in my mind. Then I received a grant that permitted me to go to opera rehearsals at the Met. I went with my friend, the poet William Meredith, who is also an opera expert, and we decided we would make a libretto out of Melville's *Benito Cereno*. When I finally left New York in the middle of the summer to do my version of *Benito*, I found I had finished it as a play before he had started on our operatic collaboration.

Q: Benito *is the last part of the trilogy, but it was the first to be written?*

A: Yes, they go backward. *Benito* was written first, then *My Kinsman, Major Molineux*, then *Endecott and the Red Cross*. But when I read them over the other day in book form I felt each play was better than the play written after it. I didn't seem to learn from doing *Benito*; I think it's much the best.

Q: *In 1967 you wrote a version of Aeschylus's* Prometheus Bound, *which turned out to be far more like an opera than* The Old Glory. *But since then you have not written for the stage. Why?*

A: I couldn't find a plot. That's the hardest thing. Once you have a plot it's very easy. I did these three plays in three months and even rewrote *Major Molineux* in that period, putting it into meter—not that anyone would notice! I found that once I got going on *Benito*, voice answered voice. I had Melville's text in front of me; I put it into dialogue and changed it, then I found it would call for an answer. That was very pleasant.

Q: *In what ways did you find the process different from writing a formal poem?*

A: Well, the beauty of a poem is that you have an absolute control over it. You can tinker with it and get the rhythms right. A poem can be read any number of times and no voice will save it. But in a play you have the shadowy solid of an actor. I wrote this for voices, but they are voices answering each other. Then, when those voices are in costume and are solid human flesh, you realize you have only written about half of the play. The actors are going to add the other half and, theoretically, could make your play much better than it is on the page. Also, the language has to be simple to get over to an audience. I think writing the poems in *Life Studies* helped me to the more rapid, simple style of the plays. But ultimately it is an entirely different thing. In the theater you are dependent on the ear hearing the actor's voice, and the eye seeing the actor. Neither of those things helps you in a poem. It's what's on the page.

Q: *The average play or TV serial is written with a terrible slackness. Do you think this discourages poets from trying to write for the theater?*

A: I don't know. I like the realistic theater of Ibsen, although I couldn't do it at all. As for modern theater, I shouldn't be too lofty about it because I'm on the sidelines, but it is ruined in two opposite ways: by being too poetic and surrealistic and unlike life, or by being exactly like life—no better, no worse—and therefore dull. And that is almost as hurtful to art as being too poetic and rhetorical.

Q: *Was it to avoid this problem that you turned to America's past?*

A: Not really. It just started with *Benito,* then I went on to the Hawthorne plots for the other two plays. I don't think I could possibly write a realistic modern play of manners, any more than I could write a novel of that kind. I want something where the realism seems to come through a poetical language.

Q: *What do you mean by realism in that sense?*

A: Well, Captain Delano, who puts down the rebellion on the slave ship in *Benito,* has to be a real person, yet his language has much more freedom than if he were a modern naval officer in the fleet off Vietnam.

Q: *Did you have Vietnam in mind when you were writing?*

A: No. It was before all that. The plays were finished in 1962, before Vietnam was really in the air as an important disaster. I think they are prophetic in a way. I made changes to fit American history into an American catastrophe which was beginning to emerge.

Q: *If you wrote the trilogy now, would it be different?*

A: I think that what I have written is almost tame compared to what has happened, but I made it rather worse than it was at the time.

Q: *You yourself have always been determinedly liberal—for instance, you were closely associated with Eugene McCarthy in his 1968 presidential campaign—but in the plays you seem extremely pessimistic about liberalism as a solution.*

A: Yes, the liberals go wrong in the plays. Of course, they are very mixed liberals, liberals mixed with affluence and power, and they fall.

Q: *Yet you also changed Endecott from Hawthorne's ironclad Puritan—a man who tramples on the English flag—into a far more ambiguous character.*

A: It was an instinct to make him a sort of crumbling figure, like Hamlet, though rather brusque and attractive when he's being a brutal ruler. That paradox starts the whole thing off. People get more and more assured as play follows play, and more and more disastrous. *Benito's* Captain Delano, for instance: I meant him to be sympathetic and put more of myself into him than into any of the other characters. I let him flow and made him as sympathetic as possible. He has American principles as much as anybody, but he is a worldly person and not superficially a Puritan at all. Yet when he finally acts it's catastrophic.

Q: *It is Captain Delano, isn't it, who says, "God save America from Americans"?*

A: Yes. The irony is that Delano is a typical American but he thinks he's not. He is much more flexible and urbane, he has seen foreign countries, speaks Spanish, and so forth. When he makes that remark he does not realize he's including himself. He is *the* American of the play.

Q: *Are you implying that there is an inevitable connection between American principles, or Puritanism, and violence?*

A: I had the idea that a simplistic, idealistic, coherent view of life turned out to be too brittle for the facts and so leads people into violence. Once you idealize the principles of the Founding Fathers and the Constitution you get something awfully simple that is bordering on hypocrisy. Yet there is something tremendously appealing about the ideals of the Constitution, they were very shrewd for the times. They gave the country a lift that was both exciting and dangerous. I don't think they properly apply now; yet I also don't think they can die. My friend the late Hannah Arendt had a great belief that the recovery of these principles, looked at very critically, would keep us alive. I don't know if we have anything better than that. I myself think that these principles are necessary for us, but they are curiously fragile in action. They bring disaster and tragedy because they simplify things beyond reality. Of course, they are also a source of great strength. For example, the Conquistadors, or nineteenth-century America, or even Fidel Castro, were helped by being principled—by having strong, simple beliefs—and everything seemed to bow before them. But as soon as those things slacken—and slacken they must with the complexity of experience—then something rather awful happens. You feel that America today is beyond prophecy in its state of indecision and chaos. We've just had one of the most disastrous wars we have ever fought, in Vietnam, and one of the most disastrous Presidents who has ever served, Nixon. It is almost as if an invincible cavalryman had stopped dead against a wall. But it's only temporary. America will go on again and keep going, because it is so big and prosperous and has so much ability. So you see that the title, *The Old Glory,* has two meanings: it refers both to the flag and also to the glory with which the Republic of America started. And my own rela-

tionship to this glory is also ambiguous. I think my principles are un-
avoidable, they are in my blood and I have to work with them. But all
the weight of my criticism is turned against them, and that is sort of
turning against myself.

1. Eric Bentley (b. 1916), theater critic and Professor of Theater at the State
University of New York at Buffalo, author of *A Century of Hero Worship* (1944)
and *The Playwright as Thinker* (1946).

17 • Conversation with Robert Lowell

D. S. Carne-Ross

Thanks to Robert Lowell, poetic translation retains much of the importance which Ezra Pound won back for it. Lowell's translations are altogether unlike Pound's, though without that example they might never have been written. And yet like Pound, and like Pope, he presents the case of a poet of great originality who is continually reworking other men's poetry. Pound, by a kind of inspired ventriloquism, almost disappears into the author he is translating. But for his name at the head of the page, would we know that The Seafarer, Cathay *and the* Classic Anthology *were from the same pen? Lowell, although he believes he has never translated a poem he could have written himself, is almost always unmistakably present in his translations. And the more intensely he engages with the original, the more Lowellian the accent and the style. He strains to the utmost George Steiner's[1] definition of poetic translation as "the writing of a poem . . . which can be read and responded to independently but which is not ontologically complete." He strains it, but he does not break it. We read his translations—and "imitations"—inadequately if we take them simply as new poems by Robert Lowell.*

He has no "method." The same flexible intelligence that informs the original poems is at work in the translations. Each text requires a different approach. In the versions from Heine or Montale[2] in Imitations, *he gave himself a good deal of elbow room; the Juvenal and the Dante in* Near the Ocean *are done at close range. When I went to see him, he was busy with Mandelstam[3] again, trying by slight changes of diction and word order to turn the literal versions he was using into formal verse. Yet he describes his* Prometheus Bound, *produced recently at Yale and soon to appear in London, as "derived from Aeschylus," a highly personal adaptation of the Greek original. I began with a question about Prometheus:*

I don't know if this is unreasonable or imperceptive, but when I opened the New York Review *and found that your* Prometheus *was in prose, I was rather disappointed. I had counted on its being in verse.*

Delos 1 (1968): 165–175. Reprinted by permission of D. S. Carne-Ross.

I no longer know the difference between prose and verse. In *The Old Glory,* the first and third plays, *Endecott* and *Benito Cereno,* are in free verse—that is, there is no scansion, the lines are of varying length. And the middle play is in four-foot lines. Well, the three sound more or less the same. I remember my friend Randall Jarrell suggested to me it would have been better if *Benito* had been printed as prose—not changing a word but printing it in paragraphs rather than lines. And quite likely he was right, but it seemed to make very little difference. I happened to write it in lines, but if it had been printed as prose probably no one would have been able to tell.

Actors turn verse into prose anyway.

I'm sure I could have printed *Prometheus* in free-verse lines and then everyone would say it's poetry. It's very queer that change, but the kind of poetry I'm interested in for the stage would have the advantages of prose. I didn't even want to worry about line length when I was doing *Prometheus* but be perfectly free to be prolix and to elaborate as much as I wanted without any metrical restrictions.

Do you feel now that the verse form of your Phaedra *isn't really suitable for the stage?*

It has never been done well. I think it was a sort of tour de force putting *Phaedra* into heroic couplets. But I don't know what to do with that material.

It's a question of formal equivalents, isn't it? With a language as near to us as French, you've got a chance of creating something that is pretty close to Racine's couplets or Baudelaire's quatrains. But there's no living equivalent for Greek verse. So what do you do? Different people try different things. Some translators use the twelve-syllable line, but that doesn't work at all—it's not a true English meter. Or there's the six-stress line that people like Richmond Lattimore use for Homer. I don't know what you think about that.

I admire Lattimore's translations a lot—they are just the opposite of what I am trying to do. I once taught the *Iliad* in Greek, with a Greek professor, at Iowa, and we used Lattimore as a trot. I was amazed to discover that each line of Lattimore's was the same as in Homer. He was actually closer than the Samuel Butler prose translation that we also used.

But he sacrifices so much.

You can't possibly call Lattimore's *Iliad* great poetry. He has invented a kind of literal verse translation, more literal than any in English, I think. He avoids the usual translator's clichés, but it's dry and unmusical. All the same, I admire it very much. When I did a passage from the *Iliad* in my book *Imitations,* I used his translation and the Greek very carefully and tried to make mine—not a critique of his, I tried to do something very different in blank verse.

I wonder if what you want from him isn't simply the closeness. When you read a translation, aren't you looking for something you could do over and improve? In a sense, if a translation is bad it's all the more stimulating.

I used his translation of *Agamemnon* for a cut version I did. I was trying there to be very brief and rapid. I think mine is about thirty-five pages shorter than Aeschylus and much shorter than Lattimore.

Yes, I can see that Lattimore is useful to you.

There are translations which interest me, like Lattimore's, or Binyon's *Divina Commedia,*[4] that are more difficult, in a way, than the original. Yet they're very accurate. I think Lattimore is probably harder to follow than Homer if you are any good at Greek. And Binyon is much harder than Dante if you know Italian. Binyon is quite accurate, but he is crippled by the *terza rima* in English.

But don't you feel that Binyon is trying for something Lattimore isn't? I mean, he tries to follow the movement, the rhythmical movement, of Dante's lines.

But I don't think it's exactly great poetry in Binyon. It's something in-between poetry. Its metrics. It's distinguished metrics, but it's very dry compared to Dante. A work of genius, but not very readable poetry. Of course the great episodes in Dante are so great that an honest poetic translator is bound to have something that sounds like pretty good poetry, but I feel Binyon's diction is cramped and knotted. I found that I was constantly looking at the Italian to discover what Binyon was saying and then I found he was saying what the Italian was saying, but he was saying it in the language of about 1910—like minor Robert Bridges. . . .

Binyon's diction is old-fashioned, sometimes deliberately archaic, but the meter isn't. For instance, he rhymes a stressed and an unstressed syllable in a way that is not traditional.

Would you admit that something could be wonderful metrics without being particularly important poetry?

Kipling?

But I think his is real poetry. It's the opposite—it's too open and easy to understand. Of course he's a much better poet than Binyon.

Kipling is a great verse-writer—I believe that is what one says.

But Binyon isn't a good verse-writer the way Kipling is. He's good metrics.

*This is a promising category. Can you think of other writers who fit into it?
Some of Swinburne, perhaps, is interesting mainly for its metrical movement.*

Well, take Auden, for example—perhaps the best poet writing in
America. His *Age of Anxiety* seems to me a masterpiece of metrics, but it
stops at that point. Auden's great poems are everything—they're metrics
and inspiration. *The Age of Anxiety* is an incredible tour de force of
alliterative poetry, but somehow it's not very interesting beneath that.
Remember Eliot's joke about Milton, that you read him once for the
sense and once for the sound. Well, you can read *The Age of Anxiety* for
its meter with great joy, but somehow the meter exists on its own.

*It's a poem I read quite often. Maybe I read it for the meter. I'm not sure, I
shall have to think about this. At any rate, it suggests another question. Given
the enormous part that meter—and rhythm—play in our experience of poetry, I
wonder what exactly happens when one translates not from the original but from
a prose crib, as I believe you have done. I mean, what is being translated? In a
crib, the sensuous body of poetry is missing, everything contributed by meter and
rhythm and the sound and shape of words is missing, and all that remains is the
"sense," the meaning. What exactly is it that the translator, in this case,
translates?*

Well, I have translated I think in five or six different ways. With
Baudelaire, for instance, all that I had were bad verse translations, not
prose crib. I did my own translation and as I read French fairly well, the
text was very available to me. When I did Pasternak, I didn't have prose
cribs either. I had rather uninspired verse translations and I tried to make
them into English poems. In other cases I have had absolutely accurate
prose versions and sometimes they were more important to me than the
originals. There you are trying to put flesh on some kind of dry bones.

Do you get someone to read you the poem in the originals?

No, it just bores me to hear a language I don't understand. People
have sometimes read me Russian and so forth. But the worst Russian
poet would sound like the best, I couldn't tell. You could get the meter,
but I don't think sound effects are transferable from one language to
another. I know what Baudelaire's sound effects are like and I try to get
something else in English.

*Yet in trying for something else, you have written lines that are pure
Baudelaire in English—*

this lying trickle swollen with your tears,

for instance, from "The Swan." That's the wonderful thing about some of those versions. The Baudelaire, and the Montale, I think—those are the two where there is the most intimate contact between you and the original.

Baudelaire was a real metrist. It was a delight to me just trying to write the quatrains. I wrote and rewrote them. The Montale comes out as free verse in my translations and there was none of that problem there. There I rewrote to improve the diction and make it more alive. I had complete freedom—nothing *had* to go in. The Baudelaire was very hard for me, just to rhyme. I first did them in blank verse, then tried to rhyme them. I really did countless versions, shifting, changing lines. I wanted a rather elegant surface. I have a feeling that Baudelaire in French sounds a little like the best parts of Pope—where Pope is being dramatic, as in the passage on the death of the Duke of Buckingham, a rather Baudelairean subject.

What do you think about the sheer amount of translation that is being produced today? It seems to me that a flourishing, let alone a great, period of translation presupposes a particular relation to foreign literature. You may need a lot of translation, as in sixteenth-century England; there was the sense that Plutarch and Ovid and Montaigne had got to be put into English. To some extent this is true of today. Or you may have the Augustan situation, the sense that England has "arrived" and is now in a comparable cultural situation to ancient Rome. Pope's imitations of Horace are so good partly because they are so confident. The Goths have been defeated, Pope is living in his villa at Twickenham just as Horace lived on his Sabine farm, a great minister like Lord Burlington is his friend just as Maecenas was Horace's friend, he can meet Horace eye to eye. That situation obviously doesn't exist today. What is it, do you think—apart from the obvious demand, which mostly produces run-of-the-mill stuff—that leads so many poets to translate now?

I think there is much more stir of poetic translation now than there was when I was in college in the thirties. I'm not sure why. I'll just give my own case—that may be more accurate. When I began writing poetry, studying Pound and his translations and Ford Madox Ford who held very similar views, I read Ford's *The March of Literature* which made it all sound attractive and I remember something he said to me. I was going from Harvard to Kenyon College. I had, as a sophomore, been majoring in English at Harvard, but I had decided to change to Classics. Ford said to me in a rather superior but kind tone. "Yes, of course you should, otherwise you'll cut yourself off from humanity." He meant not just the Classics but all literature. I think we have the feeling of discovery of what we lack. Someone like Neruda[5] has something that no North American poet has. So has Pasternak, so has some quite small-scale poet from, say, Sweden. We have a limited amount of energy to absorb these things, but we're trying to. Each person likes someone different.

And it has something to do with politics, with the terrifying world situation, with the way we can go from one country to another, the way one country can destroy another country. This is something unprecedented in human history. We have never known so many languages, we have never spread ourselves as a power into so many countries. Countries have never been so much in contact, politically and militarily.

Yes, and there's something else now, a kind of poetic koiné *or lingua franca which means that poets in different countries are writing in similar ways even though they don't know each other's works. This openness of poets to poetry in other places seems to me new. I mean, Tennyson and Browning didn't translate Leopardi[6] and Baudelaire. And even in the thirties, Auden and Spender were not translating.[7]*

But Pound was, and Eliot was very strong on different literatures. And Matthew Arnold knew Leopardi very well. He knew how Leopardi differed from other Italians and how Heine differed from German Romantics, and of course he knew French well. His whole point was that you couldn't understand Wordsworth if you couldn't understand Goethe and Leopardi and Heine. They all had inspirations that Wordsworth lacked.

Certainly, but this was part of a cultural program, part of his struggle to educate the English and make them less provincial. I was thinking of something different: the way a poet from Peru, say, can feel instinctively how a poet thousands of miles away works, even if he hardly understands his language.

It's always a difficult bridge, particularly when two poets don't know each other's language very well, understanding the niceties of another man's culture.

But somehow the bridges are built, more now than in the past.

Yes, I don't know why. But I'm very interested in this. I read a lot and stumble away in other languages and I can name about six poets I know at all well in other countries. Yves Bonnefoy in French, Voznesensky in Russian, Miroslav Holub in Czech, and there are a lot more that I admire. Enzensberger I have met and enjoyed, but I know him very slightly. I was at Expo and there was a poetry conference which like all such things was very tedious, but the best part, for me, was talking with the poets from France. We had to talk French and listen to French and this is very painful to me, but after a while with a little wine it got rather pleasant and you felt that something came over. There is something generic about poets that is hard to define, but they're not like a group of economics professors or philosophers or even novelists—even though you'd much rather meet a good economist than a bad poet.

There's another point I wanted to put to you. What do you think is the difference between the translation of a poet in the public domain—like Horace, say, or Baudelaire—a poet the reader already possesses, and someone like Mandelstam who most readers don't yet possess? What does the reader do with a translation of a new poet in a language he doesn't know? Can he read it as a translation? Is he not bound to approach it as an original poem?

Well, there's a great charm in doing a first—or a near first, nobody ever seems to do a real first. But you do an almost first Mandelstam, say, and that's wonderful. A lot of the best translations ever done are firsts—I suppose *Cathay* was largely a first. Part of the excitement is that it's news, but if it's only that, and most firsts are just news, then they soon fade as poetry.

A lot of Russian translation that appears is just that. They depend on the politically exciting fact that we can talk to the Russians now.

Well, nine-tenths of the competent translations being done today in verse, to say nothing of the incompetent ones, are of no value except as news. They get the thing over for the moment and that's very valuable, but there will be much better translations later on.

Do you agree that this sort of translation ought to be pretty close, whereas with a poet in the public domain you can afford to be as free as you like because the reader can set the original beside the translation? This is Baudelaire, that is Lowell. He can see what's happening.

You can also argue that an unknown poet like Mandelstam needs even greater freedom to be made as interesting in English as he is in Russian.

Yes, that's the line I personally am inclined to take.

I think that's perfectly valid. No one should inflict on the market a long, dull collected Pasternak done by Professor X in meter that is very bad, very uninspired English poetry. That does nothing for Pasternak, or next to nothing.

Ideally, there should be three tiers: the original, a poet's translation, then a literal trot. We need all three. This is one of the things I want to do in Delos.

There could be a law, though I don't really believe in it, that almost nobody would be allowed to do a verse translation of poetry. He'd have to do an accurate prose trot. And these trots are usually better poetry than the professor's or even the minor poet's poetic translation of a masterpiece.

I'd certainly prefer George Kay's translations of Montale if they had been in prose rather than verse.

I checked the changes of phrasing when he turned his Penguin prose into verse and two-thirds of the time they were worse. I still think his versions are awfully good, but I wish he had printed them as prose.

There is something here that has a kind of pathos to it. Innumerable people for some reason want to be poets, and the only way they can be poets is by doing Virgil or Pasternak into English verse, and it's very bad, very dull poetry. Then every so often there is an Edward FitzGerald who does an inspired translation—a man who isn't a very interesting poet except when he's translating.

Yes, but he wrote some original poetry, even if it isn't up to much. Is there any case of a man who's written no original verse at all coming up with a fine verse translation? It's particularly afflicting with the Classics. A professor who has never written a line of verse in his life seems to think he has a professional right to translate great Greek or Latin poetry just because he knows the language.

Most of them can't write prose either. . . . I remember a wonderful crack of Randall Jarrell's about translation. He said nobody thinks that some professor of Lithuanian could have written *Anna Karenina,* but everyone thinks he is the ideal man to translate it. All the same, there must be a hundred people in America who could do a readable translation of Tolstoy. But they couldn't do Pushkin, probably no one could do Pushkin unless they did it in prose the way Edmund Wilson did "The Bronze Horseman." But then he's a prose writer.

I wonder if we are not putting verse and prose translation too much in different categories, demanding inspiration from the one and accepting mere competence—"accuracy"—in the other. The verse translator is allowed to take certain liberties in order to get his text off the ground, but the prose translator is still stuck with this word-for-word thing. People complain of Scott-Moncrieff that he hasn't got this word right or the exact sense of that phrase. Only the worst kind of pedant approaches verse translation in this way now.

Scott-Moncrieff's Proust is at the least an English masterpiece.

I agree—or at least I think I do.

And it's no worse written than George Eliot. Another English masterpiece.

No comment, but one final point. One thing that translation can do is let the original language violate English just a little in order to bring something into English which wasn't there before. The only defect I see in your masterful way of translating is that you sometimes simply take possession of the original and dominate it. I am particularly interested in those places—I think they're most frequent in your Baudelaire—where you let the original language impose itself for a moment on your English. For instance, in your version of "La servante au grand coeur," you have the line

> The dead, the poor dead, they have their bad hours.

It seems to me there is something marginally un-English, something rhetorical in the repetition of "the dead, the poor dead," which has come from Baudelaire's French rhetoric. The same thing happens in your version of "Le Cygne" where the swan screams at the heavens:

> Its heart was full of its blue lakes, and screamed:
> "Water, when will you fall? When will you burst,
> oh thunderclouds?"

An English swan, even a Yeatsian Irish swan, couldn't scream at the heavens in this grand way without a touch of absurdity. This belongs to the Latin rhetoric of emotion which you have somehow made us accept in English.

I think you have raised the most important question of the morning. In a way the whole point of translating—of my translation, anyway—is to bring into English something that didn't exist in English before. I don't think I've ever done a translation of a poem I could have written myself. I wouldn't know how to answer this point. For instance, when I do a Victor Hugo poem: it's written in a way I wouldn't dare write in English myself, yet I admire it very much. To a certain extent that's true of everyone I have translated. It's a great grief to me that I can't write my original poems in the styles I have used in my translation. I wish I could use Baudelaire and write a poem like "The Swan."

Isn't your poem "The Flaw" very Baudelairean? The way you use the scene, the way the theme is dissolved in, or presented through, the scene. I feel you couldn't have written it but for your work with Baudelaire.

Well, there's a bit of "Cimetière Marin"[8] there too.

Yes, but I'm sure Baudelaire is behind it.

I can't tell, but I hope something has rubbed off. You can't go about it too deliberately. I felt this doing Juvenal—which most people criticize as being too close to Juvenal. I just wish I could write an original poem like that with historical portraits like his Sejanus[9] and Hannibal. I'd feel like the greatest poet alive if I could do Lincoln that way.

Do what Johnson did with it, you mean, and take the poem over completely, putting American figures in the place of Juvenal's Roman ones?

Well, Johnson's is one of the great poems in English. Though I'd have to say that his use of English history is much less interesting than Juvenal's use of Roman history. He's much less soaked in it. You can hardly exaggerate what good poetry his portraits of Charles XII[10] and Wolsey are, but on the whole you don't feel Johnson had much interest in history or knew much about it. Wolsey isn't a concrete person as Sejanus is, and he shouldn't be. That wasn't the way Johnson wrote.

He's more interested in the cultural parallels, perhaps, than in the characters themselves.

Again, "The Vanity of Human Wishes" has this slight defect—which I suppose makes it a great minor poem: the fact that the framework doesn't quite fit. Eighteenth-century London wasn't as awful as Juvenal's Rome, it was nothing like as murderous as the Rome of the emperors Juvenal wrote about, which in many ways is closer to us now, and yet he's forced to say that it was. This makes him slightly off key. On the other hand, Johnson did something much greater than I did in the way of transforming the poem. While I just try to give an accurate, eloquent photograph of the original, he did something much more avant-garde.

You mentioned the closeness of your Juvenal. In most of the versions in the second half of Near the Ocean *you keep nearer the original than you have usually done in the past. I wonder how far this is an attempt to make your translations complement, or balance, the original poems—which they couldn't do if they were already as nearly original poems by Robert Lowell as some of the versions in* Imitations. *In the preface you suggest that the two parts somehow match each other, though you don't quite know how. A number of obvious cross references seem to support this—like the similar risks of taking a walk in ancient Rome or in New York's Central Park.*

That would seem true except for the fact that the translations were written a year or so before. No, I don't know why but I felt you just couldn't be very original with Juvenal—or with Dante. On the other hand, two of the Horaces, the second and the third, are quite changed, and the Góngora[11] and Quevedo[12] work in about the same way as the versions in *Imitations*.

But on the whole you do keep closer to the texts in this book.

Maybe I felt ragged by people telling me I wasn't close enough in my imitations.

Do the critics annoy you?

No, it just seemed interesting to try to be more accurate.

What do you feel about the question of mistakes? Pound is deliberately very arrogant here. I fancy he refuses to look up words in the dictionary because he doesn't want his image of the poem to be sullied by what professors claim the words to mean.

I'd just as soon do a completely inaccurate translation again. Some of the versions in this book are in meter and some are not; and meter has something to do with accuracy. A metrical one may turn out more accurate, for some queer reason. It fascinates you, this sort of mosaic-work, transferring pebble by pebble into meter. Or meter may make you much more inaccurate—just the effort to handle it at all well in English. I took easy meters here: blank verse for Juvenal, two-rhyme *terza rima* for Dante. I wouldn't want to translate in any one way.

D. S. Carne-Ross (b. 1921), Professor of Greek at Boston University, is the author of *Instaurations* (1979) and *Pindar* (1985).

1. George Steiner (b. 1929), author of *After Babel: Aspects of Language and Translation* (1975).

2. Eugenio Montale (1896–1981), Italian poet, critic, editor and translator, winner of the Nobel Prize for Literature in 1975. Lowell translated some of Montale's poems.

3. Osip Mandelstam (1891–1938), major Soviet Acmeist poet and literary critic.

4. Laurence Binyon (1869–1943), English poet and art historian, translated *The Divine Comedy* (1933–43).

5. Pablo Neruda (1904–73), Chilean poet and diplomat, author of *Residence on the Earth* (1933, 1935) and *The Heights of Macchu Picchu* (1948), winner of the Nobel Prize for Literature in 1971.

6. Giacomo Leopardi (1798–1837), Italian lyric poet, scholar and philosopher.

7. In 1939 Spender translated books by Ernst Toller, Rilke, Georg Büchner, García Lorca and Manuel Altolaguirre.

8. "The Graveyard by the Sea" (1922), a major Symbolist poem by Paul Valéry (1871–1945).

9. Sejanus (d. A.D. 31), chief administrator of the Roman Empire under the Emperor Tiberius.

10. Charles XII (1682–1718), great commander and King of Sweden, 1697–1718.

11. Luis de Góngora (1561–1627), Spanish Baroque poet, author of *Solitudes* (1613).

12. Francisco de Quevedo (1580–1645), poet and satirist of Spain's Golden Age, author of *Dreams* (1627).

18 • Et in America Ego—The American Poet Robert Lowell Talks to the Novelist V. S. Naipaul

V. S. Naipaul

When I went to school in New England and talked to people, it would have been death to them to admit mine was a famous name.

Do you think it was because this linked you more closely to the old world: the fact that your family has been in America much longer?

It would seem to make you less close to the old world and more provincial. New England does mean this one peculiar thing. I was reading somewhere of a student of Leavis,[1] now a professor, who wrote a book saying that in 1800 Boston wasn't one of the more advanced American cities culturally. It was way behind Philadelphia, and even New York. But somehow by about 1830 the other cities didn't exist for a while—and I mean by "Boston," not only Boston itself, but Cambridge and Concord and New England in general, and people like James and Melville, who came from other places to New England. So it was one of the great moments of the nineteenth century.[2] You can hardly walk through Boston, even though it has been rebuilt, and not stumble on something that suggests at least 1800, or the mid-nineteenth century, 1870 or so. You go to New York, nothing. Nothing seems to have been here twenty years ago: much *has,* yet it seems to have lost all significance. That troubles me in New York, and New York and London, I sometimes think, are one city. You see the same literary people, sometimes literally the same people. But when you go to Boston there is a past everywhere. It doesn't exist here. I think that's ghastly about New York.

You have this reputation for being something of a rebel, someone who has rebelled against his New England background. The actual rebellion, perhaps, wasn't a very conscious one, but a matter of self-discovery?

Listener 82 (4 September 1969): 302–304. Reprinted by permission of Aitken & Stone, Ltd.

Self-discovery. But I didn't find the culture I was born in very nourishing, quite aside from my relations with my parents. I felt I was born in a kind of illiterate culture, a kind of decadence, and I was just very unhappy anyway. I probably wanted to go away and fish and do various things I wasn't supposed to do. Then when it came to writing, this feeling of getting away from it continued. But I really think the place had lost its seriousness, its imagination, and if you wanted to be a writer you couldn't be a conventional New Englander.

You felt the centre had shifted to New York perhaps?

No. I don't know what New York is. New York's a much more exciting city than Boston. It's a Jewish city: about a third of the city is Jewish and the talent is Jewish, all the more able people here are Jewish. New York is much better than anything we have in New England, or even in the South, which is much stronger. It's a very difficult thing for Jews and for Gentiles to float this culture, and now Negroes are coming into it. I don't think anyone should be very dogmatic about what's good and what's bad in these various strains that go into New York, but the New York I know best is Jewish New York. Most of my friends are Jewish, and the people I've learned most from, and that I like best, in New York are Jewish. It's quite strange that this tiny little minority should have such talent, and isn't anyway typical of Jews, I think, through history.

You say you've left New England and you've had to penetrate the New York literary world, which is now a mainly Jewish world. Do you feel that you have submerged your special regional identity in something larger which might be called American?

America with a capital A I find a very hard thing to realise. It's beyond any country, it's an empire. I feel very bitter about it, but pious, and baffled by it. You know, if you're standing in cold water, you wish the whole world was steaming. Living in America, I wish my own section of America—New England—were a small provincial country like Scotland, with its own capital and even customs barriers. Then it occurs to me how deadly it would be to have to live in Boston, the capital of that country, though Boston would be more lively if it were like Amsterdam, the head of a small country. But it's going to be a toothless little country, that can't throw a plastic bomb into Buffalo, or have sort of Rubens rapes of Buffalo women and carry them back to Worcester and Boston. But I think all little countries in Europe are better off than my New England. America now is not a country—it's something much larger. The melting pot's worked all too well: people have melted into one another.

From the outside, one is aware of certain people in America with reputations, and one vaguely comes here expecting they'll be much more enmeshed in the life of the country than one finds them to be.

There's an equally great danger of getting too enmeshed in these things and talking baloney about things you know nothing about. The country's cause-mad. Every day letters come to me to sign—some foolish thing or unfoolish thing I know nothing about. But I once had a queer personal experience that I'd like to get straight. It was a time when Churchill, Brendan Bracken[3] and Roosevelt met and said: we intend to burn something, and ruthlessly destroy, and we're saturating Hamburg and the northern German cities, the civilian population. They announced their policy of unconditional surrender. It seemed to me that we were doing just what the Germans were doing. I was a Roman Catholic at the time, and we had a very complicated idea of what was called "the unjust war." It is obviously a possibility that there may be two kinds of wars and one merges into the other. But this policy seemed to be clearly unjust. So I refused to go to the army and was sent to jail. I spent about five months in jail and mopped floors. Then I was paroled and was free to write. After that I felt that you weren't getting beyond your depth in protesting unjust wars.

It's very strange because writers have been involved in so many causes and have contributed so much. Yet at the same time there does persist this old romantic idea of the writer as a man who is far away from the world.

I think that poets—and this probably holds for any artist—must be removed and they must be gregarious. I'd rather use "gregarious" than "engaged" as the opposite of "removed." You won't have anything to write about if you don't see people. A novelist particularly needs people, but even a poet needs a good deal. It's very hard to tell what combination is right and no combination is right as a category of what everybody who wants to write should follow.

And so you came to the conclusion that the poet, like the novelist, had to be both in and out of the world. And you took this even further to the point of massive political intervention.

I think the arts are connected with power in a peculiar way, but it's an oblique way, and often comes when the power has faded. The great period of Italian painting, somehow, is a period not of power but of efficiency. It is no accident that Florence was the Pittsburgh of its day when the great Florentine painting came. You wouldn't call that very great power, as power goes. Still, it was there, and it's interesting that the great Spanish and Dutch periods more or less corresponded with their country's power and they tend to be best when that power is fading.

Most Americans greet the visitor with the statement that it's all falling apart. Very, very quickly. But if one probes more deeply, one finds, in fact, that there is a much deeper faith, and indeed a certain relish in the largeness of the problems. And I began to feel, particularly after reading Mailer, that what looked like concern wasn't really concern but somehow seemed to come out of a type of boredom, a sense that life is going nowhere. To have a cause was a form of intellectual self-cherishing. Is this too cruel?

Well, I think something's wrong. I've just been to two countries very unlike the United States, Israel and Spain. One country I saw rather thoroughly—I met everybody I wanted to in Israel. In Spain I met nobody but just travelled at my pleasure with my family. You immediately feel that there are innumerable irritating things about Israel, but the problems you have here, of lack of faith and strife and chaos within the country, don't exist there. While it can be exaggerated, our Vietnam is an important, horrible thing. But we'd be in almost the same situation without it. And so it's quite mysterious what has caused this situation. I think what has caused it is the terrible danger of atomic destruction, and the failure on the whole to master our machinery, to use machinery to make life attractive, and to master birth control.

What is your reaction to Mailer's description of yourself, to your first appearance as a fictional character in Armies of the Night?

His description of me is one of the best things ever written about me, and most generous—what my poetry is like and that sort of thing. He records a little speech I made about draft-dodgers and I felt he was very good on that. I am trying to think whether my reaction to the march differed from his. I don't think mine was at all his, but it's not opposed to his either. It was mainly the fragility of a person caught in this situation . . . as in that poem of Horace's where you throw away your little sword at the battle of Philippi and get out of the thing. But I believe in heroic action too.

I was wondering whether you felt a work of art could be achieved outside an accepted framework of values.

Do you think any primitive art is without a moral framework?

No, I think it is guided by all sorts of taboos and it has all sorts of purposes.

Now say there's some bad, new sort of play where everyone undresses and copulates on the stage. Is that without moral values or is it just without art? I think it probably has moral values but doesn't have any art.

I can imagine people undressing in a certain play which is linked or tied to something. But I asked this because I felt that perhaps satire—true satire—is impossible when values have been rejected.

Is it true that most, or all, satirists are conservatives?

Absolutely, absolutely.

I think that the greatest ones of our time—Ring Lardner, parts of Genet probably, Wyndham Lewis, Waugh—are all conservatives.

Instead of satire, one frequently has—if people are complaining or protesting—a dramatisation of the self. I find this quality, which I can only describe as egoism, coming through a lot in American writing, and I was wondering how far egoism reflects the American tradition. Most people seem to find life in America rather boring, they wish to step outside, they wish to express themselves, and the artist as egoist steps forward, like Mailer.

Do you think my writing has that sort of narrowness?

When I say "egoism" I mean this: all its values somehow reflect a direct personal judgment on the way the world damages or the way the world pleasures the self. The other sort of writing is the writing that turns experience into something for all.

I remember reading something by Harold Rosenberg,[4] a preface to a new translation of *The Idiot,* and he says this novel is very odd, that the hero is a spectator, you might almost say a voyeur. But he is conversed with and he's not a voyeur in the bad sense of the word, peeking on people. I'd like to appear as a voyeur in my poems, as someone watching rather than as someone running for Mayor of New York. That seems proper.

Do you think it's a passing phase, this egoism?

Of my contemporaries in poetry or prose Mailer is the most talented. There's an awful lot of fat in his writings but there's an awful lot of courage, and the ambition, I think, is correct. You should try to be something. As long as he does immerse himself in things, and write three or four bad books, then write a true book. If he didn't write the true book, then the whole thing would just be pitiful and disgusting. But he does.

You've made your life your work. You've written this long autobiographical novel, one might say, and the feeling that comes out at the end is one of pessimism, and yet this is accompanied by a very fine work of art, which, in fact, is a type of action. Are you aware, when you are actually doing the work, of a struggle between the pessimism and the effort that goes into creating the work itself?

You ask me about pessimism. I'm not sure what the word means, in the sense that I don't see why anyone would want to *intend* pessimism or optimism. You think of what you feel, then you're very astonished that what you feel falls into a groove that maybe you didn't intend. At the end of my last book I wrote this sentence, which is true but I don't quite understand why: "In truth I seem to have felt mostly the joys of living; in remembering, in recording, thanks to the gift of the Muse, is the pain."[5] I really can't tell, reading my poems, whether they're outrageously optimistic or monotonously pessimistic. You try and do the best you can, and if it comes out sour you have to stay with that. You seem to falsify a poem by improving the mood.

Tell us about Robert Frost. . . .

[He gave] the best reading I had ever heard: about twelve lines he'd read, and he showed me two lines which made all the other lines come to life. I'd never encountered anyone like that. I saw him about every two or three years. He had no interest, not only in younger poets, but in any poet living besides Frost, and he was a terribly vain man. If you said something about *Moby Dick,* he'd mention Melville's short story "Bartleby" as his favourite—it was more the likes of what Frost did himself. I won't tell about when Pasternak got the Nobel Prize and Frost's reactions. On a small scale he had the sort of quality that Gorky describes in Tolstoy. He was beyond the good and evil of the druidic rock that stood there . . . T. S. Eliot was my hero in a way. I don't think he's the best poet of the century, but a very great one—on this point he's my hero. He had a very narrow gift, I think, but he wrote, until he was about fifty-five, great poems, most of them quite long, an almost unexampled record in English. And he never quite wrote the same poem, partly by changing the metrical form, partly by changing himself, so it's the one man going from *Prufrock* through to the *Quartets.* Well, my thing is much less perfect than Eliot's. I have a lot of poems that are repeat poems. If you write a number of short poems, they're bound to be. There's a kind of model. I almost think I'm more varied than Eliot but much more repetitious. Yet I do think my books have changed. My first poems were very highly wrought: they were a young man's poems written during the war. Then, after a while, I wrote a very simple book called *Life Studies:* most of it is almost as simple as prose, in the sense that it could be read aloud and gotten on the first reading. It's about direct experience, and not symbols. It's terrible if you're bound to photograph your past, which I think I was doing in *Life Studies.* It's a decent book, but I don't want to write another *Life Studies.* Of course, you cheat and change things in giving what is supposedly the true story of your mother and father. But on the whole it seems as if it exactly happened in that kind of language.

V. S. Naipaul (b. 1932 in Trinidad), a distinguished novelist and travel writer, is the author of *Guerrillas* (1975) and *A Bend in the River* (1979); *An Area of Darkness* (1964) and *India: A Wounded Civilization* (1977).

The Latin title means: "And I am in America." The *Listener* is the official publication of the British Broadcasting Corporation.

1. F. R. Leavis (1895–1978), influential English literary critic, editor of *Scrutiny,* author of *New Bearings in English Poetry* (1932), *The Great Tradition* (1948) and *D. H. Lawrence, Novelist* (1955).

2. See Martin Green, *The Problem of Boston* (1966).

3. Brendan Bracken (1901–58), British politician and advisor to Winston Churchill during World War Two.

4. Harold Rosenberg (1906–78), important art critic and author of *The Tradition of the New* (1959). Rosenberg's preface was published in the New American Library edition in 1969.

5. Lowell, "Afterthought" to *Notebook 1967–68.*

19 • Talk with Robert Lowell

Dudley Young

[The poet Robert Lowell is presently in England, spending two years as Visiting Professor at the University of Essex, where he was interviewed by Dudley Young, a British colleague. Mr. Young recently completed a book on Yeats.]

You are often regarded as a spokesman for the American Imagination, and yet such an idea strikes you as altogether inappropriate and grandiose. Have you always felt this way?

Yes, I think so; you write for about fifty friends, twenty of them you've never met. The twenty you've never met might be like the ones you know. But you'd like them to be a little bit varied, you'd like them not all to be professors, and male. You wouldn't like them all to fall into one shop.

If that's always been your feeling about your audience, then the much-discussed decline in the literate public cannot dismay you very much.

I suppose a poet is content to be a minority. The public is a lost cause.

But isn't this a Romantic myth that alters the notion of the poet from what it was before the nineteenth century?

A minority can make a living on a lost cause; that's all one asks. One can earn a living and scrape along. That's probably the best thing for a poet and that's what they've always had. I think it's what English poets have always had, what American poets have always had. Some of them have had less than that.

What about the suggestion that Shakespeare did speak for and to a great many people; and that you cannot do this because the culture has fragmented in all the ways we know and love? Does that not depress you a bit. Would you not like to have that kind of inclusiveness?

New York Times Book Review, 4 April 1971, pp. 32–33. Reprinted by permission of Dudley Young.

Shakespeare was an unusual playwright and not typical of his age. He was much more successful than Ben Jonson and I imagine the people who saw his plays were a very small number, and the playhouse was very small, and the plays ran for a very short time; and I imagine the people who bought his folio when it came out were a very small number. I don't have the figures but I'm sure his sales weren't anything like the hundredth best seller this year. His first editors, Heminge and Condell, begged plaintively for buyers. Ben Jonson called Shakespeare "soul of the age"; he was. That didn't mean many Englishmen loved him—only much later when he was canonized. That's unfair, you see, then they all had to read him.

But isn't it true that when we admire Shakespeare, we think of the amount of life he included?

But if you include life you're almost bound to be unpopular. Shakespeare had less popularity in his life than someone like John O'Hara, but no one ever called John O'Hara "soul of the age" as Ben Jonson praised Shakespeare. So what does "inclusion" offer?

The question I'm really pushing is this: Don't you think that poetry once could give inclusive expression to a culture's experience—whether to shape it or whether to mirror it is not the point—but that it no longer can and hence the people who would ask you to "include" America are indulging some kind of nostalgia?

I don't think poetry ever did. Poets have it easier now than they did in the time of Pope and Shakespeare. I don't mean the possibilities are better for writing poetry. This is an alien age for poetry, but there's more enthusiasm and encouragement for it than there was in Shakespeare's time, at least for writers of short poems. If I lived in Rhode Island I couldn't admit that I was off the central track because I had to live there and had to make the best of it. Maybe that's what poetry is, a little unimportant state, Rhode Island, but to me it seems very important. I feel no challengers. The challenged creature bristles. Almost no movies are first-rate, the novel is in decline, it's a sad age for criticism, you snap your fingers at journalism but it's in passable shape, so what's poetry in decline to? Any of these categories I've named would feel the same about poetry, yet I don't think any of them are much better off. I happened to get into poetry and I feel a thanksgiving I didn't get into one of these other things. They all seem much sicker than poetry, poor sick poetry. What's not in decline?

Yeats thought most everything was, and yet believed he was a public poet, speaking truthfully of and for Ireland whether they liked it or not. Clearly many of your readers think of you that way, and doubtless it would come to them as a surprise that you don't.

Yeats is a good model, isn't he? He would have shivered at being called "the voice of Ireland" or "the soul of Ireland." He'd have thought it was humorless, aggressive and stiff. He always had his tongue in his cheek. He might have said, though, that he was saying what Ireland must feel. That's very different, and he had all kinds of ways of being disrespectful. He might have thought he was talking honestly but he didn't think he was the voice of Ireland: he hated the voices of Ireland. And think of his comments on the politicians who really were the voices of Ireland. He has no great poem on De Valera who turns up only in one ballad. I think a writer should think of people he knows and of himself rather deeply and compassionately, and then write as honestly as he can and use all the technique he can bring to bear. What he says may be welcome or more likely rather uninteresting and unwelcome to a large public, but at least he'll have the satisfaction of not being a spell-binder. . . . I think some writers write (and what I say applies to all the arts, I think) more profoundly than they know they have, with a deeper symbolic significance than they know they have, or perhaps have the right to have.

I wonder how that applies to your own work. "For the Union Dead" is probably your most public poem; and perhaps your best. If someone found important public meanings in it and said "This poem strikes deeply in the body politic," wouldn't you be pleased?

But I don't know what "strikes deeply" means.

It means where you were aiming and where you hit. Weren't you aiming for the midriff of some fairly large monster? Or would you refuse the question?

If you say that *Moby Dick* strikes deeply I would say that is a compliment to *Moby Dick*. If you say that Bob Dylan strikes deeply, I'd say that's an ambiguous compliment to Dylan. I'd imagine he'd feel banged on the head.

And if someone said "For the Union Dead" strikes deeply, would that be ambiguous?

I think it would be ambiguous. I wouldn't know what it meant. I know all about the poem anyway without it striking. If someone I trusted was struck deeply with "For the Union Dead," I'd be struck with wonder and appreciation. That's the only way I could know it struck deeply.

As a poet, to what extent do you mine in America?

I'm fifty-three years old and I've spent about fifty of those in America, so I have to be American. I have no choice of being anything else. I am in America.

But haven't you been spending quite a lot of energy on translation over the past few years?

That's a way to travel.

But that's not mining in America, is it?

Well, I suppose my translator–syntax is American, whatever that means. We don't have too many categories of rhetoric.

So you wouldn't be at all interested in the suggestion that when America is mined out one begins to translate?

No, I think when I'm mined out I could begin to translate. I have translated when it is more appealing to me than writing my own poems again. I just know that at times translating gripped me more than my original poems.

But you wouldn't want to generalize from that and say that America had gone dry on you?

I wouldn't think so. The distant poems I translated couldn't have been written by Americans. In that sense America is dry. There couldn't have been an American Baudelaire and there wasn't. You try to get him into English and it's fascinating.

Is that a judgment on America?

Yes, but I don't think there could have been a French Whitman. It might have been a rockslide for a French poet to translate Whitman.

What I'm hinting at is something like "God has withdrawn his blessing from America," and one of the less hysterical ways of putting this is to say that America will no longer yield rich poetry.

It's a long time since I've done much translating. For a long time I've been doing original poems which are American.

Notebook *is surely a more private book than your previous ones, which have all had at least some poems in them which have gestured toward a public space. Would you not agree with this, and also that this is not wholly a function of your own development, but has quite a lot to do with America itself?*

I don't see that it is more private. It has poems on Alexander the Great and Lincoln, the Pentagon March and things like that; but the spine of the book is my own life, more or less like an early book of mine, *Life Studies*. It's about as personal as that and I wanted to make it more difficult and complicated because more can perhaps be said thrusting through complication. I am writing in a much more difficult style. I don't think I've entirely gained by taking a complicated style but on the whole I have. What I wanted to get away from was the photograph of reality. It really doesn't matter whether one style is better than the last. When it no longer serves, you must adventure.

Some people have found Notebook *rather bad tempered and irritable, as if your hungers were not fed.*

Of all the reviews I've read only one, by Denis Donoghue,[1] made that point of irritability, so I assume that's an eccentric Irish point of view. There's a good deal of wrath in the book but I don't think that's the general temper. There are poems of diatribe but they are rare. The book is gloomy, I say that in my preface.

You also say that the good moments on the whole don't get in and the bad ones do.

That was an ironic twist but I think that's true of most poetry. Burton Feldman[2] wrote a thoughtful review of the book and said the whole thing was a New Left poster. I was jarred. I don't feel I'm a New Leftist or any kind of graduated Leftist. I think if anyone read my book, a little slowly, his eyes might smart, and he would be sad for our culture. And he might think such a view true. But he wouldn't have a campaign to do this or that. He'd feel the New Left were very shallow and superficial just like their opponents. My book is not very partisan. I've never written a poem trying to support a point. They come out as they will.

What about the speculation that you are in flight from America? Is that a myth you want to endorse at all?

No, I've been here the best part of a year and I'd quite like to stay another year and it is a vacation from America which has no sort of symbolics. I'll go back to America and be American and I'm not comparing the countries.

So we're not to see you as a disenchanted pilgrim, returning to European sources.

It's an American theme . . . the discovery, the pioneer going into the wilderness. After a while the wilderness changes into the Europe of Henry James and Eliot—a freehold almost barbaric in its newness.

Dudley Young (b. 1941), is Lecturer in English at the University of Essex, where Lowell taught during 1970–71, and author of *Out of Ireland: A Reading of Yeats' Poetry* (1975).

1. See Denis Donoghue, "Lowell's Seasons," *Manchester Guardian Weekly* 103 (26 December 1970): 58.

2. See Burton Feldman, "Robert Lowell: Poetry and Politics," *Dissent* 16 (November–December 1969): 550–555.

20 • A Conversation with Robert Lowell

Ian Hamilton

Hamilton: *You have been in England for some time now. Why have you chosen to live here?*

Lowell: Why I am in England is mostly personal and wouldn't be correct in an interview. But there are certain common reasons. I'm not here in protest against conditions in America, though here there's more leisure, less intensity, fierceness. Everyone feels that; after ten years living on front lines, in New York, I'm rather glad to dull the glare.

Hamilton: *What glare are you thinking of?*

Lowell: Our atmosphere sometimes bristles as if with little bits of steel in the rain when it falls. It strikes mostly in the mind, in argument, in our edginess. New York is a formidable city, though I've never known violence personally. One hears about it; friends' houses are always broken into. Our break-ins are rough; one would rather not be at home, because thieves are angry for dope-money. Here house-breakings are mild: thieves fear the householder.

Hamilton: *Of course, one of the reasons why your work is so admired here is that it seems to speak out of precisely that sense of danger. In other words, the situation that you describe is the situation that feeds your work in some way. Do you fear that by leaving America you might be leaving your subject, and that here you'll have, well, simply less to write about?*

Lowell: I don't know what is lost. Last week, I read for a record—poems since *Life Studies,* that is, from the last ten years or twelve. I found I wrote about only four places: Harvard and Boston, New York and Maine. These were the places I lived in and also symbols, conscious and unavoidable.

New York is our cultural city and furthest from nature; Maine is nature, and Harvard may be somewhere between, the university. Lon-

The Review 26 (Summer 1971): 10–29. Reprinted in *Modern Occasions* 2 (Winter 1972): 28–48 and *American Poetry Review* 7 (September–October 1978): 23–27. Reprinted here by permission of Ian Hamilton.

don cannot be the culture of my blood. I suppose if I spent summers in the Orkneys and winters in London I might find a contrast similar to Maine and New York, but the repetition would seem slovenly.

Hamilton: *I remember that when Donald Davie[1] left for America, one of the things he said about why he left was that he thought he could enjoy there the luxury of expatriatism, that he wouldn't get so involved in, or irritated by, what was going on around him. Nor would he feel caught up in America's destiny, and so on. Perhaps all he meant was that he'd be able to live a more peaceful life.*

Lowell: I wonder if he does? He wrote me when I was to teach at Essex in his old department saying that perhaps his reasons for leaving England for America were mine for doing the opposite. This must be partly true. I can't imagine being so predestined by Wilson and Heath as by Johnson and Nixon. Davie and I are taking vacations from our Furies.

Hamilton: *It does seem slightly odd, though, that you should leave America at a time when you seem to have become more overtly concerned in your poetry with public events.*

Lowell: I couldn't say whether I know if it is odd for me to be in England. I think wavering is a good feeling to achieve; all can't be done to push a career. I've been reading more than usual in the last months, skimming old books I loved. They grow new for me, a difference of impression more than evaluation.

I'm older than when I first met the classics, my friends are older and deafer (which I'm not)—I mean I'm older and still not deaf—total character now seems nearer. I've lived as long as most of the old writers. Once fifty-four, my age, was ancient and deep in time's turnings. It's sweet to sit back with a book and ruminate changing experience. Where is the strong woman of the late Thirties? You say I have become more overtly concerned with public events, but true public poetry must come as an inevitable accident. I grew up in anti artist-sage days, when Eliot and Picasso worked in one surprising style for some years, then surprised with another—maturing without becoming public voices or portents. Who wants to be on call to society? Have a resonant poem for each great issue?

Hamilton: *I remember you saying, in an earlier interview not long after the publication of* Life Studies, *that you couldn't go on indefinitely writing the personal poem. Sooner or later the experience would be exhausted.*

Lowell: All the veins of silver give out. Would you say that the poems in *For the Union Dead* are less personal?

Hamilton: *No, not really, although the book does seem in many ways less intimately autobiographical than* Life Studies.

Lowell: I am only thinking of my last four books. *Life Studies* was windfall. It was after six or seven years ineptitude—a slack of eternity. I remember a cousin proving to someone that I was finished—at only thirty-nine! Five messy poems in five years.

Hamilton: *These are the poems at the beginning of* Life Studies?

Lowell: Yes, but now heavily revised. Shall I say "re-inspired"? The rest of *Life Studies* was written in two years, in two lunges. Plugging in the joints was more precarious than creation. After this, continuous autobiography was impossible. In the *Union Dead,* I modified the style of *Life Studies*—free verse stanzas, each poem on its own and more ornately organized. Then came metrical poems, more plated, far from conversation, metaphysical. My subjects were still mostly personal. In a third group, probably thinner, I wrote surrealism about my life. I also wrote one long public piece, the title poem of the *Union Dead.* My next book, *Near the Ocean,* starts as public. I had turned down an invitation to an Arts Festival at the White House because of Vietnam. This brought more publicity than all my poems, and I felt miscast, felt burdened to write on the great theme, private, and almost "global."

Hamilton: *So one might say that the White House episode did, in a way, inaugurate your period as a public poet?*

Lowell: Perhaps the metre I chose, Marvell's eight-line stanza, started more. It hummed in my mind summer till fall. It's possible to have good metre yet bad intention or vice versa—*vers de société,* or gauche sprawl. All summer, as I say, the steady, hypnotic couplet beat followed me like a dog. I liked that. After two months, I had two poems, one a hopeless snakeskin of chimes. My last piece, my most ambitious and least public, was a "Dover Beach," an obscure marriage-poem set in our small eastern seaboard America.

Hamilton: *It was disconcerting for some of your admirers at that time to find you writing in tight metres. Will you go back to free verse?*

Lowell: Free verse leaves fewer clinging chips, but I think some of my later metrical poems are more myself, though clumsier. I didn't direct, I had to stumble. I read a book: *Prosody in Modern American Poetry.*[2] The author praised me for writing in Marvell's elegant baroque stanza. I remembered how twenty-five years ago, I'd found it too smooth, and left it. Reading this book coincided with the White House thing. Metre and matter—I think I'd tried free verse, and it skidded. My next poem, *Notebook,* is in unrhymed, loose blank verse sonnets, a roomier stanza, less a prosodist's darling. It can say almost anything conversation or correspondence can. I use this metre again in my last (un-published) book. I mustn't tempt it.

Hamilton: *In* Notebook *what do you feel the fourteen lines actually did?*

Lowell. Allowed me rhetoric, formal construction, and quick breaks. Much of *Life Studies* is recollection; *Notebook* mixes the day-to-day with the history—the lamp by a tree out this window on Redcliffe Square[3] . . . or maybe the rain, but always the instant, sometimes changing to the lost. A flash of haiku to lighten the distant. Has this something to do with a rhymeless sonnet? One poem must lead towards the next, but is fairly complete; it can stride on stilts, or talk.

Hamilton: *Did you find yourself falling naturally into the fourteen line unit?*

Lowell: It was a stanza, as so much of my work—a unit blocked out *a priori,* then coaxed into form.

Hamilton: *Having decided on the fourteen-liner did you find it constricting, that you had poems which would have liked to spread themselves around a little more?*

Lowell: Yes, but that's true of any fixed form, isn't it? Take one of Milton's sonnets, it could have been dragged out to a *Paradise Lost* pro-logue. I didn't find fourteen lines handcuffs. I gained more than I gave. It would have been a worry never to have known when a section must end; variation might have been monotony. Formlessness might have crowded me toward consecutive narrative. Sometimes I did want the traditional sonnet, an organism, split near the middle, and building to break with the last line.

Often a poem didn't live until the last line cleared the lungs. That's untrue of Shakespeare's sonnets, but it's true of many, and true of most of Milton's. The last line shapes to complete the motion. Shakespeare, I feel, wrote the couplets to his 150 sonnets in a single dashing afternoon. Following the inevitable music, a clang.

Hamilton: *It has been said about* Notebook *that you are less concerned with line by line excellence than in earlier books. Do you feel there is more of a hit or miss quality about it?*

Lowell: I didn't think that, when writing. I wrote in end-stopped lines, and rewrote to keep a sense of line. I never wrote more, or used more ink in changes. Words came rapidly, almost four hundred sonnets in four years—a calendar of workdays. I did nothing but write; I was thinking lines even when teaching or playing tennis. Yet I had idleness, though drawn to spend more hours working than I ever had or perhaps will. Ideas sprang from the bushes, my head; five or six sonnets started or reworked in a day. As I have said, I wished to describe the immediate instant. If I saw something one day, I wrote it that day, or the next, or the next. Things I felt or saw, or read were drift in the whirlpool, the squeeze of the sonnet and the loose ravel of blank verse. I hoped in *Life Studies*—it was a limitation—that each poem might seem as open and single-surfaced as a photograph. *Notebook* is more jagged and imagined than was desirable in *Life Studies*. It's severe to be confined to rendering appearances. That seems the perfect way, what *War and Peace* is, but it is flattening to poetry's briefer genius. . . . Sometimes free verse is like breathing naked air, and living only on it.

Hamilton: *In certain ways, the American literary scene seems more brutally competitive than ours. Do you find this so?*

Lowell: I think we have a famine for greatness, and find the English lacking in this vice. We have too many rude writers who imagine they are Emerson, or Whitman or Fitzgerald—their buildings are haystacks.

Hamilton: *Did you see the recent selection of Roethke's* Letters?

Lowell: Roethke fevered to be the best poet, and perhaps strained for the gift. Dylan Thomas is your equivalent, but Thomas may have more sceptically enjoyed his great revel. I dislike the law of the boxing ring for the arts,[4] the analogy is faulty. Many run, many win. Robert Frost had the largest ambition, but with more complication than others. He had more disguises. I loved Frost and think him as great a writer as he did, though he made no room for others. Praise *Moby Dick* to him, and he'd say "*Bartleby's* pretty good." *Bartleby* is the size of his own verse monologues. Yet Frost was infinitely civilized and possible to talk intimacy with, while Roethke, the fine craftsman, had the innocence and deafness of a child.

Hamilton: *You really feel it's a peculiarly American vice, this?*

Lowell: You have it here, I'm sure. Our noblest example of ambition was a writer who never claimed he was the best writer alive, yet may have reached it: Melville. Whitman's boastings were saved by his shyness. Pound couldn't have attempted the *Cantos* on mere vanity. You may favour the opposite kind of writer, Edward Thomas, Philip Larkin, extreme in his ambition to be witty and solid, a mocker of the Leviathan.

Hamilton: *It is really a meaner sort of vanity I have in mind—the relentless jockeying for applause, for awards and honours. Perhaps the fact that in America you can make a lot of money from literary success . . .*

Lowell: Not in poetry.

Hamilton: *Well, one reads of James Dickey making $3,500 for a poetry reading . . .*

Lowell: He is another of our champions, though very talented. I suppose men vaunt and taunt to keep up their hearts. We too have modesty: Marianne Moore, John Crowe Ransom. But I think England and America differ. Hemingway is ours; Ivy Compton-Burnett is yours. I wouldn't want to choose particularly; a literature needs lions and foxes.

Hamilton: *What do you make of the Black Mountain poets?*

Lowell: I revere Pound and Williams; I think the Black Mountain poets are their journeymen, quite powerful without being inspired or pathfinders. Pound and Williams are freer, more cultured spirits. Olson's *Maximus* is *Paterson* and the *Cantos,* though woodier. Creeley is a slender, abstract Williams, Duncan is the music of Pound without his humour or engagement. Other younger American poets, Snodgrass, Alan Dugan and Adrienne Rich, seem more original. Of the Pound people, the most personal voice is Gary Snyder.

Hamilton: *At the back of all their work there is a wish to make a distinctively American poetry. Have you ever felt the urge, or the obligation, to be more of an American poet?*

Lowell: I've been here only a year now, and am asked if I want to be British. I have finished a poem, not about England, but with an English setting, for I have to use day-to-day things. At first I hardly dared name England then found it hovered to me—the tree I see from this window and people talking. Where is America? I've had it about me for fifty remembered years; it seeps through my eyes.

Hamilton: *I had in mind the quarrel between Pound and Williams, and Williams' view that* The Waste Land, *for instance, was an act of treachery . . .*

Lowell: I know their argument, and have sat at their knees. I'd like to state Williams differently. What's good about him that Pound doesn't have is that he worked in his locale. On my next to last visit to him, he had recovered from a stroke. When he came out on Sunday, he didn't go to church but walked through the streets, and everyone said, "Dr. Williams we are glad you are better." He knew things not on the Sunday walk, how his patients talked, what happened in their marriages. His hand was on the car-wheel, as Pound's could never have been in Rapallo. Williams is more certain of image and idiom than Pound, less magnificent. I don't think *The Waste Land* would have been more authentic if Eliot had never left Boston. Williams' provincial counterpart is Philip Larkin.

Hamilton: *Williams would never write a sonnet.*

Lowell: Nor would Eliot or Pound. Both had boldness, modernity, and formal imagination. With Pound—I think of the *Pisan Cantos*—a hard, angular, in some ways shrill and artificial man by courage let the heart break through his glass ribs . . . more heart than any poet since Hardy.

Hamilton: *To go back for a moment to the current American scene, I wonder what you think of the* New York Review of Books—*its increasing neglect of the arts, and of poetry in particular.*

Lowell: I don't want to say very much about it. My wife is consulting editor and I know Robert Silvers, the editor, very well. I know Barbara Epstein very well. I'm deeply in it, in a personal sense. It never was primarily interested in the arts, nor pretended to be. It's a review for commentator and reasoner, an epic *New Statesman.* . . . Poetry reviews are more in the whirl here than with us. I wouldn't assert the quality is finer—a true review sinks into the reviewed's mind causing change and discovery, and can never be anticipated anywhere. We assign too many reporters and popularizers to poetry; you save them for plays.

Hamilton: *You once said that the last critic you found useful was Randall Jarrell. Is it the case that poetry criticism in America is less concerned than it is here with questions of evaluation?*

Lowell: Jarrell's evaluations were often more imaginative than his authors. We began in the age of the New Critics. They are a little maligned, I think, though we both grew too roughed to remain their disciples. The first had artistic genius; Winters, Blackmur, Kenneth Burke, Allen Tate . . . even Hart Crane wrote thoughtful New Criticism in letters. That age has passed; its last spirit was Randall. Of the younger English critics, I always read A. Alvarez and Donald Davie. But the king of the critics is William Empson. He's not a Messiah for the young; I don't believe he has written on anyone younger than Orwell and Dylan Thomas. But even his shortest notes change my mind. Then Leavis, the gnarled, fire-blackened oak . . .

Hamilton: *Do you read novels much?*

Lowell: I re-read old ones.

Hamilton: *You've never thought of writing a novel?*

Lowell: I couldn't. I don't have that talent. I like to put what I see and hear into poems, but to write a whole book, pages consisting of nothing but story . . . I haven't the wind of dialogue. Do you think the novel is a promising chance now? Most have the same plot with changed decor. It seems the age of shadow-novels, compared to the Twenties or

Thirties, or compared to the last century's great Russian, French and English. The trees are growing bald.

Hamilton: *Was there any sort of novelistic intention behind* Notebook? *In parts it does read like a novel.*

Lowell: I hope so. I hoped to steal from the novel—even from our new novel—because I think poetry must escape from its glass. It might be better for a long poem to be drawn from *Madame Bovary* than the *Cantos.* The *Cantos* did this; after Tennyson's *Idylls* or the *Ring and the Book*,[5] they look for a transcendence in contemporary abundance. The novel is the great form . . . little since Mann and Faulkner.

Hamilton: *I'd like to go back a bit now and ask you about your own career. The most obvious first question, I suppose, is to do with being a Lowell. How important has that been to you?*

Lowell: I never knew I was a Lowell till I was twenty. The ancestors known to my family were James Russell Lowell, a poet pedestalled for oblivion, and no asset to his grand-nephew among the rich athletes at boarding school. Another, my great-grandfather, James Russell's brother, had been headmaster of my boarding school, and left a memory of scholarly aloofness. He wrote an ironic Trollopian *roman à clef* about the school.[6] There was Amy Lowell, big and a scandal, as if Mae West were a cousin. And there were rich Lowells, but none as rich as class-mates' grandfathers in New York. Of course, we were flesh and blood, but I am talking down rumours of our grandeur. My immediate family, if you have an English equivalent, would be the Duke of Something's sixth cousins. We gave no feeling of swagger. Later I felt a blood kinship with James Russell's savage vernacular anti-Mexican war and pro–Civil War *Bigelow Papers*—they were not for the Thirties. Was Amy a rebel artist or an entrepreneur? Ours was an old family. It stood—just. Its last eminence was Lawrence, Amy's brother, and president of Harvard for millennia, a grand *fin de siècle* president, a species long dead in America. He was cultured in the culture of 1900—very deaf, very sprightly, in his eighties. He was unique in our family for being able to read certain kinds of good poetry. I used to spend evenings with him, and go home to college at four in the morning.

Hamilton: *How did it happen that you became a Catholic?*

Lowell: I don't know. I am not a Catholic, and yet I was. It came from despair and exuberance, the exuberance of learning a religion, and despair at my circumstances, a student's problem—I was just married and couldn't get a job. I was too tense to converse, a creature of spiritual severity. Christianity was a welcome. I kept following more and more for a number of years, though now it seems unbelievable. When I meet knowing Catholics, I go along with them and feel I have somewhat their geography. I don't believe, but I am sort of a gospeller, I like to read Christ's own words.

Hamilton: *It is often said that the technique of your early poems—the poems of* Lord Weary's Castle, Land of Unlikeness—*enacts a quarrel between your Calvinist background and your adopted Catholicism. Do you see it this way?*

Lowell: I was born a non-believing Protestant New Englander; my parents and everyone I saw were non-believing Protestant New Englanders. They went to church, but faith was improper. In college, I began reading Hawthorne, Jonathan Edwards, English seventeenth-century preachers, Calvin himself, Gilson[7] and others, some of them Catholics—Catholics and Calvinists I don't think opposites; they are rather alike compared to us in our sublunary, secular sprawl. From zealous, atheist Calvinist to a believing Catholic is no great leap. I overhammered the debating points. Yet Calvinism is ill-conceived, an abstract expressionist Church of Rome.

Hamilton: *Did your contact with the Southern school of poets have anything to do with all this?*

Lowell: It probably mostly came through Allen Tate. I think it connects with the New Criticism. Tate and Ransom, poets and critics, were Southerners and the line they took was that Southerners looked at the whole thing, and not just at intellect like a Yankee. If Ransom writes a poem about a man and woman, the man is a Calvinist and the woman a Southerner who knows flowers, the flesh, beauty and children. One might say that Catholicism notices things, the particular, while Calvinism studies the attenuate ideal. I have been too deep in that dog-fight to ever get out. Allen Tate would have said, and did say when I was a young man and he about forty, that I was an idealist New Englander, a Puritan and so forth: yet Allen's wife would have said he couldn't name the trees in his path. Man is always Puritan.

Hamilton: *It was presumably the presence of people like Tate and Ransom that attracted you to the South in the first place.*

Lowell: They—but not at that time their positions. They seemed the best men who wrote poetry and taught. I liked Pound and Williams and Eliot and Hart Crane and Proust and Milton, but I hadn't read Tate and Ransom. I did my cramming just before we met.

Hamilton: *Was Blackmur[8] around at that time?*

Lowell: I knew him quite well but only painfully and later. He was more of New England than anyone, and had a genius. In his prose, every sentence struggles to be poetry, form ringing on rock. He was a good poet, weird, tortured, derivative, original—and more a poet in his criticism. A side of him wanted to write novels, because he remembered everything and felt things most critics can't—people. He was more industrious than other stylist critics, wrote heavily and yet with a grace; had anarchy and discipline—perhaps he overcherished both . . . the type of the critic.

Hamilton: *Who, out of that group, was the most important to you as a poet?*

Lowell: I think the best poems were written by Ransom. Winters, a Humanist, our Malherbe[9] maybe wrote the clearest criticism . . . intuitive, authoritative, perverse. My own poetry was closest to Tate's. I couldn't write a Ransom poem. Ransom is a graceful, smoother and smaller Hardy. I think he is perfect, that is, impossible to improve on. He would say to me, "You're a forceful poet but your poems are weighty," and I knew my poems would always be weighty next to his.

Hamilton: *You first published in the South, I believe.*

Lowell: As a college junior, I published in Ransom's *Kenyon Review,* then nothing more for four years. I had grown too weighty for print. Then after a year with Tate and his wife,[10] I wrote my first rude Christian stanzas. They didn't meet universal approval, and were usually published.

Hamilton: *That "year and a day" you were sentenced to as a conscientious objector—what was that like?*

Lowell: I corrected proofs. I was quite scared going in, but I only spent five and a half months in jail, then six and a half on parole in a Catholic cadet nurses' dormitory, mopping corridors. It was filthier work than jail, but I was free and with my wife. Jail was monotonous and weak on incident. I queued for hours for cigarettes and chocolate bars, and did slow make-work like wheeling wheelbarrows of cinders. I found life lulling. I slept among eighty men, a foot apart, and grew congenial with other idealist felons, who took homemade stands. I was thankful to find jail gentler than boarding school or college—an adult fraternity. I read—*Erewhon* and *The Way of All Flesh* . . . and God knows what now . . . two thousand pages of Proust. I left jail educated—not as they wished *re*-educated.

Hamilton: *You'd recommend it?*

Lowell: No; it did. I couldn't write. When I started to think again I had a more Southern wholeness. The luck was not writing.

Hamilton: *How much hesitation did you feel about becoming a conscientious objector? You hadn't always been one, had you?*

Lowell: No, I didn't feel that way at the beginning of the war. I became an objector after the saturation bombing of Hamburg and the proclamation of unconditional surrender. I feared too the Russians would control China and half of Europe, a less dangerous possibility today. The Communists' dull, humdrum, tyrannical bureaucracies are more of a disappointment and less of a terror. Perhaps all nations are now fiercer than we feared.

Hamilton: *I believe you had volunteered for the Navy some time before?*

Lowell: Yes, I did volunteer. Later in 1943, when we'd conquered Sicily, and won the war, in a sense, I refused to report to the army, and sent a rather silly bombastic statement to President Roosevelt.[11] I still stand on it.

Hamilton: *And you'd take a similar position now, on Vietnam?*

Lowell: I would on Vietnam. But if I were young now, what would I do? It's unimaginable—if I were eighteen and coming up for the draft. I pray that I'd take the position of the draft-evader, not leave the country but go to jail.

Hamilton: *Do you feel you have much of a response among the young in America?*

Lowell: No one meets the generic young. The individuals I know are about your age, late twenties, early thirties, graduates. They are people I often get along with. Undergraduates seem to have characters still to come. I judge from a point of disadvantage. This is just another young generation and it's always good to be young—they live on. I don't find *all* youth sympathetic—maybe ours are slightly more so because of the way they dress and slop. This generation, like ours once, is hope. I hate to ape their anti-Liberalism, but the Liberal blueprints were too pure, too idealistic, too cold. My heart never beat with Roosevelt's, now the young don't salute him. Liberal heroes tarnish; but is this progress? Pollution disgusts me; dope doesn't send me. I am against violence; if I were still Calvinist I would call it *the* hell-fire.

Hamilton: *What about their literary taste?*

Lowell: I don't think the young read anything, except for a few with literary concerns. Later maybe they become readers or writers. Their taste? Suppose some writer wrote poems about violence as an essential experience—I haven't but I have written *gritting* things—he shouldn't be flattered if crowds of twenty-year-olds say violence is *the* essential experience, and then, without light or passion, begin chanting, "Guns are beautiful." I would be bored and horrified. I have a schoolteacher's conceit that I know more than my students. I really must. I've had the measure. Most professors are unwise, but a smart professor should outreach his smarter students. I find it disgusting when professors look to the young for vision. They should pay for sponging the youth of the young. Most students, now and always, are the Philistines, my old fraternity brothers. In our society, culture I fear must be *élite;* the bulk and brawn of any generation, new or past, can't tell the *Sentimental Education* from Charles Reich.[12]

Hamilton: *You were involved for a time in Eugene McCarthy's campaign for the presidential nomination. That must have been strange.*

Lowell: Senator McCarthy was a strange candidate. We were interested in ending the war in Vietnam, and finding power that could do something. McCarthy was one of various senators I went with my wife to see in Washington—she was going to write an article and I tagged along. Some people suggested to us weren't there and I think somewhat at the last minute McCarthy's name was given. We met McCarthy and Fulbright. Fulbright was an impressive nineteenth-century Southern senator, rather [like] one of my older Southern writer friends. McCarthy was interested in literary people, knew them, was one. We talked and told stories.

Hamilton: *Did you find the atmosphere of power, of big-time politics, exciting?*

Lowell: I liked to talk to McCarthy, and he liked to talk to me and blow off his tension. He didn't actually talk heavy politics—more, points made by agricultural parables, dead-pan sketches of politicians; he made Bobby Kennedy behave like a character in Ring Lardner. It was like listening to a baseball player while watching his game.

Hamilton: *So you didn't feel that here was a unique joining together of politics and poetry, or anything of that sort?*

Lowell: I doubt if McCarthy was exactly politics; it was his interest but he was a lost cause man, and ironical. He had to face terrible things: the headless crowds, the reflex applause, the ghost-written speech, the boiled eulogies. He wasn't much interested in the vote-getting abstractions, which probably someone else had written for him; such things are always written by someone else, and [for] someone else. If he had been elected one would have felt a human being was in the White House— with flaws and flare, but someone. He was something to trust. For most of the others? If an effect must be proportioned to its cause, as the Thomists[13] say, how can ghosted political shop-talk turn a horse into a rider? It didn't strike me that McCarthy would be President. I was surprised when he won New Hampshire, and there was a last high point when he carried Oregon and Northern California against Bobby Kennedy. I could feel the excitement of that, and maybe thought we were riding high tide. I wrote a poem to him that mid-summer . . . "Coldly willing to smash the ball past those who bought the park." There was allure in having a friend whose shadow had fallen on the handle of the grindstone.

Hamilton: *It was not, then, an episode that changed anything for you, for you personally?*

Lowell: I mustn't overplay what happened. In a way, it was sightseeing a new country. I spent a month and a half traveling. It was like my going to Italy for the first time, as serious maybe as that, more hurried and naked. I have never known how Italy changed me.

Hamilton: *What did you make of Norman Mailer's portrait of you in* Armies of the Night?

Lowell: I didn't know him too well—that comes out in his book— and he didn't know me very well. We'd met before. We've since grown closer. I think maybe the form of his book came from me. Not from anything I said but from contrasting me symbolically with himself. That's very heavily emphasized in the beginning. The picture of me . . . well, it isn't quite true. I am made more goy, New England, aristocratical and various things, a Quixote in the retinue of Sancho Panza. I think it's the best, almost the only thing written about me as a living person. Later, I wrote him I hoped we'd remain as good friends in life as we were in fiction.

Hamilton: *And yet it was a fairly hostile portrait, wasn't it?*

Lowell: It starts that way, in the first thirty pages or so, and then I think it's not. I had no idea he saw plots to put him down in things I said lightly. Also I didn't realize he saw everything. Moments when he didn't seem to be attending any thing, not even himself. In everything I saw and could test, I felt he was as accurate as memory should be. His story is actually, not literally, true. Accuracy isn't looking squint-eyed at faces through the eye of the needle. I am flattered I didn't step on Mailer's corns; I was treated with kindness. Is the frame of a portrait a coffin?

Hamilton: *Do you have any clear sense of an audience?*

Lowell: I don't meet it intimately. I sit here in my room, I have my life. I have my personal hopes and difficulties and interests. An audience cannot come and talk; the conglomerate voice isn't English. I can at least *read* my reviewers, but most are in a hurry. Fame? Occasionally someone sends me his poems, and writes: "You're the greatest poet, and would you annotate my manuscript?" I put it aside. I don't send it back. I don't have a large enough envelope. Once in a while a second letter comes reversing the praise, threatening to sue me for postage.

Hamilton: *What about readings, though?*

Lowell: In America a poet can make a living and shorten his life-expectancy by readings. He can make from five hundred to a thousand dollars a shot. Here it pays trainfare. I fear the performance. I expand on stage and feel bloated. One goes to Birmingham, anywhere, and takes two and a half hours to get there, and meets—I've never been to Birmingham—I meet Dr. So-and-so, I give my reading, I am promised twenty pounds which about pays for two lost days—if anything can. And I have exported my poems. Some readings were a delightful change of air.

Hamilton: *You don't find anything tempting in the availability of all that cash and applause?*

Lowell: Never quite, because it is absolutely exhausting . . . due perhaps to my imprudent habits. None shuns audiences and cash. It would be hypocritical to say I do. I hate getting to the spot, twitching in the Green Room, going on. I like answering questions better than reading poems, but my audiences don't. . . . Then the going off! I prefer teaching.

Hamilton: *You have said, though, that poetry readings helped you to find the style of* Life Studies.

Lowell: At that time, poetry reading was sublimated by the practice of Allen Ginsberg. I was still reading my old New Criticism religious, symbolic poems, many published during the war. I found—it's no criticism—that audiences just didn't understand, and I didn't always understand myself while reading. Much good poetry is unsuited to audience-performance; mine was incomprehensible. Even Dylan Thomas came over as sound. I didn't wish to be Ginsberg; I hoped to write poems as clear as conversation, so clear a listener might get every word, and I would. Shall I confess that I can seldom follow a voice without seeing the text? *Life Studies* is heightened conversation, not an act.

Hamilton: *You take a rather sceptical view of your audience, whoever they may be. I wonder, what do you think literature can do—anything or nothing?*

Lowell: Auden says poetry makes nothing happen.[14] In the teeth of this, Flaubert wrote that his *Education Sentimentale* might, if read, have prevented the bloodshed of the Paris Commune. I do think being engaged to something makes a difference. Take Flaubert who led a life even Henry James called flat—a single long love affair, a trip on the Nile, fifty years with his mother, writing, looking out on the provincial Seine at Rouen from his study. I feel he was ferociously in it, in his misses as well as his successes . . . he believed in form, a form not like the Goncourts and Maupassant, but irregular and heart-stained—the grace of anonymity, the gross of one person. I would grope up all I knew in this search. . . . The best new poems I've read in the last fifteen months are by Heine, written in Paris, when his spine was melting, and he was going to die in a month or two. He wrote a poetry beyond his power. Some of the most touching are to his wife, a simple soul, his child almost. He even fell in love with another woman at this time, even wished he could sleep with her. The first poems are almost the tenderest ones anyone has ever written to a wife; the second are spiritual, because the other woman was intellectual, read Hegel and Goethe, etc. One set of poems worked as well as the other; Heine never thought to harmonize the contradiction. The metre he took was his old rhymed quatrains—he felt no need of a new technique. I feel he was man absolutely facing reality, facing it with his old style of wit and ballad, Jewish jokes and German romanticism, spending all on his terrible experience. The last thing he wanted was to die, even though opium and morphine no longer killed his pain. He said he'd written a poetry no other German had written, only because no other German had been in his physical misery.

Hamilton: *How do you feel about the often rather melodramatic characterizations of you as a "poet of extremity"?*

Lowell: I don't deserve these eulogies. I think I've lived a life more than the average poet, but other people have lived their lives much more than I have. In *Life Studies,* I caught real memories in a fairly gentle style. It's not meant to be extremity. I agree with the critics who say it is artificially composed. I have been through mania and depression; *Life Studies* is about neither. Mania is extremity for one's friends, depression for one's self. Both are chemical. In depression, one wakes, is happy for about two minutes, probably less, and then fades into dread of the day. Nothing will happen, but you know twelve hours will pass before you are back in bed and sheltering your consciousness in dreams, or nothing. It isn't danger; it's not an accomplishment. I don't think it a visitation of the angels but dust in the blood. In *Life Studies,* I wrote about my marriage and parents; I didn't see them as desperate—though all life is askew. When I wrote, most good American poetry was a symbol hanging on a hatrack. Many felt this.

Hamilton: *Who do you have in mind?*

Lowell: There was Snodgrass. The Beats too were a breakthrough. They had little interest, most of them, in experience but had a great interest in direct utterance. *Howl* doesn't seem to have much to do with the stir of life but it is a stirring sermon.

Hamilton: *Before* Life Studies *you presumably felt that your own style had become mechanical. It can never be easy to know just when a manner one has perfected becomes played out.*

Lowell: Most of us find our standard style: an average Browning poem, an average Auden poem, where the poet's mannerisms do much of the invention. Sometimes a blessed knock comes and extends mannerism to inspiration. I think I've sometimes known this. I have a mechanical, gristly, alliterative style that does not charm much, unless . . . I try to change my spots.

Hamilton: *During these periods of depression that you've described, do you carry on writing, or does poetry come to seem meaningless?*

Lowell: Depression's no gift from the Muse. At worst, I do nothing. But often I've written, and wrote one whole book—*For the Union Dead*—about witheredness. It wasn't acute depression, and I felt quite able to work for hours, write and rewrite. Most of the best poems, the most personal, are gathered crumbs. I had better moods, but the book is lemony, soured and dry, the drouth I had touched with my own hands. That too may be poetry—on sufferance.

Hamilton: *You have quite a few imitators—indeed, there was supposed to be something called a Confessional school. How do you feel about them, about a poet like, say, Anne Sexton?*

Lowell: I don't read on with many. But Anne Sexton I know well. It would be delicate to say what I thought of her. She is Edna Millay after Snodgrass. She has her bite. She is a popular poet, very first person, almost first on personality. I had a mortifying revelation. I was reading an anthology and imagined I was reading another poet I often prefer to Sexton. It was marvellous, "much X's best poem." I thought X had become unmuddy and personal at last; but the poem was by Anne. Then the poem sank a little, I'm afraid. I knew Anne could be personal. I read with bias.

Hamilton: *What about Sylvia Plath?*

Lowell: I glory in her. I don't know whether she writes like me. In an extreme Life-and-Death style, she is as good as Sir Walter Raleigh; no, she's not as good, but no poetry has a more acid sting. Few women write major poetry. Can I make this generalization? Only four stand with our best men: Emily Dickinson, Marianne Moore, Elizabeth Bishop and Sylvia Plath. It's a rough road. Sylvia is not the most enchanting, she's perhaps my least favourite, but she belongs to the group, and has her half dozen supreme, extreme poems. Years ago, Sylvia and Anne Sexton audited my poetry class. Anne was more herself, and knew less. I thought they might rub off on each other. Sylvia learned from Anne.

Hamilton: *What about English poetry? Do you take much interest in what is going on here?*

Lowell: I like more dead English poets than I can remember; I like the living I liked before I came here. Of the older: Auden, Robert Graves, Empson, David Jones, MacDiarmid, Larkin, and Hughes in poems like "Pike" and "Pig." That's the top of it. I like Stevie Smith, Spender and Betjeman. There are many good poets; these are the ones I am wild about. There would be about the same number in America . . . and rather more, I pray.

Hamilton: *Do you take any interest in so-called popular culture? Do you take any of it seriously?*

Lowell: You mean the Beatles? I was teaching my students Stevens; I think I was, and I said to them, "What do you really like?" and they said the Beatles and Rod McKuen. So we read pop for a month. The Beatles are a cross between Noel Coward and Gilbert,[15] more polished and idiomatic than most poets. McKuen I get nothing out of. Bob Dylan is alloy; he is true folk and fake folk, and has the Caruso voice. He has lines, but I doubt if he has written whole poems. He leans on the crutch of his guitar.

Hamilton: *I'd like to ask you something about the theatre . . .*

Lowell: I wish I could be as breezy on that as I was on pop culture.

Hamilton: *Do you think there's any future for the verse drama?*

Lowell: I think there's little in this century except *Sweeney Ago-*

nistes[16] and the last short plays of Yeats. Brecht, I suppose, is the strongest modern dramatist; he is a poet even though he writes in prose—as good as a novelist.

Hamilton: *Do you see this as something you yourself are going to do much more of?*

Lowell: I am gunshy of the theatre. I've had brilliant directors, Jonathan Miller, and good, even star actors. I can't love the game. I know this is slightly paranoid, but I can't feel acted plays are literature. I'm not happy with my own, read or acted. We've never had *the* American playwright, our nearest is O'Neill. Many things are fun, Williams, Albee, many more off-Broadway; they do not breathe the same air as Faulkner or Eliot. I think it's a trapped and thwarted art—that's the challenge. And isn't it a backache to sit through a whole play? Much the best English or American writer is Shakespeare and he wrote plays and they are meant to be acted, they're not meant to be read in an armchair. Yet plays perform worse than opera; *Othello* is inferior to Verdi's inferior *Otello*.

Hamilton: *What do you feel about your own plays?*

Lowell: I wrote one play which I think well enough of, *Benito Cereno;* I'm not sure whether it is mine or Melville. Two American history plays I wrote to go with it, I find have good spots. Are they mine or Hawthorne? They were speedy to write, and took me less time than verse translation. I think of *Benito* as prose, my best.

Hamilton: *You did deviate somewhat from the original, didn't you?*

Lowell: I had to put the whole thing in dialogue; most of Melville's novella is reverie and description. Somehow the main character, the American captain, is different. Some think I've added, others see caricature. My hero is a state department autocrat. Melville's is an innocent abroad. My man is imperial, his is poignant. Mine knows everything, so steers for disaster. Some critics wish I hadn't hardened and politicized. I'm sure my play's genius is Melville.

Hamilton: *When you look back over your career as a poet, do you see a high point anywhere, or do you feel that there has been a steady development and improvement?*

Lowell: When I look back on my career, I remember high points— high in their moment. Later, they lost stature. I cannot calculate this or that was a mountain. I am always looking backward when idle, and upward when revising—revision is inspiration, no reading of the finished work as exciting as writing-in the last changes. My art, like many others, fails. The failure is dubious. Months of false cast, then a day, of strikes—something happier than anything done by me before. I mustn't assert too bravely—Leavis reading over all his essays, finding the least limiting, and saying, "I was a genius when I wrote *George Eliot.*"[17] I don't read my earliest books with full sympathy. Those I like best are *Life Studies* and my last two. The last, *The Dolphin,* is unpublished. So it's a happy ending.

Ian Hamilton (b. 1938), English editor, critic and biographer, is the author of *Robert Lowell: A Biography* (1982).

1. Donald Davie (b. 1922), English critic and poet, author of *Purity of Diction in English Verse* (1952) and *Brides of Reason* (1955).

2. See Harvey Gross, *Sound and Form in Modern Poetry: A Study of Prosody from Thomas Hardy to Robert Lowell* (1964).

3. Lowell's address in the Chelsea district of London.

4. See Lillian Ross, *Portrait of Hemingway* (New York, 1961), p. 35: "I started out very quiet and I beat Mr. Turgenev. Then I trained hard and I beat Mr. de Maupassant. I've fought two draws with M. Stendhal, and I think I had the edge in the last one."

5. Long narrative poem (1868–69) by Robert Browning.

6. Lowell's namesake, Robert Traill Spence Lowell, published *Anthony Brade, a Story of a School,* in 1874.

7. Etienne Gilson (1884–1978), French religious philosopher and medieval historian.

8. R. P. Blackmur (1904–65), influential critic and Professor of English at Princeton, author of *Form and Value in Modern Poetry* (1952) and *The Lion and the Honeycomb* (1955).

9. François de Malherbe (1555–1628), French Classical poet and influential critic, author of *The Tears of St. Peter* (1587).

10. Caroline Gordon (1895–1981), American novelist and wife of Allen Tate, author of *The Garden of Adonis* (1937) and *Old Red and Other Stories* (1963).

11. For Lowell's letter to Franklin Roosevelt, see Ian Hamilton, *Robert Lowell: A Biography* (New York, 1982), pp. 87–88.

12. Charles Reich (b. 1928), author of *The Greening of America* (1970).

13. Followers of the medieval Catholic theologian St. Thomas Aquinas (1226–74).

14. W. H. Auden, "In Memory of W. B. Yeats" (1939).

15. W. S. Gilbert (1836–1911), English playwright and humorist, collaborator of Sir Arthur Sullivan.

16. Dramatic poem (1932) by T. S. Eliot.

17. See Jonathan Swift's remark in old age about *The Tale of a Tub* (1704): "What a genius I had when I wrote that book."

II. Memoirs

21 • A Look Backwards and a Note of Hope

John Crowe Ransom

I'm glad to be enrolled on the list of those invited to say a few words of honor to so good a poet, and so great a friend, as Robert Lowell.

It was in 1937, after two years at Harvard, that Lowell came, strangely enough but as luck would have it, to stay with us at Kenyon. He did more than come under our official attention: he passed beneath the lintel of my door, and lived for a year in our house; so that now I find myself looking back fondly, with a dotard's eye, at some of those happier moments of pedagogy. Lowell was not the man, as he is not now the man, that one could hold off very long at an official distance. His animal spirits were high, his personality was spontaneous, so that he was a little bit overpowering. But a natural goodness shone from his face. We had Randall Jarrell in our house too, an M.A. graduate; and if a few others came in sometimes, our tone became that of a hilarious party, and Lowell was the life of it.

We at Kenyon were not long putting him down in our books as a "young man most likely to succeed"; shall I add, in the vocation of letters? Of course he would land there inevitably. His way of reading literature was to devour it, to get it quickly into his blood stream. But he was never the young romantic whose unearned and callow ecstasies we had to repress till he could look upon a poem with such coolness and canniness as God might have given him. Today there are few poets in Lowell's generation who are so learned and so pure; perhaps none who can manage the writing of verse with Lowell's twinned flairs of grace and nobility.

When Lowell came to Kenyon, he was at least as familiar with the range of English verse as is the ordinary man at the University with a

First printed in *The Harvard Advocate* 145 (November 1961): 22–23.

year or two of graduate studies behind him. (He could distinguish a
dozen lesser poets of the eighteenth-century school of Pope, and easily
one from another; as I could not.) Therefore he studied Latin, and after
three years graduated with highest honors. Every now and then I take up
the book again—as we are always taking up something again in order to
have another look at some rich art—and turn for example to the poem,
"Falling Asleep over the Aeneid." That is in his second major book of
verse, but already he had come that far. The old man of Concord who
falls asleep is presently Aeneas himself, in a dream-phantasy, attending
upon the funeral of the fallen Pallas, a Latin prince. He kisses the dead
youth's lips, which seem to speak. From there I quote a little further:

> His harlots hang his bed
> With feathers of his long-tailed birds. His head
> Is yawning like a person. The plumes blow;
> The beard and eyebrows ruffle. Face of snow,
> You are the flower that country girls have caught,
> A wild bee-pillaged honey-suckle brought
> To the returning bridegroom—the design
> Has not yet left it, and the petals shine;
> The earth, its mother, has, at last, no help:
> It is itself. The broken-winded yelp
> Of my Phoenician hounds, that filled the brush
> With snapping twigs and flying, cannot flush
> The ghost of Pallas. But I take his pall,
> Stiff with its gold and purple, and recall
> How Dido hugged it to her, while she toiled,
> Laughing—her golden threads, a serpent coiled
> In cypress.

The terseness of the Latin, the gravity and accuracy of Vergil, are at
Lowell's command in the English. The sweetness of the grief, the *la-
crimae rerum*[1] spilt for the fallen comrade, are indulged longer than Vergil
would have permitted to his Aeneas; but this is but a single episode, and
its poet has not on his shoulders the burden of keeping a whole imperial
epic evenly in motion. And I cannot believe that there is anything acci-
dental in, for example, Lowell's phrase, "With snapping twigs and fly-
ing"; it is not in our English idiom, but it is according to the Latin. We
might resent it in a common poet who would be mixing things up in this
phrase on his own responsibility, not knowing the inflected language.
(Perhaps we must resolve to allow it only to Milton and Lowell, who can

show Vergilian credentials.) What gives us our faith in this poet is his ability to rise to a public occasion, and to bring to it out of his own invention a great wealth of poetic "matter."

Might it be destined that, eventually, we are to come to think of Lowell as our Vergil, elevating our occasions to their proper height, celebrating our public griefs?

But there is his third book, *Life Studies*, in which his verse becomes more informal and more absolute; more according to the naked facts. Free verse is his technical medium there, and a modern poet must have it in his repertoire, for the informal, the intimate, occasions. In this book there is the piece where he remembers his childhood visit to Dunbarton, the home of Arthur Winslow his maternal grandfather, whom he seems to have revered most of all the elders of his clan. Together they raked the leaves off the family graves. It is one of Lowell's most beautiful poems.

But by now he has gone off on a fresh track, and is writing furiously again. He makes "imitations" of other poets in other languages. Already his version of Racine's *Phèdre* has appeared in book form. Shorter imitations we have seen in the magazines, and it is announced that this fall of 1961 will see the publication of the book *Imitations*, where he will furnish English versions of such poets as Homer and Sappho, Baudelaire and Mallarmé, Heine and Rilke, Pasternak. Here we are made to think of those free translations which Dryden made, though Lowell's lyre is far more capacious than Dryden's.[2]

If Lowell should turn out to be our Vergil, and our Dryden too! Will not that be something? Let us control our impatience, however. Lowell is much on our minds, but we do not mean to arrange his calendar.

John Crowe Ransom (1888–1974), a distinguished poet, critic and editor, taught Lowell at Kenyon College during 1937–40. He is the author of *Chills and Fever* (1924) and *Two Gentleman in Bonds* (1927); *God Without Thunder* (1930) and *The World's Body* (1938).

1. Latin: the sadness of things.

2. John Dryden's great translation of Virgil's *Aeneid* appeared in 1697.

22 • Classroom at Boston University

Anne Sexton

There are several teachers (and people) named Robert Lowell and I am only going to try to talk about one of them. The Mr. Lowell whom I studied with during the fall of 1958 and the winter of 1959 was a wise man and an accurate teacher. By that I mean that he was usually right about a poem.

The class met at Boston University on Tuesdays from two to four in a dismal room the shape of a shoe box. It was a bleak spot, as if it had been forgotten for years, like the spinning room in Sleeping Beauty's castle. We were not allowed to smoke, but everyone smoked anyhow, using their shoes as ashtrays. Unused to classes of any kind, it seemed slow and uninspired to me. But I had come in through a back door and was no real judge. The summer of 1958 I had made a sort of pilgrimage to meet W. D. Snodgrass at a Writer's Conference at Antioch. He asked if I had studied with Lowell and insisted that I must—right off.

I had never been to college and knew so little about poetry and other poets that I felt grotesquely out of place in Robert Lowell's graduate seminar. It consisted of some twenty students—seventeen graduates, two other housewives (who were graduate somethings) and a boy who snuck over from M.I.T. I was the only one in that room who hadn't read *Lord Weary's Castle*.

Mr. Lowell was formal in a rather awkward New England sense. His voice was soft and slow. It seems to me that people remember the voice of the teacher they loved long after they have forgotten what he said. At least, I have noticed this among poets and their teachers. Mr. Lowell's reverence for John Crowe Ransom's voice was something I wouldn't understand until today as I find myself remembering Lowell's voice and the way *he* would read a poem. At first I felt impatient, packed

---

First printed in *The Harvard Advocate* 145 (November 1961): 13–14.

with ideas and feelings and the desire to interrupt his slow line by line reading of student work. He would read the first line—stop—and then discuss that line at length. I wanted to go through the whole poem quickly and then go back. I couldn't see any merit in dragging through it until you almost hated the damn thing—even your own, especially your own. At that point I wrote Mr. Snodgrass about my impatience and his reply (which I just looked for in my stack of letters and haven't asked his permission to quote and perhaps your editors should) went this way . . . "Frankly, I used to nod my head at his every statement and he taught me more than a whole gang of scholars could." So I kept my mouth shut. And Snodgrass was right.

Robert Lowell's method of teaching is intuitive and open. After he had read a student poem he always reads another evoked by it. The comparison is often painful. He works with a cold chisel with no more mercy than a dentist. He gets out the decay. But if he is never kind to the poem, he is kind to the poet.

In November I gave him a manuscript to see if he thought "it was a book." He was enthusiastic on the whole, but suggested that I throw out half of it and write another fifteen or so poems that were better. He pointed out the weak ones and I nodded and I took them out. It sounds simple to say that I merely, as he once said, jumped the hurdles that he had put up. But it makes a difference who puts up those hurdles. He defined the goal and acted as though, good race horse that I was, I'd just naturally run the course.

Since that year and that book I have driven into Marlborough Street twice to see him in his upstairs study. The maid answered the door and I trudged up three long old fashioned flights of stairs. He sat at his large office-style desk talking in the same slow painstaking manner. One poem, a short lyric, I rewrote seven times until he was satisfied. Robert Lowell's distinction as a poet is that he knows how to control his strength and his distinction as a teacher is that he is never impressed with a display of images or sounds (those things that a poet is born with anyhow).

The last time I saw Mr. Lowell was over a year ago before he left for New York. I miss him as all apprentices miss their first real master. He is a modest man and an incisive critic. He helped me to distrust the easy musical phrase and to look for the frankness of ordinary speech. If you have enough natural energy he can show you how to chain it in. He didn't teach me what to put into a poem, but what to leave out. What he taught me was taste. Perhaps that's the only thing a poet can be taught.

Anne Sexton (1928–74), an American confessional poet, was (with Sylvia Plath) Lowell's pupil in a poetry writing seminar at Boston University in 1959. She is the author of *To Bedlam and Part Way Back* (1960), *All My Pretty Ones* (1962) and *Live or Die* (1966).

23 • From *Armies of the Night*

Norman Mailer

. . . Mailer and Robert Lowell got into what was by all appearances a deep conversation at the dinner table sometime before food was laid out, Mailer thus doubly wounding the hostess with his later refusal.

We find, therefore, Lowell and Mailer ostensibly locked in converse. In fact, out of the thousand separate enclaves of their very separate personalities, they sensed quickly that they now shared one enclave to the hilt: their secret detestation of liberal academic parties to accompany worthy causes. Yes, their snobbery was on this mountainous face close to identical—each had a delight in exactly the other kind of party, a posh evil social affair, they even supported a similar vein of vanity (Lowell with considerably more justice) that if they were doomed to be revolutionaries, rebels, dissenters, anarchists, protesters, and general champions of one Left cause or another, they were also, in private, *grands conservateurs,* and if the truth be told, poor damn émigré princes. They were willing if necessary (probably) to die for the cause—one could hope the cause might finally at the end have an unexpected hint of wit, a touch of the Lord's last grace—but wit or no, grace or grace failing, it was bitter rue to have to root up one's occupations of the day, the week, and the weekend and trot down to Washington for idiot mass manifestations which could only drench one in the most ineradicable kind of mucked-up publicity and have for compensation nothing at this party which might be representative for some of the Devil's better creations. So Robert Lowell and Norman Mailer feigned deep conversation. They turned their heads to one another at the empty table, ignoring the potentially acolytic drinkers at either elbow, they projected their elbows out in fact like flying buttresses or old Republicans, they exuded waves of Interruption Repellent from the posture of their backs, and concentrated on their

From *Armies of the Night* (New York: New American Library, 1968), pp. 29–33, 45–46, 53–59, 80, 83, 88–89, 98–101, 127–128, 143–145. Reprinted by permission of Norman Mailer.

conversation, for indeed they were the only two men of remotely similar status in the room. (Explanations about the position of Paul Goodman will follow later.)

Lowell, whose personal attractiveness was immense (since his features were at once virile and patrician and his characteristic manner turned up facets of the grim, the gallant, the tender and the solicitous as if he were the nicest Boston banker one had ever hoped to meet) was not concerned too much about the evening at the theater. "I'm just going to read some poems," he said. "I suppose you're going to speak, Norman."

"Well, I will."

"Yes, you're awfully good at that."

"Not really." Harumphs, modifications, protestations and denials of the virtue of the ability to speak.

"I'm no good at all at public speaking," said Lowell in the kindest voice. He had indisputably won the first round. Mailer the younger, presumptive, and self-elected prince was left to his great surprise—for he had been exercised this way many times before—with the unmistakable feeling that there was some faint strain of the second-rate in this ability to speak on your feet.

Then they moved on to talk of what concerned them more. It was the subject first introduced to Mailer by Mitch Goodman.[1] Tomorrow, a group of draft resisters, led by William Sloane Coffin, Jr., Chaplain at Yale, were going to march from their meeting place at a church basement, to the Department of Justice, and there a considerable number of draft cards would be deposited in a bag by individual students representing themselves, or their groups at different colleges, at which point Coffin and a selected few would walk into the Department of Justice, turn the cards over to the Attorney General, and await his reply.

"I don't think there'll be much trouble at this, do you?" asked Lowell.

"No, I think it'll be dull, and there'll be a lot of speeches."

"Oh, no," said Lowell with genuine pain, "Coffin's not that kind of fool."

"It's hard to keep people from making speeches."

"Well, you know what they want us to do?" Lowell explained. He had been asked to accompany a draft resister up to the bag in which the draft cards were being dropped. "It seems," said Lowell, with a glint of the oldest Yankee light winging off like a mad laser from his eye, "that they want us to be *big buddy*."

It was agreed this was unsuitable. No, Lowell suggested, it would be better if they each just made a few remarks. "I mean," said Lowell, beginning to stammer a little, "we could just get up and say we respect their action and support it, just to establish, I suppose, that we're there and behind them and so forth." . . .

"You know, Norman," said Lowell in his fondest voice, "Elizabeth and I really think you're the finest journalist in America."

Mailer knew Lowell thought this—Lowell had even sent him a postcard once to state the enthusiasm. But the novelist had been shrewd enough to judge that Lowell sent many postcards to many people—it did not matter that Lowell was by overwhelming consensus judged to be the best, most talented, and most distinguished poet in America—it was still necessary to keep the defense lines in good working order. A good word on a card could keep many a dangerous recalcitrant in the ranks.

Therefore, this practice annoyed Mailer. The first card he'd ever received from Lowell was on a book of poems, *Deaths for the Ladies and other disasters* it had been called, and many people had thought the book a joke which whatever its endless demerits, it was not. Not to the novice poet at least. When Lowell had written that he liked the book, Mailer next waited for some word in print to canonize his thin tome; of course it never came. If Lowell were to begin to award living American poets in critical print, two hundred starving worthies could with fairness hold out their bowl before the escaped Novelist would deserve his turn. Still Mailer was irked. He felt he had been part of a literary game. When the second card came a few years later telling him he was the best journalist in America, he did not answer. Elizabeth Hardwick, Lowell's wife, had just published a review of *An American Dream* in *Partisan Review*[2] which had done its best to disembowel the novel. Lowell's card might have arrived with the best of motives, but its timing suggested to Mailer an exercise in neutralsmanship—neutralize the maximum of possible future risks. Mailer was not critically equipped for the task, but there was always the distant danger that some bright and not unauthoritative voice, irked at Lowell's enduring hegemony, might come along with a long lance and presume to tell America that posterity would judge Allen Ginsberg the greater poet.

This was all doubtless desperately unfair to Lowell who, on the basis of two kind cards, was now judged by Mailer to possess an undue unchristian talent for literary logrolling. But then Mailer was prickly. Let us hope it was not because he had been beaten a little too often by book reviewers, since the fruit of specific brutality is general suspicion.

Still Lowell now made the mistake of repeating his remark. "Yes, Norman, I really think you are the best journalist in America."

The pen may be mightier than the sword, yet at their best, each belongs to extravagant men. "Well, Cal," said Mailer, using Lowell's nickname for the first time, "there are days when I think of myself as being the best writer in America."

The effect was equal to walloping a roundhouse right into the heart of an English boxer who has been hitherto right up on his toes. Consternation, not Britannia, now ruled the waves. Perhaps Lowell had a moment when he wondered who was guilty of declaring war on the minuet. "Oh, Norman, oh, certainly," he said, "I didn't mean to imply, heavens no, it's just I have such *respect* for good journalism."

"Well, I don't know that I do," said Mailer. . . .

Lowell has the expression on his face of a dues payer who is just about keeping up with the interest on some enormous debt. As he sits on the floor with his long arms clasped mournfully about his long Yankee legs, "I am here," says his expression, "but I do not have to pretend I like what I see." The hollows in his cheeks give a hint of the hanging judge. Lowell is of a good weight, not too heavy, not too light, but the hollows speak of the great Puritan gloom in which the country was founded— man was simply not good enough for God. . . .

Lowell sat in a mournful hunch on the floor, his eyes peering over his glasses to scrutinize the metaphysical substance of his boot, now hide? now machine? now, where the joining and to what? foot to foot, boot to earth—cease all speculations as to what was in Lowell's head. "The one mind a novelist cannot enter is the mind of a novelist superior to himself," said once to Mailer by Jean Malaquais.[3] So, by corollary, the one mind a minor poet may not enter . . .

Lowell looked most unhappy. Mailer, minor poet, had often observed that Lowell had the most disconcerting mixture of strength and weakness in his presence, a blending so dramatic in its visible sign of conflict that one had to assume he would be sensationally attractive to women. He had something untouchable, all insane in its force; one felt immediately there were any number of causes for which the man would be ready to die, and for some he would fight, with an axe in his hand and a Cromwellian light in his eye. It was even possible that physically he was very strong—one couldn't tell at all—he might be fragile, he might have the sort of farm mechanic's strength which could manhandle the rear axle and differential off a car and into the back of a pickup. But physical strength or no, his nerves were all too apparently delicate. Obviously spoiled by everyone for years, he seemed nonetheless to need the spoiling. These nerves—the nerves of a consummate poet—were not tuned to any battering. The squalls of the mike, now riding up a storm on the erratic piping breath of Macdonald's[4] voice, seemed to tear along Lowell's back like a gale. He detested tumult—obviously. And therefore saw everything which was hopeless in a rife situation: the dank middle-class depths of the audience, the strident squalor of the mike, the absurdity of talent gathered to raise money—for what, dear God? who could finally know what this March might convey, or worse, purvey, and worst of all—to be associated now with Mailer's butcher boy attack. Lowell's eyes looked up from the shoe, and passed one withering glance by the novelist, saying much, saying, "Every single bad thing I have ever heard about you is not exaggerated."

Mailer, looking back, thought bitter words he would not say: "You, Lowell, beloved poet of many, what do you know of the dirt and the dark deliveries of the necessary? What do you know of dignity hard-achieved, and dignity lost through innocence, and dignity lost by sacrifice for a cause one cannot name. What do you know about getting fat against your will, and turning into a clown of an arriviste baron when you would rather be an eagle or a count, or rarest of all, some natural aristocrat from these damned democratic states. No, the only subject we share, you and I, is that species of perception which shows that if we are not very loyal to our unendurable and most exigent inner light, then some day we may burn. How dare you condemn me! You know the diseases which inhabit the audience in this accursed psychedelic house. How dare you scorn the explosive I employ?"

And Lowell with a look of the greatest sorrow as if all this *mess* were finally too shapeless for the hard Protestant smith of his own brain, which would indeed burst if it could not forge his experience into the iron edge of the very best words and the most unsinkable relation of words, now threw up his eyes like an epileptic as if turned out of orbit by a turn of the vision—and fell backward, his head striking the floor with no last instant hesitation to cushion the blow, but like a baby, downright sudden, savagely to himself, as if from the height of a foot he had taken a pumpkin and dropped it splat on the floor. "There, much-regarded, much-protected brain, you have finally taken a blow," Lowell might have said to himself, for he proceeded to lie there, resting quietly, while Macdonald went on reading from "The White Man's Burden," Lowell seeming as content as if he had just tested the back of his cranium against a policeman's club. What a royal head they had all to lose!

The evening went on. It was in fact far from climax. Lowell, resting in the wing on the floor of the stage, Lowell recuperating from the crack he had given his head, was a dreamy figure of peace in the corner of the proscenium, a reclining shepherd contemplating his flute. . . .

Lowell's turn had arrived. Mailer stood up to introduce him.

The novelist gave a fulsome welcome to the poet. He did not speak of his poetry (with which he was not conspicuously familiar) nor of his prose which he thought excellent—Mailer told instead of why he had respect for Lowell as a man. A couple of years ago, the poet had refused an invitation from President Johnson to attend a garden party for artists and intellectuals, and it had attracted much attention at the time for it was one of the first dramatic acts of protest against the war in Vietnam, and Lowell was the only invited artist of first rank who had refused. Saul Bellow, for example, had attended the garden party. Lowell's refusal could not have been easy, the novelist suggested, because artists were attracted to formal afternoons of such elevated kind since that kind of experience was often stimulating to new perception and new work. So, an honorific occasion in full panoply was not easy for the mature artist to eschew. Capital! Lowell had therefore bypassed the most direct sort of literary capital. Ergo, Mailer respected him—he could not be certain he would have done the same himself, although, of course, he assured the audience he would not probably have ever had the opportunity to refuse. (Hints of merriment in the crowd at the thought of Mailer on the White House lawn.)

If the presentation had been formal up to here, it had also been somewhat graceless. On the consequence, our audience's amusement tipped the slumbering Beast. Mailer now cranked up a vaudeville clown for finale to Lowell's introduction. "Ladies and gentlemen, if novelists come from the middle class, poets tend to derive from the bottom and the top. We all know good poets at the bot'—ladies and gentlemen, here is a poet from the top, Mr. Robert Lowell." A large and vigorous hand of applause, genuine enthusiasm for Lowell, some standing ovation.

But Mailer was depressed. He had betrayed himself again. The end of the introduction belonged in a burlesque house—he worked his own worst veins, like a man on the edge of bankruptcy trying to collect hopeless debts. He was fatally vulgar! Lowell passing him on the stage had recovered sufficiently to cast him a nullifying look. At this moment, they were obviously far from friends.

Lowell's shoulders had a slump, his modest stomach was pushed forward a hint, his chin was dropped to his chest as he stood at the microphone, pondering for a moment. One did not achieve the languid grandeurs of that slouch in one generation—the grandsons of the first sons had best go through the best troughs in the best eating clubs at Harvard before anyone in the family could try for such elegant note. It was now apparent to Mailer that Lowell would move by instinct, ability, and certainly by choice, in the direction most opposite from himself.

"Well," said Lowell, softly to the audience, his voice dry and gentle as any New England executioner might ever hope to be, "this has been a zany evening." Laughter came back, perhaps a little too much. It was as if Lowell wished to reprove Mailer, not humiliate him. So he shifted, and talked a bit uneasily for perhaps a minute about very little. Perhaps it was too little. Some of the audience, encouraged by earlier examples, now whistled. "We can't hear you," they shouted, "speak louder."

Lowell was annoyed. "I'll bellow," he said, "but it won't do any good." His firmness, his distaste for the occasion, communicated some subtle but impressive sense of his superiority. Audiences are moved by many cues but the most satisfactory of them is probably the voice of their abdomen. There are speakers who give a sense of security to the abdomen, and they always elicit the warmest kind of applause. Mailer was not this sort of speaker; Lowell was. The hand of applause which followed this remark was fortifying. Lowell now proceeded to read some poetry.

He was not a splendid reader, merely decent to his own lines, and he read from that slouch, that personification of ivy climbing a column, he was even diffident, he looked a trifle helpless under the lights. Still, he made no effort to win the audience, seduce them, dominate them, bully them, amuse them, no, they were there for him, to please *him,* a sounding board for the plucked string of his poetic line, and so he endeared himself to them. They adored him—for his talent, his modesty, his superiority, his melancholy, his petulance, his weakness, his painful, almost stammering shyness, his noble strength—*there* was the string behind other strings.

> O to break loose, like the chinook
> salmon jumping and falling back,
> nosing up to the impossible
> stone and bone-crushing waterfall—
> raw-jawed, weak-fleshed there, stopped by ten
> steps of the roaring ladder, and then
> to clear the top on the last try,
> alive enough to spawn and die.

Mailer discovered he was jealous. Not of the talent. Lowell's talent was very large, but then Mailer was a bulldog about the value of his own talent. No, Mailer was jealous because he had worked for this audience, and Lowell without effort seemed to have stolen them: Mailer did not know if he was contemptuous of Lowell for playing *grand maître,* or admiring of his ability to do it. Mailer knew his own version of *grand maître* did not compare. Of course no one would be there to accept his version either. The pain of bad reviews was not in the sting, but in the subsequent pressure which, like water on a joint, collected over the decade. People who had not read your books in fifteen years were certain they were missing nothing of merit. A buried sorrow, not very attractive (for bile was in it and the bitterness of unrequited literary injustice), released itself from some ducts of the heart, and Mailer felt hot anger at how Lowell was loved and he was not, a pure and surprising recognition of how much emotion, how much simple and childlike bitter sorrowing emotion had been concealed from himself for years under the manhole cover of his contempt for bad reviews.

> Pity the planet, all joy gone
> from this sweet volcanic cone;
> peace to our children when they fall
> in small war on the heels of small
> war—until the end of time
> to police the earth, a ghost
> orbiting forever lost
> in our monotonous sublime.[5]

They gave Lowell a good standing ovation, much heartiness in it, much obvious pleasure that they were there on a night in Washington

when Robert Lowell had read from his work—it was as nice as that—
and then Lowell walked back to the wings, and Mailer walked forward.
Lowell did not seem particularly triumphant. He looked still modest,
still depressed, as if he had been applauded too much for too little and so
the reservoir of guilt was still untapped.

Nonetheless, to Mailer it was now *mano a mano*.[6] . . .

After the conversation with Macdonald, he had a short word with
Lowell.

"Hungover?" Lowell had asked, after a pause.

"Pretty bad."

Lowell gave a commiserative nod. Then next he asked casually,
studying Mailer, "See the papers?"

"Yes."

"Not so nice."

"I guess not. They'll be worse," said Mailer.

Lowell made a face. He had an expression in his eyes which only a
fellow writer could comprehend—it said, "We are lambs—helpless be-
fore them." It was true. . . .

The sight of Robert Lowell chatting with old friends farther up the line
did not lift his depression. He was remembering that Lowell had been a
conscientious objector in World War II, and had served time in jail.
Perhaps he was now reminiscing with old pacifist friends. But Mailer
thought not—it was more a damn Ivy League convocation that Lowell
seemed to be having; he looked for the moment like one Harvard dean
talking to another, that same genteel confidential gracious hunch of the
shoulder toward each other. No dean at Harvard had ever talked to *him*
that way, Mailer now decided bitterly. . . .

In the middle of these speakers, Robert Lowell was called up. He had
been leaning against a wall in his habitual slumped over position, deep in
revery at the side of the steps—and of course had been photographed as a
figure of dejection—the call for him to say a few words caught him
partly by surprise. He now held the portable hand microphone with a
delicate lack of intimacy as if it were some valuable, huge, and rare
tropical spider which he was obliged to examine but did not have to
enjoy. "I was asked earlier today," he began in his fine stammering voice
which gave the impression that the life rushed at him like a series of

hurdles and some he succeeded in jumping and some he did not, "I was asked earlier this afternoon by a reporter why I was not turning in my draft card," Lowell said with the beginnings of a pilgrim's passion, "and I did not tell him it was a stupid question, although I was tempted to. I thought he should have known that I am now too old to have a draft card, but that it makes no difference. When some of us pledge ourselves to counsel and aid and abet any young men who wish to turn in their cards, why then you may be certain we are aware of the possible consequences and do not try to hide behind the technicality of whether we literally have a draft card or not. So I'm now saying to the gentlemen of the press that unlike the authorities who are running this country, we are not searching for tricks, we try to think of ourselves as serious men, if the press, that is, can comprehend such an effort, and we will protest this war by every means available to our conscience, and therefore not try to avoid whatever may arise in the way of retribution."

It was said softly, on a current of intense indignation and Lowell had never looked more dignified nor more admirable. Each word seemed to come on a separate journey from the poet's mind to his voice, along a winding route or through an exorbitant gate. Each word cost him much—Lowell's fine grace was in the value words had for him, he seemed to emit a horror at the possibility of squandering them or leaving them abused, and political speeches had never seemed more difficult for him, and on the consequence, more necessary for statement.

So Mailer applauded when Lowell was done. And suddenly liked him enormously for his speech, and decided he liked him truly. Beneath all snobbery, affectations of weariness, literary logrollermanship, neutralsmanship, and whatever other fatal snob-infested baggage of the literary world was by now willy-nilly in the poet's system, worked down intimately close to all his best and most careful traditions and standards, all flaws considered, Lowell was still a fine, good, and honorable man, and Normal Mailer was happy to be linked in a cause with him.

. . . In the late afternoon they had all been naturally weary when speeches were done, but not unsatisfied with themselves. "It was a good day, wasn't it, Norman," Lowell kept asking. In the best of gentle moods, his nerves seemed out of their rack, and his wit had plays of light, his literary allusions always near to private, were now full of glee. In one sprawling bar-restaurant where they went at random to drink, a plump young waitress with a strong perfume, who looked nonetheless a goddess of a bucket for a one-night stand, caught Mailer the novelist's eye—he flirted with the sense of gravity Buddhists reserve for the cow. "Good God, Norman, what do you see in her?" Macdonald had to know. Mailer, conceivably, could have told him, but they talked instead of cheap perfume—why it was offensive to some, aphrodisiac to others.

Lowell remarked, "I like cheap perfume, Norman, don't you?" But he said this last as if he were talking about some grotto in Italy he had blundered into all by himself. It was a difficult remark to make without some faint strain of dry-as-sachet faggotry, but Lowell brought it off. The mixture of integrity (Cromwellian axe of light in the eye!) in company with his characteristic gentleness, enabled him to make just about any remark without slithering. It was as if he had arrived at the recognition, nothing lost, that cheap perfume might be one of the hundred odd scents of mystery in the poet's apothecary—let us not, however, forget the smell of gasoline which Mailer in his turn had pondered. Gasoline and cheap perfume—half the smell in American adventure.

But in fact what must have been contributing to his good mood was the knowledge that Norman Mailer seemed to like him. Robert Lowell gave off at times the unwilling haunted saintliness of a man who was repaying the moral debts of ten generations of ancestors. So his guilt must have been a tyrant of a chemical in his blood always ready to obliterate the best of his moods. Just as danger is a Turk to a coward and the snub a disembowelment to the social climber, so Lowell was vulnerable to not being liked by anyone remotely a peer. In the poet's loneliness—the homely assumption is that all talent is lonely to the degree it is exalted—Lowell was at the mercy of anyone he considered of value, for only they might judge his guilt, and so relieve the intolerable dread which accompanies this excessive assumption of the old moral debts of the ancestors. Who knows what they might be? We may only be certain that the moral debt of the Puritan is no mean affair: agglutinations of incest, abominations upon God, kissing the *sub cauda*[7] of the midnight cat—Lowell's brain at its most painful must have been equal to an overdose of LSD on Halloween.

There had been, however, a happy conversation somewhat earlier and it had made a difference in Lowell's good mood. As they were coming down the steps from the Department of Justice in the now late cold October afternoon, Lowell had said, "I was most impressed with your speech, Norman."

"Well, glad you liked it, Cal," Mailer said, "for I think your speech produced it."

"My speech did?"

"I was affected by what you said. It took me out of one mood and put me in another."

"What sort of mood, Norman?"

"Well, maybe I was able to stop brooding over myself. I don't know, Cal, your speech really had a most amazing impact on me." Mailer drawled the last few words to drain any excessive sentimental infection, but Lowell seemed hardly to mind.

"Well, Norman, I'm delighted," he said, taking Mailer's arm for a moment as if, God and kingdom willing, Mailer had finally become a Harvard dean and could be addressed by the appropriate limb. "I'm delighted because I liked *your* speech so much."

These repetitions would have been ludicrous if not for the simplicity of feeling they obviously aroused in so complex a man as Lowell. Through the drinks and the evening at dinner, he kept coming back to the same conversation, kept repeating his pleasure in Mailer's speech in order to hear Mailer doggedly reaffirm his more than equal pleasure in Lowell's good words. Mailer was particularly graceless at these ceremonious repetitions by which presumably New England mandarins (like old Chinese) ring the stately gong of a new friendship forming.

In fact the dinner was what delivered Lowell's decision to remain for the March on the Pentagon. On the whole, he had come down for the event at the Department of Justice, he had in fact a dinner party at his home in New York on Saturday night, and he did not wish to miss it. That was obvious. For whatever reason Lowell had evidently been looking forward for days to Saturday evening.

"I wonder if I could get the plane back by six tomorrow," he kept asking aloud. "If we're arrested, I don't suppose there's much chance of that at all."

Mailer had not forgotten the party to which he was, in his turn, invited. Repeat: it had every promise of being wicked, tasty, and rich. "I think if we get arrested early," he said, "we can probably be released among the first."

"By six?"

"No, Cal," said Mailer, the honest soul, "if you get arrested, you had better plan on not making dinner before nine."

"Well, should we get arrested? What do you think of the merits?"

They talked about it for a while. It was Mailer's firm conclusion that this was probably the way they could best serve the occasion. "If the three of us are arrested," he said, "the papers can't claim that hippies and hoodlums were the only ones guilty." . . .

[On the March to the Pentagon, a monitor yelled at the notables.]
"Look here," said Lowell to the monitor in a no-nonsense voice, "we're perfectly willing to cooperate with you, but there's no need to yell and get officious. Be sensible."

This emptied the pale Negro's balloon. He was sensible for the rest of the March. Mailer was now admiring again the banker manqué in Lowell—no mean banker had been lost to Boston when Lowell put his hand to the poem. . . .

[They approached the moment of confrontation with the police, amidst the fug of drugs and chants.]
"You know I like this," [Mailer] said to Lowell.

Lowell shook his head. He looked not untroubled. "It was all right for a while," he said, "but it's so damn repetitious."

And Macdonald had a harsh glee in his pale eye as if he were half furious but half diverted by the meaninglessness of the repetitions. Macdonald hated meaninglessness even more than the war in Vietnam; on the other hand, he lived for a new critical stimulation: here it might be.

But to Lowell it was probably not meaningless. No, probably Lowell reacted against everything which was hypnotic in that music. Even if much of his poetry could be seen as formal incantations, halfway houses on the road to hypnosis and the oceans of contemplation beyond,

> O to break loose, like the chinook
> salmon jumping and falling back,
> nosing up the impossible
> stone and bone-crushing waterfall—

yes, even if Lowell's remarkable sense of rhythm drew one deep into the poems, nonetheless hypnotic they resolutely were not, for the language was particular, with a wicked sense of names, details, and places.

> . . .Remember playing
> Marian Anderson, Mozart's *Shepherd King*,
> *il re pastore?* Hammerheaded shark,

the rainbow salmon of the world—your hand
a rose . . . And at the Mittersill, you topped
the ski-run . . . [8]

Lowell's poetry gave one the sense of living in a well, the echoes
were deep, and sound was finally lost in moss on stone; down there the
light had the light of velvet, and the ripples were imperceptible. But one
lay on one's back in this well, looking up at the sky, and stars were
determinedly there at night, fixed points of reference; nothing in the
poems ever permitted you to turn on your face and try to look down into
the depths of the well, it was enough you were in the well—now, look
up! The world dazzled with its detail.

Lowell, drawn to hypnosis, would resist it, resist particularly these
abstract clackety sounds like wooden gears in a noisemaker, "Hari, hari,
hari, hari, rama, rama, Krishna, hari, rama, Krishna," and the whoop of
wild Indians in "out, demons, out!" Nothing was more dangerous to the
poet than hypnosis, for the *style* of one's entrance to that plain of sleep
where all ideas coalesced into one, was critical—enter by any indiscrimi-
nate route, "Om, Om, Om,"[9] and who knows what finely articulated
bones of future prosody might be melted in those undifferentiated pots—
no, Lowell's good poetry was a reconnaissance into the deep, and for
that, pirate's patrols were the best—one went down with the idea one
would come back with more, but one did not immerse oneself with open
guru Ginsberg arms crying, "Baa, baa, slay this sheep or enrich it, Great
Deep," no, one tiptoed in and made a raid and ideally got out good.
Besides, the Fugs and Hindu bells and exorcisms via LSD were all indeed
Allen Ginsberg's patch; poets respected each others' squatter's rights like
Grenadiers before the unrolled carpet of the King.

But of course Lowell's final distaste was for the attraction itself of
these sounds (which were incidentally lifting Mailer into the happiest
sense of comradeship). Without a drink in him, he was nonetheless
cheering up again at the thought of combat, and deciding it would be
delightful to whack a barricade in the company of Ed Sanders[10] with the
red-gold beard who had brought grope-freak talk to the Village and
always seemed to Mailer a little over-liberated, but now suitable, yes, the
Novelist was working up all steam in the "Out, demons, out."

Norman Mailer (b. 1923), major American novelist, took part in the Pen-
tagon March with Lowell in October 1967. He is the author of *The Naked and the*

Dead (1948), *The Deer Park* (1955), *An American Dream* (1965), *Ancient Evenings* (1983) and a nonfiction work, *The Executioner's Song* (1979).

1. Mitch Goodman (b. 1923), Harvard classmate of Mailer and author of *The End of It* (1961), asked Mailer to join the Pentagon March.

2. See Elizabeth Hardwick, "Bad Boy," *Partisan Review* 32 (Spring 1965): 291–294.

3. Jean Malaquais, French philosopher; friend and advisor to Mailer.

4. Dwight Macdonald (1906–82), American editor of *Partisan Review* (1938–43) and *Politics* (1944–49), author of *Memoirs of a Revolutionist* (1957) and *Against the American Grain* (1962).

5. Both quotations are from Lowell, "Waking Early Sunday Morning."

6. Spanish: literally, "hand to hand"; a personal combat between two bullfighters.

7. Latin: under the tail, i.e., the anus.

8. Lowell, "1958."

9. A Tibetan invocation to the omnipresent universal spirit or divine essence of Buddha, much favored by hippies of the 1960s.

10. Ed Sanders, publisher of a poetry magazine called *Fuck You;* conductor, composer, instrumentalist and vocalist of The Fugs.

24 • Summers in Castine: Contact Prints, 1955–1965

Philip Booth

Except for the Smith's Mill picnic, which is one step out of clock time, this is a chronological strip of contact prints: views of Cal, a friendship, a decade, a place. To get back to how Cal affected me, and this peninsular village, I have fictionalized time present: the presumptive now *of a camera. Except for reviewing actual photographs, and the notes I took when Cal first looked at my poems, I have relied entirely on memory—memory checked with my wife Margaret, and with friends.*

As with any film left in a camera for years, there are, here, whole seasons left out; unexpectedly, there are two or three frames which exhibit their own sequence. What's missing, inevitably, is any sustained soundtrack: the power of Cal's talk, the gestures of Cal's voice, his hands' sprung rhythms, are partially here; I have tried to be as true as possible to who Cal was in these several—or eleven—summers. They became, finally, only an overlong August: the high stillness between McCarthyism and Viet Nam.

There were further summers, larger talk, more poems; but fewer and fewer picnics. The world changed. And Castine, now, is almost as greatly changed by Cal's leaving as it was by his coming. I miss him immensely.

1

My first year downcountry, driving John Holmes back from the Gardner house in Brookline, where we've been invited to meet Robert Lowell. The party is as big as the house, as casually elegant, to honor his homing from Iowa.

As we drive back across the river, John asks what I thought about Lowell. Isabella Gardner I met, yes; Donald Hall, yes; and more poets than I ever knew existed. But I have to tell John I didn't meet Robert

Salmagundi 37 (Spring 1977): 37–53. Reprinted by permission of the author.

Lowell. I would have remembered that sternly handsome young man peering down from the gallery of portraits in Oscar Williams' newest anthology. No, I somehow missed meeting him. But, as I tell John, I did have good talk with another Lowell about his coming to Maine—a great bear of a man with hornrimmed glasses who slumped darkly away from me in a tall Victorian chair.

"He must have been Lowell's brother," I tell John; "he said his name was Cal."

2

After we've read together at Brown, Cal's Tudor Ford ahead of Margaret and me at a Providence stoplight. Cal's head tipped down to the book he has just picked up from the seat beside him. His own poems. The light goes green, then yellow, then red again. The whole of Route 1 behind us, beginning to honk. But Cal, for minutes and minutes, keeps on reading.

3

Down over the Main Street knoll, the postoffice; and down below that—at the steep end of Main Street—the village drugstore, Ken's Market, the flagpole, the Town Wharf, and the sea.

Nothing has changed in the six years since I've been home for the summer. The same key hung in the hall still fits the same postoffice box. As I search through my take for rejections or an acceptance, I hear Cal's voice at the oak-framed postoffice window, asking Irene for mail for Lowell.

Cal seems to be as pleased to see me as I am to see him. He says I must come down to the Barn to "trade poems," the barn "behind the Brickyard House where we're staying." But I don't know his private names for his cousin's place, and he is too new here to be able to give exact directions. Never mind, I can find it. As already the mail has found Cal: I help him lug piles of publisher's and author's copies out to his Ford. In his blue buttondown and his bluejeans, Cal looks both like and unlike the poet I met in Boston. But his grin is entirely wide, the eyes behind his hornrims are glad.

Elizabeth and Cal *here*. Unlikely. For them, and for us. But what luck. For the whole rest of the summer.

4

Against sunset, against summer's end, against the prevailing sou'wester-
lies which stress and release even the peninsula's strongest elms, Cal
plays tennis almost every afternoon at one of the two courts next to the
High Road. The company at these late-afternoon sessions of round-robin
doubles is socially elect. The voices are pure Eastern Shore, West
Hartford, and Boston, but the talent is severely mixed: Cal wins one set
with Janet Hughes, twenty years his senior, then loses a second set with
Sally Austin, skilled and barely of age. His legs never get him to the right
place on the court at the right moment, but he compensates by attacking
the ball with all the immense strength of his upper body. His reflexes, if
not always coordinated, are quick: even when his stroke flails he scores
points with his running monologue—this particular game variously re-
minds him of Philip of Macedonia, his first wife, and Aristophanes.
Elizabeth, exhausted after two sets, gangles on the sidelines under the
cedars.

Cal is about to serve. Sweating hugely, he strips his shirt (violating
the only club rule ever posted), and says, "This may make me as famous
as René LaCoste. . . ." Wherever fame may reside, it will not reside in
his service: he throws the ball too low, ducks from his knees to accom-
modate the failed altitude, pushes at the ball from too short an arc, and
with great speed squashes it into his partner's left buttock. She smiles
back wildly at Cal, and he invites everybody for supper.

Everything stops. Cal glances hugs at Elizabeth, and turns back
happily to his tennis partners. "If you can't do that," he says, "at least
come for drinks."

5

A northwest wind day. Large scale clarities. In spite of shut doors, the
shoreside Barn where Cal writes (table, chair, typewriter, and cot set at
the windows fronting Oakum Bay) is a barn too September-cold for
long talk. Cal escorts me out to the lee wall of the Barn; we sit in
sweetgrass, sun glinting up off the harbor.

After thanking me for introducing him to the bluejean jacket he's
just beginning to wear from stiff to soft, Cal starts straight in on my
manuscript. Depending on the quality of his interest, he turns slowly or
quickly the pages he has had now for two days. Sometimes he reads
aloud, his head tipped forward with total focus on the poem, then looks

up at me over his glasses and smiles his reassurance: "That's what I like best—the sparse and accurate description." Then, his expression slightly pained, he says of another poem, ". . . but the resonance is too obvious." And, turning pages, he finds a lot to attack in a poem called "Red Brick": "too full of strained personification, too general, too shrill." He stops, lets up, smokes, and says I should read "say three poets for a month, maybe copying-out poems" to see what I can learn to use, to extend my range. "Empson for intellect. Marianne Moore for observation, Frost for how a poem gets organized."

Back again to the poems, he goes at them totally, liking "this rougher metric," dismissing that "intellectual indolence." He insists that all of the description, not just sections, be "as solid as the first part of *Life on the Mississippi,* or the crossing-the-river part of *As I Lay Dying.*" A lot of his touchstones are prose. But against the general dangers of "balsam pillow Maine," he again shifts to poetry; he wants to send me to Arnold's shorter lines, "Tennyson rowing out to Catullus's island," Hardy's "narrative strength," or Wordsworth's simplicity in "Michael"; and "the 'thereness' of 'Tintern Abbey.'"

All this I half know but have never before heard. My one college writing course far behind me, I begin to understand that I am for the first time hearing a master teacher. I listen and listen, reminding myself that when I get home I must write myself notes about everything Cal is saying.

The sun is across apogee, the wind has calmed and come back from the south before Cal is done with me. If he withheld anything, I'm not sure I want to know what that anything is. I feel like the new boy taken out behind the gym by a Sixth Former, being told quietly that one isn't living up to the school's best traditions.

As we get up from the shingled barn wall and the sweetgrass, Cal shakes my hand. But it is neither congratulation nor goodbye; it is, rather, as if something new had begun. I walk along the harbor, and home up the hill, stunned by Cal's impact. Nobody before has ever cared so much for my poems: cared to criticize them so brilliantly, cared so to demand of them, even in parts so cared to praise them, as Cal has this day.

6

Annually now, like my native grandmother and his summer cousin before us, Cal and I have inherited being neighbors across a mid-village back pasture. It's still hard to put together the virtuosity of *Lord Weary's Castle* with the white clapboard Augusts we're beginning to share. There's never been question who is the senior poet. Nor whose territory Cal has moved to. I less want Cal's good wine than I want to hear him talk more about Hardy; I'm continually knocked over by the intensity of his intelligence. But Cal wants to hear the Maine voice in which I tell stories, or he wants to be taken sailing. To whatever experience I'm native, Cal is deferential, with innate Boston ease.

After supper in the Lowells' barn, that tall summerroom Cal's Cousin Harriet made from the old ell back of her house on the Common, we have variously taken in dishes and come back in front of the fire. We've talked long, over wine, salad, and coffee. Now Cal has put Nadia Boulanger records on Harriet Winslow's old Magnavox; while the four of us listen, I find myself feeling that if there's another war this is the kind of civilization I'd want to remember. Or want to try to save.

Elizabeth's early to bed; Margaret has walked up the hill to let our babysitter go home. Cal's back to Hardy, and his ability to imply narrative. As we talk, I get to how circular Maine stories are. Remembering Cal's pleasure in Mace Eaton's seal story, I tell Cal about this noon on the wharf: Mace asking me if I'd been across the harbor for clams, then (literally, with his finger) ribbing me that "Clams'll makeyuh stemmy!"[1] Cal laughs, catching the aphrodisiac implication but wanting me to repeat the metaphor in my own voice.

"Oh," he says, "*stemmy!* That's nearly Shakespearian. But you haven't taken me to meet Mace yet. . . ." Cal's hands dance in front of him in pure delight. "Let's do that *soon*."

7

Chokey and fevered with a pharynx abscess, I've kept myself propped up in bed by rereading *War and Peace* for the best part of two days and the worst of two nights. This second night I dreamt the Battle of Borodino, with Cal cast as Pierre. After penicillin broke my abscess, and my fever, I woke in high relief: the battle was over. But even on this June morning the after-image sustains itself: Cal as Pierre.

8

On the waterfront here, even in the protective coloration of his bluejean jacket, Cal seems as vaguely outlandish as Pierre in his white suit.

A lot of Cal's energies blur when he can't verbally focus them. For matters simply practical, Cal has no native talent; his natural frames of reference are as historical-literary as my dream. Even his most pedestrian associations are freestyle, full of verbal leaps, until they fall into some narrative play or pivot on a phrase or a word. For instance: *submarine*.

Today, over the Fourth, we traipse our conglomerate families down to the Town Wharf to visit the submarine that the Navy has sent in, and opened to the public for the day. The ladders are vertical, the passages narrow; our wives and daughters are variously gaped at or saved from hysterics by the incredibly young submariners in their Navy dress blues. After we've been guided the length of the submarine's innards, and have asked civilian questions about torpedoes and periscopes, we climb back topside, out into the gleam of the harbor. Cal turns to me with a question which must have preoccupied him for the whole dark length of our short tour. "Tell me," he says, his hands waving awkwardly down from the wharf to the submarine moored alongside, "are the men who sail that thing *Marines?*"

I explain. Cal shakes his huge head: "Oh, I should have *known* that." He is genuinely, if momentarily, embarrassed. But it is by just such associative leaps that some of Cal's best poems get written.

9

I submarined myself this summer, having taken Cal out sailing around the bell. As we came back into the harbor on a dying breeze, I asked Cal if he wanted to take the helm. He did, accompanied by improbable tales of his sailing in Padanaram[2] as a boy. These somehow slid into a wonderfully funny story about sexual mores in Dubuque; a wonderfully funny story at which Margaret laughed more than I only because Cal was letting the boat gybe at will, all over the harbor. The air was too light to have these gyrations hurt the boat, but she was easily identifiable along the waterfront, and it hurt my pride to have her sailed badly in such public view. Aside from some suggestions, readily accepted by Cal, to head for this buoy, or that farm on the shore, I held in my frustrations until we neared the wharves. I mentioned the difficult set of the current, took back the helm from Cal, and buttonhooked up to our mooring. Margaret neatly picked up the pennant with the boathook, but then proceeded to cleat it with perhaps her right hand rather than her left. I jumped forward past Cal with all my frustrations vented on my wife, grabbed the pennant from her, cleated it the other way around, and stood

quickly straight up, puffing angrily on my pipe. Next thing I knew I
stepped one step smartly backwards, plunk into the harbor.

This event has become, variously embellished, a waterfront story
which Cal likes even better than Mace Eaton stories. Tonight at dinner,
with Fred and Andy Dupee up from the Brickyard house they've again
been renting, and with the Wannings over from Blue Hill, Cal got me to
tell Mace's seal story, then led me on to tell about falling overboard. My
version ends with some slight face-saving: I went down sucking my pipe
and surfaced with the pipe still clamped in my jaw.

"Oh," Cal roars to everybody, "that's only a *tenth* of it. He tells a
story with perfect pitch for Maine accent, but . . . ." Cal all but explodes
with delight at having so set me up. "But aboard his boat he's an abso-
lute Ahab!"

Cal's no Ahab, afloat or ashore. But at dinnerparties he's no Pierre,
either. Elizabeth's dinners in the barn are done with a grace that makes
them seem easy. And everybody is, in fact, greatly at ease. Including
Cal. But he plays a dinnerparty at the pitch at which he plays tennis.
Given an audience of more than one, Cal turns conversation into his best
competitive sport.

Cal is immensely knowing in all sorts of worlds beyond Castine:
poetry, politics, women—in every possible permutation and combina-
tion. He has many appetites, but the surest of these is for talk. Talk at the
level he must have exchanged with Randall Jarrell, and with Delmore.
But we here are, at best, intermediates to Cal's expertise. Cal serves with
high wit; his wild intelligence never misses an opportunity to score. The
dinner table is, for him, centercourt at Longwood.[3] As if in total relief
from writing, or from shop talk, Cal tries every shot in the book: drop-
shot, lob, slam. There are few long rallies; it is almost impossible to drive
Cal back to some conversational baseline. But dinnerparties, supperpar-
ties, are stunning games of intelligence at play, every exchange ending
and never ending in strokes of quick victory or happy collapse.

10

Cruising friends of ours made port late this afternoon, downeast a day
early on steady southerlies. By quick arrangement, we took them in tow
to the Lowells' barn for that rarest Lowell event: a cocktail party. A lot of
people, but even among them the cruising Blacks are literally outstand-
ing: Carol is gracefully rigged, Peter is about as tall as the mast of their

French sloop. Asked today what he does when he isn't cruising, Peter said, "I make money. I don't see much other reason for working."

In his own old Irish tweed jacket and khakis, Cal listened diffidently to Peter's tailored aplomb; but once they meet, Cal is immensely pleased to know that Peter knows his poems. Peter is expert in everything: international shipping, skippering, shooting tigers, watercolors, making fish chowder, cabinet making, and knowing how to spend old money gracefully. Cal sees all this at a glance; Peter is deeply Boston. Yet only after almost everybody has left the barn, and we're saying goodbyes and thanks, does Cal speak to Peter his recognition.

"Didn't you go to Noble's? And before that didn't you live near the Ameses?"

Peter nods his surprise.

Cal, again: "I think your aunt brought you to Revere Street once. . . ."

Peter does not remember.

". . . You're the boy my mother always tried to get me to play with." Cal's eyes blink hugely, he ducks his head repeatedly, like a zoo bird, in spondaic assent to his earliest memories. "She thought that if we played together a lot I'd be more like you." His left hand begins a circular apology. "And rather less like me. . . ."

Cal grins his widest grin. Peter roars. Boston is intact.

11

Life Studies has made Cal famous. Even here. Auden's claim that "poetry makes nothing happen"[4] to the contrary, "our fairy decorator" has already left town. *Post hoc,* maybe *propter hoc.*[5]

"Skunk Hour" isn't my favorite life study (though I feel the vested interest of having helped Cal get his yawl down from twelve knots in draft to a more realistic nine), but it's the only poem I ever heard talked about on any Main Street. And it has mightily confounded the elderly Boston ladies who here live out their handsomely furnished lives. Cal is still "Bobby" to some of them, who knew his mother; they indeed know something of his personal history. Little or much as they may understand of "Skunk Hour," what troubles them is its tone: they feel threatened by what they take in the poem to be "Bobby's not liking it here." It's difficult, if not impossible, to say simply that—save for weathers of flat depression, hanging in like day after day of fog—Cal has always been well here, that he has written well here, that he is generally happy here, and that "Skunk Hour" is about more than a man named Lowell or a town named Castine. How possibly say to the Boston ladies, or anybody else local, that Cal's poems (as Stevens says of his "Comedian . . ."[6]) "make / Of his own fate an instance of all fate."

After Cal read last year to benefit the community hospital, he seemed stranger than ever to the people who went, mostly, out of obligation or curiosity. The school gym was barren, and too hot; the acoustics were terrible, and Cal's poems turned out not to be Longfellow's.

When he was first getting at these new poems down in the Barn, and we were talking about their metrics, Cal astounded me by saying that he'd heard X give an *Advocate* reading in Cambridge, and that "I knew if he could change, so could I." Cal's new measures are demonstrably looser, the language is less dense, the resonances are buried, true; but the poet of these poems and of *Lord Weary's* is much the same poet, onto a new stage. It is not that Cal has changed, or that except for his effect on poets he has much changed the world. But the Boston Cal came from, which is still much the world of this small peninsula, *is* changing, and that is a truth the town wants nobody to remind it of. Least of all somebody "from away," somebody who seems to be "famous."

I thought that the squalls about *Life Studies* in general, and "Skunk Hour" in particular, had blown out of this harbor a couple of seasons ago. But tonight, two years after the book, I've been drying family laundry in one of the two driers in The Village Laundromat. In through thick fog, to use the other drier, comes a vacationing schoolteacher from Bangor, a woman I grew up with. After we mention the weather, the condition of the driers, and make other small change, she asks if she can ask me something. I nod.

"You write poetry sometimes, don't you?"

I nod.

"Will you tell me *how* a poet like Mr. Lowell can be so famous when he can't even get Jimmy Sawyer on the right island?"

For a moment I don't figure her sense of Cal's leeway, and say so.

"Well, you know that poem about the skunks, the one about him taking his car up into the cemetery?"

I do.

"Well! He says in that one that our selectman works for a woman on Nautilus Island, a woman whose son is a bishop. . . ."

I begin, even in the laundromat, to see.

". . . and everybody knows that that woman on Nautilus never had children, and that Jimmy Sawyer keeps the farm for Miss Harris over on *Hol*brook Island! Now you tell me, how can a poet like that get so famous?"

I cannot tell her. I try, but I do not do well at it. Not while I'm folding hot laundry, not here on the stained old table where she is sitting as we talk. Cal has never been near the laundromat; she has never been near "Notes Toward a Supreme Fiction." Not Stevens'. Not, more specifically, Cal's.

12

In the house on the Common, between the kitchen and the Barn, there is a small room which must always have been what it still is: part passageway, part storeroom, part woodshed. While Harriet was still being formula fed, it was through this dark passage that the sure smell of burning rubber once drifted out into the barn. And back through here that Cal rushed to fling the smoking sterilizer off the stove and into the sink. For weeks the event became Cal's favorite story, mostly because of the title he gave it: "The Night of the Burning Nipples."[7]

To help care for Harriet, early, Cal and Elizabeth brought with them to Maine a woman from Madrid whose English is still as nonexistent as her sense of service is fastidious. She turns down beds to perfection (an annoyance to Elizabeth, a delight to Cal), she cooks fine paella, she cares for Harriet with large fondness. Now that Harriet is no longer infant but fully little girl, the room between the kitchen and barn has become her special province. She retreats to it after being dutifully presented to guests in the barn; it is her halfway place between her parents' voices around the fireplace and Nicole's Spanish in the kitchen. Harriet, now, is at an all-but-invisible age; pudgy, melancholy-shy with everybody except her friend Johanna or the three adults of this house. She and Robin, our youngest daughter, born the same year, have since babyhood hated each other with the natural desperation of children whose various parents are affectionate friends. Except when Harriet is part of a picnic, we most often see her here: darkly near one or another doorjamb between the kitchen and the barn.

Now, as it must have been a hundred years ago, this transitional room partially belongs to the small animals that belong to a child's own growing. This year they are guinea-pigs, long-haired guinea-pigs. Their breed doesn't much matter; they are live, furry, small, and entirely Harriet's own. Or Harriet's and Cal's.

Bringing ice out from the kitchen, Cal stops in the warm gloom of the unpainted passageway, puts the ice-bucket down on the plank floor, and scootches[8] to the fruit-crate level inhabited by Harriet's pets. As Harriet tends them, Cal tends her. All this is all but wordless, as basic as pats and murmurs. Nothing more. Nothing else. Nothing less.

Whatever gets understood here must be what Cal's mother maybe got spoken to him, in some more formal hallway in his own South Shore summers. Unlike anybody else though Cal now is, he must once have been as small, as needful, and as largely adoring, as this half-hidden Harriet. Under the one dull lightbulb hung in the passage he hugs her to his shoulder with total gentleness. Then, with no perceptible transition, he picks up the ice-bucket, and lugs his whole grizzly-bear frame back over the transom into the adult barn.

13

Weir Cove, on Cape Rosier, is about six miles by boat, about twenty-six by car. Once we get there, complete with children, for our here-or-there every-year-or-so picnic with assorted Hoffmans and Eberharts, one feature is inevitable: Dick's taking everybody out around Spectacle Island in his newest prize: a thirty-year-old somewhat Gothic power yacht named the *Reve*. Given the poet each has become, that Dick was Cal's teacher at St. Mark's seems entirely unlikely; unlikely, that is, until both of them get together on the *Reve*. Once, with the two highest landmarks on the east coast clearly in sight, they talked poetry until the boat was 180 degrees off course in the middle of Blue Hill Bay. Dick has a poem about it; Cal tells it as a supportable story. If they commonly lack concentration on landmarks like Cadillac Mountain, buoys, and headings, at least they have a common compass in Cambridge: Cal, with some envy and certain delight, sees the *Reve* as "Dick's floating Memorial Hall."

Boats are rarely on Cal's mind; poems almost always are. Today, getting out of their Ford wagon at Weir Cove with his crew, as we pull up with our daughters in ours, Cal wants a moment before we walk down to the Cape Rosier poets and the *Reve*. He tugs me aside, then declaims in his high reading voice the eight lines that will be the third or fourth strophe of "Fourth of July in Maine."

He tells me where the strophe will fit, in the gap I felt this morning when we were down at the Barn, trading poems. I remember questioning the early pace of the poem, but I can't recall how the parts go. I stall: I ask when he got these lines written.

Cal's head tips sideways with a proudly shy grin: "Driving over in the car."

14

This morning at the Barn, lying on his cot in the midst of piles of mail and unopened books, Cal is reading new Roethke,[9] marking the margins of passages he particularly likes. He reads me a longish section of a long poem, apparently changes his mind about it in mid-reading, and says it feels slack when you think of the Whitman it comes from. Then—his hand angled back from the wrist over the edge of his cot—he literally pushes the contrast away to the floor. "But Ted's just *aw*fully good at things like this. . . ." He turns back to a page he has earlier pencilled, and reads again. "*No*body can do that better."

In spite of the accelerated pace of his writing (or perhaps because of it), noboby knows better than Cal the difficulty of drafting, shaping, intensifying, and—as he says—"tinkering with" a poem. Roethke, Jarrell, Schwartz, seem to be the poets he most suffers for. Or with. Long friends, long on pain. Competitive as Cal can be in semi-final conversation, his generosity to poets he values is without competitive edge. Several springs ago, when Roethke was reading around Boston, Cal gathered every known poet east of the Hudson for an evening party[10] on Marlborough Street: that they might meet Ted, that Ted might meet them. When Cal asked Ted to read, Ted said he would if Cal would; Cal said he'd be glad to if I. A. Richards would. When Mr. Richards agreed, if there was a copy of his new book in the house, it occurred to Cal that he could invite everybody to read. And up and down he climbed, to high bookshelves and low, until he'd found a book by every poet present. And we all read, one poem or two, deferring to Ted and Cal as Cal deferred to Mr. Richards. Ted had upstage center, deferred to nobody, and revelled in it. Cal let him, happily.

Last year Cal phoned from New York about the possibility of a Syracuse job for Delmore. And we took him. Cal knew how difficult Delmore was, and was going to be, and said so; but he primarily spoke Delmore's virtues, longstanding and residual. Given the number of people who had given up on Delmore, Cal's concern seems all the more typical: Cal stood by him not because he was last in line but because their friendship was in some way beyond dissolution. The old way. Remembering. Knowing how the world hurts.

It seems to me that caring for poets is, in Cal, based on root fact: having to write poems is one of the terrifying, if sometimes redemptive, joys. Yet Cal keeps at his writing (or his reading-toward-writing) on an almost invariable schedule. And his concentration is such that even being interrupted does not phase him: not if the interruption owes to distress or to poems. I've come to the Barn, unannounced, on both counts; today, our individual and family routines being so different that we haven't in weeks seen each other for real talk, we've prearranged to share sandwiches. I bring a couple of beers.

After Cal's reading Roethke, he remembers things he likes about David Wagoner, and then moves off the cot to the big door overlooking the tide. We sit there, taking our nooning, and talking about nothing but poems. Not his, though his hunt-and-peck drafts are strewn on the floor as they are strewn with inked-in corrections and Cal's misspellings. Not my poems. Today, almost everybody else's between Northumberland and Alaska: H.D. to John Haines. But below our talk, and surfacing constantly in what Cal says, are touchstones from all levels of history. Poems, painters, military tactics, Czarist politics. Even on the new sill of a sagging barn, sitting in the midst of high noon, Cal is like an archeologist at a dig-site; there are ages and ages under him. I think as I listen how incredibly much Cal knows.

No. I correct myself as I keep listening: I don't know anybody who has felt as much, who has thought as deeply.

15

From the first, Cal has needed people to talk to; I think he imported conversation the very summer he himself was first visiting. And then Cal got the Dupees[11] to rent the Brickyard House when he and Elizabeth moved to the house on the Common. The list of people who came visiting at Cal's behest, during these summers, can only sound like a guest-list out of *Gatsby:* Bill Meredith for a day or a week at a time, Bill and Dido Merwin most of one summer. Bill Alfred, quickly in and out from Cambridge, alone; and down from Cambridge, too, Peter and Esther Brooks, and the Bob Gardners—usually en route to Roque Island. Allen Tate, solo; Rollie McKenna, with her Nikons; Fred Morgan, over from Blue Hill; and Andy and Pat Wanning, too, as part of a plank-busting dance in the barn. Sometimes Blair Clark, or Bob Silvers, over-night; and Sidney Nolan from Australia; and Elizabeth Bishop, for the best of a week in the Brickyard. And Lord Gowrie, Cal's Harvard student, with the first and only miniskirted Lady ever observed in these New England parts.

16

People come to talk with Cal, to listen to how his brilliance works. What's remarkable is how steadily, even with visitors, Cal keeps to his writing routine. Almost daily, Cal's day moves from the old isolation of poems to the strong refreshment of people. Breakfast, postoffice, Barn; work and lunch there until it is time for tennis and people again. People come to talk with Cal; they also come to share Elizabeth's own brilliance, to share her table, to be part of her house. And part of the idea of summer. Almost the only exception to Cal's working schedule is dictated by that alchemy of people and weather which turns a day into a picnic.

We used to go to Ram Island, mostly by way of a couple of outboard-powered rowboats, and by ferrying people on our small sloop. This year, perhaps because the picnics have been considerably enlarged by the arrival of Mary McCarthy and Jim West, and their household, from Paris, we've gone more to Smith's Mill—a millrace cove with a clamshell beach that lies three miles across the harbor from Cal's Barn.

Over breakfast, the weather comes clear. Mary and Elizabeth, by phone, start collecting people and salads; and, beyond outboard and sail power, a lobsterboat hired from Eaton's Wharf. We all gather there at eleven, and begin to meet each other's visitors. By the time we're all ashore again at Smith's Mill, dinghy-load after dinghy-load, I figure that this has become a picnic to end all picnics. Years ago, I came here with an aged aunt, or boys my own age, to eat jelly sandwiches and dig for arrowheads in the shellheap bank above the shell beach. Today there are over twenty people picnicking by the millrace. To name them, to say the languages being spoken in this mostly lonely cove, is to suggest how much of the world, and what parts of it, have gravitated here—primarily because of Cal.

Harris and Mary Thomas, from Exeter, are in her native tongue talking about their memory of Rennes with the newest addition to our crew: An AFS[12] student just arrived from Brittany. Priscilla Barnum is with Margaret and Elizabeth, who trade Georgia talk for Kentucky talk between tending fire and attending to daughters. Margot, our seventeen year old Bikini, is putting her highschool Russian to test, listening to Olga Carlisle explaining some nuances of Pasternak's to Cal. As I take some photographs of all this, I have just had explained to me, by a Classics professor from Cincinnati, that *xai ov,*[13] the name of our dinghy, is badly spelled Greek. Henry Carlisle is talking American English to Sonia Orwell, whose English is British; Ted Draper and James West have given up on Sonia's conversation and have turned to their mutual interest in Poland. Jim, in Polish, asks something of Maria, whom he and Mary have imported from their Paris apartment to serve their establishment here. Native Pole though she is, Maria answers in French; she is helping Jim's sons, Johnny and Danny, dig for flints on the bank above us. Robin and Harriet are huddled in towels on opposite sides of the fire after a quick duck into the local edge of the Labrador current. Carol, our almost-sixteen, has stayed in longer than anybody except Mary McCarthy—who since coming to Castine has become, by general acclaim, the Champion Stayer-In of All Time. As Mary and Carol stroke slowly toward the shore, Margot comes up to me in full amazement, and speaks (though she does not know it) in that same daughterly voice Thomas Wolfe once heard at his editor's breakfast table:

"*Daa*addy, do you know how many languages people are talking here?"

I assent to her amazement.

"You know," she says, "if some Mohawks, or Penobscots, or whoever they'd be, crawled out of that shellheap, *some*body here could probably talk *Ind*ian to them. . . ."

Who, for instance?

Her eyes slide down the shell beach toward Cal in his L. L. Bean red shirt, his hands gesticulating wildly. "Well," she hesitates, "*prob*ably Mr. Lowell."

17

Cruising people often think of this as a good fogport, and we're fairly used to having old friends descend on us by boat in foul weather. But this August morning, in ample sun, we got a phonecall from an acquaintance on North Haven, asking if we could tonight take care of the friends who are chartering his boat. My father is visiting, Robin's in bed on this ninth birthday of hers; I was much relieved to find that Margaret and I were only being asked to locate rooms ashore for the charter party and, if possible, to meet them at the wharf when they made port. Then I got told who the charterers were, and how many; they took all the available rooms in the town's one inn.

I'm not used to Kennedys, even junior senators from Massachusetts, much less a whole Washington caucus of Kennedy friends. But they seemed pleased to be met at the wharf when they sailed in casually late; they were grateful for our having found rooms for them; and, yes, they'd love the ten minute tour of the town on the way to their inn. Places where history and revolution happened: the promontory where the French first landed thirteen years before Plymouth, the British fort that frightened Saltonstall into losing his fleet, the Paul Revere bell in the Unitarian Church—all these interest them. Turning, by the church, I point out the house that quartered British officers in 1812; and here, on the opposite corner of the Common, the house where the poet Robert Lowell lives. They might know that just this June, as an act of protest against our involvement in Viet Nam, he refused President Johnson's invitation to the White House. They do know. Could they meet him? I offer our Shed and drinks if that wouldn't interfere with their plans. They have no plans, beyond showers immediately and supper much later.

Elizabeth said she wouldn't come, thank you. "I've seen all I want to of those jet-set Kennedy women in their tight pants." Cal was amused, curious, pleased.

In due time everybody arrives at the summer livingroom at the ell-end of our house. Mieke Tunney, and John Culver's wife, and Joan, and Marieve and Paul Rugo, seem to have read Cal; John Tunney,[14] and Culver, and Ted Kennedy want to hear from Cal why he turned down the president. They do hear.

Talk gathers momentum though the drinking is slow. I am only on the edge of it, moving around to pass drinks and cheese, going to and from the kitchen. By the sink, Margaret and I exchange impressions; beyond liking Joan immediately, we find we're similarly astonished: these are the people who are running the country, and "they're all younger than we are."

But age is not why they defer to Cal. And as I tend the logs my father has lit in the big stone fireplace, I realize that what started as a casual symposium has mostly turned into a dialogue. Cal is at the fire-place end of the couch, Marieve Rugo and Mieke Tunney beside him, across from the big window looking out into fields. The others are variously spread round the room: in wicker chairs, on the bookcase under the window, on the floor by the fire. Just across a low bench from Cal, sitting in a ladderback chair, is Ted, leaning forward as far as his backbrace will allow. And he is conducting what has become a kind of sub-committee hearing, question after question being put to the expert witness.

Cal's grasp of politics is new to me, or newly marvellous. Out of nowhere, making analogues from his trip to Brazil, he begins naming South American names, and coming up with figures on income and distribution—figures which sound more like a Kennedy than a Cal. But the hands are Cal's, intensely moving, and so is the voice: a Beacon Hill nasality, varying always in pitch no matter how low the volume. As I go for drinks I catch only snatches:

"I didn't want to lend even tacit approval to what he's begun to do to us."

"*I* don't know what to do about it, Senator; that's up to you." His hand includes Iowa and California. "What I do know is that what we're doing in Viet Nam is only more terrible, and more visible, than what we're probably doing in Chile. Or what we've already done in Santo Domingo."

"You know more about power than I do. All I could do was do what I did. I was wrong at first, about wanting to go. It's awkward; it's painful, even, having to refuse a president. He's been good on domestic issues. But abroad we've got to stop him from using power as if it were his rather than ours. It'll take a lot of democracy to stop that."

Ted's voice now: more questions. His respect for Cal is obviously considerable; his courtesy is total. It occurs to me that Kennedy Boston is astounded to find patrician Boston so passionately informed.

". . . I'm conscience bound." Cal stops, then starts again: "We're not only corrupting them, we're corrupting ourselves in the process."

I catch this just coming back into the Shed. The fire has burned low, but none of us seems to have wanted to turn on any lights. In the heavy dusk, the voice at the center of the room is, hauntingly, the voice of an assassinated president.

Ted stops. Then everything quiets.

Cal has said his say.

They came late, and have stayed long. It is only mid-August; but now that everybody is leaving and saying thanks, we are each noticing and saying all at once the same thing: how quickly the dark has come down.

Philip Booth (b. 1925), American poet, Professor of English at Syracuse University and author of *Letter from a Distant Land* (1957), *Margins* (1970) and *Before Sleep* (1980), spent many summers with Lowell in Castine, Maine.

Salmagundi is a literary journal published at Skidmore College in Saratoga Springs, New York.

1. Sexually erect, like a stem.

2. Small town on Buzzards Bay, near Dartmouth, Massachusetts.

3. Elegant tennis club in Brookline, Massachusetts.

4. See No. 20, note 13.

5. Latin: a fallacious mode of argument—literally, "after this, therefore because of it."

6. Wallace Stevens, "The Comedian as the Letter C" (1923).

7. An allusion to Beaumont and Fletcher's play, *The Knight of the Burning Pestle* (1609).

8. Stoops, crouches.

9. Roethke, *The Far Field* (1964).

10. The party took place in April 1960.

11. Frederick Dupee, literary critic and Professor of English at Columbia University, author of *Henry James* (1951) and *The King of the Cats* (1965).

12. The American Field Service sponsored foreign students.

13. This makes no sense in Greek.

14. John Tunney (b. 1934), son of the boxing champion Gene Tunney; lawyer and senator from California, 1971–77.

25 • Robert Lowell, 1917–1977

A. Alvarez

Robert Lowell was the last of the brilliant generation of American poets who emerged after the last war—John Berryman, Theodore Roethke, Delmore Schwartz, Randall Jarrell—all of whom died before their time. Although Lowell lived longest, he was only sixty when he collapsed last Monday with a fatal heart attack in a New York taxi-cab.

He was a tall, stooping man with a benign, vaguely puzzled air but shrewd eyes which missed nothing. His thin, floating hair had recently turned white—perhaps because he had spent the last few years in England. He was born in 1917 one of the Boston Lowells—who "talked to the Cabots"—and, like Eliot, he was a Harvard man, though he did not stick it out, finishing at Kenyon College under the poet John Crowe Ransom.

Ransom, Tate and the other Southern poets of the Fugitive School influenced his speaking voice, which was full of strange Southern lifts and drawls, more than his style or his preoccupations. Technically, he was the heir of the great modernists, particularly Eliot, and began by exploring the rhetorical possibilities of their legacy while adapting it to a sensibility palpably rawer and less protected. From the start, he had an unwavering command of language, an extraordinary range of imagery and a knack of stamping each line with his own utterly individual rhythm.

He published his first two books, *Land of Unlikeness* and *Lord Weary's Castle,* in 1944 and 1946 when he was in his middle twenties. They won him all the prizes, including a Pulitzer, and established him immediately as an original, lavishly gifted new talent. This reputation was reinforced by his long poem *The Mills of the Kavanaughs* in 1951. All through the fifties Lowell's reputation grew. He became the darling of the New Criticism for which his rich, knotted poems were a godsend

Observer, 18 September 1977, p. 24. Reprinted by permission of Aitken & Stone, Ltd.

with their learning, their literary references and Catholic symbolism (he had converted in 1940, but left the Church a few years later).

Then in 1959 came *Life Studies,* a complete and unexpected change of direction and a book as revolutionary and influential in its way as *The Waste Land.* He turned his back on the symbolism and thickly textured Eliot-Jacobean language of his earlier work and began to write clearly, colloquially, about all the subjects which were taboo to the New Critics: his personal strains, domestic conflicts and the periodic breakdowns from which he had suffered for years.

> Tamed by *Miltown,* we lie on Mother's bed;
> the rising sun in war paint dyes us red;
> in broad daylight her gilded bed-posts shine,
> abandoned, almost Dionysian.
> At last the trees are green on Marlborough Street,
> blossoms on our magnolia ignite
> the morning with their murderous five days' white.
> All night I've held your hand,
> as if you had
> a fourth time faced the kingdom of the mad—
> its hackneyed speech, its homicidal eye—
> and dragged me home alive . . . oh my *Petite,*
> clearest of all God's creatures, still all air and nerve.[1]

He wrote without nagging or hysteria, and also without abandoning the skill, intelligence and tautness of line of his earlier work. The poems were not less concentrated, they were simply concentrated in a different way and for different ends: to capture lucidly and without rhetoric the experience as it really was, not as it might have been in an ideal poetic world. The result was a kind of transparency: you looked through the poems to see the man as he was, troubled, witty, vulnerable, balancing precariously between tenderness and violence.

In *Life Studies* and the books that followed, Lowell transformed poetry in much the same way as the action painters, who were working in New York at the same time, transformed the visual arts: not by turning it towards abstraction—he once told me that what he was aiming for was "a sort of Tolstoyan fulness"—but by his determination to cope artistically, with great concentration and directness, with the inner world, or with what another American poet, Hayden Carruth, called "the existential core."

In doing so, he altered the whole climate of poetry. His example set free other talented poets, most notably Sylvia Plath, who used the gains he had made to push on in their own different areas. After *Life Studies,* as after *The Waste Land,* nothing has quite been the same.

In this country his originality was acknowledged, but grudgingly, as though it were not quite the done thing for a serious poet to lay himself on the line so nakedly. Perhaps this was true of his many minor imitators, but with Lowell himself it was to ignore the great discipline and artistry which went into his apparent simplicity, and also to ignore his profound involvement in the technical skills he effortlessly deployed. He was continually rewriting his poems, as though to acknowledge both his own technical dissatisfaction and also the provisional nature of each work when measured against his artistic ambitions.

It was this aesthetic distance and discipline which set him apart from the minor exponents of the so-called "Confessional" school. It also gave his poems a curiously general, almost impersonal resonance. When he wrote nominally about his own crack-ups he seemed in the process to be describing the symptoms of crack-up in the society around him. In a liberal and individual way he had always been intensely concerned with American politics and history. In 1943, for example, he served five months in a federal prison when he refused to be conscripted because he considered the allied bombing of European cities morally indefensible. Much later, he turned down an invitation to the White House as a protest against President Johnson's Vietnam policy. He also campaigned strenuously when his friend Senator Eugene McCarthy ran for President. In his trilogy of plays, *The Old Glory,* and later in the poems collected in *History,* he was continually harping on the conflict between American idealism and American violence.

Life Studies was followed in 1962 by *Imitations,* a brilliant collection of very free translations, then in 1965 by the equally stunning *For the Union Dead,* then by the lyrical but more regular *Near the Ocean* in 1967. After that he began a long series of shorter, tighter poems first collected as *Notebook,* then expanded and republished in three separate volumes, *History, For Lizzie and Harriet* and *The Dolphin.* None of these quite achieved the marvellous power and ease of *Life Studies.* He seemed stifled, almost stultified by the condensed forms he had imposed on himself. He abandoned them, however, a couple of years ago and was writing again in the freer, more open style of his best work. A new collection, *Day by Day,* has just appeared in the USA.

He was, I think, the finest poet of his greatly gifted generation—

wide-ranging, subtle, powerful—whose influence on contemporary verse has been as profound as anyone's since Eliot. In private, he was a brilliant, allusive talker, and a courteous, most generous friend. He had been married three times, always to talented writers: Jean Stafford, Elizabeth Hardwick and Caroline Blackwood.

1. Lowell, "Man and Wife."

26 • Remembering Lowell

Michael Schmidt, Seamus Heaney, Peter Levi, Richard Ellmann, A. Alvarez and M. L. Rosenthal

Michael Schmidt: Robert Lowell died yesterday in New York at the age of sixty. The shock of his death is all the more vivid because he has been a vital presence among us for so many years, the greatest poet in an outstanding generation that included John Berryman, Randall Jarrell and Delmore Schwartz. He was the final survivor of that ill-starred generation. Last week, he was in Dublin, where he met with Seamus Heaney.

Seamus Heaney: The shock this morning was because he had been over in Ireland last week and Caroline and himself were in our house this night week, in fact, and we had a very happy occasion. He brought his new book, *Day by Day,* Caroline brought her new book, *Great Granny Webster,* and we had looked forward to meeting again. And the news this morning was—well, incredible. He was a poet who lived for his art and through his art and who maintained the status of artist, if you like.

Peter Levi: I thought he was the most engaging man, very kind, long awkward arms, big head, great beam, appeared to be almost zany, incapable of concentrating, and yet everything he said was immensely intelligent and concentrated. He was a man who one actually loved. He wanted to be loved and he did love, himself—he gave love in all circumstances, I think. When he came into some restaurant, like we used to go to Chez Victor in London, one was immediately cheered by the mere sight of him, dropping shirt buttons and magazines in his trail. Now that he has gone, we're going to feel a loss, not just personal but in poetry, which we can't appreciate yet because it's hard to know what it will be like without somebody like Lowell.

I think we've lost the greatest poet now writing, so far as I know, in any language. We've lost a huge part of our tradition which will never be replaced. There aren't going to be poets as great as that for another few years. With Robert Lowell one had the consciousness of being on this

Listener 98 (22 September 1977): 379–380. Reprinted by permission of Michael Schmidt.

earth at the same time as a poet who took everything very seriously. He had a quality of earnestness in the good Victorian sense, like Matthew Arnold. To read his poetry was to hear serious things seriously talked about by a contemporary. There isn't much of that.

Richard Ellmann: There is a continual effort in his poetry to expose himself in a particular way, a kind of Lowell way. It's not exactly the confessional mode that one sometimes assumes it is, even though there are many personal details in it, quotations from letters and the like. It's as if the universe were confessing through Lowell.

A. Alvarez: He had a curiously benign, almost saint-like manner, vaguely puzzled, vaguely confused, very nervous, very shy, very well mannered, Boston—but in fact that concealed a very shrewd, rather beady eye—he didn't miss anything.

He had a very complex relationship with John Berryman. They were both highly ambitious and highly productive people and they kind of competed. But it was on a very civilised level. Berryman had produced, over ten or twelve years, this marvellous sequence of short poems which added up to one very long poem, and I think Lowell took this form in order to show he could do it better than Berryman. That's putting it vulgarly, but I think there was a certain element of that in it. I think it was a mistake. I think he needed all through his life to get free of constrictions, and the whole history of his development as a poet is one of freeing himself from unnecessary rules. I think he is—or was until he died yesterday—the greatest living poet in the English language at this moment. But I don't think it showed in those later, rather compact, condensed poems.

M. L. Rosenthal: I reviewed *Life Studies* for the *Nation*,[1] and I was struck by the power of the book. It was the first embodiment of the fact that we had a new body of modern poetry that was powerful, that was more immediately frank; and, in fact, in that review, I coined the expression "confessional poetry," which I meant to have a very special meaning. It was a poetry that gave the game away shamelessly but was redeemed aesthetically by the artistic quality which it achieved at the same time.

Alvarez: There's a very good essay by Randall Jarrell about reviewing bad poetry, in which he says that you get these poems which are really unreviewable because they deal with the most unspeakable experiences but don't do anything with them—they just record them. He says it's as though someone sent you through the mail a severed leg and

scrawled on it in lipstick, "This is a poem."[2] Now I would have thought
that that certainly is what happens in a lot of the poems of Allen Ginsberg
and the Beats. I would have thought it unfortunately happens far too
often in the poems of Anne Sexton. But Lowell and Plath remained
artists. They were trained in the Fifties, they knew about literature, they
knew about what should go into poetry, and they had served their ap-
prenticeship, they had all the necessary skills, so that when their devil, or
muse, or whatever you want to call it, finally took them by the throat,
they had the skill to cope with it.

Levi: There are two obvious things that distinguish him from other
people: first, probably alone among poets writing now, he's the only one
to have come from a very grand traditional background, from which
admittedly he broke away—but that's rather unusual in a poet nowa-
days. And second, he's a real human being, in a way that most of my
friends and contemporaries try to hide. By that I mean that he's had
torment all his life. He was, as you know, mentally ill. There was a
physical basis for this—I knew that he wouldn't live long because I asked
a doctor about his disease. He was constantly plagued by fits of madness.
He was a very loving man but that also was affected by the madness, so
that although he could give such happiness to other people, there was
also pain, and he knew a lot about that. He was always conscious of it. I
think all the consciousness of that makes him more human, more open
than most poets now writing.

Schmidt: We have one more collection of poems that Robert Lowell
saw through press—*Day by Day,* published in America but not yet in
Britain, though we will see it next spring. Seamus Heaney has read it.

Heaney: There's something tremendously autumnal about it. It be-
gins with poems of tremendous power, the Ulysses[3] poems that ap-
peared in the *New Review,* a good bit of terror and compulsion in them.
But it relaxes out into—oh, what I remember is sunflowers, elder-
flowers—golden. And it ends with a couple of poems of repose, really,
one called "Thanks Offering for Recovery"—and the last poem is about
the difficulties and the rewards of writing and the help that the skills of
writing are and yet the challenge that the mess of life is.

Michael Schmidt (b. 1947), English editor and publisher at Carcanet Press,
is the author of *Black Buildings* (1969) and *Change of Affairs* (1978). Seamus
Heaney (b. 1939), Irish poet, is the author of *Death of a Naturalist* (1966), *Door into*

the Dark (1969), *Wintering Out* (1972), *North* (1975) and *Field Work* (1979). Peter Levi (b. 1931), Classicist, poet and travel writer, Professor of Poetry at Oxford University, is the author of *Water, Rock and Sand* (1962) and *The Lightgarden of the Angel King* (1973). Richard Ellmann (1918–87), major American biographer and critic, and Emeritus Goldsmiths' Professor of English at Oxford University, is the author of *Yeats: The Man and the Masks* (1948) and *James Joyce: A Biography* (1959). M. L. Rosenthal (b. 1917), American critic and Professor of English at New York University, is the author of *The Modern Poets* (1960) and *Sailing into the Unknown* (1978).

    1. See M. L. Rosenthal, "Poetry as Confession," *Nation* 189 (19 September 1959): 154–155.

    2. Randall Jarrell, "A Verse Chronicle," *Poetry and the Age* (New York, 1953), p. 176.

    3. See Lowell, "Ulysses and Circe."

27 • Robert Lowell

Patrick Cosgrave

In 1969 I published *The Public Poetry of Robert Lowell*. Like, I suppose, any author of a first book, I waited in anxiety for the reviews. Two weeks passed. Then, in these columns, Martin Seymour-Smith blasted my work to kingdom come.[1] I thought I was more right than Smith about the merits and demerits of Lowell's work; but I had, then, no recourse. A week later, however, I got a letter.

In its course Lowell invited me to lunch. More to the point, he agreed with my strictures on his poem, "Mr Edwards and the Spider." Indeed, he said, the last three and a half stanzas were "obtuse and irrelevant." He offered a new version of the poem, dedicated to me. Thus honoured, who needed reviewers?

We met in the flat he then had, near Hyde Park. We both drank a good deal of whisky, and walked up and down past one another for some time before I dared ask him why he had invited me to lunch: after all, the book was not, taken all in all, very friendly. "You tore four-fifths of my gut out," he said, 'but you sure liked the fifth that was left." We went out and had a good lunch, and talked late into the afternoon about prosody. My—then and still unfashionable—preference was for his early work over the collection *Life Studies,* in which he laid bare in shaky and sometimes non-existent metre the wrack of his soul and mind. I also thought, however, that he had never done anything finer than "Waking Early Sunday Morning." I remember then, and I remember now, the sense of barely controllable excitement I felt when I first read that magnificent paean to joy and despair:

> O to break loose, like the chinook
> salmon jumping and falling back,
> nosing up to the impossible
> stone and bone-crushing waterfall—
> raw-jawed, weak-fleshed there, stopped by ten

Spectator 239 (24 September 1977): 26. Reprinted by permission of Patrick Cosgrave.

steps of the roaring ladder, and then
to clear the top on the last try,
alive enough to spawn and die.

For the next few weeks I saw a lot of Lowell. Even in his lightest
moments he was forever in turmoil. Writing, even feeling, caused in him
an agony that, it seemed, could be assuaged only by drink or mania. It
was as though spiritually he had a supersensitive skin all over and this
meant, alas, that he was frequently unable to assess the real value of any
particular feeling and unable, too, to find in himself the intellectual disci-
pline needed for that tempered structure of judgement of experience
which is in his finest metres. The more I saw of him the more I felt the
truth of R. P. Blackmur's judgement that ". . . in dealing with men his
faith compels him to be fractiously vindictive, and in dealing with faith,
his experience of men compels him to be nearly blasphemous."[2] So close
to the edge of things did he seem to live that I was always amazed by—
and immensely grateful for—the kindliness and generosity he displayed
in finding time again and again to talk at length to a novice critic, always
with a kind of fitful yet blazing insight.

Then I lost touch with him. His work after *Near the Ocean* seemed to
me very rarely to reach the heights of "Waking Early Sunday Morning."
He was incapable of writing a dull line, and there was something arrest-
ing about nearly everything he did. But the superlative, racing discipline
of that great poem he could not, it seemed, recapture. His political
preoccupations, always intense, took him more and more out towards
fringe events and phenomena. My own path, anyway, led me somewhat
away from literature, and into politics. When I heard something of him,
or saw a new poem or a new volume, it was like saluting a lost friend
from afar.

Then, in 1975, he telephoned. His wife, Caroline Blackwood, was
planning a piece on Margaret Thatcher: he wanted me to talk to her, and
to arrange an introduction. "Are you still interested in poetry?" he
asked, "I suppose now you have to be, more than ever." The sentence
was a striking illustration of his complete and unforced conviction that
poetry was a necessary public activity, an essential method of judging the
affairs of men and of state.

After our meeting—where the booze and the talk flowed as though
there had been no interval—he fell into one of his deep depressions, and
was again under psychiatric care. In the most general sense his real trouble

was that he needed—and knew he needed—God, but could never bring himself to believe for any great length of time that God was there, for

> The breath of God had carried out a planned
> And sensible withdrawal from this land;[3]

To the end, however, he sustained, against all the odds, an extraordinary, almost tactile, appreciation of life and nature, a grip on beauty and on the phenomena of life, and an ability to render love and pleasure and understanding in a way no other modern poet could. He understood, too, how even inadequate religious observance "left a loophole for the soul." But the final vision, superbly rendered, instinct with a life that denied his own conclusion, was sombre:

> Pity the planet, all joy gone
> from this sweet volcanic cone;
> peace to our children when they fall
> in small war on the heels of small
> war—until the end of time
> to police the earth, a ghost
> orbiting for ever lost
> in our monotonous sublime.[4]

Patrick Cosgrave (b. 1941), English critic and biographer, is the author of *The Public Poetry of Robert Lowell* (1970), *Churchill at War* (1974) and *Margaret Thatcher* (1978).

1. See Martin Seymour-Smith, "The Lowell That Never Was," *Spectator* 225 (3 October 1970): 367.
2. R. P. Blackmur, "Notes on Seven Poets," *Kenyon Review* 7 (Spring 1945): 348.
3. Lowell, "After Surprising Conversions."
4. Lowell, "Waking Early Sunday Morning."

28 • The Things of the Eye

Robert Fitzgerald

Robert Traill Spence Lowell, James Russell Lowell's older brother, born in 1816, Harvard Class of 1833, became headmaster of St. Mark's School and taught at Union College. As Robert Lowell he published works of fiction and works in verse, including a sentimental narrative, "The Relief of Lucknow," which was still making the school readers when I was in school. Mr. Lowell died in 1891. His grandson, the third to bear the name, was born in Boston on March 1, 1917, and became the poet whom we have come here to remember. Our Robert Lowell went to St. Mark's and then to Harvard for two years, but he did not find what he wanted at Harvard. He wanted a master in poetry, and he found one in the person of John Crowe Ransom at Kenyon College in Ohio. He studied there under Mr. Ransom and a young instructor named Randall Jarrell, majored in Classics, and graduated with a *summa* in 1940. In that year he married the fiction writer Jean Stafford and became a Roman Catholic.

The poems that Lowell published six years later in the book called *Lord Weary's Castle* were tentative in no respect whatever. They were, as Mr. Ransom liked to put it, "written"—that is, written to stay. They were astonishing as formal works in verse and also as concentrated works of imagination. His Lowell grandfather of the feebly pious and breezy writings would have been stunned—an effect probably not unwelcome to the poet. Milton and Donne were behind these poems; so were Crane, Empson, and Tate. Fictional and even satiric modes entered into the imagination in question, but the drift was lyric and prophetic. As religious poetry, Lowell's hardly had a precedent even in the extremes of baroque. When the speaker in one poem besought the Mother of God with her "scorched blue thunderbreasts of love" to pour "buckets of blessings" on his "burning head,"[1] one apprehended a verse builder working with intensities close to madness.

Poetry 132 (May 1978): 107–111. Reprinted by permission of the Estate of Robert Fitzgerald.

Lowell, Jarrell, and John Berryman—all friends of each other, all a few years younger than I—became friends of mine in New York in the late 1940s and in my memory and judgment had almost no rivals but one another as poets in that generation. To some extent Jarrell kept the role of instructor that he had first had for Lowell. His long and beautiful review of Lowell's poems, a review well entitled "From the Kingdom of Necessity," in the *Nation* for January 18, 1947, announced a new major poet in America. But the instructor could also poke fun at his student. With Berryman on hand, Jarrell once amused himself by making up for Lowell a glorious new poem with such Lowell properties as Charon, Grandfather Winslow, and the Apocalypse. . . . These were brilliant, mordant, and lighthearted young men. They faced the age of anxiety with nerve and love, and they had hard lives.

In Washington in 1948, when he was Consultant in Poetry at the Library of Congress, Cal Lowell did a lot of reading or rereading in Virgil. On a visit I made, he showed me his new poem, "Falling Asleep over the Aeneid," that marvel of dreamwork as historical imagination to which I was happy to contribute the right spelling of "turms"—Roman squadrons of horsemen. His spelling, and his block letter writing, were among the many traces of boyhood that stayed with him through life. Tall, gentle, big-boned, humorous, teasing, sly; moved to glee over phrases and fantasies; devoted to friends; he loved company as he loved the labor of verse-making—but that he loved most of all. Berryman used to muse respectfully over Cal's innumerable drafts in those years and the permutations they underwent. He remembered with relish one poem first entitled "To Jean" that ended up entitled "To a Whore at the Brooklyn Navy Yard."

In Rome in November, 1948, George Santayana, august in his dressing gown at the convent of the Blue Nuns, spoke with a certain speculative wonder of the correspondence he had been having with young Lowell. It interested the author of *The Last Puritan* first that a Lowell had been a Catholic convert and, second, that he should now with enthusiasm be sending him, Santayana, the works of William Carlos Williams. "I think I understand them," he said, "but why all the excitement?" He went on to say that after at first supposing that when they met Lowell would be afraid of him "because of the writing and all that," he now foresaw being afraid of Lowell. They did later meet, with what division of trepidation I don't know, and Lowell's image of Santayana, one of his most haunting, appeared in the superb poem dated

1952, "Beyond the Alps." In this poem Lowell, as one line had it, "left the City of God where it belongs"—a departure of a kind from the Church of Rome. As to his promotion of Williams, it was very like Cal to magnify in Williams, and in Pound, as he did, freedoms and naked non-metrical beauties that at that point he felt to be beyond him. "That's genius," he said to me groaning over a line of Pound's,* "one would give anything for that."

In this hankering there is one motive for the free, or free-er, verse poems of Lowell's second period, the period of *Life Studies,* published in 1959. But what lies much more importantly behind those poems and henceforth all his work is his breakdown of 1949 and the necessity he now felt of governing his greatness with his illness in mind. Manic attacks now and again would put him in the hospital, overborne by the fever that one had felt to be just beyond some of his poems from the beginning. But now with his second wife, Elizabeth Hardwick, he traveled in Europe, taught at Iowa and Boston University, and lived for several years in Boston in the mid-Fifties.

When he was in Italy after his mother's death at Rapallo, he came out to Fiesole for dinner with the Fitzgeralds and brought his friend and translator, Rolando Anzilotti, a young professor at Pisa and mayor of a small Tuscan town. The new poem that evening concerned high Renaissance politics and, amid many grandeurs, made out Catherine de' Medici to be "round as a cannon," a phrase that has pleased me ever since. A few years later the magnolia was out in the front yard when I went to see him and Elizabeth and their baby, Harriet, in the Boston house on Marlborough Street—one of the scenes in *Life Studies.* Always a prodigious reader, in these years he began taking in armloads of the western world's best poetry and possessing it by translating it—Juvenal, Racine, Villon, Baudelaire, Leopardi, Montale. Some of these *Imitations,* published in 1962, did not work for me but some were very fine. I remember—it must have been 1961—a whole afternoon of pleasure in New York, going over with him his versions of Baudelaire: strongly knit rhymed stanzas and some great simplicities that his ear had given him, as in "The dead, the poor dead, they have their bad hours" for a memorable Baudelairean line.

By this time he and Elizabeth had adopted New York life in the winter and life in Castine, Maine, in the summer—the pattern of their

---

*"Capaneus; trout for factitious bait"; from "Hugh Selwyn Mauberley."

life in the Sixties. Cal's fame and influence had grown, and he became a public figure. By far the best portrait of him as such is Mailer's in *Armies of the Night,* the point being that the public figure and the private figure— myopic, hulking, diffident, formidable, wry, companionable, sombre— were the same. In middle age, in 1963, I believe, he found something he wanted at Harvard, as in his youth he had not—in this case a job, for the fall term usually: classes to hold, students to teach. He commuted by the air shuttle from New York. When he got sick, his devoted friend William Alfred and others rallied round and met his classes. Of the poems of those years, *For the Union Dead, Near the Ocean,* and *Notebook,* Alan Williamson has done a responsive and clarifying study in his book, *Pity the Monsters,* subtitled "The Political Vision of Robert Lowell."

After 1970, when I began to teach in the same fall term, I saw Cal regularly again. During the rest of the year he was soon now living in England, in Kent, with his third wife, Caroline Blackwood, and their little boy, Sheridan. Cal was fond of his attachment to Harvard, and Harvard felt his presence. Just as in the world at large he embodied the best of social and political protest among the young, so for a generation of students here he embodied, as a Lowell, as a great poet, something intangible but profound in Harvard tradition—and for those students Harvard without him will never be the same. In these latter years one of the joys of Cambridge life was having lunch with him, beginning with gazpacho or garlic soup, at the Iruña after his morning "office hours" in Quincy House or Holyoke Center or, last year, in Emerson Hall. When Peter Taylor was here—his old Kenyon classmate—we lunched to- gether. Beginning three years ago we heard of a heart condition and, alcohol being off his list, he drank many glasses of iced tea. But even after he had been laid up in Massachusetts General for his heart a year ago, though to some friends he seemed frail and tired, he seemed so happily his old self to me that I never guessed his death could be near him. In June each gave the other his blessing for the summer, and I never saw him again.

This is not the occasion nor am I the critic to attempt a formal estimate of Lowell's life work. Very roughly speaking, I'd say he exerted a giant's pressure on language and experience. In verse and prose, he had great intelligence and literary power. What he wrote and what he *was* dignified for many people their own metaphysical predicaments in the world of twentieth-century choices that, under great difficulties, he tried bravely to meet. What I have called the dreamwork in so many of his poems was, I think, the rare and quintessential poetic thing, that without which the imagination in words cannot move or transport us. On the other hand, the proportion of this in his work was very high. He trusted it very far. The result now and then was the "senseless" quality that even Jarrell spoke of. By comparison Auden—to take another public poet— by keeping Augustan literary standards, impersonal and empirical criteria, perplexed and burdened us less. But the strange mass and monumentality of Lowell were all his own. So was the occasional shiver of his music, like this:

> Before the final coming to rest, comes the rest
> of all transcendence in a mode of being, hushing
> all becoming. I'm for and with myself in my otherness,
> in the eternal return of earth's fairer children,
> the lily, the rose, the sun on brick at dusk,
> the loved, the lover, and their fear of life.
> their unconquered flux, insensate oneness, painful "It was . . . ."[2]

Another line of his, about a room in the dark, runs: "The things of the eye are done."[3] It is true of our dear friend now: the things of the eye are done for him. But the things of what we need not flinch to call the spirit— since it is so obvious—these are not done for him, and will not be.

Robert Fitzgerald (1910–85), American poet and translator of the *Odyssey* (1961), *The Iliad* (1974) and Greek tragedies, was Boylston Professor at Harvard and a friend of Lowell.

1. Lowell, "A Prayer for my Grandfather to Our Lady."
2. Lowell, "Obit."
3. Lowell, "Myopia: A Night."

29 • The Sense of a Life

Stanley Kunitz

On the afternoon of Tuesday, September 13, I was in Naples, in the flag-draped auditorium of the United States Information Center, meeting with a small group of university professors to talk with them about American poetry. Our informal conversation had scarcely begun when one of them leaned forward and said, "Have you heard about Mr. Lovell? He's dead. Did you know him?" I caught my breath. Did I know him! Yes, in a hundred phases, the myriad contradictions of one who was both Puritan and satyr, alternately silly and wise, modest and arrogant, tender and mean, generous and indifferent, masterful and helpless, depressed and manic.

Everywhere Cal (as he was known to his friends) went he brought his turmoil with him, hand-in-hand with his batch of stained and crumpled manuscripts. "I am tired," he had written. "Everyone is tired of my turmoil."[1] His blue-gray eyes behind his glasses were vague and restless, till they began to glitter. He seemed so full of self, so disconnected from his surroundings, that you could not believe he noticed anything; but somehow, indoors or out, little escaped him. On his next visit to your place he would inquire about a painting or a piece of bric-a-brac that had been moved, joke about the gain in weight of your fat cat Celia, or comment on the most trivial household acquisition. In the garden or on a country walk he would ply you with questions about the names and properties of flowers, about which he appeared to be totally ignorant; but then he would astonish you by publishing a poem full of precise horticultural detail.

His talk was expressive with gesture, the stirring of an invisible broth, interspersed with the shaping of a vase in air—or was it Lilith's[2] archetypal curves that he was fashioning? When he slumped onto your sofa like an extended question mark, tumbler in hand, chain-smoking,

New York Times Book Review, 16 October 1977, pp. 3, 34, 36. Reprinted by permission of Stanley Kunitz.

dropping his ashes, spouting gossip or poetry, you knew that the moon would have to drift across the sky before he would be ready to go, leaving at least one memorial cigarette hole burnt into cushion or rug behind him. You were bleary with fatigue, but you cherished the rare electricity of his presence. And you would have been desolate if he had not returned.

How could I say all or anything of that to my amiable Italian professors? To them Robert Lowell was an abstract eminence, already historical, a spirit of civilization wafted from on high over the airwaves. *The famous American poet died last night in New York.* No doubt the same report had been flashed to Rome, Paris, Berlin, Madrid, Moscow, Istanbul and beyond. After Eliot and Pound, had the death of any other American poet been treated as world news? I picked up *The Norton Anthology,* which I had brought along with me, and read "For the Union Dead" in tribute. What would a foreign audience make of its complex and highly allusive text? Their impression, I soon learned, was that the poem was somehow tied to the Vietnam War, though in truth it had been written several years before we got into that mess. Its density of local Boston color and Civil War documentation was difficult for them to penetrate: yet they listened with polite and even reverential attention. Indeed, fame has its mysteries and advantages.

Most of Lowell's poems—with the conspicuous exception of those in *Life Studies*—move too fast to be grasped at a hearing. They have the velocity of a mountain torrent precipitating silt and stones down into the valley. He himself read them rather badly, in a high nasal quaver to project emotion, lapsing intermittently into a toneless mumble. "Santayana," he told me, "spoke the truth when he said that a lecture hall is a place of mismatch. The man on the platform is racing on horseback while the audience plods ahead on foot." In order to liven the proceedings he took to telling rambling anecdotes between his poems at a reading. Once, Roethke, who preferred a more melodic line than Lowell's, accused him to his face of having "a tin ear." Cal tried to pass the incident off as a piece of drunken foolery, but I know the charge rankled, for he recalled it to me years later, after Ted had died.

I have never known anyone so singularly immersed in writing as was Cal. Berryman and Roethke may have vied with him in this respect, but his concentration on the literary landscape was more unremitting: he watched its weather with the diligent attention of a meteorologist, studying its prevailing winds, regularly charting its high and low pressure area. "All my friends are writers." With his tidy inheritance he had more leisure and fewer responsibilities than most of us. Protected by his physical awkwardness, which did not prevent him on occasion from projecting an image of noble public grace, he avoided being handy around the house; no sports or hobbies distracted him except, perhaps, for the game of rating his contemporaries—the game he loved to play at parties, especially when inferiors were present, with high-keyed zest and malice. At home the daemon drove him to his desk; even in strange hotels he kept on scribbling, covering loose scraps of paper with his shaky, nondescript block-letter hand.

One forgave Cal for much because one recognized his instability. Madness never ceased to threaten him, and periodically it struck him down. In his twenties he had already perceived his fate:

> Your lacerations tell the losing game
> You play against a sickness past your cure.
> How will the hands be strong? How will the heart endure?[3]

For a while he sought refuge in the Catholic Church, but it failed him. Eros, who perennially beckoned, only reflected his mania, adding to his tumult. The two constants that he clung to, as elements of continuum in the precarious flux, were history and friendship, whose beauty is that they abide. "We are dear old friends," he would say at parting, with the stress on "old," as if time had managed to seal this covenant. Allen Tate, Randall Jarrell, Elizabeth Bishop and Peter Taylor were even older friends, who had already been elevated, alive or dead, to angelic company. To him their works were sacred texts, though sometimes he would concede that even angels erred.

Most poets tend to resist criticism, and Lowell was no exception, fuming as others did about negative reviews. On the other hand, his method of composition was uniquely collaborative. He made his friends, willy-nilly, partners in his act, by showering them with early drafts of his poems, often so fragmentary and shapeless that it was no great trick to suggest improvements. Sometimes you saw a poem in half a dozen successive versions, each new version ampler and bolder than the last. You would recognize your own suggestions embedded in the text—a phrase here and there, a shift in the order of the lines—and you might wonder how many other hands had been involved in the process. It did not seem to matter much, for the end product always presented itself as infallibly, unmistakably Lowellian. Even so, he kept modifying his poems each time they appeared in print. Like the stream of Heraclitus, you could never dip into the same poem twice. Once the ghost of Jarrell appeared in a dream to him, scolding, "You didn't write, you *re*-wrote."[4] In a sense the representative voice of our age was a collective poet.

During the anguished period of his separation and divorce from Elizabeth Hardwick I quarreled with him about the inclusion, in his poems, of raw material from her letters to him. It seemed to me a cruel invasion of her privacy, morally and esthetically objectionable. In April 1972, after his marriage to Caroline Blackwood and the birth of their son Robert Sheridan, he wrote to me from Milgate Park, Kent, where they were living:

"Now full spring weather. Ivana [a stepdaughter] back at school. Sheridan eating everything in sight: blanket, rug, small dog, our fingers—a microcosm of James Dickey, but on the wagon. Lovely.

"About your criticism. I expect to be back in New York for a week beginning the 21st of May, and hope to unwind over drinks with you. Dolphin is somewhat changed with the help of Elizabeth Bishop. The long birth sequence will come before the Flight to New York, a stronger conclusion, and one oddly softening the effect by giving a reason other than new love for my departure. Most of the letter poems—E.B.'s objection they were part fiction offered as truth—can go back to your old plan, a mixture of my voice, and another voice in my head, part me, part Lizzie, italicized, paraphrased, imperfectly, obsessively heard. I take it, it is these parts that repel you. I tried the new version out on Peter Taylor, and he couldn't imagine any moral objection to Dolphin. Not that the poem, alas, from its donnée, can fail to wound. *For Lizzie and Harriet* doesn't go with *History*, it goes before *Dolphin*, but I thought it was too sensational, *confessing*, to bring the two books out together. I think you are right, tho, and I'll do something. *History* somehow echoes and stands aside from the other books. Do you think I could comb out enough excrescences from History to do much good? The metal too often reforged wears out. Maybe you could put your finger on a few of the worst. It must be as good almost as I can make it."

In November 1973, after the simultaneous publication, in three separate volumes, of *History, For Lizzie and Harriet* and *The Dolphin*, Lowell gave a reading at the Pierpont Morgan Library in New York. What I said then, at the conclusion of my introduction of him, sums up my understanding of the nature and meaning of his achievement:

"One of the disarming features of Lowell's work is that it does not pretend to aspire to the condition of an absolute art. He tells us the time in the right kind of voice for the day. He does not try to overpower us with a show of strength; instead, with his nervous vivacity, he hurries to build a chain of fortifications out of sand, or even dust. A revisionist by nature, he is forever tinkering with his old lines, rewriting his old poems, revamping his syntax, and periodically reordering his existence.

" 'It may be,' he has remarked, 'that some people have turned to my poems because of the very things that are wrong with me, I mean the difficulty I have with ordinary living, the impracticability, the myopia.'[5] Nobody else sounds quite like that. He makes us excruciatingly aware of the thrashing of the self behind the lines; of the intense fragility of the psyche trying to get a foothold in an 'air of lost connections,' struggling to stay human and alive. He is a poet who will even take the risk of sounding flat or dawdling in the hope that it might be true. What we get from these poems is the sense of a life . . . a life that has been turned into a style."

In the end, the effort consumed him. He felt that he had turned, at the cost of his humanity, into a kind of literary monster, a machine for producing verse:

> I have sat and listened to too many
> words of the collaborating muse,
> and plotted perhaps too freely with my life,
> not avoiding injury to others,
> not avoiding injury to myself—[6]

It had required a heroic endeavor to construct the strong persona of his poems: actually, he had only a weak grip on his identity. In manic episodes he had confused himself with Christ, St. Paul and Hitler— particularly Hitler, whose dark spirit rose violently to possess him. Men of power had always fascinated him. Once, when I visited him at McLean's Hospital in Boston, he read "Lycidas" aloud to me, in his improved version, firmly convinced that he was the author of the original.

Even his political convictions were more tentative than they appeared to be in his public statements. His eloquent rejection of President

Johnson's invitation to the White House Festival of the Arts in 1965 had won him worldwide attention and had helped mobilize the forces of opposition to the Vietnam War, the forces that eventually brought John-son down. Few realized that he had first accepted the invitation and then rescinded his acceptance at the urgent solicitation of a handful of friends. The name of Lowell was needed to catapult the story onto the front page of the *New York Times*. Politically and esthetically, a deep strain of con-servatism opposed his liberal, humanitarian and avant-garde leanings.

He had written of Flaubert, "the supreme artist," that "the mania for phrases enlarged his heart."[7] Now the doctors had warned him that his own heart was dangerously enlarged. In *History* he had described his work as "this open book . . . my open coffin." The furious compulsion to tell his story pained and exhausted him. The ants were to be envied, for not being "under anathema to make it new."[8] He longed to emulate Mallarmé, "who had the good fortune to find a style that made writing impossible." Pound, Wilson, Auden, Berryman, Ransom were all freshly dead: "The old boys drop like wasps / from windowsill and pane." Both his parents, he chose to remember, had died of heart attacks at sixty. He hoped to die as insects do in mid-autumn, "instantly as one would ask of a friend."

He had his wish, dying at sixty in a taxicab, on his way from Kennedy Airport after a flight from England. A fragment was found among his papers:

> Christ,
> May I die at night
> With a semblance of my senses
> Like the full moon that fails.

1. Lowell, "Eye and Tooth."
2. In Jewish folklore, Adam's wife before Eve was created.
3. Lowell, "Mr. Edwards and the Spider."
4. Lowell, "Randall Jarrell 3."
5. See Kunitz's interview with Lowell (No. 7).
6. Lowell, "Dolphin."
7. Lowell, "Les Mots."
8. Lowell, "The Ants."

30 • Robert Lowell, 1917–1977

John Thompson

Forty years ago in the carpenter's Gothic of Douglass House, demolished now, at Gambier, Ohio, in the long gabled upstairs room he shared with Peter Taylor, Robert Lowell had the intelligent habit of lying in bed all day. Around that bed like a tumble-down brick wall were his Greek Homer, his Latin Vergil, his Chaucer, letters from Boston, cast-off socks, his Dante, his Milton. Even in those days before he had published a word we knew he belonged among the peers who surrounded him.

The poems he wrote and rewrote and rewrote in bed then were as awkward as he was, the man of the Kenyon squad who plowed sideways into his own teammates, but strong as a bull, spilling them all over, who never won a game. He aspired to be a Rhodes Scholar, and thus had to be an all-around man like Whizzer White.[1] In those days Lowell couldn't tie his own shoe laces.

To our astonishment this nearly inarticulate fellow entered the Ohio state oratory contest. But we were not surprised at all when like Demosthenes he won the prize.

Lowell has written about his mother Charlotte and his father the Naval Commander. Charlotte was a Snow Queen who flirted coldly and shamelessly with her son. His father once ordered a half-bottle of wine for five at dinner.

Lowell brought Jean Stafford to Kenyon, shining she was, wearing a hat and gloves, tucked under her arm a mint copy from England of something mysterious to us, *Goodbye to Berlin!* They married, and, new Catholics, after a year on the *Southern Review* under Brooks and Warren, they holed up in Maine, as both have written. He went to jail as an objector to the War after attempts to get in the Navy. He didn't like it that we had started bombing cities.

New York Review of Books 24 (27 October 1977): 14–15. Reprinted by permission of John Thompson.

He lived in a fleabag under the old Third Avenue El on about a dollar a day. In the room next door dwelled an ardent couple. "Be quiet," one of them whispered, "the kid there might hear us." He read all the books, and wrote and rewrote his poems. History was his eye-opener and his nightcap. He recited Vergil with Robert Fitzgerald. When he came to supper he ate enough for three days, and then graciously said, "I'm stuffed." He got the Pulitzer Prize.

He went crazy, and being brought toward home after a cross-country charge he squatted, powerful and sweating, in the rotunda that was then LaGuardia airport. The cops came and sat down on the floor with him. They discussed Italian opera. He was taken to the first asylum. Cured, well-known now, he kept writing his wonderful poems. He married Elizabeth Hardwick who brought him up. She gave him Harriet his daughter.

They moved from Boston to New York. Many times Elizabeth, as if Alcestis[2] had had to do it over and over, faced the kingdom of the mad and dragged him home alive.[3] He wrote frankly about his illness. This did not mean he thought it a distinction. He hated it, hated making a fool of himself and being a trouble to other people, hated the time and work lost to it. Everything the doctors prescribed he did but the illness had its own power of accessions and remissions.

Some Lowell money and his own solid earnings brought him and his family a living in fair style. The elegance, grace, and power of a great man came to him without his noticing.

He was big, well-shouldered, and light on his feet but bore a notice-able physical diffidence like a polite stammer. His face was big, gnathic,[4] and classically formed, with owl spectacles that slid down his nose, and his head was feathered around later with his longish gray hair. His fingers were clean and delicate. He poked and pointed with them as he talked. Teasing or telling stories, for instance his endless saga of the tribe of bears whose misbehaviors parodied those of his friends and relations, he had a special sing-song voice. Otherwise, except in public reading, it was a Boston soar then mutter. His only sport was trout-fishing.

He had confounded his old mentors with *Life Studies,* which they said was not literature, and he should not publish. They were right, it was not literature. Blake and Whitman and the man he oddly admired so much, Hart Crane, were not literature either but they made literature move over for them.

Calligraphers recognize in one another's lettering what they call a man's "fist," his unchangeable personal style. Lowell's lines might be pentameters of Miltonic elevation,

> When the whale's viscera go and the roll
> Of its corruption overruns this world
> Beyond tree-swept Nantucket and Wood's Hole
> And Martha's Vineyard, Sailor, will your sword
> Whistle and fall and sink into the fat?[5]

Or they might be in the off-hand slang of his middle period,

> The season's ill—
> we've lost our summer millionaire,
> who seemed to leap from an L. L. Bean
> catalogue. His nine-knot yawl
> was auctioned off to lobstermen.
> A red fox stain covers Blue Hill.[6]

Or, characteristically, the lines bring old catch-phrases to a focus so sharp it hurts.

> My hopped up husband drops his home disputes,
> and hits the streets to cruise for prostitutes,
> free-lancing out along the razor's edge.
> This screwball might kill his wife, then take the pledge.[7]

The unchanging element of Lowell's poetry was that whatever he was writing about in whichever one of his many styles, the words loomed everywhere as if in some huge magnifying lens of etymology and idiom and sound—and yet were always in the stream of English speech.

Lowell's genius and his grinding labor brought to verse in English not only technical mastery on a scale otherwise scarcely attempted in this century, but then his courage and honesty brought, to crib from myself, "a new generosity and dignity to the whole enterprise of poetry." He was not afraid of mistakes and made plenty of them, or so it seemed to me, in the mulled-over *Notebooks*.

As a boy he had studied Napoleon and he liked being famous. Francis Parker,[8] who did the etchings for every one of Lowell's books, says that while he was chained in the special Nazi cells for Dieppe survivors[9] he would sometimes fancy that his school chum Cal Lowell had at last been named Commander of Allied Forces.

Lowell drank and smoked too much as became his generation, and tolerated around him an incredible number of fools. If he went to an art museum he liked everything, even nineteenth-century steel engravings; or would say one might come to it if one saw them often. He was fond of going to operas too and liked them all. To fellow poets he was cordial, and respectful of their work. But once in a while in a flash it would come out that he had them all precisely ranked and not so very highly either.

Fame, titles, great names attracted him as they do all those who know their souls belong on the upper slopes. He loved maybe five or six people and he loved them all his life. He was also dangerous, as men in his dimensions can be.

In New York, Lowell ruled a writer's roost as he saw fit, and then married Caroline Blackwood. They lived in England. She gave him his son Sheridan. He wrote every day and read everything, was well and ill, off and on. I am told that the kind of heart attack that took him, in a New York taxi on the afternoon of September 12 as he was returning to Elizabeth and Harriet, just all at once puts you to sleep.

John Thompson (b. 1918), American critic and Professor of English at the State University of New York at Stony Brook, is the author of *The Founding of English Metre* (1961) and a volume of poems, *The Talking Girl* (1968). Thompson had been Lowell's contemporary at Kenyon College.

Lowell's second wife, Elizabeth Hardwick, is an advisory editor of the *New York Review of Books,* to which Lowell was a frequent contributor.

1. Byron "Whizzer" White (b. 1917), associate justice of the U.S. Supreme Court since 1962.

2. In Classical mythology, Alcestis agreed to die in place of her husband Admetus, and was later brought back from Hades by Hercules.

3. See Lowell, "Man and Wife."

4. With a prominent jaw.

5. Lowell, "The Quaker Graveyard in Nantucket."

6. Lowell, "Skunk Hour."

7. Lowell, "'To Speak of Woe That Is in Marriage.'"

8. See author note to No. 34.

9. In August 1942 Allied troops made an abortive attempt to land at Dieppe, on the Channel coast of France.

31 • Robert Lowell, 1917–1977

Vereen Bell

In truth Robert Lowell's life may not have been much more painful and complicated than most other people's, but it certainly seemed to be because it had been made so visible in the poems. The manner of his dying was therefore all but unbearably appropriate: inauspicious, in transit, as he moved from one city to the next keeping the stressed tissues of his life connected, a last image of the unequal contest between the human will and fate. (Blandly indifferent to provinciality, one of the Boston newspapers ran this headline: "Hub Poet Dies.") At the requiem mass the rector of the Church of the Advent said, in the homily, that God had fashioned creation not in defeat of chaos but within chaos, and—with what one hopes was unconscious irony—that we were to imagine the firmament as a great bell jar, impinged upon by chaos from without. Robert Lowell, he said, had known all too well the eternal threat of chaos to the firmament. A more barbarous, though not less appropriate, way of expressing the same idea is to say that Lowell was the celebrant of the psychopathology of everyday life. Like Roethke he was intoxicated by the knowledge of his own mortality and was motivated by that knowledge at every turn. He may be said, in no facetious sense, to have died of it.

Calvin Bedient wrote of the poems in the *Notebook* and *History* phase that they seemed to unroll before us as if on a scroll, one poem appearing, imposing its impression, then moving out of sight to make room for the next, the process continuing, nothing set in bronze.[1] That was Lowell's way of dealing with time, day by day. For a poet who was considered by many, with some good reason, to have unwisely forsaken the palace of art, he seems at times to have been one of the most intensely creative and productive poets we have had. The mere volume of his work itself does not tell the whole story; in the *Notebook* alone there are countless images, observations, pairs of lines which other poets would

Sewanee Review 86 (January–March 1978): 102–105. Reprinted by permission of Vereen Bell.

have husbanded carefully and shaped into full and substantial poems but which, issuing from Lowell's imagination, are simply carried along and away with the flow.

The poems in his last volume are dense with the observed details of rooms, angles of light, pictures, walkways, ants, homely trees, houses, turtles, birds, cats, fields in sunlight, details of what cows seem to try to look like and the way they walk and sound. What thou lovest well remains.[2] Everything in *Day by Day* is connected by feeling: Lowell's friends, children, wives, and parents are prominent, but they are assimilated with all the rest; and transcending even the pain and conflicts the prevailing tone is, oddly, one of a seasoned comic love.

One always knows, or at any rate can find out, who the "you" in Lowell's last phase of poems is or was; but there is also a distinctly cumulative effect of that indirectness which causes the individual "yous," though they remain individuals, to become a generic you, a generic loved person who is reached out to: as, sadly, in the last two lines of "Obit": "After loving you so much can I forget / you for eternity, and have no other choice?" In contrast with Roethke there was never any question for Lowell that the world's humanness was what made it cherishable in the long run and gave everything else in it its meaning. To commit oneself so fiercely to the principle of the "interhuman," as Martin Buber phrased it, to the belief that "it is from one person to another that the heavenly bread of self-being is passed," means to reject the consolations of solipsism in order to enrich and therefore complicate one's life. This knowledge gave a special significance in Lowell's case to the fact that the final celebration in the requiem mass is the sacrament of holy communion.

I would not think of claiming to have known Lowell personally or well. I doubt if any but his very closest friends could. I met him on two occasions. The first was only briefly, after the dismal occasion in 1967 of his attempting to read at the annual meeting of MLA, over whose self-important conviviality and disinterested clamor the poems he read were barely audible. The second was a more sustained occasion when he read with Peter Taylor at Vanderbilt in 1974. His audience was respectful. His reading was halting, disorganized, and diffident, but thoughtful and visibly felt. Others besides myself have expressed wonder at the modesty of his bearing in such situations as if the self he wished to project was carefully not to be confused with the more or less accidental achievement of the poems. He would have been a dreadful reader of, say, the poems of Richard Wilbur, but he was the perfect reader of Robert Lowell. He flew to Washington the next day to accept an award and then dutifully returned for the second night. My chronically irrepressible son, after shouting to Lowell and his guides through the jammed front door of our house for them to go around back, gave him a critical appraisal and said, "You must be very old." "Oh, about ten," said Lowell. "Oh, come on," said my son, "you're older than that.""Well," he said, "maybe one hundred and ten." While waiting for Taylor's reading to be over, Lowell spellbound the small group of bright and attentive graduate students with his strangely neurasthenic and animated conversation. Bizarre associations sprang into his mind like enchanted crickets. He asked my wife at dinner whether we allowed our children to dine with us and expressed mystified astonishment when she, repressing astonishment herself, said yes. He said to me, or really into space, apropos of my mother's being present, that I must feel very rich to have a mother who was living. No one who was around him for more than a few hours would ever have mistaken him for anyone else. In his manic phases he must have been an awesome figure to behold. Given his known, taxing erraticness, that almost otherworldly uniqueness was surely one reason for the cherishing protective loyalty of his friends.

One of the difficult aspects of my having achieved maturity is that I no longer have any recourse against the death of anyone whom I have been close to except simple anger. When Auden died I was not only angry for his dying but angry with him for having died; it seemed an act of bad faith. Partly because of the intimate relation in Lowell's poems between the themes of his life and of his work, his dying set off in me a swarm of bitter and poignant associations. One image was of an old and cherished friend of my parents, and second father to me, whose memory one day many years ago began flaking away and then inexorably unwound in stages, despite his own discipline and the most sophisticated medical attention, until eventually, in a nursing home, he simply died, still trying to win, helplessly struggling to get one pair of trousers on over another. I remembered a dear friend, passionate and nihilistic, visiting for the first time at age thirty-seven in the Poets' Corner in Westminster Abbey and finding himself suddenly unable to speak and in tears. That in turn evoked a recent memory of going into the Abbey again myself and being shocked to see Auden's marker there already beside Eliot's, before it seemed that he had time to be truly dead. (The memorial decor of the Poets' Corner becomes plainer as history rolls on.) But there it was for sure, the new entry, Wystan Hugh Auden / 1907–

1973 / "In the prison of his days / Teach the free man how to praise." I think now in relation to the Yeats elegy that in Lowell's case the death of the poet will not be kept from the poems, because from almost the very beginning the death of the poet was the poems.

A close friend of Lowell's said in his sorrow that Cal was not ready to die; and God knows that was true. But now he has died anyway, survived by, in effect, two grief-shredded wives; by a sternly beautiful daughter of twenty who once in a poem cartwheeled upon the blue; and by an equally beautiful young son, Robert Sheridan, who already appears to know what he wants no part of, for in his correct navy suit he had to be tugged down the imposing nave of the Church of the Advent as he kneaded both eyes with his free hand. He is also survived by his old, durable friend Allen Tate, whom he once paraphrased (perhaps inaccurately) in a poem as saying of his own youngest son, "I shall not live long enough to see him through."[3] For those many others who will feel left behind, like Lowell's mother after his father's death, "as if she had stayed on a train / one stop past her destination,"[4] there will be some consolation in two thoughts. One is that his last volume is a beautiful and strong work. The other is that he went in privacy and apparently, let us hope, in sudden peace.

Vereen Bell (b. 1934), American critic and Professor of English at Vanderbilt University, is the author of *Robert Lowell: The Nihilist as Hero* (1983).

1. Calvin Bedient, "Visions and Revisions—Three New Volumes by America's First Poet," *New York Times Book Review*, 29 July 1973, p. 16.

2. Ezra Pound, *Cantos*, LXXXI.

3. Lowell, "Letter from Allen Tate."

4. Lowell, "For Sale."

32 • Robert Lowell

Seamus Heaney

In the consoling and slightly complacent idiom of some Christians, Robert Lowell has "crossed over." Yet for one who loved his Dante, whose understanding was structured on the groundplan of classical and biblical thought, the phrase has its propriety. That taxi-driver who ferried his dead body across the East River into Manhattan was Charon, and we can imagine him receiving a fare in the coin of language, from the poet's tongue, a coin stamped and welted with the impression of Robert Lowell.

We all have our memories of his vivid, confirming and enlivening presence. I can recall being shy of meeting him, and perhaps others were too, because of that nimbus of authority that ringed his writings and his actions. He already had the status of classic, when he came to settle on this side of the Atlantic. There had been a lineal descent, a laying on of hands, first by Allen Tate and John Crowe Ransom, and then by T. S. Eliot. He had come within the orbit of Ezra Pound and Robert Frost. He had been part of that coincidence of brilliant, troubled writers who had just entered or were about to enter a newer, more unsettled and unsettling pantheon—Theodore Roethke, Sylvia Plath, Randall Jarrell, John Berryman. He came seasoned by the hard weathers of his own life, with the grain of his thought and feeling worn, definite, solitary and authoritative by the lives and death of those others.

Yet because of the way he divined us when we did meet him, he bound us to him as a person. In a room full of people, his quick scanning eyes could throw a grappling hook to the person he was meeting, as he came forward, half buoyant, half somnambulant, on the balls of his feet, his voice at once sharp and sidling. At those tentative moments, and on other more leisurely occasions when he could play the stops and pull the

Agenda 18 (1980): 23–28. Expanded from the *New York Review of Books* 25 (9 February 1978): 37–38. Reprinted in *Robert Lowell: A Memorial Address and Elegy* (London: Faber, 1978). Reprinted here by permission of Seamus Heaney.

carpet in a conversation, he touched and strung in us a chord of fidelity and gratitude that we are gathered here to play once more.

That resonant medieval phrase, "the fall of princes," kept surfacing in my head for days after his death. Within the principality of poetry he was acknowledged by living poets and had been dubbed by those dead ones to occupy a princely rank. Just as in that older dispensation, the order and coherence of things was ratified in the person of the prince, so in the person and poetry of Robert Lowell, the whole scope and efficacy of the artistic endeavour was exemplified and affirmed. And his death shook the frame of poetry. He did not pitch his voice at "the public" but he so established the practice of art as a moral function within his own life that when he turned outward to make gestures against the quality of the life of his times, those gestures had been well earned and possessed a memorable force. He alone had the right to nominate his conscientious objection to the Second World War a "manic statement,"[1] but his open letter declining an invitation to the White House in 1965 was dignified and more potent than other more clamorous, if equally well-intentioned protests that followed.

He spoke at that time with a dynastic as well as an artistic voice, recalling how both sides of his family had a long history of service to the *rem publicam,*[2] and this preoccupation with ancestry was a constant one. From beginning to end, his poems called up and made inquisition of those fathers who had shaped him and the world he inhabited. As a young poet, graves and graveyards stirred his imagination, and there is a morose funerary splendour about his early meditations on the New England heritage: their rhetoric is both plangent and pugnacious, as they "lurch / for forms to harness Heraclitus' stream." The voice we hear in them is oracular and penitential, and its purpose is redemptive, as if by its effort towards understanding and its pining for transcendance it might conjure an "unblemished Adam" from what he was later to call "the unforgivable landscape."

To the very end, memory remained for him both a generating and a judicial faculty. Indeed, I can think of no more beautiful evocation of its relevance to Robert Lowell's life and work than those lines of T. S. Eliot's, another New Englander making casts in Heraclitus' stream:

> This is the use of memory:
> For liberation—not less of love but expanding
> Of love beyond desire, and so liberation

> From the future as well as the past. Thus, love of a country
> Begins as attachment to our own field of action
> And comes to find that action of little importance
> Though never indifferent. History may be servitude,
> History may be freedom. See, now they vanish,
> The faces and places, with the self which, as it could, loved them,
> To become renewed, transfigured, in another pattern.[3]

History, love, renewal, these were what possessed him, not as abstractions but as palpable experiences and consciously held-to categories of truth. His poetry embodies magnificently the integrity and wisdom of his quest, amplifies and reaffirms the possible reaches of the human spirit.

Yet this man whom we so gratefully praise thirsted for accusation. That line in the concluding sonnet of *The Dolphin* which says, "My eyes have seen what my hand did" branded itself upon me when I read it. It has two musics that contend but do not overpower each other. There is the bronze note, perhaps even the brazen note, of artistic mastery, yet in so far as the words intimate the price which poetic daring involves there is also the still, sad music[4] of human remorse. The man who suffers is recompensated in himself as the man who creates,[5] but Robert Lowell, the man who spoke of "the brute push of composition," was ruefully aware that that push could bruise others, others who were perhaps even the very nurturers of his poetic gift and confidence. When I praised the line to him, he gracefully diverted the credit for it from himself and said, "Well, it's something like Heminge and Condell said about Shakespeare, isn't it?" But the line's power and accusatory force derives from what they did not say: their sentence about Shakespeare reads, "His mind and hand went together," and was meant to celebrate Shakespeare's fluency and the felicity of his first thoughts and words. Robert Lowell bends and refracts all this to sustain the deliberated elements in his art, the plotting, as he called it, with himself and others, the unavoided injuries.

Robert Lowell, the man we so lately knew, walks perhaps in our imaginations under the aspect of a Shakespearean hero, an appeased, dishevelled, sturdy Lear, one buffeted and humble after the purgative climaxes, capable of making his "exhaustion / the light of the world," of making "the elder flower . . . champagne," to quote only two assuaging images from his last autumnal book of poems. But it is not Shakespeare whom we think of when we think of his art, not that happy medium who left scarce a blot on his lines, but rather Shakespeare's fellow maker, the learned, classical, critical Ben Jonson, that devotee of re-making and re-vision, who wrote "that he / Who casts to write a living poem, must sweat / and strike the second heat / Upon the Muses' anvil."[6] Robert Lowell's second sight often had to face the challenge of his second thoughts. He had in awesome abundance the poet's first gift for surrender to those energies of language that heave to the fore matter that will not be otherwise summoned, or that might be otherwise suppressed. Under the ray of his concentration, the molten stuff of the psyche ran hot and unstanched. But its final form was as much beaten as poured, the cooling ingot was assiduously hammered. A fully human and relentless intelligence was at work upon the pleasuring quick of the creative act. He was and will remain a pattern for poets in this amphibiousness, this ability to plunge into the downward reptilian welter of the individual self and yet raise himself with whatever knowledge he gained there out on the hard ledges of the historical present, which he then apprehended with refreshed insight and intensity, as in his majestic poem "For the Union Dead" and in many others, especially in that nobly profiled collection *Near the Ocean*.

When a person whom we cherished dies, all that he stood for goes a-begging, asking us somehow to occupy the space he filled, to assume into our own life values which we admired in his, and thereby to conserve his unique energy. This feeling was made more acute for me by the fact that six days before he died, Robert Lowell and his wife Caroline had spent a happy, bantering evening with us in Dublin. I felt that something in our friendship had been fulfilled and looked forward to many more of those creative, sportive encounters. But his wise and wicked talk, his obsessive love and diagnosis of writing and writers, the whole ursine force of his presence have been withdrawn from us, as he half-predicted they would be, in his sixtieth year.

> We are things thrown in the air
> alive in flight . . .
> our rust the colour of the chameleon.[7]

> This winter, I thought
> I was created to be given away.[8]

> No honeycomb is built without a bee
> adding circle to circle, cell to cell,

> the wax and honey of a mausoleum—
> this round dome proves its maker is alive;
> the corpse of the insect lives embalmed in honey,
> prays that its perishable work live long
> enough for the sweet-tooth bear to desecrate—
> this open book . . . my open coffin.[9]

That almost narcotic thought of death can be felt in his latest poems, some of which were like prayers, acts of thanksgiving and of contrition, acts of hope for loved ones and of charity for himself. And the mood of that poetry was very much the mood of his life during the final months. In a letter to Caroline, written last February, we can catch both the music of resignation and the old indomitable irony:

> The hospital business, despite the rough useless and dramatic ambulance at McLean's, was painless eventless; perhaps what death might be at best. A feeling that one was doomed like Ivan Illich,[10] but without suffering. There seemed to be no danger at all, except that there still may be—but all so quiet it hardly seemed to matter. . . . If that's all life is, it's a coldly smiling anti-climax. Gone the great apocalypse of departure.

The last letter he wrote from Ireland, where he had spent time with his son Sheridan and his step-daughter Ivana, shunned the apocalyptic in favour of the playful:

> I spent until about two with Sheridan. We had a merry amiable time except that he (wisely) preferred people to swans and a rubber-tyre swing to people.

And these four lines, found among papers he left behind him in Ireland, persuade us that he was indeed ready to meet Charon, to dart him one of those penetrating looks, and to allow himself to be guided, as of right, into the frail skiff:

> Christ,
> May I die at night
> With a semblance of my senses
> Like the full moon that fails.

1. Lowell, "Memories of West Street and Lepke."

2. Latin: public welfare.

3. T. S. Eliot, "Little Gidding."

4. An echo of Wordsworth's "still sad music of humanity" in "Tintern Abbey" (1798).

5. See T. S. Eliot, "Tradition and the Individual Talent," *Selected Essays, 1917–1932* (New York, 1932), p. 8.

6. Ben Jonson, "To the Memory of William Shakespeare" (1618).

7. Lowell, "Our Afterlife I."

8. Lowell, "Thanks-Offering for Recovery."

9. Lowell, "Reading Myself."

10. The physically dying and spiritually awakening hero of Tolstoy's great story, "The Death of Ivan Ilych" (1886).

33 • From *New York Jew*

Alfred Kazin

Randall certainly lived and died for excellence. To be the best poet! To be the poet of a generation! When he reviewed Robert Lowell's *Lord Weary's Castle*, his natural piety expressed itself without limitation. The uprush of his praise was the most perfect example in public of Jarrell's capacity for veneration:

> I know of no poetry since Auden's that is better than Robert Lowell's. Everybody who reads poetry will read it sooner or later. . . . *Lord Weary's Castle* makes me feel like a rain-maker who predicts rain, and gets a flood which drowns everyone in the country. A few of these poems, I believe, will be read as long as men remember English.[1]

Lowell was another addict of Hannah's. Bellow might find insupportable her instructing *him* about Faulkner. When in later years Hannah's vexing book on Eichmann and the "banality of evil" appeared, Bellow took his revenge in *Herzog:* "the canned sauerkraut of Weimar intellectuals." But Lowell, the strongest poet of my generation and given to mood swings that encouraged his gift for exaltation, responded fervently to every suggestion of her culture, her sympathy for the coming men in American poetry. . . .

Wonderfully gifted Robert Lowell, whose instinct for language worked on me with the force of a jackhammer, was more exalted by Hannah's recognition of *him* than he was by her politics. I was never to understand what Lowell's politics were. His eyesight had kept him from military service, but he was a Catholic convert and positively insisted on going to jail as a conscientious objector. When I met him again at Yaddo[2] in 1949, he was divorced from Jean Stafford and no longer a Catholic, but he sounded like Evelyn Waugh rampaging against the wartime al-

From *New York Jew* (New York: Knopf, 1978), pp. 202–205. Reprinted by permission of Alfred Kazin.

liance with Russia. He objected more to Russia than to the war. It was a gloomy time for me; listening to Lowell at his most blissfully high orating against Communist influences at Yaddo and boasting of the veneration in which he was held by those other illiberal great men Ezra Pound and George Santayana, made me feel worse. . . .

Lowell and Elizabeth Hardwick were a brilliant couple, but Lowell was just a little too dazzling at the moment. He was at the top of a psychic crest down which he would slide the next season; but at this peak he talked in tongues; he was of the great company, with Milton and Hardy and Eliot; he was wonderful and frightening. He was not just damned good, suddenly famous and deserving his fame; he was in a state of grandeur not negotiable with lesser beings. He was a Lowell; he was handsome, magnetic, rich, wild with excitement about his powers, wild over the many tributes to him from Pound, Santayana, his old friends Tate and Jarrell and Warren. Flannery O'Connor, who was also at Yaddo, seemed to be attending Lowell with rapture. . . .

I was numb, entirely closed in, then was shocked awake by Lowell's discovery that Yaddo, too, was subversive and may once have had a secret line to the Soviet Embassy. Lowell did not seem too unhappy about the frightful discovery that the charming woman director[3] of many years—my friend, his friend, a good friend to many writers—was secretly attempting to cut down our country. He went to the F.B.I. about it. He was as happily excited as a man can be. With his newfound authority as an American poet, he had the Yaddo trustees convened, confided to them the great things Santayana and Pound had said about *him,* and demanded that the director be dismissed. . . .

The lesser poets were not only the biggest cowards, but impossible to shut up in their boring, whining self-defense. They were concerned with Lowell's power to affect their reputations even when they had no reputations. Lowell, who would transcend the mannerism of *Lord Weary's Castle* and find a straightforward "confessional" mode perfect for his literary instinct and troubled life in an age merciless with guilt, later admitted that he had forgotten the Yaddo episode. I believed him.

Alfred Kazin (b. 1915), major American literary critic and Professor of English at the City University of New York, is the author of *On Native Grounds* (1942), *Bright Book of Life* (1973) and *An American Procession* (1984).
1. See No. 6, note 1.
2. A writers' colony in Saratoga Springs, New York.
3. Elizabeth Ames.

34 • Brantwood Camp

Francis Parker

Cal and I became friends our Third Form year at St. Mark's. At our desks, side by side in Study Hall, I was reading poetry—he history. On the way to meals or chapel, we would often linger together in the corridors to study the large Meissonier[1] reproductions, I for the painting— he for Napoleon.

In the school attic, a hugh miscellaneous collection of books was tumbled together into a mountainous pile. We would pillage it, chiefly for engravings from histories of Napoleon, but also for others; we both admired Gustave Doré.[2] Soon I began reading history, and he began reading poetry and taking an interest in painting.

To help him understand painting, Elie Faure's *Spirit of Forms*[3] was the commentary Cal stumbled on—and "forms" was the key. The forms of snail shells led to the lines of force in a Rubens, and the suggestion of formal construction found by tracing the lines of Dynamic Symmetry on a Leonardo inspired Cal to apply what he had learned of painting to poetry; to reading it, not writing it. The commentary he chose for poetry was Norton's on Dante's *Divine Comedy*.[4]

In Norton, *will* was the Inferno's key. Farinata[5] had put himself in the circle of Hell. Will could put a man in Heaven or Hell. This idea crystallized for Cal all he had learned since he had begun reading the commentaries. He could be whatever he decided to be—anything, if he chose to do the work. Napoleon was the proof.

Cal was now fired to try it, but he had no way of expressing himself. He felt neither poet, painter, nor musician, and had no wish to be a soldier or statesman.

St. Mark's ran a summer camp, called Brantwood, for underprivileged boys. It was staffed by volunteer Fifth and Sixth Formers, and the summer of our Fifth Form year Cal decided to go as a counselor. He insisted I do the same.

First printed in *The Harvard Advocate* 113 (November 1979): 8.

Moody, solitary, antisocial, Cal nonetheless wanted to prove that he could be a good counselor. Community life; songs; hikes; competition for the cleanest hut; best record for knot-tying and campfire-building—to all these tasks Cal brought an unnatural fervor. We were each assigned a hut with about eight boys. In Cal's were "Mohawks," in mine "Massasoits." I had never underestimated Cal's drive and sense of purpose, but I was unprepared for what was to come.

In the evenings we would gather in the head counselor's hut to discuss the day's problems with our boys. The senior counselors—relaxed and smoking—were often disconcerted by Cal, who took these sessions with a seriousness that tolerated no frivolous humor.

The two weeks drove on. Cal forced himself to sing or tell stories at the evening campfires. He cleaned his hut himself, threw himself into the contests and games, and although he cared nothing for competition, he was extremely put out if his hut was not first—for that meant to him that he had not *done the work*.

The climax of the term was the Overnight Hike. Camping after the march, free at last—our boys rounded up, bedded down, the last blister band-aided—we sat by the lake and talked for the first time since we had come to Brantwood, and we talked all night. We both felt that somehow it had been worth the effort.

But for Cal it meant that at last he knew he could do whatever he chose to do. His mood was of wonder and exaltation. He would be a writer, he said (meaning prose). He would work at it, as he had worked at Brantwood, and he would be great.

We roomed together our last year. Cal wrote his first poem.

Francis Parker (b. 1917), a classmate of Lowell's at St. Mark's, illustrated many of his books and remained a lifelong friend.

1. Ernest Meissonier (1815–91), French painter of Napoleonic battles.
2. See No. 1, note 7.
3. Elie Fauré's *The Spirit of Forms* (1927).
4. Charles Eliot Norton's edition of Dante was published in 1891.
5. The leader of the Ghibelline faction at Florence in the thirteenth century, immortalized by Dante in *Inferno* X as the savior of his country.

35 • On Robert Lowell

Blair Clark

Where did his torrent of energy come from? His father, in his mid-forties when I first knew him, was sluggish and blocked. That astonishing drive's main source was certainly his mother, but the hysterical dynamo in her had no outlet and was therefore destructive of herself and of those around her—especially, of course, her husband and her son.

Somehow he survived those quite dreadful tensions and managed to invent himself. The being he created was a spring coiled by his own strong, fumbling hand. What he made of himself was a reaction to and against his parents. We are all, of course, formed in such ways, but he had special needs to slip from that parental vise and finally he found devices that made the escape possible. It was a tight one from the start, constraining his unruly nature in grotesque ways. His parents' attempt to control him could be called "conventional" except that their nagging campaign for proper dress, manners and attitude aimed beyond mere convention. It was an effort to control or subdue a phenomenon they feared, a spirit in revolt not just against them and their narrow world but against something more frightening, perhaps dangerous life itself, as they perceived it.

These dull parents fought hard to win the battle at 170 Marlborough Street. Charlotte Lowell's white gloves sheathed steely hands determined to wrest victory from her strange, rebellious only child. The fighting raged even when his childhood obsession was Napoleon (a bookshelf on Bonaparte in his bedroom, all read by the time he was fourteen), before his heroes became Homer, Dante, Shakespeare, Milton and then the rest.

At first his defensive weapon was humor, not of the sunny or winning sort but daring and aggressive, even grotesque. I remember Thanksgiving lunch, in 1932 or 1933, he and I freed for the day from St. Mark's cloisters, sitting at the mahogany dining-room table on Marl-

---

First printed in *The Harvard Advocate* 113 (November 1979): 9–11.

borough Street and giggling almost uncontrollably at obscure yarns he spun about friends of his parents. They were indirect attacks, of course (how could one dare to take on directly the friends of one's parents?). And so they were fantastic, full of invented episodes about cheeky servants and highly exaggerated misadventures of daily life in that proper world. The two of us almost choked on the turkey as we thus separated ourselves from these two parents trying to talk about the St. Mark's– Groton football game and the details of life at a school of which his father's grandfather (or was it great-uncle?) had been the first headmaster.[1]

Critics have praised him, and some have questioned his taste, for the lacerating accounts of himself and his parents in the "confessional" writing. My view, based on much observation of him and of them in those painful days, is that he spared them, and thus perhaps himself, in his accounts of their behavior. They could well have been dealt with much more harshly, and I have marvelled at his rationalizations of what he went through at their hands. (I do have a letter from him calling them "pretty awful people," written in the 1950s).

In those schooldays "loyalty" was the first principle of our friendship. Lowell was the unquestioned leader, whose dominance sometimes chafed, of a cabal of three classmates, alienated from the values of that school. The painter Frank Parker and I were the others and there was no effort to recruit more aspiring dissidents, nor did our classmates try to join our charmed, if scarcely visible, circle. Lowell deserved that leadership because Parker and I, having less reason than him to fight for survival against the parental enemy, were even more unformed. And he had a superior drive and commitment to the search for the "serious," an idea he embraced by the time we were sixteen.

He decreed that Parker would be painter and I a musician. He would be the poet (there was no talk of mere "writing"). His allocation of the arts among the three of us was based on the fact that Parker was already doing sketches and caricatures and the circumstance that I was in the choir (and what other art was left open?). Since Lowell was tone-deaf and since I had a mere trace of musical talent, he had to accept my dropping out of that niche in our pantheon. It remained a question of what to do with me in the arts. When I spent a summer with him in a cottage on Nantucket, in 1936, working hard on our nineteen-year-old intellects all the time, he made me read all the minor Elizabethan playwrights, and I still retain a tag or two from Dekker and Middleton. He assigned himself

Shakespeare, Milton, Homer again, and the English lyric poets. It was not a fair or sensible division of labor, but I lacked the confidence to challenge him. One put up with his bullying. There were enough other rewards in the friendship, but they were tested when he chased me and knocked me down to force me to stop smoking (he who later smoked three or four packs a day).

If he invented himself in an unusually conscious and deliberate way, as I have suggested, that was as nothing compared to the way in which he created Robert Lowell the writer. He set about that task even before he had a notion of what it was to "write," or what there was for him to write about. Imagination needs material, experience, to grind, and that is famously just what is missing for the young artist. Two decades went by before Lowell could face, and deal creatively with, the matter that was closest at hand, his struggle with his family. So in the beginning the impulsion was abstract and purely moral: what is good and bad, bearable and unbearable, serious and unimportant, as one considers what to do with life? To find the answers, his answers, he went straight to literature, blindly and instinctively, I would say. He had little interest in philosophy or other sources of knowledge or wisdom. If in those early years at school he looked elsewhere than to the classics of literature for guidance (along with the scholarly commentaries on them, to learn how to read them), it was to painting, in the volumes of reproductions in the Carnegie collection in a small room near the library.

Where did the nickname "Cal" come from? The scholars will bicker about that. I have never been sure whether Caliban or Caligula was the inspiration, so to speak, for his taunting classmates in the third or fourth forms. We were reading Roman history and *The Tempest* in the same year. So both names were handy for the smooth sons of Wall Street and State Street[2] to hang on Lowell, the rough outsider with rumpled clothes and hair and untied shoe-laces. I would say that Caliban was the main source—uncouthness rather than a mania that had not yet appeared. Physically the strongest boy in the class, he was looked on as odd, not crazy.

I know little about his two Harvard years, having fallen back a year because of illness and thus overlapping only one of them. My memory is that he was not much affected by the *Advocate*'s rejection of his candidacy—it was too much of a club and he knew he was not eminently clubbable. He encouraged me to concentrate in the Classics, which I did, and to join the *Crimson,* then somewhat less clubby than the *Advocate.*

But we saw each other a great deal and I was heavily involved in his struggle to leave Harvard and all those family pressures that almost trapped him. I was of some use in this effort, presenting to his stubborn parents a conventional self and conventional careerist arguments for the move to Kenyon. But Dr. Merrill Moore, the transplanted Southern agrarian sonneteer and psychiatrist with a Harvard medical base and a Beacon Street practice, who knew Tate, Ransom, Warren, et al., was, of course, much more influential with those parents. He certified Lowell's move as sane, and it helped that Lowell's mother ended up working as an aide in Moore's office; she had something to do at last beyond chivvying husband and son. Finally it got through to them that their difficult son might be better off away from them and that they might be spared, too, if he just went away.

Students of the life and work of Lowell have noted, but not sufficiently, I think, the way in which he systematically apprenticed himself to older writers. It began at school with Richard G. Eberhart, then a young poet on the faculty whom we called "Cousin Ghormley," not out of disrespect but as a sort of joke. Then there was Ford Madox Ford, the only novelist in the list of mentors, whom he met in Boston in 1936 or 1937 and visited in Olivet, Michigan. Pre-eminently, there were Allen Tate and John Crowe Ransom, the latter moving from Vanderbilt to Kenyon, to which he attracted Randall Jarrell and Lowell, among other aspiring young poets. Later there were Pound, Eliot, William Carlos Williams and Santayana, among others at whose feet he sat. He could learn from them not just the craft of poetry but something about how to think and live as a poet. It was done for enlightenment, not careerist calculation, though Lowell did not lack ambition for success.

Later, during the long period of manic-depressive "breakdowns," as he called them, which came at intervals of about eleven months, as I once figured, I often served as a way-station in the transit from abandoned home to hospital. In these episodes, some of them quite frightening, the point was to get him as soon as possible out of some wild entanglement and into the hospital. I did this several times in collaboration with his wife, the truly devoted Elizabeth Hardwick, and his psychiatrist, the remarkably impressive Dr. Viola Bernard. Once in the early 1960s I flew to Buenos Aires to persuade him to leave a clinic and his fantasies of that moment; after four days he agreed and we came back, an Argentinian doctor named Kelly accompanying us, his tranquillizing hypodermic at the ready, as required by Pan Am.

We were close friends for forty-five years, I think, though for most of that time our worlds overlapped more than coincided, and there were periods when circumstances prevented much contact. I was his best man at his first wedding, in 1940, while Allen Tate gave away the bride, Jean Stafford. At his marriage to Elizabeth Hardwick in 1948 I again handed him the ring after trying to dilute or turn aside the usual parental hostility. Mrs. Lowell asked me in that house in Beverly Farms, where the wedding was, whether I thought Elizabeth was "suitable" and would "take good care of Bobby," the same questions she had put to me about Jean, though the Lowells did not attend that unapproved service in New York. Had his mother been around for his third marriage, I would have had to give a different answer to that insistent question, which surely would have been posed once more. I was never able to conceal my doubts about that one, but they caused no trouble between us.

I remember once, a dozen years before he died, bringing him back to my house in New York in one of his crazed escapes from home. Watching him breathe in heavy gasps, asleep in the taxi, the tranquillizing drugs fighting the mania, I thought that there were then two dynamos within him, spinning in opposite directions and tearing him apart, and that these forces would kill him at last. No one, strong as he was, could stand that for long. And, finally, the opposing engines of creation and repression did kill him in a taxi in front of his own real home.

Blair Clark (b. 1917), Lowell's classmate at St. Mark's and a close friend for forty-five years, was editor of the *Nation* and campaign manager for Senator Eugene McCarthy.

1. His great-uncle was Headmaster.
2. The financial center of Boston.

36 • Homage to a Poet

Robert Giroux

My association with Lowell as a publisher began with his first trade book, *Lord Weary's Castle,* in 1946, but I had known him as a friend since late 1940. When I first met him, through Jean Stafford, he too was an editor at a publishing house, Sheed and Ward; Jean was amazed (and I think Cal was too) that they kept him on the payroll for almost a year.

One of the most memorable incidents of our long association occurred in 1948, when Lowell was the Poetry Consultant of the Library of Congress—our visit to Ezra Pound at St. Elizabeth's. I had never met Pound and was hesitant about going, but Cal was persuasive and I tagged along. When Cal told Pound I was a book publisher, he glared at me from his seat and snapped, "What the hell do *you* want?" All I think to say—it was the simple truth—was "I want to pay homage to a poet." He slowly stood up, and made a grave and courtly bow. Soon he was reading aloud his early drafts of the Confucian Odes.

Now, thirty years later, I want to pay homage—we are all here to pay homage—to a poet, Robert Lowell. From *Lord Weary's Castle* to *Day by Day* is a whole literary generation, one of the most impressive periods of poetry in America, and Robert Lowell's was its dominant voice. Since his tragic death last September, I've been going over our correspondence, and I'd like to read several short passages—from letters on the deaths of two writers, T. S. Eliot and Edmund Wilson, and on his own work, including *Day by Day*. As the later letters show, he was one of the hardest-working poets who ever practiced the art. The letter about Eliot is dated April 8, 1965:

"Dear Bob: I have reached an age where all my elders are disappearing, and can't reconcile myself to the fact. I must say there was no one who spoke with such authority as Tom, and so little played the role of the great man. He was a good and patient friend to both of us. No other man so touched something personal in my depths."

First printed in *The Harvard Advocate* 113 (November 1979): 43.

The second, about Edmund Wilson, is postmarked London and dated June 20, 1972: "My good angel must have told me to write Edmund, out of a blue sky, about three weeks before his death; I had an answer saying he had just had a stroke. He must have somewhat recovered to get to Talcottville. I'm re-reading almost all his books since I came to England—he's the best bridge maybe for an American in Europe, and so much of him reads like great short stories for novels. Goodbye, dear old man!"

The third, dated July 12, 1972, is about his book, *History:* "My book is going to get me in trouble. It would be suicide for me not to publish. I offer the best I have. *Fresh woods*[1]—I can't do anything more till I get these books out, but I have ideas: ten or twelve cantos of Dante; prose reminiscences, more or less like what I've done, if I can find a new form that will let me write at greater length; and new poems."

Finally, a letter about *Day by Day,* dated August 27, 1976, a little over a year before the book was published: "I hope you haven't sent my manuscript to the printers, because this last month or so I've worked like a beaver, and as steady almost. I have so many changes that the simplest thing will be to give you an entire new typing by mid-October. The book's substantially the same, but there are new poems and a few heavy revisions."

It was always an honor for Farrar, Straus and Giroux to be his publisher, and I take personal pleasure in the fact that the first book to bear this imprint was one of his—*For the Union Dead,* in 1964. I treasure Cal's inscription in my copy: "For Bob—This first book with both our names, with affection and gratitude, Cal."

Robert Giroux (b. 1914), Lowell's American editor at Harcourt Brace and at Farrar, Straus and Giroux, is the author of *The Book Known as Q: A Consideration of Shakespeare's Sonnets* (1982).

1. An allusion to the concluding lines of Milton's "Lycidas" (1638).

37 • Robert Lowell in the Sixties

Richard Tillinghast

Antiques and quarrels from "91 Revere Street" mix in memory with Kentucky bluegrass and whitewashed fences seen from the backseat of my father's white Buick: my parents were driving me from Memphis to Cambridge in 1962 to begin graduate school; I was reading *Life Studies* for the first time. The *angst,* the vulnerability, the exposed nerves of the author led me to expect someone other than the man who as poet, teacher and friend was to have an effect on my life I could not, even now, begin to calculate.

Physically Robert Lowell gave an impression of force, with strong shoulders and an unusually large head—not a head that revealed the skull and hinted at the brain as with Allen Tate: one, rather, that gave a powerful but awkward, elemental impression, making one think simultaneously of a bull and a creature of the sea. He was born under the constellation Pisces, and fishing was the one sport he found meaning in. The sea was his element; I can think of no other poet who has evoked the sea so often and so tellingly. Fish, gulls, whales, turtles, seals appear again and again in his work; the dolphin was both muse and self.

I picture him at Harvard slouched in a leather chair, a penny loafer dangling from one foot, shoulders scrunched up toward his massive head—his hands framing a point in the air, held up before his face as though to protect it from attack, now and then righting the black-rimmed glasses that kept sliding down the bridge of his thick nose, one of many True cigarettes between his fingers. With his broad face and "oval Lowell smile," he bore an uncanny resemblance to the pictures of Amy Lowell and James Russell Lowell in *The American Heritage Dictionary.* The jaunty, pastel shirt-and-tie combinations—the opposite of traditional—that he would sometimes wear, made one cringe, yet they were typical of one who loathed conventional "good taste" and who delighted in things that were jarring and vivid.

First printed in *The Harvard Advocate* 113 (November 1979): 14–16.

That Lowell's speech bore subtle but well-defined traces of a Southern accent was only one of many paradoxes about him, but it said something important about this complex and often contradictory person. Perhaps the accent had rubbed off in the course of many years of marriage to Elizabeth Hardwick, who was born in Kentucky. I fancy, though, he picked it up from the crowd of Tennesseans and Kentuckians, teachers and friends, whom he had met in his early twenties when he left Harvard after his sophomore year to study at Kenyon and LSU: Allen Tate, John Ransom, Randall Jarrell, Peter Taylor, "Red" Warren. Probably it was a sign of his rebellion against a New England heritage which he both rejected and thoroughly embodied—a heritage which for him carried a lot of guilt and was inextricable from his feelings toward his family. To me his speech was reassuringly familiar at Harvard in the Sixties, where I found that a Southern accent was usually greeted with incredulity or hostility. Coming from him, no one seemed to mind it.

Lowell had apparently been pretty humorless as a young man. The torture and enervation (a word that recurs in his poetry) of recurrent mental breakdowns, and perhaps worse, the treatment for them, had not left him with a sanguine attitude toward life. Yet in his late forties and early fifties, one could see him unbend and "mellow" as he came to a slow acceptance of the world and himself. In *Day by Day* he wrote (of his mother):

> Your exaggerating humor,
> the opposite of deadpan,
> the opposite of funny to a son,
> is mine now—[1]

A gifted alien, a stranger to the ordinary, sometimes hardly human at all, he relished broad humor, the ridiculous, the common. In his healthy periods, I think he was often overcome with joy at the feeling of being "normal," and thus delighted in the obvious. The "exaggerating" element in his humor, which could be charming or tiresome, was the counterpart of his extravagant poetic style.

Once during the term at Harvard, perhaps during 1965, I got Lowell and James Dickey, who was reading locally, together for lunch. Circumstances, and the two men's temperaments, had cast them as rivals. Peter Davison, in a widely noted article in the *Atlantic,* had just coupled them as the nation's two leading poets.[2] While differing greatly in background and style, they had more in common than is obvious: their genius, the scope of their ambition, their boundless energy, and a radical originality that set them apart from most of their contemporaries. Both were hypersensitive to criticism; both had recently been the subjects of full-scale critical broadsides in *The Sixties* by Robert Bly—one of the few sure signs of distinction in contemporary poetry.

We ate at Chez Dreyfus in Cambridge. Dickey and I had been drinking beer since breakfast, and had just come from my writing class, where he had put in a splendid guest appearance. Lowell was not supposed to be drinking, as alcohol was incompatible with the lithium pills he took for his illness. He made an exception (not unusual) for the occasion; food was soon forgotten, vodka flowed. Sparring between the two poets was in evidence, some of it good-natured, some of it not. Dickey, who hunts with bow and arrow, showed us a large bandage on his back and started telling us about a recent trip to the West Virginia wilderness. It was a good story. Having stopped to drink from a mountain stream, he had looked up just in time to see a huge bear reared up on its hind legs, making straight for him in the most unfriendly way. Just as the bear had attacked, raking his back and shoulder with razor-sharp claws, Dickey had got off an arrow that killed the bear. "But the bear wasn't dead, Jim," Lowell interrupted, himself suddenly bearlike, clearing his way with his gesturing hands, laughing as he always did at the remark he was about to make—"When you got back to your office, the bear was sitting at your desk. It was Robert Bly."

Lowell was slow to fall for political solutions to complex problems. One irony of his career was his position in the Sixties as a poetic spokesman for the Left (not that he didn't want it and work for it). Few critics have seen that in this profoundly divided person, radicalism was balanced by a rock-ribbed, atavistic sense of tradition. It is well known that Lowell was a Conscientious Objector in World War II, protesting the Allied bombing of civilians at Dresden and elsewhere, and that he went to jail for it; few people are aware that he had earlier tried to enlist in the Navy but had been rejected because of poor eyesight. In all events, the divisions in his own personality afforded him an unusually good opportunity to understand both sides of most political issues.

In 1969 Lowell was offered a visiting professorship for the following spring in the English Department of the University of California at Berkeley. I was on the faculty there at the time and backed up the offer with a glowing description of the political struggle at Berkeley and of the overall atmosphere of the place. Those were heady times; it really did look as though the walls were about to come down. My enthusiasm was genuine, as was my naïveté. Lowell used my letter as the basis of a poem, "The Revolution," in *History*. (Anyone who has had occasion to study Lowell's methods of quotation will know that with him, poetic license was a way of life.) Whatever its relationship to what I wrote in my letter—I can hardly say after ten years—the quoted part of the poem reads:

> "We're in a prerevolutionary situation
> at Berkeley, an incredible, refreshing relief
> from your rather hot-house, good prep-school Harvard riots.
> The main thing is our exposure to politics;
> whether this a priori will determine
> the revolutionary's murder in the streets,
> or the death of the haves by the have-nots, I don't know;
> but anyway you should be in on it—
> only in imagination can we lose the battle."

It's clear that lines five to seven and line nine were Robert Lowell's work, though trying to attribute them reminds me too much of an episode in the literary career of Mr. B. Baggins at Rivendell.[3] The following excerpt from his reply to my letter gives the flavor both of his warmth and of his ironic sense of humor:

> About Berkeley—the big classes, the two public lectures (described to me by Professor [John] Raleigh) are out of my style. Then the being away from home—I don't think I can decide this year about 1971. Still I feel drawn by Berkeley. Maybe less now. Your saying that I "should be in on it" is as tho I were to offer you Castine by saying "we seem likely to have a tidal wave and you should see the morale of a village in danger." I have so little faith in any of the sides, tho some in some things. Or rather, it's a joy this summer to be back to real life (real rest?). The contentions, the revolution, the counter-revolution will all come back to me, I cannot doubt it, and perhaps they'll be welcome.
>
> Well, Lizzie and I miss your old visits, and wish you were back.
>
> Affectionately,
> Cal

Lowell in Castine, Maine, in his studio, a converted barn by the ocean, painted a hideous aluminum color inside: him barefoot, wearing a crusty old Harvard blazer, cooking lobsters and drinking beer like any Bostonian up for the summer. Trying to describe the wind-filled shape of a striped jib while watching a sailboat regatta through binoculars, which he then turns on a rabbit crouched in the dry bracken—fascinated by the blood pulsing through magnified veins in the rabbit's pink, alert ears.

I hope I have conveyed what a terribly endearing person Robert Lowell could be, and something of his nature. To those of us whom good luck led to study writing with him, he taught almost by indirection, yet managed to touch us with a sense of his own struggle for the absolute in poetry. He transmitted a total dedication to the effort of saying something like a fresh coat of paint. In the tradition of his own youth—of Ford Madox Ford, John Crowe Ransom, and Allen Tate—he showed that a poem "must be tinkered with and recast until one's eyes pop out of one's head." At the same time he believed that the goal and meaning of writing lay beyond the mere process of writing; he was in his way as much a transcendentalist as Emerson. I have heard of his unkindnesses, and I don't doubt them, but to me he was always kind and, indeed, helped me through a very low period of my life. I feel he was a pure and simple soul trapped by fate in a tragically flawed personality and life. I went for years without seeing him, but when he died—too young, at sixty—I felt the roof had been ripped off the sky. How strange it is to be sitting here in the air conditioning in Memphis, to look at his picture on a book, and to think of him as not being alive. I always knew that when I had finally written something I could be really proud of, my greatest pleasure would be in showing it to him. But for that pleasure, there was not enough time in the world.

Richard Tillinghast (b. 1940), American poet and critic, was Lowell's pupil at Harvard. He is Professor of English at the University of Michigan and author of *Sleep Watch* (1969) and *Our Flag Was Still There* (1984).

1. Lowell, "To Mother."

2. Peter Davison, "The Difficulties of Being Major: The Poetry of Robert Lowell and James Dickey," *Atlantic* 220 (October 1967): 116–121. If the Lowell-Dickey meeting took place just after the appearance of Davison's article, then it must have been in 1967 (not 1965).

3. In J. R. R. Tolkein's *The Hobbit* (1937).

38 • Robert Lowell: A Reminiscence

Alan Williamson

I met Robert Lowell when I came to Harvard as a graduate student in 1964, and, being a little diffident at presenting myself as a poet, went to take his literature course, called The Craft of Poetry. So I saw him for the first time on the tenth floor of Holyoke Center, his large head silhouetted against its northern exposure: the Yard; the Victorian brick steeples aligned toward North Cambridge, like an architectural junk-shop of the ages of faith; and, mainly, pale gray early autumn sky. It was not unlike the setting he chose to describe in his own memoir of Sylvia Plath, high places suited him. And his talk, his reading, that fall seemed to dwell on the paradox of our consciousness above, but never freely above, its material nature and end: Hardy remembering his dead wife in her "original air-blue gown"; Emily Dickinson's "surmise," which, for Lowell, was not securely "Immortality," but a finite existence trying to grasp an infinite prospective non-being. . . . He ranked the English Victorians, and put Hardy and Arnold first; I believe for the syncopated, conversational wrench of individual pain they gave to the common elegiac cadence of the age—a combination he himself was then using masterfully, in poems like "Water," "The Old Flame," "Near the Ocean." However well I came to know him later, the larger-than-life image I formed of him at that time never entirely faded from my mind.

He could be a man of terrible and wonderful moral impressiveness. Shortly after that course in The Craft of Poetry ended, Lyndon Johnson began bombing North Vietnam, and Lowell's refusal to attend the White House Festival of the Arts made the front page of the *New York Times.* The next fall, I heard him read "Central Park" and "Waking Early Sunday Morning" in Sanders Theater, at a benefit for an anti-war organization called Massachusetts PAX:

First printed in *The Harvard Advocate* 113 (November 1979): 36–39. Revised and expanded from the *Real Paper,* 24 September 1977, p. 14. Reprinted by permission of *The Harvard Advocate.*

> Only man thinning out his kind
> sounds through the Sabbath noon, the blind
> swipe of the pruner and his knife
> busy about the tree of life. . . .

In the question period, a man—I think a reporter—rose from the second row and said, "You speak in your poem of 'man thinning out his kind.' Do you regard the [*largo;* all capitals] UNITED STATES OF AMERICA as the agent of this thinning out?" Lowell said, "Don't you?" He let at least two minutes go by in total silence, then insisted, "I asked you a question, and I'd like an answer." Another minute of silence; then, his point made, Lowell continued very softly, "I said *man* thinning out his kind; and that's what I meant; and it's going on all around us; and pray God it will stop."

In recent years some people—notably Louis Simpson[1]— have wondered how Lowell, with his pessimism, his pacifist breadth of sympathy, his aversion to sloganeering, could have been a figure of comfort and inspiration to a radical movement. One answer might be the simple contrast between the usual journalistic poem on napalm and the lines I have quoted—a Poundian ideogram allowing the Bible, American defoliation tactics, and that tidy old conservative metaphor of statecraft as gardening, to comment on each other by superposition. Another answer might be that Lowell's very ambivalence, his refusal to fall for easy hopes or to relinquish any imaginatively valuable point of view, gave a special meaning to his radical, and even illegal, actions, at a time when others used "complexity" as an excuse to avoid uncomfortable choices. Lowell's mere presence, like Montale's in Fascist Italy, seemed to prove that the best, the living edge, of traditional culture was on the dissenting side. Perhaps his unwilling extremeness—that seemed "to wince at pleasure, / and suffocate for privacy"—had a special appeal in Massachusetts, where students did not burn their draft cards but laid them in the collection plate at the Arlington Street Church, while the congregation sang the words of an earlier Lowell:

> Once to every man and nation
> comes the moment to decide,
> In the strife of Truth with Falsehood,
> for the good or evil side.[2] . . .

Robert Lowell spent much of his life criticizing the implications of that ancestral absolutism about politics, but one can't help reflecting that he would have been a less interesting and less admirable man if it had not been so deeply ingrained in him; if relativism had been his essence, and not a deliberately cultivated corrective.

His private personality, on the other hand, was genuinely casual, even languorous (and yet still more vivid, I think, in the memory of anyone who knew him well). He preferred to speak in impressions rather than judgments: "One feels that . . .". He carried his large body in a headlong, fumbling way he himself called "fogbound"; and preferred slumped, lounging postures when seated. (He was happiest of all lying full length on a sofa.) He liked to live in a certain amount of disorder; he joked in a poem that the President of Columbia's study after the student takeover was "much like mine left in my hands a month," and once scandalized and delighted a friend by saying that his cat lived "on what she picks up around the house." His talk was counterpointed and qualified by an endless vocabulary of hand gestures—chopping, hovering, smoothing; the hands held crosswise before him and then pushed out to the side, as though separating unruly conglomerated masses; the circling index finger of vertigo and resolution—gestures suggesting a kind of psychomachia latent in the ordinary conversational facts of balance or overstatement, banality or precision.

Perhaps as a kind of escape-valve for this inner battle, a peculiar, teasing, fantasy-laden humor tinged almost everything Lowell said in his last years. I remember my wife telling him about the troubles a friend—a student of Marcuse[3]—had had living in the tightly-knit household of her Communist, but none the less traditional, Bengali mother-in-law. Instantly Lowell had Marcuse himself moving into the house, trying to take things in hand, writing a Constitution . . . "The mother-in-law would win," was his conclusion. Sometimes the same humor glimmered darkly in his public actions: when asked for a Bicentennial poem, he obliged with one comparing Nixon's antics in his "final days" to the madness of George III. But most of his humor was personal and affectionate, and does not carry well without his voice, which was, to the slight shock of most people meeting him for the first time, Southern: not broad Southern, but the mild, pleasant drawl of Kentucky and Tennessee, where so many of his intimates—Elizabeth Hardwick, Peter Taylor, Allen Tate, Randall Jarrell—had grown up. He had a way of deliberately intensifying that accent's natural purrs and pauses that could set a whole room laughing, even when his joking was at its undergraduate nadir: "The great mystery about Peter [Taylor] . . . is his *age*. . . . Nobody really knows . . . how *old* he is. . . ." (And yet, the fact that this unforgettable voice was acquired, largely, from the same friends he teased with it suggests one of the vital contradictions in his character: his relation to others was at once dominating and expansive and curiously, even poignantly, dependent.)

I came to know Lowell better through attending his "Office Hours" from 1966 to 1968. These Office Hours were a Harvard institution over many years, but the English Department would not tell one exactly when and where they were held; one knew, or one did not. In my day, it was Wednesday morning, from 9:30 to 12:00, in a windowless, cement-block seminar room in Quincy House. Lowell's best undergraduate students came, as did a slightly larger number of graduate students, and some already recognized poets living, or visiting, in the area. In the late Sixties the regulars included—among many others—Jean Valentine, Helen Chasin, Richard Tillinghast, Frank Bidart, Grey Gowrie, Lloyd Schwartz, Courtenay Graham, and James Atlas. Most mornings, we waited tensely—though doing our best, under the influence of the Master's serene lassitude, to conceal it—for our poems to come up and be judged; but occasionally Lowell would read his own work in manuscript, or simply talk, about history, religion, or politics as often as about poetry. (Once a whole morning was spent on Churchill's history of the Second World War, with unorthodox comparisons between its author, Hitler, and Stalin.)

Lowell was a casual teacher, and economized the effort he put into understanding any single student poem; so it's a little hard to pin down why he defined, for me, the only imaginable way of trying to teach "creative writing." He managed to avoid the two easiest, but in some ways most limiting, paths a teacher can take: to be too readily pleased with work that is merely sincere, and does what it sets out to do; or to make the student better by rules, whether the old rules of rhyme, meter, impersonality, or the new rules of whatever style is most in vogue. He made us feel how rarely we touched the hem of truly memorable poetry. He would listen to the student read the poem once, then read it aloud himself, his hand hovering like a divining-rod until he reached a particular detail or turn of phrase, then plumping down: "it comes to life here." As often as not he would hand the student back a new poem, constructed on the spot out of the two or three passages that "came to life." If one had the temerity to object—after the manner of well-trained English majors in those days—that certain omitted elements formed a *pattern* with those retained, he would say something like, "if it's there already, why bring it in twice?" Provided that the poem belonged to a style and genre he found sympathetic to begin with, he was often uncannily right as to where the emotional center, the possible originality, lay. He came as near as I can imagine anyone coming to teaching the intuitions—about one's real subject; about diction; about structure—which so often distinguish good, let alone great, poets from journeymen.

This is not to say that he was a perfect teacher. His taste had its rigidities. He was partial (some of us felt, too partial) to a kind of generic 1960s poem vaguely influenced by his own style in *Life Studies:* a freshly observed detail in every line, but a quiet, everyday, even slightly depressed, tone of voice. Poems influenced by his own high style, or any hermetic mode, left him deeply ambivalent ("good lines, but . . ."); he was also unsure how plain poetry could dare to be, in the interests of ascetic truthfulness ("underenergized"). The same conflicts expressed themselves in his judgments of his peers and predecessors: fascinated irresolution over Hart Crane; high praise for poets like Dugan and Snodgrass; gingerliness toward Ginsberg, the Black Mountain School, Ashbery (though he admired *Kaddish,* and had a late change of heart with Ashbery, over "Self-Portrait in a Convex Mirror"). One was not altogether encouraged to argue with these judgments in the classroom; yet in the long run Lowell often showed greater interest in the students who revered him, but disagreed.

It was not always easy to pass from being his student, or his acquaintance, to being his friend (in my own case, real friendship came only after I had left Harvard, when we were, geographically, far apart). He had, and needed, his barriers; his own hypersensitivity mixed badly with the hypersensitivity and self-consciousness his fame evoked in most people who met him. But the other half of the story was the almost inexhaustible pleasure he took in being at leisure with his friends— spending a whole day together, reading each other's new work, taking walks, drinking white wine through dinner, and long after. He showed affection easily and without embarrassment, beginning a letter to an old (male) friend who has been ill, "Well, old dear . . .". He willingly used his own prestige to "throw a lifeline" to others (his own words about Randall Jarrell). I well remember the only long-distance call I ever had from him, which came the day after I had been refused tenure in the English Department where I was then teaching. He loved gossip, and liked enlisting others in boyish conspiracies: I remember him regretfully eyeing the empty wine bottles on the table--too near dessert-time, with too slow-drinking a party—then whispering to me, "Let's just ask the waiter for another round." Nobody else caught on, until three newly opened full bottles sat in our midst. . . . That story came back to me, reading the passage in *Day by Day* where he imagines heaven as

> a sensual table
> with five half-filled bottles of red wine
> set round the hectic carved roast—[4]

and then, even more wonderfully, as "the familiars of a lifetime . . . running together in the rain to mail a single letter."

This is not the time or place to go into what little I know about Lowell's experience of madness. What—beyond his poetry, even—made him a hero to a great many people was the fact that, living in the imminence of an internal chaos that would have wrecked many lives, he so often seemed stronger and not weaker than the normal person: in his steady and enormously ambitious work, which even illness could not interrupt; in his political courage; in the importance he gave to friendship; and in his ability to synthesize harsh truths with deeply felt values. I believe R. D. Laing[5] wrote somewhere that one should wish to be able to see the things a mad person sees, while remaining sane. Lowell would probably have distrusted the romanticism of that statement, but the need constantly to recognize and accommodate the undersides of motives, the irrational theatricalities of the mind, was part of the stature of his character: the swimming balance of a violent man who liked languor, a helpless *voyant* who overvalued realism. (When he was told, once, that smoking pot helped one to see one's own mental states through external things, he replied dryly, "I never had any trouble doing that.")

In his last years—when his life was made a great deal easier by lithium, and breakdowns tended to come mainly in the wake of external crises—he tried, almost as a kind of spiritual exercise, to see his peculiar fate as a mere variant of the generic tragedy, and pleasure, of being human and an individual. A curious, joyful feeling of being—not in the ordinary sense—beside himself, beside his own life, runs through his late poems. I think, particularly, of one of the very best, "Thanks-Offering for Recovery":

> The airy, going house grows small
> tonight, and soft enough to be crumpled up
> like a handkerchief in my hand.

In this detachment, Lowell becomes a kind of Everyman, "the *homme sensuel,* free / to turn my back on the lamp, and work." Later in the poem, he stands beside himself in a more drastic, even grotesque, sense; the story requires retelling. When he was recovering from a breakdown, Elizabeth Bishop sent him, as a get-well present, a Brazilian *ex voto*[6]— the replica of the afflicted part of the body which Latin Catholics give to the saint believed responsible for the cure. Too late, Miss Bishop realized to her chagrin that this particular object was specific to "head-injury or migraine." (I can still almost hear Lowell's voice relishing these words, just as he relished his own joke about "Peter's age.") In the poem, the *ex voto* becomes, with wonderful ambivalent wit, an emblem of Lowell's problematic specialness, of madness, of the closed-in self-observation and self-recording which apparently grew more unremitting with depression:

> a head holy and unholy,
> tonsured or damaged,
> with gross black charcoaled brows and stern eyes
> frowning as if they had seen the splendor
> times past counting. . . .
> It is all childcraft, especially
> its shallow, chiseled ears,
> crudely healed scars lumped out
> to listen to itself, perhaps, not knowing
> it was made to be given up.
> Goodbye nothing.

It is terrible, no doubt, to come to regard a great part of one's life, spent in pain, as a "nothing"; but it is also freedom. . . . In many theologies, it is at the threshold of a beatific vision that one feels that evil is not substantial but merely privative; that the self-conscious self is the "shadow" of a larger universal one. This much is explicit: Lowell has, however shakily or temporarily, escaped the sense that he is merely the self, and plaything, of fate, "created to be given away." The *ex voto*—like his autobiographical poetry, though the analogy is never leaned on—has taken his place as scapegoat, allowing him to float free into a dimension, "airy," undefinable, where mere existence is its own purpose and recompense.

Such a serenity and ease seemed to radiate from Lowell, though he talked freely of depression, the last time I saw him, during the great European heat wave of July, 1976. Perhaps for that reason, when I try to distinguish these late poems from the poems of loss and determinism in

For the Union Dead, I think of the distance between Holyoke Center and the scene of our last meeting. The wavering of London under the heat; the floor-through townhouse room, another high place, almost as bare as a classroom, but with a seventeenth century mounting around the one mirror; and Lowell opening a drawer where a hundred of those family photographs which, in life as in his "Epilogue," he loved so specifically, lay unmounted, rising on each other like waves in the sea.

Alan Williamson (b. 1944), American critic and Professor of English at the University of California, Davis, was Lowell's pupil at Harvard in the late 1960s. He is the author of *Pity the Monsters: The Political Vision of Robert Lowell* (1974) and *Introspection and Contemporary Poetry* (1984).

1. See Louis Simpson, "Robert Lowell's Indissoluble Bride," *A Revolution in Taste* (New York, 1978), pp. 131–167.

2. James Russell Lowell, "The Present Crisis" (1844).

3. Herbert Marcuse (1898–1979), German philosopher and educator, adopted by the New Left in the 1960s. He is the author of *Reason and Revolution* (1941) and *Eros and Civilization* (1955).

4. Lowell, "The Withdrawal."

5. R. D. Laing (b. 1927), Scottish psychiatrist, author of *The Divided Self* (1960) and *The Politics of Experience* (1967).

6. Latin: from a vow.

39 • Robert Lowell

Frank Bidart

In Elizabeth Hardwick's *Sleepless Nights,* there is a passage about Robert Lowell that eloquently expresses his relationship with many people.

> He remembered what a disappointment he had been to his grandfather, how the old man, dying of cancer, would call out to him, the only male around since a handsome son had died at thirty. Who are you? Grandfather would ask. One year thin and handsome and the next year bulky and brooding. Cannot shoot a gun, cannot ride a horse. What prizes have you won, except for collecting snakes and mismatched socks? On a sailboat, a menace. Where are you standing, why are you standing gazing at the water? You will drown us all.

The scene suggests the inextricable mixture of love, expectation, frustration, *rancor* Lowell aroused in many. The fact that this was true was always a source of pain for me. *Why* did it happen? Was it Lowell's "fault"—or others'? Did "fault" or "blame" even apply?

He once said to me, "When I'm dead, I don't care what you write about me; all I ask is that it be *serious.*" This sentence reflects, I think, the relentless mind that disturbed so many people, even friends and family. In a central way, Robert Lowell was not quite civilized. However courtly or charming, casual or playful he was by turns, in his art and his personal relationships Lowell was unfashionably—even, at times, ruthlessly—*serious.*

He knew that his poems destroyed the decencies, the privacies of family life as these are ordinarily understood. He was haunted by the pain the poems caused.

First printed in *The Harvard Advocate* 113 (November 1979): 12.

> Can I be forgiven the life-waste of my lifework?
> Was the thing worth doing worth doing badly?
> Man in the world, a whirlpool in a river—
> soul cannot be saved outside the role of God.[1]

Lowell's dark night, as a writer, came after the publication of his second book. For about five years, he wrote almost no poetry. The kind of poem he knew how to write, technically, couldn't embody his experience: "I couldn't get my experience into tight metrical forms."

After *Life Studies,* he never allowed that to happen again. At whatever cost—the dismay, the disappointment of reviewers, family, friends—the poems proceeded from what at the deepest level absorbed and obsessed his mind.

The issues, agonies, dilemmas of his personal life were an essential (by the end, *the* essential) part of this. As a whole, the poems attempt to "take on," catch, embody, express the whole world. (The unrhymed sonnets are, I think, an attempt to ingest the whole world.) "Soul cannot be saved outside the role of God." The poems don't pretend to resolve the moral issues, or justify the pain, the "life-waste," that the fact of writing them caused. They can only dramatize, "play out" the shape and nature of these dilemmas.

Van Gogh, in his letters, says that we must "truly love" what we in fact do love.

> *Love what we love,* how superfluous a warning this seems to be, and yet it is justified to an enormous extent! For how many there are who waste their best efforts on something that is not worth their best efforts, whereas they treat what they love in a stepmotherly way instead of yielding wholly to the irresistible urge of their hearts. And yet we venture to call this conduct "firmness of character" and "strength of mind," and we waste our energy on an unworthy creature, all the while neglecting our true sweetheart. And all this "with the most sacred intentions," thinking "we are compelled to do it," out of "moral conviction" and a "sense of duty." And so we have the "beam in our own eye," confusing a pseudo- or would-be conscience with our true conscience. . . . The man who damn well refuses to love what he loves dooms himself.

Lowell's presence and being had a peculiar *density.* He seemed to carry around within his body the whole of his past life, past art—both as grace and as burden. Valéry's words about Mallarmé irresistibly come to mind: "Near him while he was still alive, I thought of his destiny as already realized." Several months before he died, he said to me with an air of resignation, despair, and pride: "I don't know the value of what I've written, but I know that I changed the game."

Frank Bidart (b. 1939), American poet and Professor of English at Wellesley College, was Lowell's pupil and is his literary executor. He is the author of *Golden State* (1973) and *The Sacrifice* (1983).

    1. Lowell, "Dear Sorrow 2."

40 • Robert Lowell: The Teacher

Judith Baumel

Robert Lowell was a powerful, commanding man. He could take over a room with his energy which wasn't a dynamic energy. When I knew him, the last years of his life, he was ill and this may have contributed to the contradictions I saw. He was tall but he stooped. He had a quick wit but spoke and moved slowly. He was brilliant and social but would behave like the absent minded professor. We would be on our way to the steamy classroom in Holyoke Center and find him slowly walking in the other direction down Mass. Ave. toward Levitt and Pierce. Fifteen minutes later he would appear with the French cigarettes he would chain smoke through two hours of class.

Without exception student writers wanted to take Robert Lowell's poetry workshop. The fact that not many advanced workshops were offered at Harvard and that Lowell had a reputation for choosing his classes quixotically added to the anxiety everyone felt on the first day of class. The seminar room was packed. Lowell didn't seem to know what to do with the large group although he must have had equally large first classes before. When he started talking about literature some student was anxious to discuss the most obscure texts to impress Lowell and he seemed to know this and enjoy it. In the end he selected an astrophysicist at the Observatory who'd never written a word, a social studies concentrator who was beginning to be interested in poetry and only then a few of the writing students. I had just switched from chemistry to English and hadn't written much. He delighted in the combination, the possibility of fresh or skewed insight and we felt lucky to be in this class, drawn together as if for a formal dinner with surprises.

Students took the class because he was a great poet and a great man but few realized beforehand that Lowell was a great teacher of literature and an awful workshop teacher. I'm not sure that that sort of teaching is

First printed in *The Harvard Advocate* 113 (November 1979): 32–33.

necessary or even possible, but Lowell had very little help to offer in the form of direct, constructive criticism of line, structure, intent, execution of student drafts. He would say, rarely, "this line is quite nice," or "I like it, this is my favorite part." Such praise was enormously welcome. Rarely "supportive," he was usually harsh, sometimes summarily so. I once brought a terrible poem about my childhood fear of nuns and of their habits touching me and in it compared the nuns to ravens. He didn't see why anyone should be afraid of the sisters of mercy and argued not that I failed to express the fear well but that it wasn't possible. He hated the ravens. Later in the class we talked about a poem called "The Invalid" or something equivalent. The invalid was in his hospital bed for an awfully long time when Lowell looked up from the poem and with a boyish smile in his eyes asked the poet "Is he a Catholic?" "I don't know, I never thought about that." To which Lowell replied "I asked because if he were, some ravens might fly in and comfort him."

In his criticism, Lowell could be arbitrary, petty and even cruel but I never felt he meant to hurt. Perhaps this came from the democracy of his discussions. He talked about the published work of "real" poets from Shakespeare to Jarrell or Berryman. And our work was placed beside theirs and treated as if it should be, though never was, equal. He liked a line or he liked a phrase and we learned much more listening to him talk about poems other than our own. During the first hour of each class he would choose some poet and talk about a few poems. Sometimes the work was in the assigned Ellmann *Norton Anthology* in front of us, sometimes not. One clear memory is an eloquent explication of W. C. Williams' "The Yachts." Lowell found the uncharacteristic long lines full of wonderful rhythms and tension and he compared them for an hour to Crane's "Voyages I." He could explicate well but he also gave marvelous personal readings: just how this line or that struck him. He delivered these insights as if they were parlor conversation. He seemed capable of getting very very close to the poem itself—of knowing exactly what the verse was doing.

He was a gossipy reader and teacher of poetry. In his nineteenth-century class we read Wordsworth's "Anecdote for Fathers" and he joked about what a tyrannical father Wordsworth was. He told stories as if they were the latest news. He enjoyed bringing the lives of poets to bear on their work. Lowell could sum up an entire poetic career with an epigrammatic sentence: "Tennyson is an intense, moody, clumsy young man with enormous metrical skill. Pound, who loathed him, has a Tennysonian splendor." Of Blake: "His whole conflict is that man isn't free but when he doesn't write in fetters he isn't good. I find his long poems very tiresome. In a way they're about sex. They're not professional." Of Browning: "His life had no plot, no romantic flair, even though he married Elizabeth Barrett. But he invented the mystery novel in verse and wrote more good lines than any nineteenth-century poet." Individual lines were important to Lowell. He would ask which was the best or the worst line in a poem and told the workshop that in his own poems he didn't go on to the next line until the one he was working with was finished. For Lowell poems seemed to come together in a single line.

He talked for the majority of all these seminars and he read the poems out loud, that was important too. And then he'd ask his few questions. He once made an offhand apology about all the talking and reading, saying his favorite class at Kenyon was one where the Professor talked and read and they all listened rather passively. Lowell's comments were intimate like his poems. He was, to the students at least, a shy man who wanted to reveal things so the details became confidences and we were privileged to share them. When drawn into discussing the famous incident where he turned down a White House invitation to protest Johnson's foreign policy he chuckled and told how Johnson's speechwriter quoted Arnold when he said he liked Lowell's poetry. Lowell said "It was really an epigraph (The opening of 'The Mills of the Kavanaughs'), the lightest thing he could find."[1] The intimacy was increased by his soft voice, sometimes impossible to hear, the reticent approval-seeking mannerisms, the tilted head, crooked glasses.

In class he talked but outside he could listen avidly. He was the Poet at the Signet Annual Dinner my senior year. When I arrived with another student for cocktails, Lowell stood there alone, tall and obvious, in the middle of the crowded library. It didn't seem possible that he was as awkward as he seemed. We were thrilled that he recognized us as we approached. We brought him a drink, went to one of the dining rooms where he leaned on the mantle and listened to us joke together, talk about, as I recall, Jews at Harvard then and now. His interest in us was genuine. Lowell wanted information, had an appetite to know everything, and our exhilaration when we realized we were entertaining him let us continue, made us, we hoped, funnier. The reading that night was wonderful, his introductions the usual biographical intimacies. He read

some of the new poems later published in *Day by Day;* Robert Fitzgerald
sighed and clucked his appreciation of the more beautiful lines and every-
one felt, as always, that they were sharing something very very special.

A friend from the poetry workshop wrote recently about discover-
ing him in Flannery O'Connor's letters and remembering other por-
traits, *Armies of the Night* particularly. She shared what she labeled a
universal fascination with Lowell among those he touched. When we
were undergraduates, my writer friends and I behaved, with regard to
Robert Lowell, as we would never dare with a movie star. We followed
him on the street, ate at Iruña's on Wednesday afternoons where he came
in after office hours and before classes, discussed his odd suits or ties,
read every interview with him, all he wrote, all he was interested in. He
gave me marvelous introductions to Crane, Williams, Browning,
Hopkins. We studied these poets because of Lowell's love for them and
we adopted that love. My very first poetry teacher, Peggy Rizza, had
been taught by Lowell and she told the class that it was dangerous to read
Lowell because one's writing would never be the same and never be clear
of his great influence. It was impossible to avoid imitating the seductive
charm of the poems; their mixture of history and personal memory. And
it's true we all struggle against his influence in our work. But the over-
whelming memories remain without struggle. The feeling of the man
and teacher, the feelings he evoked, are years later still powerful and
fresh.

Judith Baumel was a pupil in Lowell's poetry workshop at Harvard in the
1970s.
   1. The epigraph, "Ah love, let us be true / To one another! . . ." is from
Matthew Arnold's "Dover Beach" (1867).

41 • Remembering Cal

Esther Brooks

When someone says Robert Lowell to me, or Cal, as he was known to his friends, an instantaneous picture comes to mind: Cal sitting in a chair, his head inclined a bit to one side, his chin pressed slightly down, his magnified eyes peering through their lenses at you, one hand holding a drink, the other raised in front of his chest, palm out jabbing at the air, a cigarette between the index and middle finger, dropping ashes all over his shirt front, talking and talking and commanding your whole attention. The only variation is the expression on his face. Depending on my own mood, I suppose, I can see him looking introspective and intense; at other times, choking back his merriment, his lower lip becoming thicker with some impending verbal mischief, or again a look of anguish brought on by some thought of doom, of man's fate, or of the world gone so madly awry.

When Cal was well he was enormous fun to be with. His way of looking at things was so completely original that you yourself began to see everything from a different perspective. Hours meant nothing to him when he was interested. Day turned into night and night back into day while he, with his seemingly limitless stamina, worried an idea, rejected it, discovered another, built mental pyramids, tore them down, discoursed on the habits of wolves, the Punic Wars, Dante, Napoleon, Shakespeare, Alexander the Great, politics, his friends, religion, his work, or the great noyade at Nantes.[1] Whatever the subject it all came forth as though it were being pushed at you, helped on its way by that outward prodding palm. Sometimes this incredible energy of his would exhaust you and you would suddenly feel like screaming, or running away in search of some undefined moment, some unexamined fact, some purely sensuous reaction to beauty.

But if you did run away you would soon come back, because you

---

Robert Lowell: A Tribute, edited by Rolando Anzilotti (Pisa: Nistri-Lischi, 1979), pp. 37–44.

knew that this was without a doubt one of the most knowledgeable and original minds you would ever encounter and not just knowledgeable and original, but often wonderfully, marvelously funny.

I think he was probably the most entirely cerebral person I have ever known. His creativity was not diffuse as it so often is with great artists. There were no signs that his talent spilled over into other fields. He didn't sing, didn't play an instrument, didn't draw. He wasn't a linguist. He couldn't dance, nor did he have, in spite of his unusual physical strength, any athletic skill other than a puffy game of tennis. In other words all his genius was concentrated entirely in his mind—a mind so original, so perceptive, so finely wrought, that seemed able to intuit sensory experience without reacting directly to it. He could discourse on music as brilliantly as any trained musician but he could not hear whether a note was higher or lower when played for him on a piano. He had only the meanest, most rudimentary grasp of foreign languages and yet he translated foreign poetry brilliantly. He had an extraordinary sense of metre but no physical sense of rhythm. He visited churches and museums, avidly seeking out works of art by the great masters. Yet if over there in some small chapel within a great church you found a madonna and her infant sitting tranquilly as she had these last three hundred years or more under a perfectly carved cupola, touched by a beam of unexpected sunlight, and he found you there almost hypnotized, moved nearly to tears, he would pause to ask "Who is it by?" and if it was not by some famous master or was simply ignoto,[2] he would pass it by as though blind. Once in Venice when I had become impatient with being asked to locate yet another masterpiece—this time it was a particular painting by Titian in the Basilica of the Frari—I said "Why don't you find it just by looking?" He didn't like this at all and began to cajole me into finding it for him, telling me I was being childish, that Titian was more important than guessing games, etc. But when he understood that I was not going to locate it for him he intercepted a monk hurrying to his prayers and asked him "Dov'è Tiziano?" and the monk pointing to heaven replied "In Paradiso, speriamo bene,"[3] crossed himself and hurried on. I was trying to stifle my laughter when Cal asked "Is he a friend of yours?" Then he appealed to me again. I was tired. We had been sightseeing all day. I bolted from the church and made for the nearest bar. Still trying to persuade me, he came puffing along behind me, calling out "Wait! Stop this! This is a bad joke!" As we entered the bar he suddenly gave up (for the moment) and ordered "caffè in bicchiere."[4]

That was one of his oddities. In Italy he always ordered "caffè in bic-chiere." I never heard him do it anywhere else. Anyway, that much Italian he had mastered. He had his coffee in bicchiere, and I had mine in a cup. Afterwards, feeling somewhat revived, I agreed to lead him back to the Frari. Once there, standing before Titian's great work, Cal with-out any embarrassment whatsoever, began a discourse on its merit as a painting, on Titian and his times, on beautiful women, on Titian and beautiful women, on old men, on the works of old men. And as always he was riveting, fascinating, funny, odd, and completely, interestingly original and serious.

I have always felt that Cal stood at a different angle to experience than most people I've known. Most of us, I believe, encounter something, then we feel it, and then we think about it. With Cal it would seem that whatever he encountered he thought about first, then he turned it into metaphor, and then he reacted with feeling toward that abstraction. In other words the feeling, though no less intense, was once removed from the actual experience. Metaphor was his reality, not the original fact.

One time when we were all in England together, one of his step-children came dashing into the room shouting "Melanie's stuck in the bog and can't get out! Please come help her, Robert!" (Melanie was her friend down for the weekend). Cal didn't move. Instead he looked around the room in anguish and said, with his outward prodding palm jabbing at the air, "We are all stuck in the bog. Nobody can help us. It's impossible to help someone out of their bog when we can't get out of our own bog." At first I was mesmerized by the truth of what he was saying, but seeing the panic on the child's face, I dashed from the room and screamed back over my shoulder, "This is a real bog, damn it all!" I tore down the soggy pasture land and found there at the foot of the hill a small and terrified child sinking quite above her knees in the mud of a very real and very dangerous bog. It didn't take too much strength to pull her out, but her boots were left behind in the process and they may still be there as some sort of testament to reality. We met Cal and his friends as we came back up the hill. He had belatedly taken in the fact that a real bog rather than a metaphoric one had existed.

With this story, after the laugh is over, one might say that he was a cruel man. But I believe that instead he was once removed from the actual bog. He certainly wasn't cruel if cruelty means not caring. He cared enormously about human life and he cared enormously about his friends and would do anything for them within his realm of possibility.

If you were the victim of some deep personal tragedy, he could be the first to comprehend your suffering. He could take your pain apart, verbally dissect it, study it, expound upon it, until you almost felt the pain no longer belonged to you. But I wonder if he could comprehend the kind of pain that brings you into an isolated world of tears and rage where no thought is wanted or even possible.

Robert Traill Spence Lowell had become well known in literary circles by the time he was barely thirty. From then on his fame steadily increased, and he seemed to enjoy every moment of its consequences without losing his sense of humor, or becoming a victim of his own notoriety.

When America began to be torn apart by the tragedy of Viet Nam he thought about it and reacted to events in a deeply personal way. He never got caught up in shrill causes or violent reaction. His anguish was extreme, but he somehow managed to remain lucid, independent, and courageously non-violent. This was much harder than it might sound, for during the late Sixties in the United States and particularly around the universities, there was the most terrible confusion of purpose. Nevertheless, somewhere in that seemingly apocalyptical breakdown of human reason there were genuine grievances which could not be resolved until our government ended its illegal war in Viet Nam. Towards that end Cal did all he could and he seemed to have an almost infallible instinct for making the right gesture at the right time. It wasn't always easy to distinguish the motives of the various groups who arranged themselves under the banner of the peace movement, and in 1967 for example, he found himself committed to read at Harvard for a group which, as it turned out, was one of the many disruptive organizations abounding on the campus at that time. The major part of its members weren't students at the University at all but were outsiders, there for the purpose of stirring up violence. When my husband and the poet William Alfred and I arrived at the theatre and took this fact in, we tried to warn Cal, but he was late getting in from New York and suddenly he was there before us on the readers' platform—tall, awkward, disheveled, somewhat diffident, and gazing around him in what appeared to be a rather vague and absent way. Then he sat down. Someone wearing a red arm band came from the back of the hall to introduce him as "the great poet of the Revolution," and a voice somewhere in the back of me yelled "Let's have the poem 'Che Guevara!'" Then another voice—"Yay man, Che Guevara, viva la Revolución!" Cal stood up, muttered something about being a poet, not a revolutionary, and began to read a poem he had written to his daughter Harriet. And so for forty minutes or more he read some of his early poems and some more recent ones, while from time to time a voice from somewhere in the audience would call out for "Che Guevara, man, let's have the Che Guevara!" But Cal kept on: a new poem for Allen Tate, an older one for George Santayana, something from *Life Studies* but no poem for "Che Guevara," no "Caracas," no "The March, 1" or "The March, 2," not a single political poem. However vague or diffident or vulnerable he had seemed at the beginning, he had grasped the situation almost instantaneously and he had set about to defuse its potential explosiveness. He had turned a radical protest meeting into a poetry reading. He had fulfilled his commitment to read but he had not been used.

Cal was also a tragic figure, and that sense of tragedy was as much a part of his aura as was his gaiety, his love of life, and his extraordinary intelligence. There is nothing odd in this when one contemplates his memory for he was, more than anyone I've ever known, all contrast and contradiction—a sort of Push-me-pull-you of opposite motives and directions. In a paper as brief as this one there is no time or desire to discuss at length the terrible curse of his recurrent madness but it cannot be avoided entirely for it was his obverse side and an important part of his poetic inspiration. For those of us who loved him there never could have been a Jekyll so opposite to his Hyde, nor a figure who could have suffered more from being so inwardly at odds with himself. After one of his breakdowns I asked him if when he was well he could remember all he had said and done when he was ill. "Yes," he replied, "everything. And that is the worst part of it." He felt himself responsible for everything he was, regardless of his state, sane or deranged, manic or depressed, or on the thin edge of illness or recovery. At a certain point in the early Sixties he was put on lithium, a drug which was supposed to control the effects of schizophrenia. For a while this seemed to work and he appeared to be released from the terrible ordeal of more and more frequent breakdowns. But lithium, like any drug not properly monitored, can become a boomerang as much as a cure. As the years wore on he became more and more careless about its use and the consequent effects were subtly noticeable to those who knew him well. The well person and the unwell person seemed to rub together in a strange kind of muted euphoria. One no longer feared that he would go mad but one kept waiting for the delicate and exquisite side of his mind to assert

itself once again. Of course it did but at other times he seemed to deterio-
rate, becoming the victim of a kind of breezy sarcastic teasing egotism
which left him frequently deprived of any judgment and drove him to
make the worst kind of decisions for himself as a man, and in my opin-
ion, as a poet. In this state he expatriated himself to England. He left his
wife and his daughter, he took upon himself another wife, three step-
children, and shortly afterwards fathered a son. "This is much better,"
he said to me when I visited him in his new home in England. But was it
really? I didn't believe it for a minute and I don't think he did for he
protested too much and too insistently that he was only as he said "let-
ting the great force of life" act upon him and lead him where it would. In
his case the great force of life proved to be of crushing strength, totally
belying the weakness of the literary cliché.

He was, as he so often repeated, "crazy" about his new wife (crazy
was a word he used nearly as often as the blind refer to seeing) but the
chaos of their life together brought in its wake so many problems that
both his health and his passion declined. For four years he wrestled with
divided loyalties which caused him enormous mental suffering and two
more breakdowns, and all the while his homesickness increased. By 1976
this totally American man, whose poetic inspiration seemed wrenched
from New England granite, could no longer resist, in all its various
meanings, the tug of home. He arrived in the U.S. in October of 1976,
delayed some few weeks by an illness which was only later diagnosed as
having been a minor heart attack. For those of us who were close to him
there seemed no great cause for alarm, for in every other way he seemed
so much better. Looking back now one could almost say that his mind
had begun to heal itself just as his heart had begun to fail him. Gone was
the breezy egotism. He seemed not only in touch with his own feelings
but with the feelings of those whom he had caused to suffer so very
much. A delicacy of judgment returned along with humility, and com-
passion replaced once again the rather offhand insensitivity of past years.
In May of 1977 over a long lunch Cal told me that he planned to remain
in the United States for good. "America and teaching at Harvard are my
life's water," he said. "I don't want to divide what's left of my life
between two continents and two cultures." "Where will you live?" I
asked. And then he told me of his intention of returning to his former
wife, Elizabeth Hardwick. "She has been awfully good about all this.
Awfully good to me through all these difficult seven years." And so she
had, this extraordinary brilliant woman.

That summer I visited them in Castine, Maine. The last evening we listened to American Civil War songs on the record player which very soon became background music to Cal's thoughts on American history. Should the Civil War have been fought? He thought probably not. Would the slaves have been freed without such a terrible conflict? He thought they probably would have. Would the United States have been better split in two? He thought there were good arguments that it might have been. As always, these thoughts, these speculations, were totally interesting whether you agreed with him or not and they all came forth at you, helped on their way by that outward prodding palm, with his head inclined slightly to one side, his beautiful intelligent face looking slightly bemused, slightly pained, while with a drink in one hand, a cigarette in the other he dropped ashes all over his shirt front.

The rest of the story has been widely reported. In September he left for Ireland to see his son and put that part of his life in some sort of order. Due to stay there two weeks he arrived back in New York sooner than expected. Leaving the airport in a taxi he died on his way home. It is said that in his dying he had not suffered at all.

Esther Brooks, a long-standing friend of Lowell, was a ballet dancer and teacher who lived in Florence in the 1960s and 1970s. Philip Booth notes that she was a house guest at Castine, Maine.

1. French: drowning. In 1793 Jean-Baptiste Carrier, ruthless envoy of the revolutionary Committee of Public Safety, replaced executions by guillotine with mass drownings at Nantes, in western France.

2. Italian: by an unknown artist.

3. Italian: In heaven, I dearly hope.

4. Italian: coffee in a glass.

42 • Lowell in the Classroom

Helen Vendler

In 1955–56, Lowell was teaching at Boston University, where I was a special student in transit from chemistry to English. I sat in, off and on, unofficially, on his course in literature, but I was unprepared (as I now realize) to receive what he had to give—casual remarks, *obiter dicta*,[1] a slant of light, a polemic too concealed to be visible. I had read his poems, and admired them, and expected a prophet, denunciatory and theatrical; instead, a mild, soft-spoken, and myopic man, his voice lost in the hard-surfaced room, offered disconnected sentences that were more musings than messages. I thought learning came in sterner packages, and could not understand a form of teaching that had nothing to do with the imposition of a body of knowledge, but rather aimed at the example of a mind in action, a mind brooding as much on life as on literature. Our tastes differed; he had an inexplicable love of Hardy, and dwelt prodigally on "The Convergence of the Twain": it was to be twenty years before I was to read Hardy—so awkward, so lumbering, so unsatisfying to my adolescent wish for finish—with any sense of his crabbed honesty and painful candor.

When I came to know Lowell, in the last three years of his life, I thought back often to my earlier ignorance; finally I plucked up courage enough to ask him whether, when I was in town, I could come to his Wednesday class at Harvard on nineteenth-century poetry. I did not tell him it was a reparatory gesture, too ashamed to admit its origin. He was, as he was so often, amused; but he was seigneurial enough not to make the self-deprecatory remarks commonly offered in such cases. I missed a lot of the meetings because of work or journeys out-of-town; to my regret, I missed the Keats classes, the Hardy classes, the Tennyson classes, the Browning classes. I had asked him, earlier, if someone were

First printed in *The Harvard Advocate* 113 (November 1979): 22–26, 28–29. Reprinted in *New York Times Book Review*, 3 February 1980, pp. 9, 28–29. Reprinted by permission of *The Harvard Advocate*.

taping his courses, and he laughed and said no, nobody had ever asked to. This took me aback. I should have taped them; but then, I thought there would be more years, and more classes. In fact, they were the last classes he taught in the spring of 1977.

I used to jot down things he said, and this seems the place to record some of those things, but first I should say something—which will eventually be supplemented, I hope, by others—about his way of talking about poetry. The first thing to be said is that he came at poetry by way of poets, not by way of single texts or a theory of creation. It may be that all poets think this way, as Blake thought of Milton, as Keats hoped to be "among the English poets" after his death. In one of the poems of *History,* Lowell echoed Keats and questioned the sufficiency of his hope: the poem, "In the Back Stacks," written on the publication day of one of Lowell's books (I don't know which one), bleakly reflects that "everything printed will come to these back stacks" of Harvard—forgotten, or imposed on unwilling students:

> It's life in death to be typed, bound and delivered,
> lie on reserve like the *Harvard British Poets,*
> hanged for keeping meter.[2] They died with Keats.
> Is it enough to be a piece of thread
> in the line from King David to Hart Crane?

Lowell began his classes on each successive poet with an apparently indolent, speculative, and altogether selective set of remarks on the poet's life and writing; the poet appeared as a man with a temperament, a set of difficulties, a way of responding, a vocation, prejudices. The remarks were indistinguishable from those Lowell might have made about a friend or an acquaintance; the poets *were* friends or acquaintances; he knew them from their writing better than most of us know others from life. This, in the end, seems to me the best thing Lowell did for his students; he gave them the sense, so absent from textbook headnotes, of a life, a spirit, a mind, and a set of occasions from which writing issues— a real life, a real mind, fixed in historical circumstance and quotidian abrasions. Arnold, for example, appeared before the class roughly as follows (I reconstruct from notes, and the sentences are here isolated in a staccato unlike Lowell's actual talk):

He was born only ten years after Tennyson, but into a wholly different world. He married at 31, and then spent thirty-three years as a School Inspector. His fury against the Philistines—the middle class—is at least partly explained by what he had to see in the course of his official duties. He seems witty and energetic in writing, but he's always complaining about fatigue and the fluctuations of the spirit. He gave bouncy, eloquent, and impertinent lectures; but the poems are uneven—when he's uneven, he's stiff and abstract, and insists too much—a lack of art, strange in someone who knew so much about art. You'd almost say all his good passages are description—and of course description with meaning, it's not imagism. He's an interesting poet because you feel great eloquence and great difficulty in the writing.

This sort of thing was followed by a set of comments on "Dover Beach," ranging from the wittily malicious ("Arnold was a great Francophile, but the French coast is still something frightening to an Englishman") to the piercing: about Arnold's remarks on "the Sea of Faith," Lowell said that Hopkins "would not have said 'the Sea of Faith'" (it is characteristic of Lowell to have used the word "said" instead of the word "written": he regarded poetry as utterance more often than as writing, at least when teaching it) "because one only talks that way after having ceased to believe: Belief is very alive—more alive than anything." It interested me that Lowell, when reading the poem, which he knew, as he knew most of the poems he taught, by heart, substituted "*tumultuous* cadence slow" for "*tremulous* cadence slow"—an instance of the way in which he turned every poet he read into a version of himself. (In the first long conversation I had with him he said, accusingly, "You don't like 'Esthétique du Mal' as much as I do." "No, I guess not," I answered, and then he said assertively, "I think it's the best thing Stevens wrote." "Why?" I asked. He stopped, and said with some glee, "Because it's the *most like me*.")

Lowell was never embarrassed to be heartfelt. At the end of "Dover Beach," he said, the poem turned to love because "nothing else has, at that point, any validity, any moral sweetness." It was, of course, phrases like "moral sweetness" that I missed the drift of when I was twenty-two, but that I waited to hear in these later classes. At the same time, after such a depth, Lowell could ascend to the anecdotal and the personal—in this instance, saying to us, "You know, Auden regretted that line, 'We must love one another or die,' saying 'You die anyway'[3]—and I said to him, 'But you didn't mean it that way, you meant "die spiritually,"'" and he

said, 'Yes, of course, but they didn't seem to get that.' So he refused it."
The anecdotal then turned personal: "After I refused to go to the White
House, a critic who decided not to like my poems on that account said
'But I like some of Lowell, like "Ah love, let us be true to one another."'
(I had used it as an epigraph.)" The excursus became moral: "'We must
love one another or die' is about loving one's neighbor, but 'Dover
Beach' is about loving one other person, which is more impressive. We
don't love our neighbors—we don't know them well enough—or know
them too well."

This sort of commentary would continue (and I have by no means
reproduced all that Lowell would say) from poem to poem. "Arnold's
language was much fancier than Wordsworth's—much more dressed up.
There's no childhood or adolescence in Arnold." With a sentence like
that, Arnold's constriction is put into a psychological setting that re-
moves the sting of criticism. Lowell was always sympathetic with his
poets, but sympathetic with what they were, with Arnold's "slightly sad
wit" at the end of *Sohrab and Rustum* ("not enough to save the poem, but
enough to end it"). Arnold was, for Lowell, "a preacher with no
church—it's hard to preach poetry in a poem." The practical difficulties
of writing linked Lowell to his predecessors: "When you write poetry
you do it by instinct and by ear," and when those are in tune, as in the
end of "The Scholar-Gypsy," the poem succeeds. The poet's freedom to
feel and act, his freedom to invent and to disobey, hovered as a constant
subject beneath all that Lowell said. "In the old days of the New Critics,
'Dover Beach' was criticized for not continuing the sea imagery in the
last stanza, but I think by then you've had quite enough of it." Lowell
wanted books like his own commentaries: "I like those books that give
you an idea of how the poem was composed and who it's addressed to,
all the circumstances—instead of telling you Marsyas was flayed by
Apollo[4] and so on." He ironically praised teachers of his own ilk: "The
best teacher I ever had was Fred Robinson. All he did was read aloud
from his own edition [of Chaucer], giving his agreeable interpretations,
explaining words explained in his own edition."

From time to time, Lowell would be seduced away from the poet of
the day by recollections of another poet, another poem, or simply by the
idea of poetry itself. The lyric, he said, quoting Keats's remark about
"one eternal pant," is "a monument to immediacy," a "play of mysti-
fication and demystification." A poem "*is* an event, not a record of an
event." "It makes a claim to produce an event—it is this for which lyric

strives and which it sometimes brings off." Lowell instanced "Keats's most fascinating poem," "This living hand," as a case in point in which, as Keats "eschews apostrophe for direct address," he produces an event. Lowell's sense of the poem as event, together with his equal sense of the living voice speaking the lines out of some occasion, made the poems instantly available as experience, as "To Marguerite" was about "the rending pain of parting." But nothing escaped his irony. The next sentence was "Of course it's slightly tiresome as an idea—people as islands—you wouldn't think you could keep this up for three stanzas."

Lowell's genius for description was never long submerged. I regret not having heard him on his contemporaries, where his conversational descriptions always had glints of combativeness. He did diverge from the nineteenth century long enough to say in class one day, about Frost's poetry, that it was like a "landscape of overhanging crags, lit by a lurid gloom of volcanic outbursts, with occasional appearances of a Troll, dressed perhaps like the Virgin Mary, but a Troll nonetheless." He was equally irreverent about the poets he most respected, remarking on "Resolution and Independence" that "Wordsworth liked talking to those old imbeciles." Such a gibe, with its frivolity, would have seemed rude to me in my innocent youth, and it would have pained me; perhaps Lowell's more recent students have the irony to see the wonder underlying the satire—Who would have thought great poetry was to be made out of talking to old imbeciles? And if it can be, what poet has the right to complain of a lack of subject?

Wordsworth's name recurred. (I missed the Wordsworth classes too.) He had "great genius in spreading out a sentence"—this said in conjunction with talk of Whitman, in the category of "loose" poets. "Lots of Wordsworth," Lowell said, "is commonplace and uninspired, but when Wordsworth is inspired he writes in the same way he does when he's uninspired; the syntax is wonderful." On the other hand, "Wordsworth had a genius for meanness and condescension—he left out 'The Ancient Mariner' from the *Lyrical Ballads*." There were also odd, slanting, comments: about the lines from "Christabel" on "the one red leaf, the last of its clan" hanging "on the topmost twig that looks up at the sky," Lowell said, "In a Wordsworth poem it wouldn't be on the topmost twig; it would be somewhere else." His *obiter dicta* were often of that sort; behind this example there lies a sense of Wordsworth's generality and Coleridge's pointed idiosyncrasy, a difference that could as well be illustrated by the difference between the old Cumberland beggar and the Ancient Mariner—but Lowell preferred to speak in parables; those who had ears to hear could hear.

Clare, Coleridge, and Hopkins, all in different ways, seemed to Lowell like himself, I think, though, as I have said, he tended always to rearrange poetic features till they resembled his own. "I Am" seemed to him about depression, and "Secret Love" ("It's about adolescence") seemed about mania. Clinical depression, he said, speaking of "I Am," is "just what depression is like in other people, only more so. Everything seems very bad, and only likely to get worse." The grandeur embodied in the very size, breadth, scope, and duration of clinical depression makes it need a vocabulary hard to come by for the modern poet: Lowell regretted that "nowadays you have to get along without language like 'the ship-wreck of my life's esteems.'"

The Coleridge who appealed to Lowell was not the discursive Coleridge, but the domestic Coleridge first of all, and second the wild Coleridge. The verse letter to Sara, which was later revised into "Dejection: An Ode," seemed to Lowell preferable to its later, formal incarnation. The letter, said Lowell, is "an embarrassing poem—a long apologetic masterpiece. Something is lost by making it an ode." The domestic revelations were the passages Lowell read aloud: "And thou art weak with sickness, grief, and pain: / And I—I made thee so!" There is, Lowell claimed with some satisfaction, a "morbid Romantic declarative in Coleridge." As for the three narrative poems—"Christabel," "Kubla Khan," and "The Ancient Mariner"—Lowell rebuked I. A. Richards[5] for calling these (if indeed he did) "Coleridge's least important poems" (the phrase is not in Richards' *Viking Portable Coleridge*). For Lowell, Coleridge had perfected "a hallucinated concentration on description"; "Christabel" was "genuinely both beautiful and spooky—Poe couldn't do it at all compared to Coleridge." Coleridge could be "showily simple and get away with it":

> The thin gray cloud is spread on high,
> It covers but not hides the sky.
> The moon is behind, and at the full;
> And yet she looks both small and dull.

Lowell's envy of Coleridge's two styles—the fullness of domesticity, the air of the simple and the inevitable—came out of his own last struggle, I think, to render the domestic, in all its tangles and dailiness

and anguish, in a language aspiring to the casualness of intimate ex-
change and unemphatic realism. What he admired in "The Ancient Mar-
iner" was the way in which madness was inserted into the prosaic: "It
starts merrily enough, and the bird is made quite real in a very few
stanzas; it's a surprise, after all that rather domestic detail in the sea-
description, for the guest to say, 'God save thee, Ancient Mariner, from
the fiends that plague thee thus.' It's as if someone, just as you're giving a
nice sea-description, says to you, 'You're mad!' But the guest hits the
bull's eye, because the Mariner then confesses." Lowell thought "The
Ancient Mariner" "obviously an opium poem," full of "phantasma-
goria" and "fetters clanking." Coleridge knew "what words do on the
page to each other" (that was one of the remarks about Coleridge's
careful simplicity); about the "moral," Lowell knew, like Coleridge, that
"the poem *per se* does not illustrate a point." The most personal thing
Lowell said about the poem was, "The tenderness is explicit; not yet is
the rage explicit."

When he turned to Hopkins, a poet he had known well since his
earliest years as a Roman Catholic, Lowell dismissed the old conflicts
about Hopkins' life by commenting simply that he was "a man with a
second vocation—or maybe a first vocation—like a soldier; a Jesuit
priest." Lowell rather skipped over middle Hopkins (except to say of the
"Wreck" that it was written in "Anglo-Saxon baroque" about one of
Hopkins' great subjects, "despair"). He dwelt instead on the sonnets,
perhaps because he had been so recently engaged in sonnets himself,
talking about how well Hopkins "did" ecstasy and despair—the early
sonnets of ecstasy, the late ones of despair. Nature, he went on to say,
disappears from the "terrible" sonnets, which he liked most of all, say-
ing, "the later ones, if you take only the pentameter ones, can be seen as a
sequence," repeating words like "wring," "comfort," "hell." They
show the "alliteration of exhaustion and force—'I weary of idle a being
but by'—'dark heaven's baffling ban bars.'" "In the nineteenth cen-
tury," said Lowell, looking back to a more congenial time, "born
Catholics were *all* skeptical." He made little (rightly, to my mind) of
sprung rhythm, saying, "In Hopkins, there's a strong shadow of regular
meter: behind every line of sprung rhythm is a scanned line."

I am conscious of the degree to which these remarks seem scattered
and diffuse, and I despair of giving a sense of how they were inserted into
a musing narrative occasioned by a text. Those who have heard Lowell's
conversation, and know the apparent diffidence and drawl concealing a

mind of ferocious force and outrageous irreverence, will know the sub-
merged authority present even in his most offhand remarks, whether
they were remarks on life or on art. The authority coexisted with an
intense affection, a brotherliness of affection, for the poets, which lay
comfortably side by side with a brotherly rivalry. There was no poet he
spoke of with more rueful affection than Whitman, beginning with
moral admiration ("He had a stroke at fifty-four, and took it well") and
immediately joining to it moral distrust ("He had sly eyes"). Whitman
"invented free verse" of "great rolling power": the Preface to *Leaves of
Grass* is "a windy, magnificent document, but there is not one single
name of a predecessor mentioned in it, and he said what isn't true, that he
didn't care about the rhythm of the line, but only about what he was
saying." *Leaves of Grass* is "full of waste and repetition, but it is the only
place where someone's collected works are called by a single title." Whit-
man was "a New York poet"; he "had to sympathize with everything."
His method was adjectival; "if he were doing Blake's 'Sunflower' he'd
give it an adjective—call it 'broadfaced' sunflower."

Lowell was candid: " 'Song of Myself,' if you read it in the right
mood—as I couldn't this time—*all* works. The revisions didn't improve
it." "Whitman's later poetry—the tender poems at the end—are differ-
ent in tone from the poetry of his great healthy days." (There was
something in Lowell's regret that may have been self-reflective, with
respect to *Day by Day,* but I am not sure.) Lowell made the Freudian slip
"Milton," for "Whitman" at one point, and excused himself for it,
claiming "they rhyme." He was not taken in by Whitman's own claims
for brotherhood, saying, "There are no human beings in Whitman, just
one human being, very sympathetic, with marvellous visual powers. It's
hard to get people into poetry—it's not a good medium for it." When
Lowell turned to consider Whitman with other poets, he thought first (as
Hopkins himself had) of Hopkins, commenting that "The Mating of
Hawks" was "like Hopkins, but more spread out than Hopkins, full of
sadness rather than despair." He thought Eliot's *Quartets* ("When the
fourth Quartet came out I felt I had read a masterpiece") had learned
from Whitman, but concluded that "if anyone's going to benefit from
Whitman, it will be someone quite unlike him." "Thoreau was tense,
but Whitman was sly, lazy, relaxed, sympathetic."

There were things in poets that Lowell seemed to envy: I noted
down three of them. On Keats: "The large unhurried gravity of negative
capability"; on Williams, "A wistful optimism"; on Frost, "Faith incor-

rupt from subversion, subversion unillumined by faith." But on the whole he spoke without envy, and with generosity, scarcely ever stopping on a bad poem, and finding, as I've said, the best passages to take up even in poems, like *Sohrab and Rustum,* that he didn't care for as wholes. He had a gift for pointing out true qualities obscured by critical clichés; for all the claim, he said, that Whitman was full of bluster and noise, it was remarkable how often he used the word "noiseless" (noticing it in the poem about the spider, where its unexpectedness suddenly, under Lowell's gaze, took on luster).

With that, I come to the end of my notes, except for two remarks he made in conversation, which I add here; one is literary, one not. I worried, like every mother, about whether my child would turn out well, and said something to Lowell about being concerned that he had acted with "selfishness" in some instance, wondering what this boded about his "character." Lowell's reply, dismissing the cant of motherhood, cast light on his own self-defining in his college years: "But you have to remember that for children selfishness *is* character." Like most of his aphorisms, it came effortlessly. Another time, I had been saying how hard it must have been for Flannery O'Connor to have to return to live with her mother. Lowell said mildly, "But I'm told they got along quite well—sat on the porch and talked about people." I: "But in the stories she's so clearly not the little Southern Shirley Temple her mother seems to have wanted, but a malign little girl, ugly and watchful." Lowell: "But you know, what's in the stories is the *idealized criminal form* of Flannery." It was in such gaiety—the Platonic forms redefined in a flash—that Lowell's best humor issued, a humor at once descriptive, personal, and philosophic.

Lowell did not do many of the things recommended in current pedagogy, at least not in his literature class as I observed it. On the whole, he did not know his students' names; there was no "discussion" (though anyone was welcome to make observations, few did, and if an observation was incorrect or unlikely, Lowell had no hesitation about saying so). Occasionally Lowell would make a stab at soliciting opinion, but what he generally did was to murmur a monologue. (This was unlike his practice in conversation, where he loved give-and-take.) What his privileged students heard was original discourse; what they experienced was the amplitude of response stirred by past poetry—which, in Lowell's hands, always seemed poetry of the present—in a poet who had earned his place "on the slopes of Parnassus." It was a response in which familiarity and reverence went hand in hand, in which technique and vision were indissoluble; it made the appearance of poetry in life seem as natural as any other action. I felt, always, that a scanning faculty quite unlike anything I could describe was reviewing and judging and annotating the lines or stanzas he took up; it made one feel like a rather backward evolutionary form confronted by an unknown but superior species. And when one asked what the name of the species was, the answer came unbidden: Poet. Lowell's classes were a demonstration in the critical order of what those mysterious beings in the anthologies had in common—a relation to words beyond our ordinary powers. In that sense, his classes were as inimitable as his poems.

Helen Vendler (b. 1933), influential American critic and Professor of English at Harvard, was Lowell's pupil at Boston University during 1955–56. She is the author of *On Extended Wings: Wallace Stevens' Longer Poems* (1969), *The Poetry of George Herbert* (1975) and *The Odes of John Keats* (1983).

1. Latin: passing remarks.

2. An allusion to Ben Jonson's remark, in *Conversations with William Drummond of Hawthornden* (1619), "that Donne, for not keeping of accent, deserved hanging." See *Ben Jonson* (Oxford Standard Authors), ed. Ian Donaldson (Oxford, 1985), p. 596.

3. Auden, "September 1, 1939." In his Foreword to B. C. Bloomfield, *W. H. Auden: A Bibliography* (Charlottesville, 1964), Auden explained his reasons for suppressing this line and the poem.

4. A legendary Greek figure who challenged Apollo to a contest with his lyre and was flayed by the god.

5. I. A. Richards (1893–1979), influential literary critic, author of *The Meaning of Meaning* (1923), *Principles of Literary Criticism* (1925) and *Coleridge on Imagination* (1934).

43 • Robert Lowell's Last Days and Last Poems

Helen Vendler

The last years of Robert Lowell's life, when I knew him, were ones of almost emblematic location. He and his wife Caroline Blackwood were in Kent in a manor house called Milgate Park; when that house was sold, they lived at Castletown House in Ireland; he taught at Harvard one term each year, giving a course in nineteenth- or twentieth-century poetry, and holding open Office Hours in which he commented on the writing of those presenting work; he was, during his last summer, in Maine with his second wife Elizabeth Hardwick. In England and Ireland he was an expatriate; at Harvard he was at home by virtue of birth and name but exotic by virtue of his life and his poetry; in Maine he was returning to a scene long-familiar. In his final summer, he went for the first time to Russia. After his sudden death on his return from Ireland to New York, there was a funeral at his childhood church, the Church of the Advent, not far from that Revere Street which appears in *Life Studies;* finally, he was buried in the Winslow and Stark family cemetery, still in Dunbarton, New Hampshire, though moved from the original location described in several of his poems.

These various places—Boston, Maine, England, Ireland, New York—the old-fashioned, the urban, the rural, the foreign, the sophisticated—respond to facets of Lowell's complex character, and appear in his last poems, collected in *Day by Day* (1977). In these poems, Lowell becomes not only the New England poet of Boston, Dunbarton, and Maine, not only the American poet of New York, Washington, and Ohio, but also the expatriate poet of Kent and Ireland. Besides new places, he added new experiences, writing for the first time as the father

Robert Lowell: A Tribute, edited by Rolando Anzilotti (Pisa: Nistri-Lischi, 1979), pp. 156–171. Reprinted in Helen Vendler, *Part of Nature, Part of Us* (Cambridge, Mass.: Harvard University Press, 1980), pp. 161–173. Reprinted here by permission of Helen Vendler.

of a son—a son uncannily resembling him. He wrote of physical ill-ness—he was hospitalized briefly in January of 1977 for congestive heart disease—and of the expectation, not unfounded, of his death.

Like the books which preceded it, *Day by Day* was attacked. "Slack and meretricious," one fellow-poet said of the later poetry, accusing it of "the lassitude and despondency of self-imitation." In twenty years, he prophesied, no one would praise *Day by Day*, which would remain "a sad footnote to the corruption of a great poet."[1] Without attempting to usurp the function of time, which will decide whether *Day by Day* is a stern and touching volume, as I believe it to be, or whether it deserves no such praise, I would like today to glance at a few of its poems and a few of its claims, beginning with its own description of itself; but I must look first, briefly, at its predecessors.

Lowell began as a writer of an obscure and oblique poetry, which struggled violently with murky feeling, invented baffling displaced suf-ferings like those in *The Mills of the Kavanaughs*, resisted interpretation, and discovered original resources in traditional forms. This poetry, in spite of its difficulty, attracted wide attention and praise, so much so that its very strength was the greatest obstacle to Lowell's poetic progress. *Life Studies* disappointed readers attached to Lowell's earlier "Catholic" manner, and the lean and loose-jointed poems which are now his most famous work had to wait some time for popular acceptance. Just as *Life Studies* entered the anthologies, Lowell returned to a species of formality, writing innumerable sonnets (collected in *Notebook* and subsequent vol-umes), compressing life with what seemed extraordinary cruelty and candor into a Procrustean and unyielding shape. These poems have not yet been assimilated—except in a voyeuristic way—into the American literary consciousness. "It takes ten years," Lowell said dryly of popular acquiescence.

Now he has ended, in *Day by Day*, as a writer of disarming open-ness, exposing shame and uncertainty, offering almost no purchase to interpretation, and in his journal-keeping, abandoning conventional structure, whether rhetorical or logical. The poems drift from one focus to another; they avoid the histrionic; they sigh more often than they expostulate. They acknowledge exhaustion; they expect death. Admirers of the sacerdotal and autocratic earlier manner are offended by this di-minished diarist, this suddenly quiescent volcano. But Lowell knew bet-ter than anyone else what he had given up: "Those blessèd structures, plot and rhyme— / why are they no help to me now," he begins his closing poem, "Epilogue." He had been willing to abandon plot and rhyme in writing poems about things recalled—in order to make that recall casual and natural. But now, in his last poem, he wanted "to make something imagined, not recalled," and wished to return to plot and rhyme. But the habit of the volume held, and the last testament is unrhymed and unplotted, as unstructured, apparently, as its companions. Despairingly. Lowell contrasts himself with the "true" artist, the painter, feeling himself to be—like Hawthorne's Coverdale[2]—only an American daguerrotypist:

> sometimes everything I write
> with the threadbare art of my eye
> seems a snapshot,
> lurid, rapid, garish, grouped,
> heightened from life,
> yet paralyzed by fact.

Lowell here anticipates all that could be said—and has been said in criticism of his last book: that his art does not go clothed in the gorgeous tapestry of his earlier work, but is threadbare; that he is making capital of the lurid and garish episodes of his life—adolescent cruelty, family scandal, madness, three marriages; that his poems are rapid sketches rather than finished portraits; that he is hampered by his allegiance to fact without even the compensating virtue of absolute truthfulness, since all is heightened by compression and focus. After this devastating self-criticism, the only self-defense can be the anti-bourgeois question: "Yet why not say what happened?"

Howard Nemerov has called the poet "the weak criminal whose confession implicates the others": and Lowell's "saying what happened" is not a cowardice of the imagination but a subversive heroism of the memory. "Memory is genius," Lowell said once at a reading, regretting how little remained even in his own prodigious memory, and regretting as well the poverty of language as a vehicle for the preservation of the past:

> How quickly I run through my little set
> of favored pictures . . . pictures starved to words.
> My memory economizes so prodigally
> I know I have suffered theft.

Abandoning the showy "objective correlatives" of his life, which fill the earlier poetry, Lowell prays, in his last poem, for "the grace of accuracy," which he found in the Dutch realists, from Van Eyck to Vermeer. There is, in this volume, a painstaking description of Van Eyck's Arnolfini marriage portrait.[3] The couple are not beautiful: the husband stands "long-faced and dwindling," the wife is pregnant; the husband "lifts a hand, / thin and white as his face / held up like a candle to bless her . . . / they are rivals in homeliness and love." In the background of the portrait, Lowell sees all the furniture of their common life: "The picture is too much like their life— / a crisscross, too many petty facts"—a candelabrum, peaches, the husband's wooden shoes "thrown on the floor by her smaller ones," the bed, "the restless marital canopy." This "petty" domestic inclusiveness is what Lowell now proposes to write about in place of his former metaphysical blazes, even in place of his former carefully casual "life studies." We know at least, then, that the aesthetic of the last work was not an unconscious or an unconsidered one. Whether it is, as some would say, a rationalization after the fact, justifying, *faute de mieux,* an exhausted invention, only history can tell; some will see in these pieces a shrewdness of choice and an epigrammatic wit that suggest consummate art.

These last poems, so random-seeming, were nonetheless composed with Lowell's characteristic severity of self-criticism. The worksheets, as always, are innumerable, incessant. Lowell lived for writing, was never happier than, as he said, when revising his revisions. Successive versions were exposed to the criticism of friends; spurred by questions, objections, suggestions, he would return eagerly to his drafts, and change, transpose, rewrite. "He loved to tinker," he said of God; it was equally true of himself. His brilliant adjectives were not achieved by chance; his inspired aphorisms took time to perfect themselves. His manuscripts may be the most interesting since Yeats's.

Lowell would have been sixty on March 1st of this year. To honor his birthday, and commemorate his death, the Houghton Library of Harvard University exhibited a selection from his papers on deposit there. His unremitting work appears in his earliest notebooks, in the drafts for such famous poems as "The Quaker Graveyard" (originally entitled "To Herman Melville") and "Skunk Hour" (which had begun as a poem of personal desolation but had acquired, late, its first three stanzas of tolerant, if biting, social description). The Houghton exhibit included a letter Lowell wrote, at eighteen, to his father, declaring his vocation as a writer: "If I fail at this, I would fail at anything else," he wrote, as I recall the page.

How, then, are we to read these late poems? Not, certainly, for the blessed structures of plot and rhyme; not for the hard-driving compression of the late sonnets; not for the transforming and idealizing power of lyric; not for the diamond certainties of metaphysical verse; not for the retrospective and elegiac stationing of figures as in *Life Studies;* not for the visionary furies of youth. One afternoon last spring, I walked with Lowell through Harvard Yard. "Did you see that Christopher Ricks[4] had written a piece about me?" he said. "No, what did he say?" I asked. "He said I'm violent," said Lowell with a mixture of humor and irony. "And Ehrenpreis says you're comic,"[5] I said. "Why don't they ever say what I'd like them to say?" he protested. "What's that?" I asked. "That I'm heartbreaking," he said, meaning it.

And so he is. If this book is read, as it should be, as a journal, written "day by day," as a fragment of an autobiography (Lowell called his poems "my verse autobiography,") it is heartbreaking. It records his late, perhaps unwise, third marriage; the birth of a son; the very worst memories suppressed from *Life Studies,* the memories of having been an unwanted child and a tormented adolescent; exile in Britain and Ireland; the death of friends; clinical depression and hospitalization; love-making and impotence; distress over age; fear of death. Against all this is set the power of writing—"universal consolatory / description without significance, / transcribed verbatim by my eye."

Readers who demand something more than the eye's verbatim transcript—who do not ask whether in fact there is anything more—may not find these poems heartbreaking. But the Wordsworth who said that the meanest flower that blows could give thoughts that do often lie too deep for tears[6] would, I think, understand the tears underlying these "petty facts" of one man's existence. Let me quote some of Lowell's memorable descriptions.

Of sexual impotence, recalling sexual capacity: "Last summer nothing dared impede / the flow of the body's thousand rivulets of welcome." "Rivulets" is, in its pastoral and Wordsworthian tenderness, the word carrying all the delicacy of reference. On depression: "a wooden winter shadow," with the paralysis of that state hiding in the word "wooden." On ants, and their pragmatic and logical errands: "They are the lost case of the mind." On death: "My eyes flicker, the immortal / is scraped unconsenting from the mortal." On old age: "We learn the spirit is very willing to give up, / but the body is weak and will not die."[7] On the anticipation of his own death and burial:

> In a church,
> the Psalmist's glass mosaic Shepherd
> and bright green pastures
> seem to wait
> with the modish faithlessness
> and erotic daydream
> of art nouveau for our funeral.[8]

And yet, for all their air of verbatim description, these poems, like all poems, are invented things. They are invented even in little. Lowell once handed me a draft of a new poem, called "Bright Day in Boston." It begins, "Joy of standing up my dentist, / my X-ray plates like a broken Acropolis . . . / Joy to idle through Boston." I was struck by the *panache* of standing up one's dentist, and said so; "Well, as a matter of fact," said Lowell sheepishly, "I actually *did* go to the dentist first, and *then* went for the walk." But in the poem, "the unpolluted joy / And criminal leisure of a boy"—to quote earlier verses—became fact, where in life they had been only wish. The life of desire is as evident in these poems as the life of fact. Medical prescriptions are both named and rejected: "What is won by surviving, / if two glasses of red wine are poison?" The Paterian[9] interval becomes ever smaller: "We only live between / before we are and what we were." Lowell looks in terror to "the hungry future, / the time when any illness is chronic, / and the years of discretion are spent on complaint— // until the wristwatch is taken from the wrist." These deathly truths, unrelieved by any prospect of afterlife or immortality, are I think what dismay many readers. How squalid and trivialized a view of death, they may feel—chronic illness, complaint, and that last hospital gesture, the wristwatch taken from the wrist. But over against that end, Lowell sets a flickering terrestrial Eden: "We took our paradise here—how else love?" That "a man love[s] a woman more than women" remained for him an insoluble and imprisoning mystery: "A man without a wife / is like a turtle without a shell." "Nature," says Lowell who is part of nature, "is sundrunk with sex," but he would "seek leave unimpassioned by [his] body." That leave was not granted him: he stayed with women till the end of the party, "a half-filled glass in each hand— / . . . swayed / by the hard infatuate wind of love."

In this last accuracy, the poet cannot even see himself as unique, unusual, set apart. There is the humility of the generic about this volume, in spite of its pride in its poetic work. As far as he can see, Lowell tells us, each generation leads the same life, the life of its time. No one in the present is wiser or more foolish than those in the past or the future. No fresh perfection treads on our heels; nor do we represent any decay of nature. This attitude, too, distresses those who come to poetry for hope, transcendence, the inspiriting word. "Really," says Lowell to Berryman in his elegy for Berryman, "we had the same life / the generic one / our generation offered."[10] First they were students, then they, as teachers themselves, had students; they had their *grands maîtres* as all young writers do, they had their "fifties' fellowships / to Paris, Rome and Florence," they were "veterans of the Cold War not the War." Thousands of other intellectuals of their generation had the same "generic life." If he were young now, says Lowell, he would be indistinguishable from the other young, listening to rock, "lost / in unreality and loud music."

In a class lecture on Arnold, Lowell once said that "Dover Beach" had been criticized, "in the old days of the New Critics," for not continuing the sea imagery in the last stanza; "But I think by then," Lowell went on, "you've had quite enough of it." His sense of the fluidity, of life's events and of human response pressed him into some of the same discontinuity of imagery, and drew the disapproval of purists in structure. Lowell believed—I am quoting another class—that the poem "is an event, not the record of an event"; "the lyric claims to produce an event; it is this for which it strives and which it sometimes brings off." Like an event, the lyric can be abrupt, odd-shaped, irregularly featured, and inconclusive. The important thing is the presence of "exciting or strenuous writing"—what one finds in Henry James, he said, on every page, good or bad. Power and wistfulness stood, for Lowell, in inverse relation: he praised the "tender" poems at the end of *Leaves of Grass* while remarking nonetheless how different in tone Whitman's later poetry, written when he was ill, was from the poetry of his "great healthy days." We might say the same of Lowell's last collection. The impetuousness of the "manic statement" is gone: "mania is now viewed with apprehension and horror": "I grow too merry, / when I stand in my nakedness to dress." Even poetry itself can seem to want conviction: it becomes merely a compulsive "processing of words," a "dull instinctive glow" refueling itself from "bits of paper brought to feed it" which it blackens.

In the transparent myth which opens *Day by Day,* a weary Ulysses tires of Circe, returns to a deformed Ithaca, to a Penelope corrupted by living well, and finds rage his only authentic and vivid emotion. A shorthand of references has substituted for the luxuries of description, while a desultory motion has substituted for youth's arrowy energy. No-one would deny that this poetry has destructive designs on convention. Lowell once quoted Eliot on Coleridge: "By the time he wrote the *Biographia Literaria* he was a ruin, but being a ruin is a sort of occupation."* The remark, if it is authentic, reveals a good deal about Eliot, but Lowell's citation is interesting in itself: it conveys the conviction of the artist-survivor that there is always something to be made of life, even of its orts and offal, its tired ends, its disappointments and disgusts, its ironies. The sense of the end of life must find some expression, even if in what Stevens called "long and sluggish lines." Without endorsing an imitative form, we can yet find in Lowell's casualness, his waywardness, his gnomic summaries, his fragmentary reflections, authentic representations of a sixty-year-old voice and a sixty-year-old memory.

Not every poem, I suppose, succeeds in giving "each figure in the photograph / his living name." But the poet who had decided that "we are poor passing facts," felt obliged to a poetry of deprivation and of transient actuality, lit up by moments of unearthly pained happiness, like that in his last aubade:

> For the last two minutes, the retiring monarchy
> of the full moon looks down on the first chirping sparrows—
> nothing lovelier than waking to find
> another breathing body in my bed . . .
> glowshadow halfcovered with dayclothes like my own,
> caught in my arms.[11]

The poetry of "poor passing facts" entails the sacrifice, in large part, of two aspects of Lowell's poetry that had brought him many admirers: his large reference to European literature, through his allusions and translations (which he called "Imitations"); and his political protest. In that earlier grandeur of literary scope, as well as by the moral grandeur of

---

*T. S. Eliot actually wrote in *The Use of Poetry and the Use of Criticism:* "Sometimes, however, to be 'a ruined man' is itself a vocation."

defiance and protest, Lowell seemed to claim a vision and power for poetry that many readers were happy to see affirmed. Others were more pleased by the development, beginning in *For the Union Dead* and culminating in Lowell's final volume, of a humbler style, that of a man, in Rolando Anzilotti's fine description, "who confronts directly and with courage his own failures, his faults and despairings, without seeking comfort, without indicating solutions to cling to. Feeling is revealed with the subtlest delicacy and candor, in its essential being." "The eye of Lowell for the particular which becomes universal," Anzilotti continues, "is precise and perfect; . . . we are far away from the oratory, from the bursting out of emotion in tumultuous rhythms, that appeared in 'The Quaker Graveyard.' "[12] This line of writing, as Anzilotti points out, remained in equilibrium with the national and moral concerns evident in *Near the Ocean* and *Notebook;* not until this final volume did the precise eye and the quotidian feeling become the dominant forces in Lowell's aesthetic. The allusions in this last collection come from an occasional backward glance to favorite passages—a line of Dante, a line of Horace—but the poetic mind turns less and less to past literature, more and more to the immediacy of present event. There is only one poem in the volume springing from a political impetus—the poem called "Fetus," prompted by the trial, in Boston, of a doctor accused of making no effort to keep an aborted fetus alive; and even this poem quickly leaves its occasion behind, and engages in a general meditation on death, that "black arrow" arriving like a calling-card "on the silver tray." And it is perhaps significant that this poem is the least successful, at least to my mind, in the group, in part because Lowell no longer has to hand the moral sureness to condemn or approve the abortion. He sees only the grotesquerie of the medical procedure, of the trial court, and of the biological shape of "the fetus, the homunculus, / already at four months one pound, / with shifty thumb in mouth— // Our little model. . . ." A poem which, by its title, "George III," might seem to be prompted by Anglo-American relations turns out, in the event, to be in part a reflection on Nixon but even more a reflection on a fate Lowell feared for himself: a permanent lapse into madness, like George,

> who whimsically picked the pockets of his page
> he'd paid to sleep all day outside his door;
>
> who dressed like a Quaker, who danced a minuet
> with his appalled apothecary in Kew Gardens;

who dismayed "his retinue by formally bowing to an elm, / as if it were the Chinese emissary." George's later mania bears a strong resemblance to phases of Lowell's own illness:

> addressing imaginary congresses,
> reviewing imaginary combat troops. . . .
>
> Old, mad, deaf, half-blind,[13]
>
> he talked for thirty-two hours
> on everything, everybody,
>
> read Cervantes and the Bible aloud
> simultaneously with shattering rapidity. . . .

Social forms disappear in this last phase of Lowell's writing, and public moral witness disappears with them. The solitary human being, his life extending only as far as the domestic circle, becomes the topic of attention. Epic ambition is resigned: the *Odyssey* is reduced to a marital triangle. The personal is seen as the locus of truth, insight, and real action.

And when Lowell writes about the personal, he spares himself nothing, not the patronizing doctor in the asylum addressing Caroline, "A model guest . . . we would welcome / Robert back to Northampton any time"; not the susurrus of public or private comment about madness having attacked him even in this third, scandalous marriage:

> If he has gone mad with her,
> the poor man can't have been very happy,
> seeing too much and feeling it
> with one skin-layer missing;

not a murderously detached self-portrait among the other mad:

> I am a thorazined[14] fixture
> in the immovable square-cushioned chairs
> we preoccupy for seconds like migrant birds.

After the scene-setting in the asylum comes the distracted interior monologue, much as it had in "Skunk Hour": but whereas in the earlier poem the poses struck were tragic, and then comic, redeemed in some way by the animal appetite of the skunks, the monologue in the asylum, forebodingly called "Home," is one of pure childlike pathos:

The immovable chairs have swallowed up the patients,
and speak with the eloquence of emptiness.
By each the same morning paper lies unread:
January 10, 1976.
I cannot sit or stand two minutes,
yet walk imagining a dialogue
between the devil and myself,
not knowing which is which or worse,
saying,
as one would instinctively say Hail Mary,
I wish I could die.
Less than ever I expect to be alive
six months from now—
1976,
a date I dare not affix to my grave.
The Queen of Heaven, I miss her,
we were divorced. She never doubted
the divided, stricken soul
could call her Maria,
and rob the devil with a word.[15]

The grand drama of the manic has ended, and it is the depressive side of illness, without the illusions of mania, which gives its tone to these latter poems. As the horizon narrows, the smallest sensations of living—waking up alive, seeing the spring—suffice. "I thank God," says Lowell, "for being alive— / a way of writing I once thought heartless." Heartless because selfish, solipsistic—or so he thought when he was young, and had heart for all the world, or so it seemed. Recognizing the fury of political statement as a displacement of fury against parents, he can no longer permit its unmediated and thoughtless energy. In the poem to his mother, he admits, "It has taken me the time since you died / to discover you are as human as I am . . . / if I am." In the poem to his father, he confesses,

It would take two lifetimes
to pick the crust
and uncover the face
under our two menacing,
iconoclastic masks.[16]

His father refuses the sympathy proffered, when Lowell implies that now he understands his father's life through the similarity of his own life to that of his father: "It can't be that, / it's your life," says his father, "and dated like mine." The failure of Lowell's father is reflected in his own failure, just as Lowell's childhood innocence is reflected in the innocence of his little son:

> We could see clearly
> and all the same things
> before the glass was hurt.
>
> Past fifty, we learn with surprise and a sense
> of suicidal absolution
> that what we intended and failed
> could never have happened—
> and must be done better.[17]

The old paternal hope that the child's life will be lived better struggles with the conviction that each generation repeats the generic life of all its predecessors. The very motive for action is removed by such resignation to the common fate.

What remains for Lowell, then, after he has jettisoned formal religious belief, social protest, a twenty-year marriage, even residence in America, except memory and the present moment. When asked why he wanted a formal funeral in the Episcopal church, Lowell said, "That's how we're buried"—that was the custom of the family. At the funeral, his second and third wives, his grown daughter and his small son, and his three stepdaughters, sat in the first mourners' pew, existing side by side as they did in his life and his poetry. He is buried in Dunbarton next to his father and his mother. His parents' tombstones both bear inscriptions he composed; in an odd flash of authorship, he had a signature incised, in cursive script, below the Roman lettering—"R. Lowell Jr." There were memorial services for him in New York, at Harvard, and in London. When Voznesensky[18] came to America last winter, he asked to be driven to Lowell's grave, and laid on it berries which had grown above the grave of Pasternak. Already there have been elegies; though none, as yet, equal to the many elegies he wrote for the friends who preceded him in death.

In writing this last volume, Lowell pleased himself, listening with some inner ear to the inner life of the poem, deciding with mysterious certainty when it was finished, when it had found its equilibrium. I think that the instinctive principles on which he worked will become clearer with time. One writes poetry, he said, by instinct and by ear, and his own instincts and ear were pressing him towards a poetry ever more unconventional, ever less "literary." He admired the way Coleridge, in his ballads, could be "showily simple and get away with it." He sought that ostentatious simplicity himself. He added that though Coleridge's verse epistle to Sara Hutchinson—the first version of the Dejection Ode—was embarrassing, yet it was "a long apologetic masterpiece—something is lost by making it an ode." What is lost is the spontaneity, the heartbreak, the domestic anguish—all that appears in Lowell's journal written day by day. No doubt it could all have been transformed into odes; that was his old manner. But the something that was lost, in such a case, now seemed to him more precious than the something that is found. His last book, however casual it may seem, is not a collection of unconsidered trifles. Lowell wrote justly: "My eyes have seen what my hand did." His metaphor for this book was not one of arrangement, but one of accumulation:

> This is riches:
> the eminence not to be envied,
> the account
> accumulating layer and angle,
> face and profile,
> 50 years of snapshots,
> the ladder of ripening likeness.

If, to Lowell in a Shakespearean mood, we are "poor passing facts," in a more Keatsian moment we resemble the "camelion-poet":

> We are things thrown in the air
> alive in flight. . . .
> our rust the color of the chameleon.[19]

"Not to console or sanctify," says Stevens, speaking of the aim of modern poetry, "but plainly to propound."[20] The plain propounding—of things thrown in the air, alive in flight, and rusting in change to the color of dust—if too severe for some tastes, is to others profoundly assuaging. We are lucky in America in our poetry of old age: Whitman's, Stevens', and now Lowell's. Such poetry never can speak to the young and form their sensibilities as can the poetry of passion and hope and revolutionary ardor; but it sums up another phase of life, no less valuable, no less moving, no less true.

1. See Donald Hall, "Robert Lowell and the Literature Industry," *Georgia Review* 32 (Spring 1978): 7–12.

2. Miles Coverdale, autobiographical hero in Nathaniel Hawthorne's *The Blithedale Romance* (1852).

3. Jan Van Eyck, *The Arnolfini Wedding* (1434), National Gallery, London.

4. See Christopher Ricks, "Robert Lowell at 60," *Listener* 97 (10 March 1977): 314–315.

5. See Irvin Ehrenpreis, "Lowell's Comedy," *New York Review of Books* 23 (28 October 1976): 3–6.

6. See Wordsworth, "The Immortality Ode" (1807).

7. An allusion to Matthew 26:41.

8. Lowell, "Our Afterlife II."

9. Walter Pater (1839–94), English historian and novelist, author of *Studies in the History of the Renaissance* (1873) and *Marius the Epicurean* (1885).

10. Lowell, "For John Berryman."

11. Lowell, "The Downlook."

12. Rolando Anzilotti, Introduzione a *Robert Lowell, Poesie, 1940–1970* (Milano, 1972), pp. 20, 22–23.

13. See Shelley on George III in "England in 1819": "An old, mad, blind, despised and dying King."

14. Thorazine, a sedative for the treatment of mental illness.

15. The last three quotations are from Lowell, "Home."

16. Lowell, "Robert T. S. Lowell."

17. Lowell, "For Sheridan."

18. Andrei Voznesensky (b. 1933), Russian poet, author of *Antiworlds* (1964) and *The Fifth Ace* (1967), wrote "Family Graveyard," an elegy for Lowell.

19. The last two quotations are from Lowell, "Our Afterlife I."

20. Wallace Stevens, "Notes Toward a Supreme Fiction" (1942).

44 • Life with Lord Lowell
   at Essex U.

Dudley Young

We first met Robert Lowell in the spring of 1970 when he was shopping for a University and came down to inspect us. The lunch was long and animated, such a success that dessert was followed by whisky and more so. This was our introduction to the Robert Lowell marathon. The party ended in the early evening; and I remember driving him to the station in my two-seater, the softness of spring, a female colleague on his knee, himself still in spate, and one hand absently cupped to her breast all the way there.

Expansive, careless, and yet needful: a disconcerting mix it then seemed, and so it remained. Compelling too: that voluminous brain, the relentless talk, the charm, the wit, the malice: all driven by a deceptively powerful body burning manic energy and whisky at about twice the rate of us who were half his age. He was the large and lethal Carnival King, the Candlemas Bear come to release us from common prose; sublime, sexy, and frequently mad.

When not this, of course, frighteningly depressed, a condition almost as infectious, at least to his intimates, as the mania. As he often admitted, his grasp of the middle register was insecure.

Essex in those days provided a fitting theatre for such magic, as we too had been running on a manic-depressive curve since our own rather admirable version of the glorious revolution had been presented in the spring of 1968 (sparked off by a visiting chemist from Porton Down,[1] which at the time was making poisons for Vietnam). By the fall of 1970, when Lowell joined us, the music had begun to turn sour, and many of the causes were looking lost. But the energy was still high (just turning vicious), and what we would today call normalcy nowhere in sight:

PN Review 28 (1982): 46–47. Reprinted by permission of Dudley Young.

politics, dope, music, poetry, sex, apocalypse, mysticism, and more politics—yes, the carnival was still on.

The students were brash, unbuttoned, and street-wise; and though suspicious of anyone as old or as famous as Lowell, they enjoyed telling him Dylan's stuff was more important (an argument he would engage with some ferocity). It was a measure of the lateness of the hour that his radical credentials, which would have appeared impeccable in 1967, were by then looking dubious to many. The big themes of the Sixties, which had produced such unanimity amongst staff and students, were breaking into smaller subjects, subjects and objects, us and them, a return to grammar.

The Department of Literature, having been largely assembled by Donald Davie, was, unsurprisingly, agreed upon the preeminence of poetry, and its members sufficiently young and enthusiastic still to care about each other's literary conversation. Although Lowell was approached warily by the Williams–Black Mountain[2] faction, who distrusted both his rhetoric and his class, he was welcomed by all, certainly; and all were certainly flattered by his having chosen us over the dullards of Oxford, about whom he was delightfully scathing.

For almost all of his two years here he would stay with me in Wivenhoe one or two nights a week, and then return to base camp in London, leaving me to put my house in order. From the outset our relationship was a fierce one: we had so much in common, and so much to fight about. The Candlemas Bear, lacking a middle register, insisted on a blow-out every night; and I, with no woman to help defend my domestic pieties, which were in any case insecurely rooted against my own carnival spirits, found it hard to say no. To say no would bring forth the Lowell depression, which was truly harrowing.*

Evening festivities in the first year were variously attended, by staff and students, and were not unlike those conducted by Delmore Schwartz as transcribed in Bellow's *Humboldt*. At submanic velocity the man was truly amazing, the range dazzling, the anecdotes endless and funny and fine. To bring us back from high talk, or just to silence some bore, he

---

*In fact I didn't effectively say no until the fall of 1971, his second year, when I finally dared to bring a woman home on one of his nights. This upset him considerably, and occasioned "Morning away from you," a remarkably accurate premonition of death. Soon after that, Madam moved in, and for his last term at Essex, Lord Lowell withdrew to University digs, amicably of course.

would ask Deg, my sagacious labrador, lying by the fire, what *he* thought; and there would follow a doggy discourse, regal and hilarious, usually along the lines of "What fools these mortals be."[3] Cal loved the dog, and these bouts of ventriloquism were altogether wonderful. But often, as the evening progressed the speed increased; and the monomania would sound, the language come unstuck, and we'd all go to pieces. With any luck it would then be bedtime.

Beneath the fun, never far away, was the seriousness; for they were seriously crazy times. Gradually a resistance to milord's monomania developed amongst us, particularly in me, his man-servant, more exposed to it than anyone else. When told at breakfast that last night, once again, his imperial voice had ignored every one (and every *thing*) in the room, he would grow quiet and sad, genuinely contrite, for he knew his vice; and he would ask me to sit on him next time it happened.

More difficult to manage was the not unrelated resistance to what his poetic voice was then doing. None of us was altogether happy about *Notebook;* and the unease was naturally most pronounced amongst those who most admired the earlier work. To a more or less unreconstructed Puritan like me, it was a matter of the highest importance. The problem was finally theological, and it covered just about everything; and so it grew between the two of us, into a kind of theme song, some part of which we would sing every week, in cheerfulness or rage, playfully or very fierce. We could even sing each other's part. Although most of it was scored for two voices, others would occasionally join in.

The song was called "Colonel Shaw[4] and the Monsters," and though we would doubtless sing it rather differently now (*piano, piano*)[5] I think the raucous version is worth recording. It went something like this:*

"Do you want me to go on re-writing that poem forever?"

"Yes, yes, you must. It's the last public poem. Without it we'll all drown in privacies; as your friend Miss Arendt has taught us."

"But the Colonel's statue *is* in the ditch now: his father has had the last laugh. The ditch is flooded and the monsters are loose. So let's move on."

"You and I will never move on from fathers, our common obsession. Perhaps you're rushing the apocalypse now because you knocked

---

*A rather sourpuss rendition of the song was published in an interview in the *New York Times Book Review* in April 1971, in which he deftly blocked most of my questions. [See No. 19.]

daddy down then, and couldn't either kill him off or get him to stand again. I'm afraid you're ditching Shaw and going over to the monsters."

"Ad hominem, below the belt."

"O.K. But the Colonel is *not* out of bounds, because the poem binds us to him. *Fiat iustitia*[6] and bugger Boston."

"We tried that, and look where it got us."

"The statue is not down, because your poem keeps it standing; which keeps both you and many of us on our feet—against the odds."

"Statues get dull, unbending. I want to go dark and downward."

"You are king of the human fish and reptile when your hand constructs the aquarium poem that keeps them contained. You may even burst the odd bubble; such violence is permitted the last Caligula, when he makes Colonel."

"My, my, that's kind of you, High-Priest. But I don't want to be king. Why must I wince at pleasure?"

"The logic of renunciation: You get what you give up. Your monster is licensed to stomp only by your fight against him. Your Colonel winces in order to rejoice."

"Strange. I thought *I* wrote that poem."

"If you give up that logic you lose your law—and your unlicenced monster swims forth; no glamorous whale but something horrible, lawless, ungrammatical, mad. Your hand, that cannot (will not?) even boil a kettle, yet dares to hammer the most audacious poems. That's a *dangerous* hand! Where is its piety? Lose that law, Hephaestos,[7] and your hand will be burned into a monstrous flipper."

"Pity the monsters."

"That's God's job. Man's is to hate and fear them, as the poem does, in the name of God the father. Perhaps God the son has pity; but if so it's beyond human understanding, and besides, you ain't Him."

"But the monsters are loose and the water is rising. Gabriel is kinder—and more intelligent. You sound a little bit tidy, and behind the times. You should get married; and go teach theology, in Toronto."

"I have my untidy side. Don't forget my generation was born nearer the ditch than yours was. We were suckled on savage servility; and some of us actually *believe* in the monsters that bring you metaphors for poetry. If our heads are still above water asking you to remind us of the Colonel, most of our bodies are down in the flood: the ground is gone, and *en attendant*[8] the sea-change of hands into fins there are prayers to be said: 'Let the fins be not greasy, Lord, and teach us to float.' "

"We're in the same sea. I'm hoping to catch a ride on the dolphin."

"Caroline is a sometime dolphin,[9] but you often seem to be riding one of those badass sharks, all teeth and appetite, no repose. The decade's dire conclusion is that speed kills. Time to exorcize. But your hand no longer draws back. *Notebook* is famished for human chances, and it *does* swallow them, as you say. Much of it burns the brain, burns syntax, burns history, burns the orders of space and time without which human significance cannot appear. Colonel Shaw suffocates for privacy, does he? And what of Lizzie and Harriet? It looks as if Ahab the shark has come for you at last, and you too tired to resist him any more."

"The ancestral curse. Perhaps he has come for all of us."

"Perhaps he is also a bad dream. Some of us are still trying to wake up."

And so on and on. Wonderful knockabout stuff, week in, week out. But we did get knocked about.

Two parties, two anecdotes. In the winter of '71, an American friend in London arranged a title bout between R. Lowell and R. Laing, two tigers of the Sixties who had never met. The referee was William Burroughs (who knew their tricks) in his banker's suit. The audience consisted of two warrior wives and five discerning hippoids. Would there be an exchange of whatever? Would the grownups talk to each other? Would they talk to us?

The food was good, the audience keen. In the red corner Laing was warming up in the lotus position, humming a mantra. In the blue corner Lowell, representing the Homeric party of sex and violence, was cleaning his glasses and taking a few final swigs from his flask.

Things opened slowly, with general exchanges on Apocalypse, which all agreed was imminent, if not almost finished. Shadow boxing mostly. Dr. Laing was sane but very subtle, very zen. In an effort to get things going, the ref began telling some hippoids about being in a Mexican jail on a murder rap, and the worry was, not the judge, but getting gang-fucked by the inmates. And then, from across the room, that loping and resonant southern drawl: "You evah bin gang-fucked, Bill?" Well, heavens to Betsy, that was it: sex and violence had made its move, and the quietists were henceforth in retreat. Final decision: some kind of draw, though the hippoids felt, as the young often do, somewhat ignored.

Second anecdote. About Easter 1971, I gave a large party in Wivenhoe, an encyclopedic gesture, manic certainly, from George

Gale[10] on the extreme right to various intellectual thugs on the extreme left. Girls in their finery. We might just have gotten away with it, except the Angry Brigade rump turned up. Tension mounted, until a fight broke out and the blood flowed. Feeling rather isolated (where were my friends?) I managed to eject five of the mischievous, with no further casualties than a treasured rose bush by the front door; and the party continued. Over our bedtime nightcap, Cal, who had been in another room, recounted with satisfaction his verbal triumphs over the vulgar lefties who had gone for him. I replied with my sad tale. "Why didn't you come and get me?" he said, shaking his silver mane; "Together we could easily have thrown them out."

In retrospect I see that party as our little local Altamont,[11] carnival's end.

PN [*Poetry Nation*] *Review* is a conservative journal of poetry and criticism published in Manchester, England.

1. Government scientific institute in Salisbury, Wiltshire, notorious for research in chemical warfare.

2. An experimental college in North Carolina founded in 1932 by Charles Olson; and the school of poets, led by Olson and Robert Creeley, who worked there. Olson's theory of Objectivism was derived from William Carlos Williams.

3. Shakespeare, *A Midsummer Night's Dream*.

4. An allusion to the military hero of Lowell's "For the Union Dead."

5. Italian: softly, softly.

6. Latin: let there be justice.

7. Greek god of fire and forging.

8. French: while waiting for.

9. Lowell's third wife, portrayed as a dolphin in his late volume of poetry, was Lady Caroline Blackwood (b. 1931). By association, Young calls the aristocratic poet, and author of *Lord Weary's Castle,* Lord Lowell.

10. George Gale (b. 1927), English journalist, author and broadcaster.

11. The California locale for a notorious Rolling Stones rock concert, where someone was stabbed and died.

45 • Robert Lowell in Cambridge: Lord Weary

James Atlas

When I stepped out of the elevator on the tenth floor of Holyoke Center, in Harvard Square, one afternoon in the fall of 1968, the corridor was already crowded. Students leaned against the wall, sprawled on the crimson carpet, or stood around in clusters. I sat down on a bench near the elevator bank, away from the others; their eagerness put me off.

We were waiting for Robert Lowell. The year before, I hadn't been eligible for his advanced poetry seminar—Lowell accepted no freshmen—but this year I was sure he would be impressed with my "work" (as I had taken to calling it). Somber meditations on history in a time of crisis and on the predicament of Jews who never quite found a home in America, my poems addressed the big issues yet were movingly personal. I considered myself a good candidate.

The elevator doors opened, and Lowell emerged amid a coterie of graduate students, a Mafia don surrounded by his lieutenants. Leonard Wiggins, my freshman poetry instructor, was by his side. I rose to greet him, but he hurried past with a brusque nod, clearing a path through the crowd. Lowell shuffled down the corridor, an aging professor in a fullback's body, staring ahead with the prescient gaze of the blind. We pushed into the classroom after him, so many that we spilled out into the hall.

Lowell glanced around in bewilderment; his eyes, magnified by black-framed glasses, flicked warily from face to face. The students fell silent, like birds before an eclipse. His wrinkled suit hung from his shoulders as if it were a size too large. Flecks of spittle formed at the corners of his mouth. "I can only take ten or twelve of you," he said in a tentative voice that had a faintly southern accent. He winced beneath the bright panels of light in the acoustic-tile ceiling, and smiled through taut lips. "I'm sure everyone is qualified." We were to leave our poems with

Atlantic Monthly 250 (July 1982): 56–64. Reprinted by permission of James Atlas.

him, and he would post a list in Warren House[1] before next week's meeting. That was all; he was making his way toward the door.

Well, at least I had seen him. Like a bird watcher elated by a rare sighting, I noted the characteristics I had studied on book-jacket photographs and in the *Time* cover story that had appeared the summer before I went off to Harvard. (I could still recall my excitement when I walked into Hoo's Drugstore in Evanston, Illinois, and saw the cover, with Sidney Nolan's portrait of Lowell wreathed like an emperor.) I had that sense of recognition one gets from seeing a celebrity in person; he seemed at once familiar and remote, someone I knew and someone different from other people by virtue of his known image. Our first glimpse of the famous is often disappointing; they seem diminished, ordinary. Lowell seemed, if anything, larger; he was taller than I had expected, and his corolla of whitening curls trailed back from his broad, marbled forehead.

I felt as if I had known him for years. I had been gathering Lowell's biographical lore since I was a sophomore in high school. I had read every reference work, every literary essay, every biographical note I could find; he was the greatest living American poet, so it was natural that I, an aspiring poet myself, should be curious about his life. I had read every book of Lowell's, from *Land of Unlikeness* and *Lord Weary's Castle* to *Life Studies,* that astonishing chronicle of his nervous breakdowns, his conflicts with his parents, his precocious, moody childhood. "I used to sit through the Sunday dinners absorbing cold and anxiety from the table"—I knew all about it.

Of course, Lowell, for all his complaints of belonging to a shabby, impoverished branch of the aristocratic Boston Lowells, was from another world. After all, what did that family have to do with the Atlases of Illinois and, before that, of Poland and God knows where else? This discrepancy troubled me; it was one thing for Lowell to write about himself and another for me, a mere boy, to go about denouncing my relatives and disclosing my wracked soul's every secret. My experience, however charged with significance I found it, could hardly have been more inconsequential in comparison with Lowell's. Even the proper names in his poetry—the Porcellian, Beverly Farms, Blue Hill in Maine—evoked a class so far beyond mine that I scarcely knew it existed. The names in *my* story—Eli's Delicatessen, the Skokie Indoor Tennis Club, Howard Johnson's Nassau Beach Lodge—were hopelessly suburban. How could I ever get poetry out of this unpromising material?

It wasn't enough simply to *feel* the poignance of life, a poignance that graced even Evanston on humid August nights when I coasted on my bicycle through the lakeside parks, swerving up and down the graveled paths with an exalted heart. No, you had to move in a more privileged realm, I suspected, to get poetry out of life.

This is why I had gone to Harvard—to find that more authentic experience, to dwell in a literature-producing region. Never mind that Dreiser, James T. Farrell, and Nelson Algren had been inspired by Chicago, that Saul Bellow lived there now, or that in the early decades of the century there had been some kind of Chicago Renaissance. (I was amazed to learn from Henry James's *The American Scene* that he had visited Chicago in 1905 and been introduced to a literary salon; the only salon I knew was the beauty parlor in the Orrington Hotel where my mother had her hair done once a week.) Much as I loved Chicago, it was impossible to imagine actually living in that soot-coated city. It was the East that held out promise, the East where writers lived and wrote; it was the East that I dreamed of, the New England of Hawthorne, Emerson, Melville (or was he from New York? Anyway, you get the idea), the crucible of culture, a world with a tradition.

Tradition: what a significant word that was! I couldn't open my mouth anymore without complaining about its absence. Everything is new! I sneered, casting a cold eye on our Danish-modern living room. I was off to where the American past was visible, where the furniture in the common rooms was burnished to a dark patina. The summer before freshman year I had spent whole afternoons in a plastic-webbed lawn chair on our patio perusing the 1967 Harvard course catalogue. "The Romance in America"; "The American Novel from the Civil War to 1900"; "The Poet in America": I read this catalogue with the "wild surmise" of Keats looking into Chapman's *Homer* "like some watcher of the skies / When a new planet swims into his ken."

But there was a still greater revelation in store for me, and that was the discovery that Harvard offered *writing* courses. Why, this was news! Here was William Alfred, the popular Harvard English professor I had read about in the *New Yorker*'s "Talk of the Town." And here was . . . "Mom!" I rose out of my lawn chair with a glad cry. My mother hurried to the door and looked out through the screen. "This is unbelievable! Guess who teaches poetry at Harvard? *Robert Lowell*." I read aloud: "English Sa. Writing (Advanced Course). . . . The emphasis will be primarily on poetry. Not more than ten students will be enrolled."

"Only ten?" my mother said doubtfully. "That's not so many."

"Oh, for God's sake, Mother. How many poets can there be at Harvard?"

When I arrived in Cambridge and learned that Lowell's seminar was closed to freshmen, I could scarcely imagine how I would get through the year. To console myself, I boarded the MTA,[2] got off at Charles Street, and headed for 91 Revere Street, where Lowell had lived as a child. Standing before the "flat red brick surface unvaried by the slightest suggestion of purple panes, delicate bay, or triangular window-cornice," I was as disappointed as Lowell had been by its bland façade, which blended in with the other houses on the steeply descending street. For once I was unstirred.

I got no closer to Lowell that year. Now I was sweating out his decision. On the crucial day, I consulted the bulletin board in Warren House every few minutes until a secretary wandered in and tacked up the list. There it was! My name.

Elated, I rose in the Holyoke Center elevator that afternoon and hurried toward the seminar room—only to find it nearly as crowded as it had been the week before. There must have been forty people, perched on the broad windowsill or the metal-hooded radiator, sitting cross-legged on the floor among piles of coats and notebooks, or lounging by the door. Tutors and graduate students, local poets, elderly women with crests of billowing white hair and vein-threaded cheeks, a reporter with a notepad balanced on his knee: the list, I soon discovered, was a formality. Anyone could attend.

Lowell passed around copies of a poem—the ritual of poetry seminars—and asked who the author was. A girl with kohl-encrusted eyes and silver stars pasted on her cheeks raised her hand. Lowell nodded and began to read the poem in a low, droning voice—the same voice I had listened to on a Caedmon album in high school, sprawled on the carpet in my bedroom late at night, while the TV boomed up through the floor. His broad Boston accent blended with a southern drawl acquired during his undergraduate years at Kenyon, where he had been a disciple of the Agrarian poet John Crowe Ransom:

> The night when you became my lover,
> goats cavorted above the star-dappled sea,
> I saw the whitewashed villages whiten,
> the moon intensify its beam of light.

Lowell's hand, the fingers splayed, moved in circles over the page, as if he were conjuring it to rise off the Formica surface. "You feel this last stanza's almost a parody, it's so weird," he said. "You could almost say it's a satire on the genre." The girl gnawed a fingernail and lit a cigarette. "It reminds me of Swinburne's '*Cor Cordium,*'" Lowell persisted. "It has Swinburne's florid energy." He turned a mild, inquisitive face to the girl, tucking a feathery wisp of hair behind his ears. "Isn't that what you had in mind? It's a translation of an English poem."

"I guess so," said the girl.

"How do others feel about the poem?" A few tentative hands rose, but Lowell was studying it again. "Or you could have the goats cavorting first: 'Goats cavorted when you became my lover.'" Pleased with this variation, he tried another: "'The star-dappled sea cavorts . . .'" His eyes had a hectic glint. "Why doesn't someone else talk now?" he said softly.

"I wonder if that last image is really earned," ventured a boy in a motorcycle jacket. "I mean—"

"But then you couldn't really say Swinburne." Lowell cut in, his hands circling above the poem. "It doesn't have Swinburne's lushness." He stared out the window, thinking hard. "And you could queer my argument by saying that it doesn't rhyme."

Through the picture windows that made up a wall of the room, the needle-like spire of Memorial Church divided the sky. A line of geese floated over the Yard. Lowell studied the poem for a while, then turned again to the author. "It's as good as Edna Millay."

Eventually we got used to these peculiar associations. Lowell would sit before the poem, seemingly transfixed by it, one cigarette cradled in his hand, another smoldering in the ashtray. Glancing up, he would suddenly offer some terse summation—"How many others in the room have grandfather poems?" he once asked after reading my contribution to the genre—or impossible advice: "Have you tried writing this in couplets?" "What if you made the speaker a priest instead of a young poet? Then maybe his sins would seem more real."

Lowell's interruptions seemed involuntary. Hunched down in his chair, smoke dribbling from between his thin, moist lips, his forehead shiny beneath the recessed lights, he would spin his manic fantasies, imagining how the poem would have gone if Wallace Stevens or T. S. Eliot had written it. Once, discussing a poem by an athletic, fresh-faced boy who stood out in that pale, needy crowd, Lowell peered intently at the page and stated, "You've been reading Hardy."

"Not really," said the boy, in obvious confusion. Wasn't Hardy a novelist? Then, not wishing to be impolite, he amended his answer: "I mean, no more than usual."

"But you could see these stanzas in *The Dynasts*," Lowell insisted. "Only with Hardy it would require eight hundred lines instead of eight." He leaned back in his chair and gazed at the ceiling. "You have Hardy's grim sense of humor—his enjoyment of misery. Fate was something he could mock at and not be called cruel." The boy stared at him like a tourist trying to make out a foreign language. "But then Hardy wrote his poetry out of genuine despair," Lowell mused. "You feel he wasn't so much inspired by his misery as driven mad by it." And then he was off on a long account of Hardy's two marriages, his reclusiveness, his cruel behavior toward his wives.

Lowell gossiped about the English poets the way other people gossip about their friends; he spoke of them as if they were colleagues and contemporaries, and thought nothing of disparaging them. "You feel that Arnold's trying too hard here," he remarked once, poring over "The Buried Life." "You'd almost say he wants to feel more than he does; the terse lines are there to goad on his emotion." It would never have occurred to me that Arnold could have tried too hard or pretended to feel more than he did; Arnold was only a name in the canon. He came after the Romantics and before Swinburne. He was represented in *The Norton Anthology of English Literature*. But to Lowell he was a school inspector, a thwarted poet, a man who had once lived.

Lowell had the infuriating habit of devoting hours and hours of our precious class time to older poets—and I mean old. Bored with our unmetered cries of anguish, he would turn to a well-thumbed *Oxford Book of English Verse* that he carried with him, its dark-blue cover faded with age. "This reminds me of Wyatt," he would say quietly, contemplating one of our poems. (He never seemed ironic about these comparisons; to him, poetry was poetry.) Flipping through the compact blue volume, he would read with a weird, urgent lilt, his voice gathering tension, then dropping to a nearly inaudible murmur. The Elizabethan diction of "The Appeal" or "Forget Not Yet" was as natural in his mouth as a poem from *Life Studies*. Once he recited from memory Sir

Walter Raleigh's "What Is Our Life?" and when he came to the last four lines—

> Our graves that hide us from the searching sun
> Are like drawn curtains when the play is done.
> Thus march we, playing, to our latest rest,
> Only we die in earnest—that's no jest.

—his voice grew rapt with terror. Eyes wide, he stared sightlessly out at the vision summoned up by Raleigh's words, a premonitory hallucination remote from our innocent classroom with its shiny Formica table and Fiberglas chairs, our heap of ski parkas and pea coats on the floor.

We listened dutifully to Lowell's monologues about these dead poets. Only why didn't he understand our unappeasable hunger to discuss our own work? Week after week, we entered the classroom tense with expectation; whose poems would be handed out this time? You could feel the frustration when the unlucky ones glanced down like poker players appraising their hands and learned that they would have to devote the next two hours to someone else's work. What bitter disappointment!

Lowell, though, was curious about our poems. Looking up from the mimeographed sheet before him, he would ask in his mild voice whose it was, then fix upon the author an uncertain scrutiny. The first time a poem of mine was discussed, read out in Lowell's quaking intonation, I could feel him trying to bring me into focus; it was clear he had never seen me before.

"It's an odd poem," he began, pawing the air like a blind man groping down a corridor. "It's all sensibility. You've written yourself back to the nineteenth century, to Baudelaire." He studied the poem, as absorbed as a scientist examining a slide, then read a line again: "'My wracked frame wastes on a Tangiers balcony.' You've told us that you're suffering, but not how or why." He gave me a kindly look. "And this pathetic fallacy: 'The stars' mad vacant stare'—it's too outlandish. The reader balks."

Was my poem pathetic, then, on top of everything else? And after so many years of waiting for this moment, waiting for approval from the highest authority in the land? A fallacy! Pathetic! I eyed the poem in disgust. "But I like its strangeness." Lowell broke in on my despondent reverie. "It's as if Keats had come out and told us how much he wanted to be a great poet." He smiled. "The poem's all about you, a good subject—even if it's a you that's entirely made up."

I didn't hear another word in class that day. Like a patient cut off by his psychiatrist at the end of the hour, I was uneasy, resentful; I hungered for more. My audience had ended all too quickly. I tried to remember everything he had said, but the message was ambiguous. Had I been compared favorably with Baudelaire? What about "sensibility"? Was that a good thing to have? My memory, cruelly accurate for once, restored the disparaging phrase: "all sensibility." But it was the word "pathetic" that tormented me the most; what a hateful idea. Not even "I like its strangeness" could cancel out that distressing epithet. (It wasn't until many years later that I came across Ruskin's discussion of "pathetic fallacy" in *Modern Painters*.)

I was hardly alone in my hunger for Lowell's attention. Everyone clamored for a share: the Brattle Street ladies who invited him to dinner; the undergraduates who clustered around him after class on the thinnest excuse—a late assignment, a clarification of some stray remark he had made about their work; the graduate students and tutors who accompanied him to the Faculty Club for a drink. Nothing dejected me more than to watch Lowell moving off down the sidewalk surrounded by his coterie.

Denied direct access to him, I cultivated his disciples. Leonard Wiggins had organized a workshop of his own, which met once a week in the basement of Kirkland House, and now that I was in Lowell's class, he invited me to join. It was in that dreary room, beneath plaster-swaddled pipes and next door to a quivering, ancient boiler, that I came to know the core of Lowell's Cambridge following, that handful of zealous graduate students who dined out and corresponded with the poet, even visited him in New York.

It was from Lowell's disciples that I learned the main details of his life: that he lived in New York and came up to Cambridge for two days a week; that he was married to the writer Elizabeth Hardwick; that he had a suite of rooms in Quincy House; that he was writing sonnets now. But they knew far more: the identities of the people mentioned in his poems; the variants of celebrated lines ("That poem used to have two more stanzas," Leonard would say, or "The *Sewanee Review* version was much better"); his itinerary at any given moment ("Cal's in London," or "Cal's campaigning with McCarthy").

I was greatly impressed by these knowing discussions, and envious of the casual talk about "Cal"—short for the Roman emperor Caligula, a prep school nickname that had stuck (with Lowell's own connivance, I suspected; I hadn't had any trouble getting rid of "Fatless," *my* nickname). To speak of Cal was to claim an intimacy with Lowell that forever eluded me; even later on, when I knew him well enough to call him on the phone, I would murmur with stilted English formality, "Is that Robert Lowell?" But Wiggins had clearly earned the right. "Cal read this poem aloud the other night, and thought it was one of my best," he would say; or, "Cal says you have to tinker with a poem until your eyes pop out of your head." The name in itself was poetry; it suggested a world one could know if one were only patient enough—a world in which great men were colleagues.

The other disciple of Lowell's I got to know that year was Winston Walker, a graduate student from New Orleans who attended the Kirkland House evenings and was writing a Ph.D. thesis on religious imagery in Lowell's early work. The son of an amateur historian from an aristocratic southern family, Walker had grown up in a household that must have been, from what he told me of it, as old-fashioned as mine was progressive. The strict father, the vine-covered house where servants glided noiselessly through the halls, the theological debates at the dinner table (Walker had converted to Catholicism while still in high school): had I read about such childhoods in Faulkner? I imagined Winston seated at a mahogany dining-room table, a Latin primer open before him, translating Catullus, while his father, behind a closed door in the upstairs study, put the finishing touches on a book about how the South could have won the Civil War.

However fanciful this image, it represented for me the rigor of Winston's character, its archaic formality. He was hopelessly awkward—I had once been riding with him in his old Chevrolet when he smashed a rear headlight trying to park, then sideswiped two cars as he drove off in disgust—but somehow powerful; in his cream-colored linen suits and flesh-tinted glasses, he was at once vigorous and professorial, refined yet possessed of a nervous animal strength. Nowhere was this strength more evident than in his voice, a penetrating nasal whine that made heads turn. Once, while crossing a street together in Paris against the light, we were nearly run over by a Frenchman who leaped screaming from his Citroën; Walker protested in a sonorous drone that emanated like a mantra from deep within his diaphragm, "*Ça ne vous donne pas le droit de parler comme ça*"[3]—upon which the driver backed off, gaping in astonishment, and drove away.

Nothing mattered to Walker but poetry; I never heard him mention a novel. On the rare occasions when he found himself in the company of people who didn't write, he sat with a drink in his hand and the nervous look of a patient in a dentist's waiting room, tossing back one highball after another. Fiercely impatient but too polite to interrupt, he crouched forward in his chair, as eager as a hunting dog about to be unleashed, and waited for a chance to bring the conversation around.

He was maddeningly thorough, and would go through some minor poet's oeuvre book by book, assessing the poet's development and reputation, concentrating on a thin volume destined for oblivion a laborious scrutiny that made me feel boorish for dismissing it out of hand. "How can you say that?" he would interrupt when I declared a poet "stupid" or "no good." "What about the sequence of poems on the death of his father in *Waiting Out the Winter?* There are some good things there." His impulse of fairness shamed me.

It was Walker who introduced me to Lowell's "office hours"—not voluntarily but by chance, when I happened to encounter him turning in at the gate of Quincy House one morning. He was on his way to see Lowell, as it happened, and had no choice but to invite me along. I followed him down a flight of steps, past a janitor's closet, and into a tiny, windowless cell with cinderblock walls, a scuffed linoleum floor, and a few metal folding chairs around an old wooden table. It was in this cheerless dungeon that Lowell spent every Wednesday morning from nine until noon. The procedure was no different from his Tuesday class, except that those who wished to have their poems discussed could volunteer. Anyone could attend, the only requirement being that one knew about the office hours in the first place; and since no one who did know was anxious to share the information, word didn't get around.

Promptly at nine, Lowell would shuffle into the crowded room looking hung over and pale, his forehead damp, a watery remoteness in his eyes. "Who has a poem?" he would ask shyly, lighting a cigarette.

I could never figure out why he submitted himself to this needless torture. Perhaps it was because so many of our poems were imitations of his own—a form of homage. The brutal candor of *Life Studies* was our model, Lowell's madness our literary myth. Every few semesters he had to be confined to McLean's, the Boston-area mental hospital described in his poem "Waking in the Blue." I had never witnessed one of these breakdowns, but I had heard about them in grim detail: Lowell showing up at William Alfred's house and declaring that he was the Virgin Mary; Lowell talking for two hours straight in class, revising a student's poem in the style of Milton, Tennyson, or Frost; Lowell wandering around Harvard Square without a coat in the middle of January, shivering, wild-eyed, incoherent. In the seminar room on the top floor of Holyoke Center, we waited nervously—perhaps even expectantly, given the status accorded anyone who had been present at one of these celebrated episodes—for it to happen before our eyes, watching eagerly for any manic soliloquies, references to Hitler, or outbursts of unnatural gaiety. These were the signs that Lowell had "gone off" and would have to be put away.

Encouraged by Lowell's willingness to write about such episodes, his disciples turned out confessions of madness, attempted suicide, and sexual miscreancy that made the revelations in *Life Studies* seem as tame as a country priest's confession. "When you slit your wrists," began a poem by a genial midwestern boy whose work Lowell admired, "the blood made a crimson gully on the floor." "I could feel his heart lunging like a rabbit flushed from cover" was another line I recall, from a poem in which a three-hundred-pound diva laments the sudden death of her lover, seized by a fatal coronary as she rode above him on a couch in her dressing room. The day a thin, mild-mannered divinity student whose piping voice, disheveled beard, and wire-rimmed glasses made him a dead ringer for Lytton Strachey read out the dramatic monologue of a mass murderer of boys that began, "I was only happy when I had one in the trunk," I gazed around our cell in wonderment: just how many Loebs and Leopolds[4] were there in this room?

My own poetry revealed few homicidal inclinations; the only violence I did was to the language. But in every other respect it was so close to Lowell's as to verge on plagiarism. Once I brought in a poem for discussion at office hours and Lowell read it aloud, interrupting with his usual digressions, until he came to the last line. Instead of reading it, he paused as if studying a word that he was uncertain how to pronounce, then said in his gentle, murmurous drawl, "I see you've taken a line here from one of my poems." I faced his unreproachful gaze, and suddenly Lowell's line came to mind, a line from which my own diverged by only a single word.

"Huh!" I said. "I guess it is a lot like it." I could feel myself blushing, and stared down at the poem, my head cradled in my fists.

"It's a good line," Lowell said kindly, and everyone laughed.

Even in my embarrassment, I felt a certain pride. The plagiarism had troubled him, I noticed, and to register in his mind, however fleetingly and under whatever conditions, was to exist. I used to walk back to my dorm from office hours calibrating the amount of attention I had gotten over the past three hours; every glance in my direction, every casual aside, was rehearsed and evaluated. "What do you think, James?" Hadn't Lowell turned and spoken those words? Hadn't he referred to me by name? My need to be noticed was obsessive—an obsession shared, I suspect, by many who came to class or office hours. Like cripples thronging about a healer, we longed to be anointed by the great man's recognition.

What was it that gave Lowell this gravity, this nearly shamanistic power? Perhaps it was that the one question that tormented everyone else had been decided for him: he had made it into the pantheon of great American poets. His work would last, while we were condemned to doubt; our poems were so provisional, so rudimentary that we despaired of ever giving utterance to what we felt. "Oh Lord, how beautiful must have been some of the faces trampled in the dust." I was moved by that lament, from an Urdu poem I had read somewhere, awed that so much effort might come to so little. "The unspoken question," Winston once confided, "is which of us will last." It reassured him that Keats had gone largely unappreciated in his lifetime, that Tennyson had been ridiculed by his early critics.

He was haunted by thoughts of immortality. But I was haunted by other thoughts—thoughts of oblivion. I wrote to preserve the memory of my own existence, to record for the sake of the dead their forgotten history. This vanished past was the only tradition I knew, and it was to thwart its terrible anonymity that I sat hunched over my desk night after night, turning out what Lowell once called my "Jewish homelife" poems: chronicles of my grandparents' arrival in America, the crowded households of immigrants on Chicago's West Side, the new prosperity and dispersal of children to the suburbs; the accumulation and divestment of carpets and looms and paintings and sideboards and gold-framed photographs. They were like geologic strata, these possessions and lives, each generation burying the previous generation deeper.

Elated by the discovery of office hours, regular attendance at which had raised me above the common lot of the undergraduates in Lowell's poetry class, I was disappointed to find that there was still another, more privileged status—those who joined Lowell for lunch every Wednesday at Iruña, a Spanish restaurant in Harvard Square. It was with the keenest regret that I emerged from the Quincy House basement at noon on those days and lingered on the sidewalk while Lowell and his select group drifted off in a cluster. It was strange; no matter how old I was, there always seemed to be an "older crowd" around to exclude me. Just because I was twenty rather than ten made no difference in the humiliation I suffered as I made my way back to Dunster House and pushed my tray along the barred counter, peering in through the steamed-up glass at the metal bins heaped high with carrots and lima beans, mashed potatoes and Salisbury steak. I could still have been the boy unwrapping his bologna sandwich on a bench while sides were chosen for the scrub baseball game; still the seventh grader new to Evanston, trailing after the eighth-grade boys who smoked, carried switchblades, and slipped out to the luncheonette on the other side of the viaduct during lunch period; still the high school freshman trudging home after school, my Harvard bookbag crammed with work, while the upperclassmen hurried off to their extra-curricular activities. Would there ever come a time, I wondered, scanning the Dunster dining hall for an unoccupied table, when I would belong to the "older crowd"?

One day, after a sparsely attended office hours, I noticed Lowell glancing around and realized that no one from the inner circle had shown up. Who would join him at Iruña? I happened to be sitting beside him— rather, I had arrived twenty mintues early and claimed the seat. Lowell registered my presence and said, "Let's have lunch." It was a command, but spoken in such a diffident voice that I scarcely heard him.

As we headed off down the street, I glimpsed one of the other undergraduates who had managed to find out about office hours. A burly, taciturn young man who specialized in dramatic monologues by martyred religious figures—Jan Hus,[5] Giordano Bruno,[6] Thomas More—he seemed capable of the violence the others only wrote about; there was a taut, furious shape to his mouth, and his blue eyes behind rimless glasses had an angry glint. He was angling toward us with a determined stride, his big shoulders thrown forward, as if he were muscling his way through a crowd.

I tried to hurry Lowell on, hoping to screen him from the intruder's view. But he came right up—and Lowell, the distracted, indiscriminate Lowell, invited him to join us. What the hell are you doing? I raged inwardly. How can you waste your time on this ominous character? I could scarcely restrain myself from seizing the intrusive poet and hurling him into the snow. But it was too late; he had fallen in beside us. Fuming, I kicked a stony lump of ice. The great event ruined! What was so special about having lunch with Lowell if this boorish lout, this lumpen bully, could push his way in? I was too exasperated to join the conversation or even hear what they were saying until we were seated at Iruña, and Lowell was filling our glasses with sangría. Oblivious of the malevolent stares we exchanged—the other poet was no happier than I at the prospect of having to share the occasion—Lowell posed his favorite question: "Who do you read?"

Some younger poets were mentioned, neo-surrealists with a weakness for hallucinatory images and weird, improbable metaphors. I knew Lowell didn't care for their work.

"Oh, I just don't believe them," I broke in. "Their poems aren't *about* anything. I mean, don't you get tired of all those speaking stones and streetlamps that turn into stars? It's become a style, the latest fashion." My voice quavered with vehemence.

Lowell lit a cigarette and caressed the tablecloth, smoothing out wrinkles and brushing away crumbs. He was in his element, ranking poets, assigning them their place on the ladder—beneath him, it was understood. Flattered as I was by his invitation, I had been anxious on the way over to the restaurant; how would I ever hold his interest or find enough to say? But I realized that it didn't matter; all one had to do was mention a few poets and he was off, judging, dismissing, now and then offering a shred of praise. This exercise could entertain him for hours. "Who else?" he would prompt during a lull in the conversation; or, "What about so-and-so?" Whenever a new name was introduced, he leaned forward eagerly, his hands spread out on the table, a glad look in his eye. "He's written two good poems," he would say in that mild but definite voice of his; and he would name and discuss them as if the poet's work were right in front of him, open to the page. I was amazed by how much he kept up with even minor poets; I don't recall ever hearing him say he didn't know someone's work.

"You think they're really so bad as all that?" My rude outburst had made Lowell more charitable. Why be the first to attack? "I find Norman interesting in his own small way," he said. "He's written some good poems." Lowell's eyes behind his glasses bulged. "Only you feel he has nothing to say."

I nodded—a victory for our side—and glanced at my sullen opponent, but he was busy gnawing the husk of a shrimp. Lowell signaled the waiter and ordered another pitcher of sangría. He hadn't touched his dish, an omelette in a cream sauce. The ashtray was heaped with bent and broken half-smoked cigarettes. Lowell wasn't one of those smokers who exhale in vigorous plumes; he smoked as if it made him ill. His skin had a mushroom-like pallor; his tie was streaked with ash. But he was talking with great energy now, recalling the time he and this poet had met. "He wanted me to come read in Milwaukee or somewhere like that against the war, but I'd already been to Washington and marched against the war, and felt I'd done my part." He gave an apologetic smile, as if asking us to absolve him; had he done the right thing?

Lowell had a way, I noticed, of soliciting opinions from his listeners in order to draw them out; it flattered us to know that our ideas mattered—though I couldn't imagine why they did. What difference did it make what I, a long-haired, unkempt boy in a worn corduroy jacket and Frye boots, thought of Pound's *Pisan Cantos* or the later Hardy? But Lowell was achingly well mannered. He was working his way through Yeats's whole career now, starting with the florid Pre-Raphaelite verse in *The Wanderings of Oisin* and moving brusquely through the various phases of his development, encouraged by an occasional nod or murmur of approval.

"I guess my favorite is 'Under Ben Bulben,'" I volunteered.

"Really?" he said in surprise, as if I were F. R. Leavis reversing an opinion put forth in *New Bearings in English Poetry*. "What is it that you like about it?"

What, indeed? The only line I could remember was "Horseman, pass by!" God, why hadn't we been taught to memorize?

"Uh, it's such a mature statement about death," I babbled, reaching for my glass. My brutish colleague probably knew the whole poem by heart, and half the plays! But he too was silent. Couldn't Lowell understand that others simply didn't live for poetry the way he did? We had been sitting here for an hour comparing Dryden with Pope, Coleridge with Wordsworth, Edward Thomas with Wilfred Owen, and the two pitchers of sangría had made inroads on my attention. It seemed odd to be drunk in the middle of a winter afternoon, with the ice-etched windows glinting in the sun. Ecstatic as I was to be in Lowell's company, I felt groggy from alcohol and talk; and besides, I was eager to get word out about the momentous event. How could any experience, even this one, compare with the joys of reporting it? To refine, elaborate, revise what happened, to polish and edit the afternoon . . . I could hardly wait to get out of there. "Guess who I just had lunch with?" I heard myself saying over the phone. (No need to mention what's-his-name in these accounts; from now on it was Lowell and me.) "He was fascinating, just incredible. He's every bit as brilliant as he is in class . . . ."

But Lowell, done with English literature, had started in on the poets who came to office hours. "I find Bennett's poems too much like mine," he said benignly. "You wonder where he can go from here." Bennett Lamsdon was one of Lowell's most devoted disciples, and had written several essays on his work. I was surprised that Lowell had reservations about him. He admired Bennett's poems and had even recommended him for a fellowship. "I mean, he's very good," Lowell said, turning to me with the look on his face of a child caught drawing on his bedroom wall, "but can you really get away with some of what he gets away with in a poem? Or can you say anything now?" There was a slyness in his eyes that dared reproof. No one had challenged him in years, I was sure, apart from a few easily discredited critics, and he must have grown bored at times by adulation. His disloyalty was a game, a way of diverting himself.

Of course, it was a game that required another player, someone to feed him names. "What about Leonard Wiggins?" I said. He had gone out to California for the semester and "been through a lot of heavy changes," he reported in a letter I now quoted to Lowell.

"Yes, I gather he's brimming with revolutionary zeal," Lowell said, leaning forward to concentrate on my words. (What a keen pleasure that was!) He loved news of anyone he knew. "I like his early poems, but I can't follow what he's writing now. You wonder if there isn't too much California in it." (He always switched from "I" to "you," as if attributing his opinions to someone else.) I introduce another name. "His poems are grotesque, too truthful," Lowell said. And of an undergraduate whose work he had praised in class: "She has a schoolgirl's bright enthusiasm, but you feel she hasn't lived."

Everyone did this, I reflected as we left the restaurant. How many of us would choose loyalty over the chance to say what we really thought— or even to display our wit? And how often I disparaged my own friends just for the sake of camaraderie, for the atmosphere of good fellowship that agreement about the failings of others invariably produced. There was no reason why Lowell should be any less vulnerable or calculating than anyone else.

Yet the deference, the gentle drawl, the bowed head, were no pose: they were the visible signs of his ordeal. That he had been through so much was intimidating and made people shy away from him. One evening I spotted him at the Boston Athenaeum, where a young painter who had attended office hours on occasion was giving a slide show of his canoe trip through Alaska. Sitting in the dark among that crowd of ruddy-faced Bostonians, I wondered what Lowell made of the seals and caribou, the trout surfacing on ponds, the vistas of barren tundra that flashed on the screen; it was all so remote from his populous, incident-crowded, human world. Afterward, when the lights came on, he made straight for me, glad to see a familiar face.

More often he was oblivious. I used to see him shuffling down Massachusetts Avenue in his crepe-soled rubber boots. One afternoon, loitering by the magazine rack in the Pangloss Bookshop, I looked up to find him staring in the window, cupping a hand against the glass. I nodded and smiled, hoping to be noticed, but the face squinting with a wrinkled brow at the dust-flecked books registered nothing. He didn't know what he was looking at, I realized; his mind was elsewhere— circling, I imagined, the thought of death that had come to haunt his poetry. It wasn't that he thirsted to live; then only in his early fifties, he seemed wearier than anyone I had ever known. It was that he couldn't believe he would ever die; he had seen and known and felt so much. His bleak eyes in the sunlight were moist, as if he were holding back tears.

James Atlas (b. 1949), American editor and biographer, was Lowell's student at Harvard in the late 1960s. He is the author of *Delmore Schwartz: The Life of an American Poet* (1977).
1. The location of the Harvard English Department.
2. Metropolitan Transit Authority, the Boston subway.
3. French: that doesn't give you the right to talk like that.
4. Nathan Leopold and Richard Loeb, celebrated Chicago murderers, were defended in a famous trial of 1924 by Clarence Darrow.
5. Jan Hus (1372–1415), Czech religious reformer and Protestant martyr.
6. Giordano Bruno (1548–1600), Italian philosopher, astronomer and occultist, author of *On the Infinite Universe and Worlds* (1584). He was burned at the stake as a heretic.

46 • *Le Byron de Nos Jours*
(Robert Lowell)

Anthony Hecht

> *Everything is real until it's published.*
> —"Flight to New York"

In *Robert Lowell* (Random House) Ian Hamilton has written an extraordinarily careful and well-researched biography. It runs to four hundred and seventy-four crowded pages, and it's easy for the reader to believe that Hamilton's chief problem may well have been deciding what to leave out. For, long and meticulous as his book is, there's a good deal that has mercifully been eliminated. Lowell's life was so public and publicized, so redolent of scandal, so meshed with the lives of others whose biographies have been, or are about to be, written, so prominent in the reminiscences of other writers, of students, politicians, poets and intellectuals, that almost any reader of this book who knows anything about literature and the world since the Second World War will be able to think of texts that Hamilton might have drawn on had he cared to, and may possibly have chosen to disregard.

So it is a mark of the care and success of his winnowing that this book should have been saluted with what may fairly be called rave reviews by Helen Vendler in the leading article in the *New York Review of Books;* by Richard Ellmann on the front page of the *New York Times Book Review;* and by Stephen Spender on the front page of the *Washington Post*'s *Book World*.[1] There is in this a rather poignant irony that is not likely to be lost on Hamilton, who is himself a notable poet. Of all the work of a lifetime dedicated to poetry, and abundant in its production, the only volume of Lowell's to receive front page notice in the *Times Book Review* was his last, *Day by Day,* reviewed there admiringly by Helen Vendler on August 14, 1977, less than a month before Lowell's

Grand Street 2 (Spring 1983): 32–48. Reprinted as *Robert Lowell* (Washington, D.C.: Library of Congress, 1983); and in Anthony Hecht, *Obbligati* (New York: Atheneum, 1986), 264–289. Reprinted here by permission of Anthony Hecht.

death on September 12. Mr. Hamilton's book bids fair to be something
of a best-seller, and may be so already; and, like the reviewers who are on
record in praising it, I wish it every success. But he and I will not be
alone in imagining that this book will be devoured by many who have
little or no interest in poetry, and scarcely any knowledge of Robert
Lowell's work.

The sort of prurience that is bound to contribute to the public's
interest can be illustrated by an anecdote, true in its major outlines, and
from which I have merely deleted the proper names. Some years ago,
when Lowell was a firmly acknowledged celebrity, the editors of a popu-
lar magazine invited one of New York's leading intellectuals, a critic-
author-editor of impeccable credentials, to lunch at one of the city's best
restaurants to discuss some sort of possible article about the poet. The
distinguished critic was intrigued by the emergence of this proposal from
so unlikely a source, and perhaps engaged by the excellence of the restau-
rant. It was during the second, soothing martini that the editors began to
make clear what it was they hoped the projected article would cover:
they wanted to have as much in the way of particulars as could be
managed about (a) Lowell's girlfriends and extramarital affairs, and (b)
his episodes of violence and incarceration in mental hospitals. The critic
listened silently, savoring his drink, as these guidelines were laid out for
him, and when they seemed to be quite through he asked the editors,
"And how much space do you think should be devoted to the *poetry?*"
The answer he received convinced him that, of their kind, these were real
pros. "Roughly eighty percent of our readership," he was told, "hold
B.A.'s, and of those perhaps twenty percent have more advanced de-
grees. So I think you can safely assume that they will *know* the poetry,
and you won't have to bother with it."

And indeed this book, though sparing in both numbers and details
(not a few women will doubtless be outraged to find their names omitted
from the chronicle), makes it clear that Lowell's manic cycles almost
always involved episodes of sexual adventurism. So much was this the
case that at one time his New York psychiatrist, a woman, convinced
that somehow Lowell's wife, Elizabeth Hardwick, had a deleterious ef-
fect upon the poet, and needed to be kept from him at all costs, neverthe-
less found herself so mystified by the urgency with which Lowell spoke
of someone he was newly obsessed with (or so goes the story as I heard
it) that, for all the therapist's hostility to Hardwick, she phoned her to

ask, "Who is this Gerta he talks about now all the time?" Hardwick replied truthfully that her husband was talking about the author of *Faust*.

Hamilton's book deserves praise for many things, but I think chiefly for being astonishingly fair to all the major figures in the story he has set out to tell—not in itself an easy task, given a tale so congested with pain and cruelty, infidelity, wildness, and violence—but he is also to be congratulated on his respectful and intelligent dealings with the poetry. He is very keen, subtle, and knowing, for example, about Lowell's poem, "Home After Three Months Away," indicating with great care the stratified, geological layers of reference that work down through the poet's entire biography. He is even more helpful, and helped in his turn by the painter Sidney Nolan, in the unraveling of an all but impenetrable poem, "The Misanthrope and the Painter," which seems otherwise defiantly hermetic and private. (It's impossible to tell whether the poem was meant to be cryptic, or was not sufficiently worked out.) In his honest dealings with his large cast of characters, and in his valuable comments on the poetry, Hamilton has done, I think, rather greater justice to Lowell than has been done to Byron by most of his biographers, some of whom, like Peter Quennell and Harold Nicolson, appear not really to be interested in the poetry at all. So responsible does Hamilton prove in most regards that I hope he will not mind my pointing to two small errors which, together with a handful of solecisms and typos, compose the only small faults I have found. John Crowe Ransom did not study at Cambridge, as stated on page 45, but at Oxford: "I pernoctated with the Oxford students once. . . ." And Lowell's celebrated poem, "Waking Early Sunday Morning," is declared on page 327 to be written "in a meter borrowed from Andrew Marvell's equivocal 'Ode upon Cromwell's Return from Ireland.'" Many another Marvell poem—any of those, like "The Garden," or "Upon Appleton House," composed in rhymed tetrameter couplets—might have served Lowell as a model, but the ode on Cromwell's return is written in alternating tetrameter and trimeter couplets, and is metrically unrelated to Lowell's poem.

The Byron comparison, while not to be pursued with Euclidean precision, and not Hamilton's but mine, is a fair one in some respects. Both poets were public figures and involved in the political events of their time; both were capable of devastating expressions of scorn for their opponents; both were powerful and handsome men; both were crippled, each in his own way; both were astonishingly attractive to women; both were aristocrats by inheritance (somewhat shabby aristocrats) and democrats by generous instinct; both were the subject of scandalous gossip during and after their lifetime; and both were poets of acknowledged international stature, who *found themselves famous* quite early in life. It may be added that both were bedeviled by a strict and relentlessly Puritan conscience, and Calvinistic anguish. Hamilton reports that Lowell's nickname, Cal, was meant to stand for Caligula (as Lowell himself acknowledges in a poem) and Caliban. Robie Macauley has told me that it also stood for the Calvin in Calvin Coolidge. While there was something strikingly Julio-Claudian about Lowell's huge head, the Calvin of Geneva, a dim but satanic presence in "Children of Light" ("Pilgrims unhoused by Geneva's night, / They planted here the Serpent's seeds of light; . . ."), has, I think, a legitimate part to play in the poet's psychic genealogy.

The nickname was curiously prophetic because it was assigned to, and adopted by, Lowell before his madness had yet exhibited itself in any forms graver than eccentric recklessness and untidiness. Later, of course, the news of his periodic breakdowns spread with amazing speed, penetrating without difficulty to even the most remote recesses of the world. News of his Salzburg collapse reached me somehow in provincial Ischia, and I remember passing it on to Auden, expecting from him some grunt of commiseration, at the very least. I could not have been more astonished by his response. He regarded Lowell's whole tortured history of crack-ups as pure self-indulgence, and undeserving of any sympathy. It took me many years to come to even a partial understanding of this chilling reaction, and I can only guess that it may be due to Auden's medical fascination with Georg Groddeck, Homer Lane,[2] and other psychosomatic theorists who believed that virtually all illnesses are *willed,* along with his parental inheritance of clinical detachment, and the fact that there was no history of madness in his immediate experience. In fairness it should be added that he may have been at least partly right: Hamilton quotes Jonathan Raban's account of the dolphin binge Lowell went on during the writing of *The Dolphin,* a binge that clearly represented a huge exertion of will power ("So the obsession was with dolphins—it never got into great men. Which was a triumph") directed towards avoiding a crack-up, and which, in this lone instance, worked. But Auden's lofty, condemnatory tone was to exhibit itself again when Lowell later, in *The Dolphin,* published poems of unprecedented intimacy, with details and even language frankly rifled from private conversations and correspondence, chiefly with his abandoned wife, Elizabeth Hardwick, but with others, like Allen Tate, as well. Hamilton quotes from a letter to Lowell from William Alfred, who had just met Auden for the first time: "He spoke of not speaking to you because of the book. When I said he sounded like God the Father, he gave me a tight smile. I write to warn you." Alas, in both these cases Auden sounds less like the Ancient of Days than like a prim English nanny with a rigid sense of decorum. In fact, Auden is permitted to voice his objections in one of the book's sonnets, called, with some point, "Truth":

> The scouring voice of 1930 Oxford,
> "Nothing pushing the personal should be published,
> not even Proust's *Recherche* or Shakespeare's *Sonnets*,
> a banquet of raw ingredients in bad taste. . . ."

Undeniably, as Lowell's best and most admiring friends forced themselves to point out to him before publication, the book would be excruciatingly painful to Elizabeth Hardwick. Elizabeth Bishop wrote Lowell an agonizing letter, urging him not to publish the book: " . . . *art just isn't worth that much.*" And Stanley Kunitz must have raised objections no less strong and direct, as he indicates in a memoir published in the October 16, 1977 *New York Times Book Review*. . . . Hamilton reports these terrible debates and dilemmas without passing judgment, though at least one review that I have seen (in the *Washington Times Magazine)* matches Auden in righteous indignation.

The problem is not easily solved, nor does solution lie in some considered compromise between Auden's snooty evasions and Lowell's ruthless candor. Somehow Lowell must have clung to a fuddled conviction expressed in the line I have used here for an epigraph: "Everything is real until it's published," whereupon, I think he may have felt, it becomes art, which is beyond the real but nearer the truth. Whatever theorizing may have lain behind this attitude, it took no account of the human pain it would engender. But Lowell's sense of the transformations wrought by art, removing its matter from the realm of the literal, is wonderfully documented in this book. Jonathan Raban is quoted as observing that Lowell's revisions were usually

> a kind of gaming with words, treating them like billiard balls. For
> almost every sentence that Cal ever wrote if he thought it made a

better line he'd have put a "never" or a "not" at the essential point. His favorite method of revision was simply to introduce a negative into a line, which absolutely reversed its meaning but very often would improve it. So that his poem on Flaubert ended with Flaubert dying, and in the first draft it went "Till the mania for phrases dried his heart"—a quotation from Flaubert's mother. Then Cal saw another possibility and it came out: "Till the mania for phrases enlarged his heart." It made perfectly good sense either way round, but the one did happen to mean the opposite of the other.

While it may be argued that there is a considerable difference between tampering, on the one hand, with the words of Flaubert's mother, and, on the other, appropriating the most intimate domestic communications of an abandoned wife with whom the poet lived in great happiness for many years, and who is the mother of his daughter, I think two other points must also be made. First, that any poet who habitually treats words and facts "like billiard balls" is likely to be convinced of their transmutability into a realm that is immune and indifferent to the literal. And, secondly, there is in this revision of the Flaubert poem an allegory of what Lowell must have felt about himself: if to others it appeared that his heart had dried, to the artist, to Lowell/Flaubert, it was clear that his heart was enlarged by the very act of finding words, by the very mania for phrases that so obsessed them both. It is a self-granted absolution of the sort Auden granted to Yeats—and to all who give life to language— in the first version of the final part of his famous elegy:

> Time that is intolerant
> Of the brave and innocent. . . .
>
> Worships language and forgives
> Everyone by whom it lives;
> Pardons cowardice, conceit,
> Lays its honors at their feet.[3]

This is not a justification—the book is full of instances of Lowell's personal cruelty, attested to by Xandra Gowrie at some length, and in Hardwick's declaration that at certain times for the poet "the deep underlying unreality is there, the fact that no one else's feelings really exist . . ."—it is merely an attempt at an explanation.

In an essay called "Fifty Years of American Poetry," Randall Jarrell says, "Lowell has always had an astonishing ambition, a willingness to learn what past poetry was and to compete with it on its own terms."[4] This driving ambition and sense of competition was with him from the first, and plays its role in other realms besides poetry. Hamilton quotes the first draft of "Waking in the Blue," then titled "To Ann Adden (Written during the first week of my voluntary stay at McLean's Mental Hospital)," from which these lines are taken:

> The bracelet on your right wrist jingles with trophies:
> The enamelled Harvard pennant,
> the round medallion of St. Mark's School.
> I could claim both,
> for both were supplied by earlier,
> now defunct claimants,
> and my gold ring, almost half an inch wide,
> now crowns your bracelet, cock of the walk there.

And in a letter of tribute and admiration addressed to Theodore Roethke, Lowell says

> I remember Edwin Muir arguing with me that there is no rivalry in poetry. Well, there is.

This keenly competitive drive accounts in some ways for his wholesale appropriations of The Western World's Great Poetry, all converted into what someone has called "Lo-Cal" in the volume *Imitations*. But it also exhibits itself in more covert ways. For example, the most ambitious poem in *Lord Weary's Castle* is probably "The Quaker Graveyard in Nantucket." This poem is deservedly admired, studied, and commented upon by astute critics, who have located prose passages in Thoreau, as well as more conspicuous references from Melville, that are woven carefully into the fabric of the poem. It first appeared in what amounts to two installments, in the Spring 1945 and Winter 1946 issues of *Partisan Review,* and longer by a great deal, when those two installments are assembled, than would appear in the final, careful pruning of the poem as the text we now know. Lowell's editing of his own poem was brilliant and right in every way; everything he eliminated was excessive, and even sometimes rather shabby, and so it is not entirely out of order to wonder why such material had ever been included in the first place. The answer seems to me clear. If the two original installments are brought together, they come to one hundred and ninety-three lines of poetry, which is precisely the number of lines in "Lycidas."

In that chapter of Eileen Simpson's fine book of recollections, *Poets in Their Youth,* where she focuses on Lowell, she records the matching excitement and enthusiasm both Lowell and Berryman felt about Milton's poem. Describing a visit to Lowell and Jean Stafford in Maine, she writes:

> After Mass Jean repeated what she had said the previous evening; John and I mustn't think of leaving as originally planned. We must stay, Cal said. How could John even consider going when they hadn't discussed "Lycidas"? . . .
>
> The days of our visit, which stretched from a weekend to two weeks, fell into casual order. Although neither Cal nor John was supposedly working, there was never a time when they were not working. After breakfast and a good long recitation:
>
> > Bitter constraint, and sad occasion dear,
> > Compels me to disturb your season due;
> > For Lycidas is dead, dead ere his prime,
>
> and explication of "Lycidas," which they had no trouble agreeing was one of the greatest poems in the language (though there was the usual push/pull over the Three Greatest Lines), . . . Cal went up to his room.

A moment's reflection ought to make clear why this paradigm meant so much to Lowell when he came to write "The Quaker Graveyard." Here was one of the world's indisputably great poems, a marine elegy, formidable in its overt and hidden debts to its classical predecessors, distinguished for its striking outburst of moral indignation, the superlative work of a young but limitlessly ambitious poet, who not only composes a masterpiece but ends by announcing that he looks to even greater undertakings in "pastures new." As a model of substance, of congested and densely packed style, of concealed prophecy and covertly declared ambition, nothing could have served Lowell better.

But Milton, rebel and symbolic regicide, and "Lycidas," trumpet voluntary of independence and ambition disguised as a pastoral elegy, served Lowell in an even more intimate and psychologically far more important way, being bound up with his primal act of rebellion against his father, who had written a prudish and insinuating letter to the father of a girl young Lowell regarded as his fiancée. The letter was eventually turned over to the poet, who went home and knocked his father down, an event remembered again and again in a series of poems that have been examined with great sensitivity and understanding by David Kalstone in his book *Five Temperaments*. Hamilton furnishes two versions, one from *Notebook 1967–68* and the other an unpublished poem, written about 1956, and now in the Houghton Library at Harvard, from which these lines are taken:

> I hummed the adamantine
> ore rotundo of *Lycidas* to cool love's quarrels,
> and clear my honor
> from Father's branding Scarlet Letter . . .
> "Yet once more, O ye laurels"—
> I was nineteen!

In his excellent chapter on Lowell, Kalstone quotes Jarrell thus: "If there were only some mechanism . . . for reasonably and systematically converting into poetry what we see and feel and are." That somewhat wistful yearning of Jarrell's took on the quality of a ravenous appetite in both Berryman and Lowell. And it is true that lyric poetry in our days has conceded vast territories to the writers of fiction, of which the impelling narrative drive is merely the most obvious advantage to the novelists. By its concentration, its narrowly focused point of view, its determined elimination of anything but the absolutely pertinent, its inviolably single tone, the lyric has elected to exclude all the contingent, chancy shifts of event, character, atmospherics, the alterations of time and consciousness that are the chief textures of our lives, and the vital substances of our very sense of reality. Novels are omnivorous, capable of assimilating everything, whereas the lyric has, since the Victorians, become more and more emaciated. Lowell's commendation of Elizabeth Bishop's volume, *North & South and A Cold Spring,* makes his own craving clear: "Her abundance of description reminds one, not of poets, poor symbolic, abstract creatures—but of the Russian novelists."[5] And of Anne Sexton's first book he wrote, ". . . an almost Russian abundance and accuracy."[6] Hamilton indicates how admiring and competitive Lowell felt about Berryman's *Dream Songs,* which were performing feats everyone assumed were denied to poetry. In Lowell's own words of 1964: "The scene is contemporary and crowded with references to news items, world politics, travel, low-life, and Negro music. . . . By their impertinent piety, by jumping from thought to thought, mood to mood, and by saying anything that comes into the author's head, they are touching and nervously alive. . . . All is risk and variety here. This great Pierrot's universe is more tearful and funny than we can easily bear."[7] And Frank Bidart, recalling Lowell as a teacher in the Spring 1977 issue of *Salmagundi*, a salute to Lowell's sixtieth birthday, writes, "One day in Robert Lowell's class, someone brought in a poem about a particularly painful and ugly subject. A student, who was shocked, said that some subjects simply couldn't be dealt with in poems. I've never forgotten Lowell's reply. He said, 'You can say anything in a poem—if you *place* it properly.' "

Out of this appetite and ambition came *Notebook 1967–68*, reissued in 1970 in a "revised and expanded edition," and ultimately enlarged into *History* and *For Lizzie and Harriet*. From that vast richness I want to single out two versions of an unrhymed sonnet about Sir Thomas More.

> Hans Holbein's More, my friend since World War II,
> the gold chain of S's, the golden rose,
> the plush cap, the brow's damp feathertips of hair,
> the slate eyes' stern, facetious twinkle, ready
> to turn from executioner to martyr—
> or saunter with the great King's bluff arm on his neck,
> feeling that friend-slaying, terror-ridden heart
> beating under the fat of Aretino—
> some hanger-on saying, "How the King must love you!"
> And Thomas, "If it were a question of my head,
> or losing his meanest village in France . . ." Or standing
> below the scaffold and the two-edged sword—
> "Friend, help me up," he said, "when I come down,
> my head and body will shift for themselves."

This poem remained unaltered in the revised and enlarged edition of *Notebook* that came out in 1970. And for the moment I wish only to offer a guess that Aretino may have suggested himself because, besides being fat, like the King, and something of a womanizer, again like the King, and a poet, as the King was, too, his portrait by Titian hangs in New York's Frick Collection, directly across the room from Holbein's More.

> Holbein's More, my patron saint as a convert,
> the gold chain of S's, the golden rose,

the plush cap, the brow's damp feathertips of hair,
the good eyes' stern, facetious twinkle, ready
to turn from executioner to martyr—
or saunter with the great King's bluff arm on your neck,
feeling that friend slaying, terror-dazzled heart
ballooning off into its awful dream—
a noble saying, "How the King must love you!"
And you, "If it were a question of my head,
or losing his meanest village in France . . ."
then by the scaffold and the headsman's axe—
"Friend, give me your hand for the first step,
as for coming down, I'll shift for myself."

This is the 1973 version from *History*. Before any comment on the differences, it may be worth remarking on the similarities, provided by Lowell's two main sources: the Holbein portrait and the first biography of More, written by his son-in-law, William Roper, the husband of More's favorite daughter, Margaret. Lowell makes use of two passages in Roper, which are worth quoting here.

The King, allowing well his answer, said unto him: "It is not our meaning, Master More, to do you hurt, but to do you good would we be glad. We will therefore for this purpose [an arduous and dangerous embassy to Spain] devise upon some other, and employ your service otherwise." . . .
And for the pleasure he took in his company would his grace suddenly sometimes come home to his house in Chelsea to be merry with him. Whither on a time, unlooked for, he came to dinner to him; and after dinner, in a fair garden of his, walked with him by the space of an hour, holding his arm about his neck.
As soon as his grace was gone, I, rejoicing thereat, told Sir Thomas More how happy he was, whom the King had so familiarly entertained, as I never had seen him do to any other except Cardinal Wolsey, whom I saw his grace once walk with, arm in arm. "I thank our Lord, son," quoth he, "I find his grace my very good lord indeed; and I believe he doth as singularly favor me as any subject within this realm. Howbeit, son Roper, I may tell thee I have no cause to be proud thereof, for if my head could win him a castle in France (for then was there war between us) it should not fail to go."

And, later, this:

> And so was he by Master Lieutenant brought out of the Tower
> and from thence led towards the place of execution. Where, going
> up the scaffold, which was so weak that it was ready to fall, he said
> merrily to Master Lieutenant: "I pray you, Master Lieutenant, see
> me safe up and, for my coming down, let me shift for myself."

These passages are so well known, as is indeed the whole Roper text, that
we may be astonished at some of the liberties Lowell has chosen to take,
and a few I find either unfortunate or inexplicable. More's own terse,
nearly jaunty gallows humor, being far more offhand than either of
Lowell's more cumbersome versions, is by just so much the more felici-
tous. And since Roper makes it clear that it was he himself who re-
marked with awe and joy upon the King's benevolent intimacy with
More, made the observation directly to More himself, and he to whom
More gave his shrewd reply, we must wonder why Lowell provided a
nameless hanger-on in the first version, followed by a nameless noble in
the second. I am not persuaded that he gains anything by either choice;
instead, he loses a sense of the intimacy and candor of the statement:
what one confesses, regarding the moral character of a monarch, to a
family member one trusts, will be quite different from what one might
divulge to some courtier—and More was a prudent man.

What next puzzles is the retained line in which More is said to be
"ready / to turn from executioner to martyr . . . ." Obviously, More
has no executioner's part in Roper's biography; these accusations were
raised against him by Foxe,[8] and later by Froude,[9] among others. I
believe they have been convincingly refuted by R. W. Chambers,[10]
though it may be added that Robert Bolt's pietistically worshipful play,
A Man For All Seasons, has aroused impatience in some, and the old
charges of persecution are once more being voiced. What is strange,
however, is to find them voiced by one who had chosen More as his
patron saint, and who clearly knew More as the firm, mild-mannered
and compassionate man he is represented as being in Roper. And for this
puzzle I will venture a conjectural answer.

With a sound instinct both for drama and self-lacerating honesty,
Lowell identifies himself with both the king and the saint; and he is too
cagey to reduce these wily antagonists into anything so allegorically
simplified, or so crudely doctrinal, as The Good and The Bad. Opposed

they are to one another, king and saint, but curiously alike in their divided inward selves. And not only do they resemble one another: in their determined opposition they are destined to enact the poet's personal torment. Fated by history to irreconcilable positions, they are also fated identities of the poet, More being able to be both intransigent fanatic and meek victim; Henry being able to be both benevolent patron and friend-slayer, whose "terror-dazzled heart" can go "ballooning off into its awful dream," presumably of lunatic omnipotence; the saint being able to "feel" the crazed heart of the king, in part, perhaps, because they are somehow alike, and are both linked to the poet, one by being his patron saint, the other by being like a famous licentious poet (now suppressed) as well as in other, more heartrending and body-rending, ways. The conversion of Roper's "castle" to "the meanest village" merely insists on Henry's ruthlessness, though it misses the overtones of a chess game, implied in More's comment. But the charges of no less ruthlessness against More are revived for the sake of the divided symmetries of the poem, which is terrifying in its awareness of the hideous cost of great-ness. As for its relation to Lowell, Hamilton tells us, ". . . it always unnerved him to make enemies of friends."

Some years ago John Malcolm Brinnin toyed with the idea of writing a biography of Lowell, and at that time he had a number of long talks with me. Once, he asked me point-blank whether I thought Lowell was in any way an anti-Semite, and after a moment's thought I answered flatly, "No." I would still answer that way now, though there are those who might feel entitled to think otherwise. Of Lowell's final lecture at the University of Cincinnati, when he was in perilous mental shape, Hamil-ton quotes Elizabeth Bettman as saying that he talked about "Hitler, more or less extolling the superman ideology. . . ." This was neither the beginning nor the end of Lowell's fascination with "great men" who were characterized by their "ruthlessness." But my own experiences with him were not only free of this particular dementia (though I was with him in several of his manic periods) but rather the reverse. Once, in his gentlest manner, Lowell asked me whether I was a believing Jew. For reasons that might not bear a too critical inspection, I said I was. He then said, "That means you think the Messiah is yet to come," and I assented. He asked whether I thought it might not be possible for the Messiah to be born, unrecognized, right in this country, and in our time. Given his pronounced excitement about the topic, together with my by now slightly informed sense of the symptoms of his illness, I was able to bring the whole conversation to a quiet conclusion by remarking that I thought it would be extremely difficult for any modern man to trace his ancestry irreproachably back to the House of David. But it was never my lot to cope with him as others were made to cope, and this book is, among other things, a genuine tribute to those who were closest to Lowell, and suffered accordingly. Blair Clark, Peter Taylor, William Alfred, John Thompson, and Frank Parker were devoted and unfailingly helpful friends. And Lowell was not less blessed in being deeply loved by each of his wives. But it seems to me that the most selflessly devoted of all those who were close to him and loved him, the most patient and enduring, generous, sympathetic, and forgiving, has been Elizabeth Hardwick. His gift was enormous, but of a disobedient, costly, Promethean kind; hers, too, has been heroic, and comparable in strength to his, though different. She and Cal were extremely warm and generous to me, and I think of them always with gratitude for many and unusual kindnesses. Hamilton comes near doing them justice.

Anthony Hecht (b. 1923), American poet and Professor of English at Georgetown University, is the author of *The Hard Hours* (1968), *Millions of Strange Shadows* (1977) and *The Venetian Vespers* (1979).

1. See Helen Vendler, *New York Review of Books* 29 (2 December 1982): 3ff; Richard Ellmann, *New York Times Book Review,* 28 November 1982, pp. 1ff; Stephen Spender, *Washington Post Book World,* 14 November 1982, pp. 1ff.

2. Georg Groddeck, a forerunner of Freud, wrote *The Book of It* (1923). Homer Lane was a crackpot American psychologist. Both had an unfortunate influence on Auden in the 1930s.

3. W. H. Auden, "In Memory of W. B. Yeats" (1939).

4. Randall Jarrell, "Fifty Years of American Poetry," *Prairie Schooner* 37 (Spring 1963): 27.

5. For Lowell on Elizabeth Bishop, see "Thomas, Bishop, Williams," *Sewanee Review* 55 (Summer 1947): 497–499.

6. For Lowell on Anne Sexton, see "Anne Sexton," *Anne Sexton: The Artist and Her Critics,* edited by J. D. McClatchey (Bloomington, 1978), pp. 71–73.

7. Lowell, "The Poetry of John Berryman," *New York Review of Books* 2 (28 May 1964): 3–4.

8. John Foxe (1516–87), English Protestant religious historian, author of *The Book of Martyrs* (1563).

9. James Anthony Froude (1818–94), English historian, author of *History of England from the Fall of Wolsey to the Defeat of the Spanish Armada,* 12 vols. (1856–70).

10. See R. W. Chambers, *Thomas More* (1935).

47 • Robert Lowell: A Memoir

Kathleen Spivack

In 1959 I came to Boston on a fellowship to study with poet Robert Lowell as an alternative to my senior year at college. I worked with him both privately, in tutorial at his house on Marlborough Street, and in a class, alongside Anne Sexton, Slyvia Plath, and others who were in the first bloom of their careers. As my poems and friendships with these poets set roots, I continued to work with and to be associated with Lowell until his death in 1977.

Lowell taught and encouraged an unusually large number of poets in Boston. I had the opportunity to observe and develop in his atmosphere. Later, as a writer and teacher of writers myself, I reflected on how Lowell managed to train so many writers, and, more generally, on how poetry, the value of it, was communicated in his teaching. Both by example and by his approach to literature in his classes, Lowell conveyed a sense of the central importance of poetry; he alternately scolded, prodded, encouraged, ignored, protected, and pitted his students against each other to spur their own development. It was not so much what he said about a student-writer's work that made an impact, but rather what he showed in his approach to the literature of the past, as well as his assiduous attention to his own multiple drafts and revisions.

Historically, it seems important to look at this, although my friendship with Lowell covers only one period in his life, and within that, only one aspect, Lowell in his middle and late years, in Boston.

To a young woman, arriving in Boston from the Midwest, some of the social aura surrounding Lowell was forever overwhelming, and, for the most part, our friendship existed outside of that ambience. Also, over the years I felt myself incapable of dealing with Lowell's breakdowns, so I stood outside his inner circle in that respect. Grateful for others who were more capable, I was an observer of, although not a partaker in, those more difficult and complex aspects of Lowell's life.

Antioch Review 43 (Spring 1983): 183–193. Reprinted by permission of Kathleen Spivack.

Our friendship existed in a place of poetry, good conversation, light, and laughter. We enjoyed long walks and late-afternoon tea. We shared—as did all those writers who came in contact with him—a belief that poetry was the central thing in life; and, like other writers, I was struck by the penetrating power of his mind. There were darker aspects of the man, too, and I have tried to voice my impressions of these.

Over the course of eighteen years we grew comfortable with each other, and, near the end of Lowell's life, the warmth that had been there from the beginning was manifest and simple. Lowell had been a part of my major decisions in my work; he knew my marriage, my family and children, as well as my poetry; and the friendship became reciprocal. Throughout this time he carried an aura of greatness, and this was more and more evident as the personal ambitions fell away.

This memoir is an attempt to look at Lowell's greatness as poet and teacher, as well as at some of the personalities surrounding him. I hope to catch the spirit in which poetry is written and, as Lowell showed, transmitted, and taught. Seen through my eyes, quite subjectively, this is in no way a "biography" of Lowell, for in it you will see myself as well, a young woman, at first a student, sometimes confident but often overwhelmed, groping toward her own realization as a person and poet.

I had come to Boston my senior year to study with Robert Lowell on a fellowship from Oberlin College, where I had written for the undergraduate newspaper. The *Cleveland Plain Dealer* had reprinted some of my stories, and I was given a Gage Foundation Fellowship. Ostensibly for my last year of study at Oberlin, the fellowship was later changed to allow me to study writing with a poet "acceptable to the Oberlin English Department." The chairman of the department, Professor Andrew Bongiorno, commented, "Man is a social animal" as he set about signing the necessary papers for me to leave Oberlin during my senior year. It was arranged that I should take that year away, handing in the first draft of my honors thesis before I went, and would then return in June to take final honors exams and be graduated with my class. The thesis was, unfortunately, on Andrew Marvell's "The Garden," already too much written about, but with the help of friends I was able to construct something barely acceptable. "Metaphysics" and the "seventeenth century" were English department catchwords then, and the pressure to write something original about the lines "Ripe apples drop about my head," etc. etc. was high:

> What wondrous life is this I lead!
> Ripe apples drop about my head;
> The luscious clusters of the vine
> Upon my mouth do crush their wine;
> The nectarine and curious peach
> Into my hands themselves do reach;
> Stumbling on melons, as I pass,
> Ensnared with flowers, I fall on grass . . . .

Originally I had wanted to spend my senior year in San Francisco rather than Boston, as I hoped to have a lot of "Sin" during this year away. But San Francisco, alas, housed Allen Ginsberg. This was 1959, and the Beat poets were considered an outrage. The "beatniks" lived in "pads" on mattresses (something I was longing to do) and wrote works like "Howl." They believed in "free love." But Oberlin did not: there was no way the college would give me senior-year credit for studying with Allen Ginsberg, whose morals were considered questionable. Modern Poetry, at Oberlin, stopped at Thomas Hardy.

(Later that year, a classmate was expelled from the college for getting pregnant. Her chief crime appeared to be that she had conceived during men's visiting hours, with the door to the room open the requisite ten inches. The "ten-inch rule" was strictly enforced, with housemothers coming around during visiting hours to check the doors and literally measuring the space. The young woman had been visiting her boyfriend's dorm when "The Act" had occurred. Prior to her expulsion there were long and solemn discussions and meetings of the faculty and deans. The chief puzzlement seemed to be not the pregnancy, but the question of how it could have occurred during these carefully monitored visiting hours.)

Since Oberlin would not accept Allen Ginsberg (and therefore San Francisco) in lieu of senior year, I went to my second choice. Boston, which stood in second place as "Sin City," happened to house Robert Lowell, a poet I had heard of, but whose work I could not understand at all. Lowell had published *The Mills of the Kavanaughs* and *Lord Weary's Castle,* which seemed to me thick, clotted, and obscure. But Lowell was affiliated with Boston University, and the Oberlin English department found him "acceptable." Lowell agreed to take me on. I quickly finished an appalling version of my thesis on Marvell's "The Garden." Friends typed it for me. A classmate went with me to the train station in Cleveland and, as he said goodbye, confessed that he was "an invert."

This left me puzzled. The train pulled out of the station. At the end of that academic year I returned to Oberlin, took exams, went to parties, and was graduated. During that time I had firmed up my decision to be a writer, had learned to take poetry seriously, had begun friendships that would continue for twenty years with Lowell and others, and had met and was already living with my future husband.

Robert Lowell had no recollection of having agreed to work with me when I arrived at his office at Boston University. He was eating his lunch and looking abstracted. I arrived in a rainstorm, in blue jeans and boots. "I never take anyone under thirty," he said coldly. He didn't remember getting my letter or the arrangements with Oberlin. I was stunned. I knew no one in Boston, had taken a room in a rooming house and felt overwhelmed by the city, by the circumstances, and by having to take subways and find my way around. (At Oberlin, cars were forbidden, and everyone rode bikes.) As I stood in Lowell's office, wet and depressed, not knowing quite how to handle his amnesia, Lowell took pity on me. He was eating a hurried lunch in one of the back offices of the English department. "Would you like part of this sandwich?" he offered. We sat in silence for a while. Finally he offered an "Oh yes, I do seem to remember *something*." There was more silence; Lowell looked into space. By the end of a half hour he had arranged that I would audit his class at Boston University and would come to his house on Marlborough Street one afternoon a week for individual tutoring. "Whom have you read?" he asked. I had not read much beyond Marvell. This ignorance was to be remedied, Lowell decided.

Shortly after making this arrangement, Lowell proceeded to have a breakdown. As it was slow in coming, and as I had never seen anyone have a breakdown before, the whole series of swings in Lowell's moods seemed very mysterious, and what later struck others as "signs" seemed, in fact, to be normal Lowell behavior. I never was able to shake a slight fear of his unpredictability, the flashes of cruelty that could and did emerge, the wit at others' expense. This, coupled with my awe at the working of his mind, kept our relationship formal. I called him "Mister Lowell," and though he asked me to call him "Cal," as did so many of his friends, there was always a slight catch in my throat as I did so. Privately, to myself or to friends, I referred to him as "Lowell": some kind of compromise between the formality of "Mister" and the slangy "Cal," with its associations to Caligula and to the cruelty of both man and emperor. "Cal" was always hard to say—I admired the way Elizabeth Hardwick (his second wife) assumed a gently teasing, laughing way of addressing him; I was never able to feel that comfortable with him. The unpredictable, quixotic nature of the man, the manic swings, all were beyond my eighteen-year-old perspective. Although I was, during our association, to come to know his mood swings well, I preferred, in our dealings, to remain the friend at a formal distance. Though I talked fairly freely with Lowell, much of our relationship was a jokey, laughing one, which made possible a deeper intimacy not directly approached.

Though impatient with the quality of most of the student poems Cal addressed, one always knew, in the classes or office hours, that Cal too was much more interested in, and would rapidly turn to, "real" poems. If students hoped for praise from Cal for their own work, they often were disappointed. But the reading of the classics, the "genuine article," as Cal said, made the whole afternoon worthwhile; and for that reason, such professional writers as Frank Bidart, Robert Pinsky, James Atlas, Sidney Goldfarb, Bob Grenier, Lloyd Schwartz, Gail Mazur, and many others continued to attend, year after year, whenever Cal was holding "office hours." The level of talent and ability of the people who passed through the "office hours" was amazing—writers Jonathan Galassi, as an undergraduate, Andrew Wylie, Sandy Kaye, Roger Parham Browne, and others; poets Richard Tillinghast, Steven Sandy, Jane Shore, with her alert gaze that seemed to take in everything, Bill Byrom, Anne Hussey, and others. We would meet each other randomly, outside the Lowell context, and friendships developed. Occasionally I would run into James Atlas, browsing morosely through the magazines at Reading International, taking a break from his biography of Delmore Schwartz. Later, when I read his book, I understood how difficult it must have been to write. He not only chronicled Delmore's work and life, but also had a definite moral point of view on the poet and his work, a sympathy as well as a detachment.

Many of the people who were in that early class at Boston University were serious writers. To list a few: Henry Braun, Helen Chasin, Don Junkins, Plath, Sexton, Starbuck, Jean Valentine. I am sure there are poets not included on this list, either because they didn't overlap with me or because I did not learn their names. The awe, reverence, and timidity in Lowell's classes were too overwhelming for many introductions. Years later I met Roger Rosenblatt, then director of the National Endowment for the Humanities, and realized that we had sat opposite each other in class for an entire year without identifying ourselves. It was interesting, however, that eight years later we could still remember each other's poems and the devastating comments about them.

Elizabeth Bishop and Anne Sexton were eager to meet each other, and since I was a friend of both, they asked me to arrange it. "Invite her for lunch at my flat," suggested Elizabeth. "Have her come out to Weston," said Anne. Both women were reluctant to meet on the other's turf. I found myself in the middle of delicate negotiations. The summit meeting took weeks to arrange. "I'm shy," each protested. Well, that was only partially true, as I watched the prima donna aspects of each poet surface. Finally a restaurant was agreed upon, a time and a date. There were, of course, several cancellations and postponements. Also, each poet insisted I pick her up and accompany her. Anne was afraid to meet Elizabeth Bishop because Lowell had touted her as the best woman poet in America and because she admired Bishop's work so much. But Elizabeth was afraid to meet her because she feared that Anne would be "confessional," and she was repelled and appalled by what she considered Sexton's raw and sexual outpourings, and because of Anne's openness in writing about her breakdowns, a topic Elizabeth feared and about which she could never bring herself to write directly.

However, Lois Ames agreed to serve as Anne's second, to pick her up and bring her into Cambridge to the Iruña, a Spanish restaurant where we would all meet. After I had met Elizabeth Bishop in her apartment and we had played a rousing set of ping-pong games, the four of us actually managed to sit down at a restaurant table. I waited for great words of literature to fly about my ears. Here were my two favorite woman poets meeting. What a wonderful conversation would ensue, I thought.

"Tell me, Anne"—Elizabeth leaned over—"how much money do you get for a reading nowadays?" "At least a thousand," was Anne's immediate answer. And the two poets were off, talking about contracts and money and publishers who had or hadn't done them wrong. Lois and I sat there amazed. If we had thought one word about poetic process was to be exchanged, we were mistaken. The two women talked about business until the dessert course, when Anne dramatically turned to Lois and exclaimed, "Lois, did I ever tell you how much it hurt, having my babies?" Now it was Anne's and Lois's turn to talk, while Elizabeth and I sat silent, as Anne and Lois outdid themselves on each gory, painful detail of their various childbirths. As I walked Elizabeth back home she was thoughtfully silent. "Well, really," she said at the door, dismissing the whole encounter. As far as I know, the two women never saw each other again.

Although Cal was helpful to Anne Sexton in her work, distance grew between them as Anne's illness continued to surface. Also, Cal did not approve of the turn Anne's poetry had taken into a looser, more unstructured expression. Perhaps her poetry was too close, or threatened his control. It was hard to tell. Also, the relation had always been an uneasy one of teacher and student; Anne wanted to lean on Cal for support, and he was unable to give it. Most of all, Cal grew uncomfortable with Anne's personal expressiveness, particularly of her anger. When Anne's play appeared at the American Place Theatre,[1] a play that dealt mostly with the self-pity of the unstable female central character, Anne, in an interview with the press, made uncharitable remarks about her husband, which alienated Cal. Anne, as a person and poet, did not have enough restraint to put either Cal or Elizabeth Hardwick at ease, and she was spoken of nervously in their household on more than one occasion while I was visiting.

Adrienne Rich was a poet whom Cal admired greatly. She had won the Yale Younger Poets Prize, was a classical poet, with restrained feeling, and clearly, he felt, his intellectual equal. He spoke of her highly and arranged for me to meet her. Her work had a clear, noble, crystalline quality, and she had a strong, opinionated way of looking at poetry. I sat in her kitchen, drinking tea, and listening to her beautifully intelligent sentences while her children puttered about upstairs, and she seemed to me outstanding not only in her promise, but in her achievements at that time. She struggled with painful arthritis, with motherhood and writing, all with an apparent grace. Only years later did I realize at what a cost such grace and control were obtained. I remember offering, feebly, to babysit, an offer she refused. She was far into her life as a faculty wife at Harvard, and that entailed stylistic reserve, a show of strength that I could not possibly understand. In the face of her articulateness, I felt my own clumsy, inarticulate intuitions about poetry groping and painful; my brain was slow, I could not think fast enough to be the least bit interesting to Adrienne as a poet or a person. I was afraid to show her my poems.

Cal loved talking poetry with Adrienne and respected her highly. So it was a terrible blow to him when, in 1972, during his divorce from Elizabeth Hardwick and his subsequent marriage to Lady Caroline Blackwood, Adrienne publicly rebuked him in the *American Poetry Review* for using "Lizzie's letters" in books (*The Dolphin* and *For Lizzie and Harriet*).[2] That review broke the friendship. Cal staggered, wounded from a side he hadn't expected, and Adrienne took Elizabeth Hardwick's part, loudly and publicly, in the marital breakup.

After that issue of the *American Poetry Review* came out, Cal's obsession with it invaded even his classes and "office hours." He talked painfully on and on about it. He talked of Adrienne as a poet. ("Major? or Minor?" he asked the group. "Minor, definitely minor," he answered his own question. "Wouldn't you say so?" he sought reassurance from Frank Bidart, who tried to hedge.) I recognized in Lowell's spiraling about Adrienne and the letters the precursor to what, in fact, turned out to be a breakdown. Lowell was at this time spending the term in Boston with Caroline Blackwood, whom I had come to know, and I spoke to her about this. She was aware of the situation, but felt quite helplessly outside of it and unable to do anything.

While Lowell supported the work of Sexton and Plath, he could be very hard on a poet who violated his canons of taste. Denise Levertov was a poet he admired, but she fell from grace in the following way. We were walking toward the inevitable late-afternoon cup of tea at a café; puzzled, Cal took my elbow. "You know," he said, in a strained, careful, musing way, "Denise used to be a very good poet. One of the best women writing in America today. But I just heard her read in New York. And she read her poems—some good ones—and then"—here Cal paused, lowering his voice, with half-concealed mischief in his eyes—"she read a poem about her cunt! How she didn't like it, and oh, how horrible it was, she described it in detail. . . ."[3] His voice trailed off, only to resume in a musing way, "and then"—long, wondering pause—"she decided she liked that cunt poem so much she read it to us a second time. . . ." Cal was shocked, and Denise, alas, was relegated to the ranks below "Minor." With her usual courage, Denise wrote on, whatever Cal or anybody else might think.

Later, when I did my M.A. thesis under the supervision of John Brinnin, I chose Doris Lessing's *The Golden Notebook* as a topic. This was before the interest in literature by women; no one, including Lowell, had heard of Lessing. Brinnin wondered, with much distaste, why I wished to be so "clinical," as he put it. Was this necessary? Lessing, Levertov, Sexton all wrote far too graphically about women's bodies to be fully acceptable to graduates of St. Mark's School—either distaste or sniggers were then the typical male reaction. Certainly members of the elite club called Harvard would never commit such crimes. And Lowell, having flunked out of or left Harvard, returned to its fold a greater snob than the group he had rebelled against.

Reading aloud was not a thing poets were expected to be good at, back in the early Sixties—with the exception of Dylan Thomas, who read like a dream; Allen Ginsberg, who has always been a phenomenal reader; and Anne Sexton, who projected a wistful, vulnerable quality, even when she read with her rock back-up band, made up of Weston high school teachers. Named, I believe, the Manic Depressives, the band chanted, "Yeah, yeah, yeah," as back-up to Anne's pensive reading of such classics as her poems "Menstruation at Forty" or the "Ballad of the Lonely Masturbator." The total effect of Anne's reading with her band was not to be believed; and, most surprisingly, it was good. But Anne reading alone could magnetize an audience.

Among the academic set, and I include Lowell in that, it was considered slightly vulgar to be "good at" reading poetry aloud, and most poetry readings were, and in fact still are, agonies of boredom. There was not yet much money around for readings. That situation was altered for a time; as poetry became more "popular," as more colleges and universities added creative writing programs, people were willing to pay to hear poets read their work. This has changed once again, in line with what is vaguely referred to in the academic world as "The Economy." Cal, as well as Elizabeth Bishop, were very boring readers of their own poems. Elizabeth read, a friend said, "like a buyer at Macy's," so terrified was she. Roethke came to Harvard and refused to read his poetry; instead, he sang little ditties he had composed against the Republican presidential candidate, and disappointed everyone by merely swaying and dancing to tunes heard somewhere in his head. Cal mumbled, and his obscure poems became even more obscure in his soft, slightly Southern voice. Even his most rapt students had trouble not falling asleep at his B.U. poetry readings.

However, Cal's last reading at Harvard was different. In the gloomy lecture hall Cal unbent, explaining his poems in a clear, gentle way before reading them. His student audience was with him all the way;

during the time of being a poet, he had become, in his presentation of his work as well as in the work itself, less obscure, more clear and direct and accessible and at ease.

My intent has been to take a walk through a friendship, and an era, with a man who happened to be a great poet, teacher, and an immensely complex person. I hoped, by looking at various facets of my relationship with Lowell, to understand not only my own roots as a poet, and those of my contemporaries, but the relationship of teacher to student, the handing down of tradition throughout generations of writers, my own continued interest in teaching, and my joy in the successes of students. Lowell was part of a great tradition of which we are all the descendants. He fostered not only our careers as writers, but the growth of our abilities, our understanding of poetry and what it means to read and write it, and my continuing belief in the apprenticeship system of training writers. Encouraging of my work as a writer, Lowell also was an integral part of my personal life, and he did not hesitate to advise on love, marriage, or priorities in writing and the work I did to support it (teaching and counseling in writing, language, and cognitive psychology). This professional teacher-student relationship became a very personal one, and continued to be so throughout eighteen years. Lowell found money for me, took poems to publishers, wrote references, and, in his personal friendship, exhibited kindness and concern.

His generosity in training younger poets explains why Lowell remained a part of so many of our lives. Most importantly, he taught us to read poetry. For that reason alone poets flocked to study with him. I had ample opportunity, over the course of nearly twenty years, to observe Lowell at work, carefully, endlessly reading and analyzing poems, studying, penetrating them. Assessing Lowell's contribution as a poet is one thing: he was daring, he took risks, he made things possible in his poems that no one else had done. But his contributions as a teacher and reader and friend were invaluable, and I have found myself looking at some of the circle surrounding him as well. In fact, the people I met through Lowell—Plath, Sexton, Bishop, and others—demanded their due as I rethought the years with Lowell. Among them, Stanley Kunitz continues to shine as an uncorrupted beacon of poetic life in what is in fact a very corrupt poetry-politics world of low stakes, huge yet fragile egos, "payments in copies," and a lot of despair.

Lowell was complex, tortured, and difficult, with multiple breakdowns, a horror of them, and a lot of ambition and dark streaks mixed in. And in writing this piece, I found that these aspects of his character needed to be included. At the same time, his darting sudden insights, humor, kindness, and generosity prevailed, despite and beyond the illness and difficult parts of his character. He had enormous understanding and talent, both personally and poetically. It was his endless interest in and generosity toward poetry itself that made Lowell, as it does Kunitz, a magnet toward which other poets flocked. He shared our obsession—in fact, urged us on. Lowell's obsession with poetry and with "being a poet" was total. Could there be any other life?

Kathleen Spivack (b. 1938), American poet, was Lowell's pupil at Boston University (in the same class as Plath and Sexton) during 1959–60. She is the author of *Flying Inland* (1973), *The Jane Poems* (1974) and *Summer in the Spreading Dawn* (1981).

1. Sexton's play, *Mercy Street,* was performed in 1969.

2. See Adrienne Rich, "Carydid: A Column," *American Poetry Review* 2 (September–October 1973): 42–43.

3. See Denise Levertov, "Hypocrite Women," *O Taste and See* (New York, 1964), p. 70.

Index